Resilience and the Humanities

The Humanities in the World

ISSN 3070-2879

The series addresses vital issues facing the humanities and humanistic inquiry. Volumes will advance the conviction that, despite the unceasing drumbeat of stories bemoaning the "crisis" in the humanities, the current moment represents not so much a crisis as a critical opportunity for the humanities.

The series' aim is to demonstrate how the humanities can be prominently and permanently reinserted into public and scholarly discourse. Political science desperately needs to draw on history and ethics to repair our increasingly perilous and authoritarian global political landscape. The climate sciences desperately need to draw on the environmental humanities to understand not just how our environment is changing but what notions of justice must change with it. Artificial intelligence has gone and will continue to go wrong if it is not guided by the principles of equity, privacy, and care taught to us by the humanities. *The Humanities in the World* brings this recuperative, emancipatory promise of the humanities to the fore through a mix of both thematic edited volumes and topical scholarly monographs. Topics that might be at the forefront include, in addition to those already mentioned, antiracism, cosmopolitan ethics, the value of creativity, and care and stewardship.

Forthcoming

Beyond the Crisis: The Humanities as a Force for Global Renewal
Edited by Peter H. Christensen and Tatyana Bakhmetyeva

Other titles in this series may be found on our website, www.urpress.com

Resilience and the Humanities

Critique and Testing

Edited by
Stephen M. Hart, Camila Gatica Mizala and
Nicolas Lema Habash

University of Rochester Press

First published 2026

University of Rochester Press
www.urpress.com
and Boydell & Brewer Limited
www.boydellandbrewer.com

Our Authorized Representative for product safety in the EU is Easy Access System Europe – Mustamäe tee 50, 10621 Tallinn, Estonia, *gpsr.requests@easproject.com*

ISBN-13: 978-1-64825-182-5 (hardback)
ISBN-13: 978-1-64825-185-6 (paperback)

Cataloging-in-publication data available from the Library of Congress
A catalogue record for this title is available from the British Library

Contents

General Introduction: Contested and Contesting Resilience 1

Stephen M. Hart, Camila Gatica Mizala and Nicolas Lema Habash

Part I: Critique (Philosophy, Ecology, Sustainability)

1. Towards Destruction: An Essay on How Resilience Affects Resistance 23

   Nicolas Lema Habash

2. Countering Resilience and its Consensual Logic: Persistence, Resistance, Re-existence 45

   Laura Quintana

3. 'How Each Particle, When It Bangs into Another, Either *Bounces Back* or Passes on a Part of Its Motion': On a Famous Spinozist Occurrence about the *Resilience* Problem, and Its Inadequacy 70

   Vincent Legeay

4. Resilience and Sustainability as Complementary Concepts in Political Thought 88

   Anna Wienhues

5. Resilience, Ecosystems and Places: Can Resilience Delineate Dynamic Entities? 112

   Patrik Baard

6. Adapt Creatively or Perish: How Resilience Dug the Grave of Strong Sustainability 130

   Andrea Lehner

Part II: Application

7. Resilience and Race in the Hagiographic Tradition of St Martin of Porres 161

Celia Cussen

8. Resilience in Gabriel García Márquez's *One Hundred Years of Solitude* 173

Stephen M. Hart

9. Discovering Women's Resilience: The Development Film since the 1970s 190

Molly Geidel

10. Reimagining Home: Exile and Resilience in Chilean Film, 1970–90 209

Jennifer Alpert and Camila Gatica Mizala

11. 'A Time that Has Not Yet Been'. Futurity and Survival in Marta Aponte's Caribbean Archive 237

Carlos Fonseca

12. Beyond Resilience: Débrouillardise in Civil War Novels 251

Hannah Grayson

13. Resilience in the Latin American Anthropocene Western 270

Leidy Paola Bolaños Florido and Wolfgang Fuhrmann

14. 'Now Where Am I?': Endurance in Peter Loizos's *Sophia and Her People* (1985) 290

Ignacio Albornoz and Katerina Hatzikidi

15. When I'm Down I Just Get up—or Do I? Contentiousness of Resilience in the Face of Natural Disasters in Jamaica 309

Victoria Carpenter and Lakhbir Singh

List of Contributors 334

Index 339

General Introduction: Contested and Contesting Resilience

Stephen M. Hart, Camila Gatica Mizala and Nicolas Lema Habash

As a concept, resilience is all around us. It is a buzzword in domains that range from Engineering, through Moral Psychology, coaching and self-help manuals, to military strategy. It does not always have the same meaning across these fields, but all of them seem to share the idea that resilience is a useful notion to account for the protection and maintenance of different kinds of (artificial and natural) environments, through the adaptation of its individuals to the changes or disruptions they might undergo. In our context, the use of the notion of resilience has normative connotations. As it happens with most catchwords that become integrated into a normative discourse, its potential usefulness starts to be taken for granted and becomes naturalised. But resilience also has a history, and its different uses also resonate and echo with the development of knowledge and power-relations occurring in society as a whole. The apparently obvious meaning of resilience and its normative consequences are the result of a series of intellectual, social and epistemic processes. *Resilience and the Humanities: Critique and Testing* assumes that, regardless of its ubiquity, resilience is a concept that cannot be accepted without interrogation and testing its value vis-à-vis the objects and the fields in which it is being deployed. The volume aims at exploring resilience by proposing that, rather than being a notion whose meaning is immovable and whose consequences are fixed, resilience is a contested concept.

This volume thus resonates with some very recent attempts to question, dispute and contest the idea of resilience and its applications. Indeed, from a historiographical perspective, Brendan Gillis has drawn attention to the different meanings the idea of resilience has adopted throughout the twentieth century, to the point of becoming a term that has acquired completely opposing connotations in different disciplinary fields and in the hands of ideological opponents.[1] From a different disciplinary perspective, that of socioecology, the recently published *Críticas y contrastes a la resiliencia socioecológica*, edited by Tlacaelel Rivera-Núñez, Laura Collin Harguindeguy, Elena Lazos Chavero,[2] also illustrates the contested nature of resilience. The volume mostly features articles that attack the notion of resilience from different perspectives or advocate for its radical transformation.[3] In his Introduction, Rivera-Núñez goes on to explain that throughout the twentieth century there was a conceptual struggle between socioecological resilience-based approaches and the perspective of Political Ecology. The dispute over the usefulness of the notion of resilience has been fuelled by decolonial and postcolonial approaches that reject the normative outcomes of resilience, most especially when applied to postcolonial contexts. However, Rivera-Núñez likewise addresses the complexity of this issue in the socioecological sciences when he recounts that, during the 2022 conference that gave birth to this volume, people gave evenly mixed answers to the question: 'Is socioecological resilience possible?'[4]

Our approach also resonates with another recent debate on the nature of resilience which was opened up by the psychologist Boris Cyrulnik. In his 2024 collection of essays, titled *The Two Faces of Resilience: Against the Appropriation of a Concept* (*Les deux visages de la resilience*: *Contre la récupération d'un concept*), Cyrulnik argues that the technical and extremely useful notion of resilience as developed in the domain of scientific and psychological research has been appropriated and transformed by other fields and public discourses for purposes that result in strengthening its deployment

1 See Brendan Gillis, 'Historicizing Resilience: Public Humanities and Emergency Management in the Anthropocene', *Transactions of the American Philosophical Society*, 114: 1, 99–116, doi: https://doi.org/10.1353/tap.2025.a957550 (accessed 10 October 2025).

2 *Críticas y contrastes a la resiliencia socioecológica*, ed. Tlacaelel Rivera-Núñez, Laura Collin Harguindeguy and Elena Lazos Chavero (Tlaxcala: El Colegio de Tlaxcala, 2025).

3 See, for example, Elena Lazos Chavero, 'Resilencia: Antítesis de luchas y movimientos sociales de transformación', in *Críticas y contrastes a la resiliencia socioecológica*, ed. Tlacaelel Rivera-Núñez, Laura Collin Harguindeguy and Elena Lazos Chavero (Tlaxcala: El Colegio de Tlaxcala, 2025), pp. 67–96.

4 Tlacaelel Rivera-Núñez, 'Una introducción crítica a la resiliencia socioecológica desde la ecología política', in *Críticas y contrastes a la resiliencia socioecológica*, ed. Tlacaelel Rivera-Núñez, Laura Collin Harguindeguy and Elena Lazos Chavero (Tlaxcala: El Colegio de Tlaxcala, 2025), pp. 14–40 (p. 15).

within neoliberalism.[5] The very notion of resilience having 'two faces' points to the idea of contestation, of performing a struggle over a concept.

While Cyrulnik points to two dimensions of the concept, however, the notion of contesting resilience that this volume collectively develops perhaps points to the larger strategy of critique of the concept. At least in one important philosophical line of thought, the concept of critique designates much more than an attack. In the Kantian tradition, the idea of critique has been analysed and used as a tool to establish the 'limits' of an object under scrutiny.[6] Such an object may well be a concept like 'reason' as occurs, for example, in Kant's *Critique of Pure Reason*. An important theme and goal of this volume is to undertake a critique of the concept of resilience following in the footsteps of this idea. A critique of resilience is not necessarily an attack on the concept. It is rather an exploration of the limits of resilience. In an epoch such as ours, where the notion of resilience is ubiquitous and permeates many instances and domains of our social life, critically assessing its limits becomes an ethical as well as a political task. Following on from this perspective, we may say that what distinguishes the chapters in this volume is their use of critique. Critiquing the concept of resilience, in the sense of exploring its limits, may take many forms. Although this volume is not exhaustive, it does provide a myriad of ways in which this critique may be carried out. It is not simply a matter of word-use, but of how a certain terminology fills a discourse with ideas that have consequences upon subjects and bodies on a social, cultural and political level.

Before delving into the contents of the volume, it is necessary to give a brief presentation of the term resilience and some of its diverse uses in different disciplines. Although this presentation is not exhaustive, it does provide a useful panorama against which we can then map out the specificity of the transdisciplinary Humanities approach we have taken in this volume.

5 See Boris Cyrulnik, 'Résilience: notion, définition et divagation du mot', in *Les deux visages de la résilience: Contre la récupération d'un concept*, ed. Boris Cyrulnik (Paris: Odile Jacob, 2024).

6 We draw here from the very insightful perspective on Enlightenment and critique by Michel Foucault, 'Qu'est-ce que les Lumières', in *Dits et Écrits. 1954–1988*, IV, ed. Daniel Defert and François Ewald (Paris: Gallimard, 1994), pp. 562–78; and then prolongued by Judith Butler, 'What is Critique? An Essay on Foucault's Virtue', in *The Political: Readings in Continental Philosophy*, ed. David Ingram (London: Basil Blackwell, 2002), pp. 212–26.

I Resilience Across Disciplines

Francis Bacon was probably one of the first scholars to use the term 'resilience'—derived from the Latin *resilire* meaning 'to bounce back'—in the English language in his 1626 *Sylva sylvarum*. Since then, the term has been transformed in leaps and bounds, such that, nowadays it is a one-size-fits-all concept. Since its use in the early seventeenth century, the term has its own history of semantics and uses based on the disciplines that have explored and 'thought through' the notion. Indeed, since the 1970s, in particular, a growing scholarship has developed, giving the word's capacity to bounce back different meanings to us. We can say that the concept itself is resilient, and it has been able to absorb over time both disruption and critique, while coping and adapting to new semantic situations. In short, and paraphrasing Kathleen Tusaie and Janyce Dyer, resilience is not a static concept.[7] When thinking through the history of the concept across different disciplines, some guiding questions inevitably appear: Why did the term become so pervasive? Why is everyone talking about resilience? Why is it such a pervasive concept in today's world? One of the reasons is that the term epitomises one way of dealing with instability.

First, we should refer to the perspective that came from Engineering, where resilience has been an important concept underpinning critical infrastructure and disaster response. Here, the problem of resilience is a physical one: understanding how a material can be or is resilient has been key to how engineers use different materials and build edifices with them. Alastair McAslan traced the origins of the concept.[8] In 1818, the term was introduced in a scholarly journal by Thomas Tredgold, an engineer known for his work on railway construction, who used 'resilience' to refer to a material characteristic of timber.[9] In the 1860s, Robert Mallet developed the idea of resilience as a term of measurement: the *modulus of resilience*, which is the maximum energy that can be absorbed per unit volume, meaning the ability of a material to resist harsh conditions.[10] The measure was included

7 Kathleen Tusaie and Janyce Dyer, 'Resilience: A Historical Review of the Construct', *Holistic Nursing Practice*, 18: 1 (2004), 3–8, doi:10.1097/00004650-200401000-00002 (accessed 12 December 2024).

8 Alastair McAslan, *The Concept of Resilience. Understanding its Origins, Meaning and Utility* (Adelaide, Australia: Torrens Resilience Institute, 2010).

9 Mr. Thomas Tredgold, 'On the Transverse Strength and Resilience of Timber', *The Philosophical Magazine*, 51:239 (1818), 214–16, https://doi.org/10.1080/14786441808637536 (accessed 12 December 2023).

10 Robert Mallet, 'On the Physical Conditions Involved in the Construction of Artillery, and on Some Hitherto Unexplained Causes of the Destruction of Cannon in Service', *The Transactions of the Royal Irish Academy*, 23 (1856),

in the *Manual of Civil Engineering of 1867*. Another definition was given by Mansfield Merriman in 1885, which focused on the ability of a material to withstand the impact or shock of a falling body. The main point of the definition given by Merriman was to measure whether the material had the 'capacity to endure work that may be performed upon it'.[11] As such, the use of the concept highlighted two active elements: energy and elasticity.

The concept jumped from the disciplines of Physics and its uses in Engineering to the field of Ecology. Ecology emerged as the main discipline that focused on resilience in relation to managing ecosystems for understanding how they are dynamically sustained through time. Within the field of Ecology, particularly in the 1970s and 1980s, the use of resilience turned to ecosystems in order to establish how they can absorb and deal with change and disruption without losing their key elements and thus sustain themselves over time. Within this scope, a foundational view was presented by the ecologist Crawford S. Holling, who, in his 1973 paper 'Resilience and Stability of Ecological Systems', used the term as a means of understanding the property of ecosystems and extinction. He defined the term as 'a measure of the persistence of systems and of their ability to absorb change and disturbance and still maintain the same relationship between populations or state variables'.[12] Following Holling, it is the resilience of these systems that gave them the capacity to persist. One of the ideas the author introduces is the impact that diversity and interplay can have on how resilient a system is (the more diverse, the more resilient), thereby linking the term to those of stability (less resilient) and instability (more resilient). Holling's groundbreaking study is also responsible for extrapolating the resilience approach from ecological non-human systems to human individuals and communities.

Holling's use of the term resilience would result in its generalised use in the domain of population management. From this perspective, the discipline of Political Development stands out as a field that began to engage with the concept in the 1990s. Within this framework, resilience moves towards governance, international development, and more political areas, emphasising preparedness vis-à-vis events and situations leading to traumas (such as terrorist attacks, war scenarios or ecological catastrophes).[13] Although Holling's work was never only descriptive of environmental systems and always tended

---

141–36, https://www.jstor.org/stable/30079308 (accessed 12 December 2024).

11 Mansfield Merriman, *A Text-book on the Mechanics of Materials and of Beams, Columns and Shafts*, 1st edn (New York: J. Wiley and Sons, 1885).

12 Holling, C. S., 'Resilience and Stability of Ecological Systems', *Annual Review of Ecology and Systematics*, 4 (1973), 1–23 (p. 14).

13 P. H. Longstaff, 'Security, Resilience, and Communication in Unpredictable Environments Such as Terrorism, Natural Disasters, and Complex

to assert the normative dimension of the resilience paradigm,[14] the move of the concept into the arena of politics made this normative component more explicit. In this sense, as many critical takes on the concept have highlighted, it is difficult to separate the genesis and development of resilience from the deployment of the neo-liberal agenda that establishes that one must learn to adapt to an ever-changing and complex world.[15] This take on resilience received pushback from the Humanities and the Social Sciences, areas in which the concept began to be perceived as being used by governments as a strategy allowing them to dismiss the possibility of structural changes.[16]

Following on from this genealogy, Psychology became one of the main disciplines in the Social Sciences to focus on resilience, linking it to studies on responses to traumatic events or the ability to cope with trauma and undesirable situations.[17] The focus moved from the plural (ecosystems, governments) to the individual, and resilience was understood not so much as bouncing but as coping.[18] Much of the early work on the term focused on children began to appear in the 1970s and does not necessarily use the concept 'resilience' but, instead, equivalent terms like the verb 'to cope'.[19] When psychologists do use the term resilience, the focus is on the idea of

---

Technology', Program on Information Resources Policy (Cambridge, MA: Center for Information Policy Research, Harvard University, 2005).

14 See *Adaptive Environmental Assessment and* Management, ed. C. S. Holling (Chichester: John Wiley & Sons, 1978).

15 Without using the term resilience, adaptation is the main topic the analysis of neoliberalism in Barbara Stigler, *Il faut s'adapter. Sur un nouvel impératif politique* (Paris: Gallimard, 2019).

16 See, for example, Brad Evans and Julian Ried, *Resilient Life: The Art of Living Dangerously* (Cambridge: Polity, 2014).

17 For a history of the term within psychology, see Zlata Grygorenko and Ganna Naydonova, 'The Concept of "Resilience": History of Formation and Approaches to Definition', *Public Administration and Law Review*, 2023, pp. 76–88, doi:10.36690/2674-5216-2023-2-76-88.

18 George A. Bonanno, 'Loss, Trauma and Human Resilience: Have We Underestimated the Human Capacity to Thrive After Extremely Aversive Events?', *American Psychologist*, 59 (2004), 20–8.

19 Norman Garmezy, 'Vulnerability Research and the Issue of Primary Prevention', *American Journal of Orthopsychiatry*, 41 (1971), 101–16; H. B. Kaplan, 'Understanding the Concept of Resilience', in Handbook of Resilience in Children, ed. S. Goldstein and R. B. Brooks (New York: Springer, 2005), pp. 39–47; Michael Rutter, 'Protective Factors in Children's Response to Stress and Disadvantage', in *Primary Prevention of Psychopathology: Vol. 3. Social Competence in Children*, ed. M. W. Kent and J. E. Rolf (Hanover, NH: University Press of New England, 1979), pp. 49–74.

thriving *despite* adverse conditions. Terms such as 'vulnerability',[20] 'social influence', 'adversity' and 'stress', to name a few, converged around resilience and gave content to it in order to understand how the social world has an impact on individual lives. Here, the topic of adaptability is one that has concentrated an important amount of the secondary literature,[21] as it is one of the main characteristics linked to resilience (McAslan, *The Concept of Resilience*, pp. 9–10).

Our approach to the concept of resilience in this volume will be deployed from the perspective of the Humanities. The Humanities are here broadly and not exhaustively understood as covering disciplines such as Philosophy, History, Cultural, Film, and Literary Studies. In the process, a number of questions have arisen: what are the possible uses of the notion of resilience in the Humanities? When the term 'resilience' is actually used in these fields, what are the hermeneutical, ethical and political consequences of doing so? Are there other alternative concepts to that of resilience that may be better suited for the Humanities? Is resilience a politically conservative concept? Is it useful for understanding the current ecological crisis? The chapters in this volume attempt to answer these critical questions, not necessarily providing straightforward answers, but by scrutinising the concept of resilience in order to test its applicability within various fields such as those proposed by the authors.

II The Chapters

As we mentioned above, countering or critiquing the notion of resilience is not simply a matter of word-use, but of how a certain terminology fills a discourse with ideas that have consequences upon subjects and bodies on a social, cultural and political level. The opening chapters explicitly take up this approach. In 'Towards Destruction: An Essay on How Resilience Affects Resistance', Nicolas Lema Habash carries out a critique of resilience through the recuperation and rehabilitation of the concept of resistance. He starts from acknowledging the adaptive imperative present in the resilience approach. He mostly focuses on the use of the concept of resilience

20 R. Cantor and S. Rayner, 'Changing Perceptions of Vulnerability', in *Industrial Ecology and Global Change*, ed. R. Socolow, C. Andrews, F. Berkhout and V. Thomas (Cambridge: Cambridge University Press, 1994), pp. 69–83.

21 Carl Folke et al., 'Resilience Thinking: Integrating Resilience, Adaptability and Transformability', *Ecology and Society*, 15: 4 (2010), Art. 20, https://doi.org/10.5751/ES-03610-150420 (accessed 12 December 2024).

in public discourses in order to account for how the resilience imperative to adapt tends to capture and eliminate the disruptive potential of the notion of resistance. Drawing on Barbara Stiegler's *Il faut s'adapter*, Lema Habash links the resilient imperative of adaptation to neoliberalism; and partly following Michel Foucault, he also adds that this imperative establishes a form of subjectivity whereby the subject is forced to live situations of trauma and catastrophe on a purely individual level, cognitively erasing or forgetting the structures that allow for those traumatic and catastrophic events to take place and that exceed the individual. By recovering the notion of resistance present in the work of postcolonial thinker Amílcar Cabral, who states that resistance integrates a destructive and creative dimension, Lema Habash argues that resistance opposes resilience in that it points to the transformation of structural conditions that allow for the possibility of violence and suffering, thus moving away from an adaptative imperative.

In the same vein, Laura Quintana's chapter, 'Countering Resilience and Its Consensual Logic: Persistence, Resistance, Re-Existence', argues that, when extrapolated from the Natural Sciences to the political and ecological field, resilience becomes a tool for strengthening what she calls a 'consensualist' regime. Drawing mostly on the work of Jacques Rancière, Quintana points out that, attached to neoliberalism, this consensualist regime supposes an imposition to a certain way of structuring the political, social and cultural field; an imposition that attempts to eliminate all dissident and conflictual strategies. Consensus is about a closure to change and becoming, no matter how destroyed or ruined the world we inhabit may be. For Quintana, the model of resilience becomes an ally of this consensualist logic, because it aims at developing a form of subjectivity that should be able to adapt to what is always-already there, thus contributing to blocking forms of dissent and conflict that may envisage other possible futures. Taking up and studying a series of strategies from indigenous populations and social movements and communities, especially in the Global South, Quintana develops a different conceptual palette anchored in the notions of 'persistence', 'resistance' and 're-existence'. This pallette does not point to the adaptative imperative of 'bouncing back' to the structures that are in place, but to forms of re-inhabiting and transforming a devastated world beyond the neo-liberal consensus.

Also following an openly critical line about resilience, but now from a philosophical historical perspective, Vincent Legeay's study on the notion of *resilire* in Baruch Spinoza's work, titled 'On a famous Spinozian Occurrence about the Resilience Problem and its Inadequacy', explores a very early critical approach to resilience. By reconstructing a case given by Spinoza in one of his letters, where he criticises an approach to the study of nature whereby each of its parts is considered a full 'whole', Legeay points out that, in Spinoza, the concept of resilience inadequately describes nature and things existing in nature. This inadequacy is given by the fact that a resilient approach to how natural things encounter and affect each other precisely considers things as 'wholes' in nature and not as 'parts' of nature. In this context, to consider a thing 'resilient' means to consider it 'isolated' from the rest of nature. Legeay thus reconstructs a line of critical thought vis-à-vis resilience, which he hypothetically says that may be directed against Francis Bacon's use of resilience in his natural philosophy. If the interrelated structure of the whole of nature and its parts is not adequately accounted for by resilience, then Legeay proposes that, within a Spinozist framework, other concepts are better suited to the task of providing a more adequate account of how natural things are related to each other. This is the case of a notion such as 'aptitude' (*aptitudo*), which designates an interrelated and complex account of how a body affects and is affected by other parts of nature even if those affective relationships refer to disturbances in their structure.

The suitability of the concept of resilience is also examined for the specific domains of environmental philosophy and philosophy of nature. In his chapter, Patrick Baard answers the following question in the title of his study: 'Resilience, Ecosystems and Places: Can Resilience Delimit Dynamic Entities?' Baard answers positively: resilience can make a great contribution to environmental ethics, because the concept can help identify long-term identity and persistence, key aspects to delimit a specific ecosystemical entity, even if such an entity is highly dynamic and has vague borders. The chapter highlights the normative relevance of ecocentric axiologies and thus further argues that defining the 'whatness' of a specific ecological entity is relevant for reducing observer-dependent analysis.

Anna Winhues's chapter, 'Sustainability and Resilience as Complementary Concepts in Political Thought', proposes that, despite criticisms and attempts to replace the idea of sustainability by other concepts, such as resilience, we should not give it up. She argues that there are political and ethical advantages present in analysing human-nature relationships through the notion of sustainability. This does not mean, however, that the resilience framework would be discarded. Rather, her argument is that both concepts fruitfully complement each other and fulfil different non-exclusive functions.

The last chapter of the first part of the volume, Andrea Lehner's 'Adapt Creatively or Perish: How Resilience Dug the Grave of Strong Sustainability', adopts a different perspective on the relationship between sustainability and resilience. By sketching out a brief history of the term resilience in environmental analysis—focusing especially on texts by C. S. Holling—she proposes that the concept has been transformed: from a promising idea that may have fostered change and transformation to a conservative notion useful to maintain the new securitarian and neo-liberal status quo. According to Lehner, this issue has had detrimental consequences for environmental activism: the resilience imperative to adapt, as well as the emphasis on the complexity of systems and uncertainty, have hidden some of the straightforward causes of the ecological devastation and have prevented agents from attempting most needed structural changes to tackle the climate crisis.

However, conceptual inquiry of a certain terminology is not the only way of undertaking the task of critiquing. If the first part of the volume has a strong philosophical bent in that it proposes this kind of critical conceptual inquiry, the book also proposes a series of studies when the authors 'test' the notion of resilience in a different key. Indeed, critique may take many forms, and testing the limits of a concept concerning its suitability is also about 'using' or 'rejecting' it for analysing a particular object and developing singular case studies.

In 'Resilience and Race in the Hagiographic Tradition of Saint Martin of Porres', Celia Cussen focuses on the celebrated and innovative Afro-Peruvian saint, St Martin of Porres (1579–1639), canonised in 1962 by John XXIII as the patron saint of racial justice. Cussen asks in what ways we can see his life and works in terms of resilience. She rejects the interpretation of the racist and sectarian treatment he received as proof that St Martin was the accepting victim of his condition; this reading has even led some to see his sainthood as helping to promote, sanction, and excuse white mastership. Instead, she probes the relevant documents in order to assess whether St Martin's life is more appropriately seen as a story of wisdom gained from pain; this would suggest that his ability to adapt to hardship and finally overcome it was an example of resistance and resilience rather than abject meekness. Cussen relates St Martin's experience of hardship and social exclusion, for example, to the specifically Johannine theology of resilience. Things changed drastically in the twentieth century and St Martin came to be seen as a pioneer who had fought against and conquered the barriers created by a regime of racial prejudice during the preceding three hundred years, thereby preparing the way for his eventual canonisation in 1962, when he became a symbol of resilience for Catholics around the world.

Stephen M. Hart, in 'Resilience in Gabriel García Márquez's *One Hundred Years of Solitude*', argues that the Colombian novelist's masterpiece is the archetypal story of Latin American resilience. The novel is a story about the birth of Latin America followed by the story of its struggle to achieve political and then economic independence. The characters in the novel are resilient and they fight for their ideals against what seem to be almost impossible odds. If we focus exclusively on the ending of *One Hundred Years of Solitude*, however, we will see the novel as the depiction of a tragedy. But if we see Chapter 15 as the central episode of the novel, we are more likely to see the novel as a story of Latin American resilience. That chapter describes the so-called Banana Massacre that occurred on 6

December 1928 in Ciénaga in Colombia when the plantation workers went on strike. There have been bitter and as yet unresolved debates about what exactly happened on that day, including how many people were killed by the army. García Márquez's novel suggests that 3,000 people died that day. But, however one calculates the numbers of dead, it was during the collision of the Right and the Left at that precise moment in time that Colombia's 'pueblo' stepped forward into the limelight of world history. As a result, *One Hundred Years of Solitude* can be seen as a story of political resilience rather than simply a modern-day version of Aristotelian tragedy.

In 'Discovering Women's Resilience: The Development Film since the 1970s and 1980s', Molly Geidel puts tension on the definition of resilience developed in the Global North by analysing two 1970s development documentaries that allow her to question the resilience of Latin American women. By focusing on these two films, the author traces visual strategies to centre Global South women's resilience to understand the glorification of girls' resilience in more recent film productions. In her chapter, Geidel explores the concept of resilience as a keyword linked not only to neoliberalism, where the person can recycle pain into success through self-development, but also to gender, where the aim is for the main character, girls or women (depending on the film), to overcome the challenges they are faced with.

Camila Gatica Mizala and Jennifer Alpert explore Chilean film production in exile as a way to construct an idea of home that was both tangible and imagined in 'Reimagining Home: Resilience, Resistance, and Exile in Chilean Cinema, 1973–1985'. Given the traumatic experience of being forced to leave or being prohibited from returning after the 1973 coup d'état, Chilean filmmakers set out to face the uprooting by making films that helped to reconfigure their positions as exiles, allowing them to reimagine spaces (their country, a specific city, or a house), as well as making sense of recent history that helped to develop a locus of resistance where bouncing back was not enough to deal with the trauma of displacement. The authors state that the reconstruction and reimagination of Chile abroad took shape in three distinct ways: (1) by making home tangible through community and belonging, (2) by displacing space and time to reproduce a version of the home that is no longer there, and (3) by reimagining the past to create a material history of the home lost.

In his chapter, '"A time that has not yet been": Futurity and Survival in Marta Aponte's Caribbean Archive', Carlos Fonseca draws on a reading of Marta Aponte's *PR 3 Aguirre* (2018), itself based on an analysis of Puerto Rico's old company town, Aguirre, in order to create a post-catastrophic literary aesthetic, one which encapsulates not only Kamau Braithwaite's adage that 'Art must come out of catastrophe', but also recalls and records Aponte's heightened sense of the need to endure and to outlive catastrophe. Aponte's work shuttles back and forth between her trips to Boston to research the roots of the founding fathers of Aguirre, her search for the transatlantic route of the slaver that gruesomely inspired J. M. W. Turner's *The Slave Ship* (1840) and her present-day conversations with former residents of the company town. Fonseca sees this shuttling movement in *PR 3 Aguirre* not only as an unearthing of the buried potential of a set of individuals forgotten by History but also as a broader political call to reconfigure world history from the perspective of the Caribbean itself; the Caribbean was, after all, a space where the relations of the modern world emerged as a result of the paradoxically globalizing forces of colonialism. Their testamentary trace stubbornly refuses to be simply erased by the catastrophic passage of history. As a result, *PR 3 Aguirre* becomes not only a new beginning for the Latin American novel but also a new beginning for a community that refused to die.

In her chapter, 'Beyond resilience: *Débrouillardise* in civil war novels', Hannah Grayson, like Hart, focuses on the portrayal of resilience in literary texts. She asks a number of questions that are highly pertinent: How do novels reflect and respond to political catastrophe? How do people 'get by' during conflict? How does a city wear the fractures of civil war? How might a poetics of movement illuminate the practice of negotiating ever-changing circumstances? To answer these questions she analyses two novels from the Ivory Coast, Ahmadou Kourouma's *Quand on refuse on dit non* (*When You Refuse You Say No*, 2005) and Tanella Boni's *Matins de couvre-feu* (*Curfew Mornings*, 2005), using a theoretical frame composed of the theory of Patrice Nganang, AbdouMaliq Simone and Achille Mbembe. She proposes a new term for the understanding of the ways in which communities cope in times of war, that is, *débrouillardise*, which she defines as a 'situated, creative expertise informing a way of being in the world', which avoids the often Eurocentric connotations of resilience. As she suggests, the 'road' is the key space that fiction has provided for us to examine how resourcefulness works, and the expertise underpinning it is shown as emerging in two ways, first, in mobility, and, second, via networks. This original approach allows for new readings of contemporary African reality. Instability is revealed to be—not so much a temporary state—rather a way of being. Kourouma's novel, for its part, promotes the value of a more mobile and streetwise knowledge that is essential for surviving contemporary circumstances. Boni's novel, for its part, shows resourcefulness to be an active, networked stance towards who is with you where you are with what you have. In both *When You Refuse You Say No* and *Curfew Mornings*, the Ivory Coast subject is shown to survive in appallingly difficult circumstances once they reject the false mechanistic ontology of stability and manoeuvre a new dynamic and fluid relationship with life based on *débrouillardise*.

In 'Resilience and Resistance in the Latin American Anthropocene Western', Leidy Paola Bolaños Florido and Wolfgang Fuhrmann focused on the dialogue between genre, resilience, and the Anthropocene. They discuss how Latin America has developed a particular understanding of the Anthropocene that varies from the European and United States' approach to the concept because it follows a different timeline. This timeline is linked to extractivist processes that have impacted the region for centuries and have led to violence and displacement. The latter means that resilience and resistance are often intertwined due to their particular historical conditions in Latin America. This theoretical proposal is explored through three Latin American Western films, which allows the authors to tension what is understood by film genre, highlighting the dynamics and flexibility of film genres, being resilient in their own right in that they can adapt to tell universal stories that can take on the particular form of the national contexts in which they are set. In this chapter, the authors discuss violence, the environment, and the possibility of film to actively challenge and participate in current debates.

In the same vein, in '"Now Where Am I?": Endurance in Peter Loizos's Sophia and Her People (1985)', Ignacio Albornoz and Katerina Hatzikidi place the question of cinema's capacity to reflect on displacement and dispossession. In doing so, the authors move away from the concepts of resilience and resistance, introducing the idea of endurance. What Albornoz and Hatzikidi suggest is that endurance helps to connect to experiences and time while focusing on the duration and strength of certain experiences, particularly those captured in Peter Loizos's *Sophia and Her People*, an ethnographic film from 1983. As in the case of Gatica Mizala and Alpert's chapter, questions of displacement, forced movement, and dispossession appear as pivotal themes in the film. The idea of being able to show the experience of the film's main character, Sophia, and her affective community is key in tensioning resilience as the main concept to explore. By shedding light on the human aspect (the experience) of the protagonist, the chapter interrogates the 'adaptative' quality of resilience, since what allows the refugees to move on is precisely that sense of community built on memories and the habits of life.

For their part, Victoria Carpenter and Lakhbir Singh, in their chapter, 'When I'm Down I Just Get up—or Do I? Contentiousness of Resilience in the Face of Natural Disasters in Jamaica', begin by pointing out that the abundance of definitions of resilience suggests that it is either something amazing that is capable of morphing into a solution for anything, or it is an artificial construct that conflates different realities and is, therefore, highly problematic. Its applicability is even more contentious when the term is used to define 'resilient' communities that are faced with the prospect of dealing with the aftermath of natural disasters. In this context, they argue, resilience is nothing more than an empty signifier that obscures the complexity of a strained relation between the social actors involved in recovery after a cataclysmic event, that is, the communities affected by the natural disaster itself and the government agencies that are charged with implementing the path to recovery. They draw on Thierry Ribault's recent book, *Contre la résilience* (*Against Resilience*, 2021), which argues passionately against the idea of saddling communities that have been struck by a natural disaster with the responsibility of becoming resilient 'on their own dime', and propose that, as far as the affected communities are concerned, the 'bounce back' should be not to pre-disaster conditions but should involve an element of 'bounce-forward'. In order for this to happen, the hegemonic top-down approach adopted by governmental and/or international agencies needs to be downplayed in favour of a steer provided by the community's innate resilience which, rather than being hegemonic, is, in fact, transhegemonic. Based on a number of case studies related to natural disasters that occurred in Jamaica, this chapter argues that the best type of recovery from a natural disaster occurs when the state, the media and the public come together in a tightly knit collaboration in which unity, pride, self-investment and planning successfully converge.

III Where Do We Go From Here?

As suggested above, resilience can be a concept that helps the Humanities to understand change, whether it be gradual or sudden. Because of the different definitions coming from a multiplicity of disciplines, as a notion, it can provide another way to explore how human beings respond to those changes. Climate change is a good example of this. The floods that devastated the region of Valencia along the eastern coast of Spain in October 2024—ranging from the tragic death of over 200 people with 2,000 missing, the destruction to property and societal infrastructure, as well as the anger of the Spanish people towards their king and their prime minister—suggests we need a much more nuanced understanding of ecological disasters and how, as human beings, we might cope with such extraordinary events. What we are offering in this book is not much a toolkit allowing societies and individuals to 'get back on their feet' as a call to re-think the way we deal with disasters and trauma in the modern-day world and how they are conceptualised and named. Re-thinking issues such as these involves dealing with everyday problems but it also involves critiquing—if the needs arise—the conceptual tools we are prone to use when faced with emergencies such as these. This may involve re-tracing the history of a term in order to provide a more nuanced historical understanding of the present. Perhaps we need to think through the words rather than simply 'jumping to re-construct'.

This volume has been organised and composed so that the multiplicity strategies of critiquing and testing a concept comes to light. In this sense,

Vicent Legeay shows that a critique of resilience is not something totally new, going back in time to seventeenth-century philosophy. From a contemporary perspective, Nicolas Lema Habash and Laura Quintana show that the prevalent meaning of resilience as 'bouncing back' points to a political ontology where the imperative is 'to adapt' to a specific social organisation; the suitability of the concept of resilience is also philosophically examined for some specific fields. In these terms of particular interest is the methodological proposal by Anna Wienhues, Patrick Bard and Andrea Lehner, all of whom conceptually question as to whether the idea of resilience is useful for the study of nature, natural environments and the climate crisis, or the latter's representation, as in the case of the study by Leidy Bolaños and Wolfgang Furhmann.

A positive use of resilience appears in historical studies about specific people, such as those of Stephen M. Hart and Celia Cussen on Gabriel García Márquez and Martin of Porres, respectively. Both authors find a powerful resource on the notion of resilience in order to explore the experience of these two figures and their historical construction. On the other hand, studies such as those of Hannah Grayson and Ignacio Albornoz and Katerina Hatzkidi propose alternative uses of the notion of resilience when analysing artistic media such as documentary films and literature. Their critique of resilience concerns the cross-checking of the concept against different terminologies. They choose other terms, such as *débroullardise* and endurance, for being better suited to describe the experience of the characters they study. What is interesting in all of these cases is that this alternative terminology is modelled by a critical discussion with resilience.

An overall view of these different treatments and, most especially, of the method of critique used in this volume allows us to continue the discussion we mentioned at the beginning on the contested nature of the concept of resilience. This is, indeed, the main conclusion we can draw from the different studies presented in this volume. The idea of critiquing resilience as a method has resulted in the overall conclusion establishing the non-univocal nature of the idea of resilience when used in different disciplines in the Humanities. Put more simply, there is no single way of using and applying the concept of resilience in these disciplines.

In addition, we may say that resilience becomes contested precisely because objects of study such as historical figures, literature and films suggest that it is not a matter of a simple 'application' of the concept. In fact, these objects themselves may 'resist' the use of resilience; or, as a result of a critical dialogue with resilience, a particular object of study may lead us to other conceptual formulations. This is what happens, for example, in studies such as those of Camila Gatica Mizala and Jessica Alpert and Molly Geidel. In studying films about Latin American exiles, Gatica Mizala and Alpert conclude that these films resisted being even framed within the notion of resilience. By the same token, the developmental films from the 1970s studied by Geidel provide a powerful resource with which to question, from a gender perspective, the narrative about resilience, especially when applied to women.

If the objects of study themselves sometimes contest the use of the framework of resilience, at other times, they allow for a nuancing of the concept depending on its site of enunciation. This is precisely what is meant by the 'contentiousness of resilience' described in Victoria Carpenter and Lakhbir Singh's article. In adopting a theoretical perspective which establishes that resilience is an 'empty signifier', their chapter invites us to consider the different perspectives in which the concept of resilience may be filled and modified. In this sense, the notion of a contested concept of resilience may also be framed by its site of enunciation, that is, by paying attention to who is talking about resilience, from where resilience is being enunciated, and for what purpose.

This is why it is important to highlight that critique is also a praxis. Resilience is not only a contested concept that has stayed stagnant with two faces, as Cyrulnik has stated. The idea of contested resilience also has to become a praxis of contesting: if the concept itself changes, its critique, namely, the exploration of its limits, must also transform itself in light of the new formulations and content the concept may acquire.

IV The Result of a Project

The research on which this book is based grew out of a co-designed and international research project funded by UCL Global Engagement and hosted by the Institute of Advanced Studies, University College London (UCL), in the United Kingdom, and funded and hosted by the Department of Engineering at the Pontificia Universidad Católica de Chile (PUC), in Santiago, Chile. The project was highly interdisciplinary, bringing together researchers and scholars in the fields of Geomatic Engineering, Philosophy, Earth Sciences, Geotechnical Engineering, Psychology, Environmental Engineering, Social Studies, Education, Literary Studies, Film Studies, and History while working closely with units such as UCL's Department of Mining and the Hazard Centre, as well as external think-tanks such as the Sustainable Minerals Institute—International Centre of Excellence in Chile (SMI-ICE-Chile), which is part of the University of Queensland, Australia.

The group held five international workshops (on 24–25 November 2020, 26–27 May 2021, 8–9 November 2021, 4–5 July 2022, and 7–8 November 2022) and discussed issues such as the various natural, environmental and mining hazards that exist in the Atacama Desert, the importance of adopting a multi-disciplinary approach to resilience, and how to invigorate education so that it supports pupil resilience. We also addressed the conundrum of how societies should best address major world challenges such as earthquakes, tsunamis, and the COVID-19 pandemic. Finally, we took a long, hard look at the different approaches to the concept of resilience that we find in the Natural Sciences, the Social Sciences and the Humanities. We assessed the ways in which History, Philosophy, Education, Social Studies, and Literary and Film Studies have grappled with the meaning of resilience in the modern world. This book, indeed, grew out of a desire to bridge the gaps between our various disciplines and thereby create a new, enhanced, critical, and multi-disciplinary understanding of the concept of resilience.

We take this opportunity to express our thanks to UCL Global Engagement for their support of the UCL-PUC 'Resilience' research project, as well as our gratitude to the Institute of Advanced Studies, UCL, and the Department of Engineering at the Pontificia Universidad Católica de Chile, for hosting the project, and to the British Embassy in Santiago for their advice and encouragement. Last, but not least, thanks to Mariana Luna, Antonia Faccini and Luis Miguel Viaña who assisted us in putting together this volume.

Bibliography

Bonanno, George A., 'Loss, Trauma and Human Resilience: Have We Underestimated the Human Capacity to Thrive After Extremely Aversive Events?', *American Psychologist*, 59 (2004), 20–8.

Butler, Judith, 'What is Critique? An Essay on Foucault's Virtue', in *The Political: Readings in Continental Philosophy*, edited by David Ingram (London: Basil Blackwell, 2002), pp. 212–26.

Cantor, R., and S. Rayner, 'Changing Perceptions of Vulnerability', in *Industrial Ecology and Global Change*, edited by R. Socolow, C. Andrews, F. Berkhout, and V. Thomas (Cambridge: Cambridge University Press, 1994), pp. 69–83.

Cyrulnik, Boris, 'Résilience: notion, définition et divagation du mot', in *Les deux visages de la résilience: Contre la récupération d'un concept*, edited by Boris Cyrulnik (Paris: Odile Jacob, 2024).

Folke, Carl, Stephen R. Carpenter, Brian Walker, Marten Scheffer, Terry Chapin, and Johan Rockström, 'Resilience Thinking: Integrating Resilience, Adaptability and Transformability', *Ecology and Society*, 15: 4 (2010), https://doi.org/10.5751/ES-03610-150420 (accessed 12 December 2024).

Evans, Brad, and Julian Ried, *Resilient Life: The Art of Living Dangerously* (Cambridge: Polity, 2014).

Foucault, Michel, 'Qu'est-ce que les Lumières', in *Dits et écrits. 1954–1988*, IV, ed. Daniel Defert and François Ewald (Paris: Gallimard, 1994), pp. 562–78.

Garmezy, Norman, 'Vulnerability Research and the Issue of Primary Prevention', *American Journal of Orthopsychiatry*, 41 (1971), 101–16.

Grygorenko, Zlata, and Ganna Naydonova, 'The Concept of "Resilience": History of Formation and Approaches to Definition', *Public Administration and Law Review*, 2023, pp. 76–88, doi:10.36690/2674-5216-2023-2-76-88.

Holling, C. S., 'Resilience and Stability of Ecological Systems', *Annual Review of Ecology and Systematics*, 4 (1973), 1–23.

Holling, C. S., editor, *Adaptive Environmental Assessment and Management* (Chichester: John Wiley & Sons, 1978).

Kaplan, H. B., 'Understanding the Concept of Resilience', in *Handbook of Resilience in Children*, edited by S. Goldstein and R. B. Brooks (New York: Springer, 2005), pp. 39–47.

Lazos Chavero, Elena, 'Resilencia: Antítesis de luchas y movimientos sociales de transformación', in *Críticas y contrastes a la resiliencia socioecológica*, ed. Tlacaelel Rivera-Núñez, Laura Collin Harguindeguy, Elena Lazos Chavero (Tlaxcala: El Colegio de Tlaxcala, 2025), pp. 67–96.

Longstaff, P. H., 'Security, Resilience, and Communication in Unpredictable Environments such as Terrorism, Natural Disasters, and Complex Technology', Program on Information Resources Policy (Cambridge, MA: Center for Information Policy Research, Harvard University, 2005).

Mallet, Robert, 'On the Physical Conditions Involved in the Construction of Artillery, and on Some Hitherto Unexplained Causes of the Destruction of Cannon in Service', *The Transactions of the Royal Irish Academy*, 23 (1856): 141–436, https://www.jstor.org/stable/30079308 (accessed 12 December 2024).

McAslan, Alastair, *The Concept of Resilience. Understanding its Origins, Meaning and Utility* (Adelaide, Australia: Torrens Resilience Institute, 2010).

Merriman, Mansfield, *A Text-book on the Mechanics of Materials and of Beams, Columns and Shafts*, 1st edn (New York: J. Wiley and Sons, 1885).

Rivera-Núñez, Tlacaelel, Laura Collin Harguindeguy, Elena Lazos Chavero, editors, *Críticas y contrastes a la resiliencia socioecológica* (Tlaxcala: El Colegio de Tlaxcala, 2025).

Rivera-Núñez, Tlacaelel, 'Una introducción crítica a la resiliencia socioecológica desde la ecología política', in *Críticas y contrastes a la resiliencia socioecológica*, edited by Tlacaelel Rivera-Núñez, Laura Collin Harguindeguy, Elena Lazos Chavero (Tlaxcala: El Colegio de Tlaxcala, 2025), pp. 14–40.

Rutter, Michael, 'Protective Factors in Children's Response to Stress and Disadvantage', in *Primary Prevention of Psychopathology: Vol. 3: Social Competence in Children*, edited by M. W. Kent and J. E. Rolf (Hanover, NH: University Press of New England, 1979), pp. 49–74.

Stigler, Barbara, *Il faut s'adapter. Sur un nouvel impératif politique* (Paris: Gallimard, 2019).

Tredgold, Mr. Thomas, 'On the Transverse Strength and Resilience of Timber', *The Philosophical Magazine*, 51:239 (1818), 214–16, https://doi.org/10.1080/14786441808637536 (accessed 12 December 2023).

Tusaie, Kathleen and Janyce Dyer, 'Resilience: A Historical Review of the Construct', *Holistic Nursing Practice*, 18: 1 (2004), 3–8, doi:10.1097/00004650-200401000-00002 (accessed 12 December 2024).

Part I

Critique (Philosophy, Ecology, Sustainability)

I

Towards Destruction: An Essay on How Resilience Affects Resistance

Nicolas Lema Habash

During the aftermath of the hurricane Katrina disaster in New Orleans, in 2005, a poster with a quotation attributed to the local lawyer Tracie Washington widely circulated. It said: 'Every time you say, "Oh, they're so resilient," that means you can do something else to me.'[1] The political message in these words is equivalent to that of a blog, also about the Katrina disaster, whose title reads: 'The next person who calls me resilient, I'm gonna stab in the neck.'[2] These references point to an awareness that resilience has become a way of treating people's behaviour and attitudes towards catastrophe through the mode of privately absorbing the consequences of disaster. In opposition to what many advocates of a resilience approach say, resilience here is not perceived as a source of appeasement of social conflict. The discourse on resilience rather triggers suspicion and anger. In these phrases, resilience is seen as an imposition, a normative ought one is called upon to perform in order to adapt to a disastrous reality.

1 Reference reported by John Patrick Leary in the entry 'Resilience' in his *Keywords: The New Language of Capitalism* (Chicago: Heymarket Books, 2018). On similar references against resilience, see Malaka Shwaikh, 'Beyond Expectations of Resilience: Towards a Language of Care', *Global Studies Quarterly*, 17 (2023), 1–13.

2 'The next person who calls me resilient I'm gonna stab in the neck', Catfish for Lunch, https://catfishforlunch.wordpress.com/2012/08/31/the-next-person-who-talks-about-resilience-ill-gonna-stab-in-the-neck/ (accessed 8 December 2024).

The aim of this chapter is not to provide a thorough study of the ways in which the population perceives resilience. The critical remarks in these references cannot be extrapolated to collective ways of considering resilience. However, I start mentioning these references about resilience to acknowledge that this term—which has become a "sexy" concept in order to describe how life should cope with catastrophe, insecurity, destruction and stress—should be further examined critically. Insofar as resilience has become pervasive, it is necessary to establish the shortcomings of this concept, the limits of its promises when articulated in public discussions and its relationship with the current social-historical context within which it is used.

My argument in this chapter establishes that there is an entanglement between the notion of resilience and neoliberalism. It is in this context that an imperative to *adapt* fills the resilience discourse and transforms it into a disciplinary device integrated into everyday life. I will contend that one key aspect of resilience is that it affects another concept, resistance,[3] thus rendering the latter a merely submissive instance facing trauma and catastrophe. By drawing on the work of the Caboverdian thinker Amilcar Cabral, I recuperate a different perspective on resistance that challenges the adaptive imperative of resilience.

I

The genealogies of the concept of "resilience" tell us that it derives from the Latin and means 'bounce', 'leap back' or 'rebound'. Francis Bacon used the word in a philosophical context to describe how a sound 'rebounds' or 'bounces back' when it hits a surface, thus producing and echo.[4] What goes

3 Other approaches to the (exclusionary) relationship between resilience and resistance can be found in Marc Neocleous, 'Resisting Resilience', *Radical Philosophy,* 178 (2013), 2–7; and Álex Mesa, 'Resistencia en vez de resiliencia. Plasticidad en vez de flexibilidad', *Papel Máquina,* 20 (2024), 139–52.

4 Bacon's key passage reads: 'The echo cometh as the original sound doth, in a round orb of air: it were good to try the creating of the echo where the body repercussing maketh an angle: as against the return of a wall, &c. Also we see that in mirrors there is the like angle of incidence, from the object to the glass, and from the glass to the eye. And if you strike a ball side-long, not full upon the surface, the rebound will be as much the contrary way. Whether there be any such resilience in echoes (that is, whether a man shall hear better if he stand aside the body repercussing, than if he stand where he speaketh, or anywhere in a right line between, may be tried. Trial likewise would be made, by standing nearer the place of repercussing than he that speaketh; and again by standing further off than he that speaketh; and so knowledge would be taken,

often unnoticed in Bacon's 1627 *Sylva Sylvarum* is that he was not only *describing* the phenomenon of sound bouncing off surfaces, but actually attempting to establish the conditions of possibility of how this 'bouncing back' could be *improved*—in relation to the angle of the hit—so that the echo may be better heard. In other words, Bacon's use of the term resilience gestures towards the possibility of 'experimenting' with the ways to 'reproduce' sound as accurately as possible, by considering the multiple physical obstacles against it clashes.

I use the word 'reproduce' as another way of explaining the result of the 'resilience' or 'bouncing back' of a sound. Bacon's guidelines to experiment with sounds lead to a notion of resilience establishing that the best reproduction of sounds would come from its bouncing back so perfectly, that it may be heard as neat as when it was first produced. Resilience in this context is about reproducing, repeating; it is about suffering a shock (like hitting a wall), but being able to bounce back—almost unaltered—from the shock. This is why it is so important, for Bacon, to measure (among other things) the angle of this shock, so that the sound may not lose its qualities and be able to bounce back, in the form of an echo, almost as the same sound first produced.

I would argue that Bacon's use of the concept of resilience in the sixteenth century is incredibly similar to its current one. Resilience seems to still define (as in Bacon) the possibility of a certain material or person to 'rebound' from a shock; or to be able to absorb a trauma in such a way that the person, or the object, is capable of 'bouncing back' from that trauma. This 'bounceback-ability'[5] implicitly supposes (just as in Bacon) that we try to design a material or train a person to being able to reproduce, as best as possible, its previous state after the shock or trauma. The material and the person have changed, of course, but we attempt to go about *almost as if* nothing had happened, just as in Bacon's example the sound has gone through physical changes but we can still hear it, in the echo, as best as possible.

What is interesting about Bacon's notion of resilience is that the idea of an object bouncing back is also present in many current mainstream uses of the concept, when applied to individuals, societies and non-human systems. Indeed, two bestsellers on resilience assume from the start that the most appropriate way of understanding the notion of resilience is by following the idea of bouncing back: Linda Graham's *Bouncing Back: Rewiring*

---

whether echoes, as well as original sounds, be not strongest near hand (Francis Bacon, *Sylva Sylvarum*, in *The Works of Francis Bacon*, 4, ed. James Spedding, Robert Leslie Ellis, Douglas Denon Heath (Boston: Brown and Taggard, 1862), §245, p. 284).

5 I borrow this term from Brad Evans and Julian Reid, *Resilient Life: The Art of Living Dangerously* (Cambridge: Polity Press, 2014), p. xii.

Your Brain for Maximum Resilience and Well-Being[6] and Andrew Zolli and Ann Marie Healy's *Resilience: Why Things Bounce Back.* In the latter, the authors open the first chapter by explicitly stating that their book 'is about why things bounce back'.[7] They are aware that bouncing back is not equivalent—at least not always—to *recovery* (Zoli and Healy, *Resilience*, p. 28). They thus recognize that resilience is not the same as coming back to an unaltered first state. As Bacon's sound hitting a wall and bouncing back, they recognize that an object may change and still be called 'resilient'. While recovery may be one of the outcomes of a resilient system, bouncing back rather means that an object is able to maintain its main purpose without being altered to the point of total destruction.

Thus, Zolli and Healey say that resilience may be defined 'as the capacity of a system, enterprise, or a person to *maintain* its core purpose and integrity in the face of dramatically changed circumstances' (*Resilience*, p. 17. My italics.). This idea of maintaining purpose and integrity is something key to understand current uses of the notion of resilience in the public discourse. It relates, once again, to Bacon's use of the term as applied to sounds creating an echo, because the most important is to calculate how a system of relations works, so that the desired outcomes may be maintained or conserved. In the case of Bacon, the relationship of the sound with the walls should be calculated—and, out of that calculation, managed—so that the purpose of the echoed sound (being heard well) could be maintained. Although Zolli and Healy refer to much more complex systems (such as the financial market, coral reefs or a human community), the same elements establishing what resilience amounts to are present in their definition and in Bacon's use of the term: by the specific bouncing back of the elements within a system, the outcome should be maintained, either in the case of coral reef survival or in the proper hearing of a sound. Their studies may be separated by some centuries, but the consideration of things in a network of systematic relations, able to maintain their purpose or goal, is maintained.

I would thus point to a specific *conservative* imprint on the concept of resilience that extends from Bacon all the way up to the twenty-first century. This conservative imprint could be further illustrated in the public discourse, for example, when Barack Obama used the term in his 10-year Twin Towers attack commemorative speech:

> These past ten years tell a story of resilience. The Pentagon is repaired, and filled with patriots working in common purpose. Shanksville is the scene

6 Linda Graham, *Bouncing Back: Rewiring Your Brain for Maximum Resilience and Well-Being* (Novato: New World Library, 2013).

7 Andrew Zolli and Marie Healy, *Resilience: Why Things Bounce Back* (New York: Free Press, 2012), p. 39.

> of friendships forged between residents of that town, and families who lost loved ones there. New York remains a vibrant capital of the arts and industry, fashion and commerce. Where the World Trade Center once stood, the sun glistens off a new tower that reaches toward the sky. Our people still work in skyscrapers. Our stadiums are filled with fans, and our parks full of children playing ball. Our airports hum with travel, and our buses and subways take millions where they need to go. Families sit down to Sunday dinner, and students prepare for school. This land pulses with the optimism of those who set out for distant shores, and the courage of those who died for human freedom. (Quoted in Evans and Read, *Resilient Life*, p. 27)

Obama's speech supposes that the United States, as a nation, has precisely this capacity to 'bounce back' from the traumatic event of the catastrophe, thus conserving a specific way of life. The nation is able to deflect, as it were, the shocks and traumas, so as to maintain what it already had as best as possible; as if nothing had happened.

After reading Obama, let us be even more specific about the conservative bent of the notion of resilience. What does resilience help to conserve exactly? As Zolli and Healy remind us, resilience cannot be reduced to recovery, so it does not conserve the *same* state of the object that has undergone a trauma. I would rather argue that what is conserved is a specific *relationship* between this object and the other entities surrounding it; or, put differently, it refers to a specific relationship of the parts composing the object, a relationship ultimately allowing the object to maintain its purpose. This specific relationship renders the object pragmatically, practically and axiologically operative in a concrete context. In the case Bacon studies, this relationship is marked by 'hearing well' the sounds produced, even if those sounds have bounced on and off several surfaces, thus changing their trajectory. The echo remains capable of conserving the relationship articulated between the listener and the listened object; a relationship verified precisely by the act of 'hearing well'.

The conservation of specific relationships on a social level is to what resilience refers in the Obama speech. The United States has continued to operate on the basis of specific relationships between human beings, articulated via institutions such as the workplace, the school system, the family and the entertainment and culture industry. By the same token, those relationships between human beings are accompanied by other kinds of relationships established between people and objects, such as inhabiting buildings or using public transportation. Conserving all of these relationships is what I would call 'conserving normality'. Thus, resilience *qua* 'bouncing back' supposes maintaining a state of normality, where 'the normal' is defined according to a specific operative relationship, even if the particular objects of which that relationship is composed have changed.

We may therefore provide a first characterization of the notion of resilience: it is a conservative concept, because it refers to the '"conservation" of a specific state, or set of practices, after the unavoidable changes produced by a shock or trauma'[8].

Thus far, I have been exploring the notion of resilience as equally applied to any object, human and non-human. In fact, resilience research seems to establish that the way in which different systems bounce back and maintain the operative relationship between their parts can be extrapolated to understand the behaviour of human and non-human living beings, as well as their relationships with non-living entities. This is what is at stake in Zolli and Healy's previously quoted definition of resilience, which refers to 'systems,' 'enterprises' and 'persons'. The issue here is that extrapolating to human behaviour the study of how an inanimate object (like a building) or a collective non-human living organism (like a coral reef) may resiliently conserve their core structure (so that it is not destroyed) is not something done in a vacuum. I am not saying that humans should be studied in isolation from other non-human systems. However, the application of the notion of resilience to the case of human beings entails concrete results that need to be critically studied.

II

Current uses of the concept of resilience should not be detached from the cultural, social, economic and biopolitical context in which we are located. Why has a concept, mostly used in natural sciences, recently acquired a key role in social and mental health sciences, such as sociology and developmental psychology? Why has it been densely integrated into the technocratic public discourse and security reports? And, perhaps most importantly, why are we, humans, called upon to be resilient?[9]

An answer to these questions has been sketched in two significant publications on the concept of resilience: *Resilient Life: The Art of Living Dangerously* by Brad Evans and Julian Reid; and *How Capitalism Will End?*

8 On the conservative characteristics of resilience, see also Anna Wienhues' contribution in this volume.

9 Zolli and Healy title the first chapter of their book 'The Resilience Imperative'. The reader discovers that this 'imperative' refers to a normative element that should be present in human and non-human systems in order to operate well. The idea of applying interchangeably the idea of an imperative to human and non-human systems is highly problematic, as it entails an implicit equivalent idea of agency for human and non-human entities.

by Wolfgang Streeck.[10] These works stress that the current implementation of a resilience approach responds to a cultural phenomenon pertaining to contemporary capitalism, namely, the generalization of insecurity as a mode of existence and the naturalization of catastrophe and risk.

It is not difficult to see, from our previous discussion, how resilience is framed within a larger context where things are always insecure and constantly run the risk of being destroyed. If, as I have stressed, the concept of resilience refers to the strategies of 'conservation' of an object or system, then we immediately understand that we have implicitly or explicitly framed that object or system within a context of 'danger'. In other words, for resilience to be operative as a concept, there is the supposition that something bad may happen to the object or system in question. If we suppose that the object or system is and will be totally safe, then there is no need to be resilient and the concept would be inoperative to study any phenomenon.

The critical issue here is not that bad things may happen to natural objects,[11] but the way in which catastrophe is framed as an ongoing threat menacing us. Interestingly enough, both critiques and advocates of the resilience approach agree on this point. For Evans and Reid, resilience has filled the public discourse accompanied by 'the catastrophic imaginary of contemporary liberal rule' (Evans and Reid, *Resilience*, p. 9). Zolli and Healy support the resilience approach, by arguing that, since our contemporary world has become more and more interconnected and complex, the probability of risk grows higher and higher: 'what resilience researchers call [resilience is a] preserving adaptive capacity—the ability to adapt to changed circumstances while fulfilling one's core purpose—and it's an essential skill in an age of unforeseeable disruption and volatility' (Zolli and Healy, *Resilience*, p. 18).

What is interesting about Zolli and Healy's work is that they tend to merge an ontological approach with a normative-cum-ethical one. Resilience appears as something like a property that natural systems (such as coral reefs) inherently have. It is as if resilience was part of their essential constitution, because otherwise they would not have been able to survive. That is why survival and adaptive strategies can be described and studied in non-human entities as a 'property'. On the other hand, however, this property present

10 Wolfgang Streeck, *How Capitalism Will End: Essays on a Failing System* (London: Verso, 2016).

11 After all, everything that exists as a specific singularity will be destroyed by something else existing in nature. On this point, I follow Spinoza, *Ethics*, IV, axiom: 'There is no singular thing in nature than which there is not another more powerful and stronger. Whatever one is given, there is another more powerful by which the first can be destroyed.' I quote Edwin Curley's translation in *The Collected Works of Spinoza*, vol. 1 (Princeton: Princeton University Press, 1985).

in natural non-human systems is a 'skill' humans need to develop in order to withstand risk and catastrophe, most especially in our age of unexpected volatility and disruption. A natural property of a system is extrapolated into the human species, as a behaviour this species should acquire. Furthermore, acquiring this behaviour is transformed into a normative imperative. Zolli and Healy could reply by saying that resilience has always been present in all systems, human and non-human. Just as a coral reef requires resilience to survive, so did the Roman Empire: we could map out the strategies of Roman imperial survival under the conceptual apparatus of resilience.

However, my point about an imperative of acquiring the 'skill' of resilience still stands. It would be certainly possible to analyse the strategies of survival of any community at any time of history. But the fact that we are advocating *now* for resilience, in a context conceived of as *more* risky and volatile, talks about a specificity of the normative statement in our age; an age perceived as constantly threatened by impending catastrophe. In other words, it is not a random fact that resilience has become a token word, in *our age*, to describe and prescribe a specific way of preparing us for catastrophe and for withstanding it.

The lexicon of this normative prescription for acquiring resilience in our age has become attached to the concept of adaptation. On this point, advocates and critiques of the resilient approach agree once again. As we saw in the previous quotation from Zolli and Healy, they establish that resilience entails the preservation of an 'adaptive capacity' (Zolli and Healy, *Resilience*, p. 18). This is very close to the definition that Wolfgang Streeck gives of resilience: 'resilience is not resistance but, more or less voluntarily, adaptive adjustment' (*How Capitalism Will End*, p. 40). We will return to the distinction between resistance and resilience proposed by Streeck. It is important to understand, first, the context within which he places this definition of resilience, because it gives us clues about the political implications of extrapolating the resilience-cum-adaptation discourse into human individuals in our context.

According to Streeck, we live in a phase of capitalism that he calls 'a post-capitalist interregnum'. This concept defines what for him will be the last phase of contemporary capitalism, which as a system is coming to an end due to its own contradictions, without any foreseeable alternative.[12] This so-called post-capitalist interregnum is characterized by a state of permanent crisis, lacking institutional devices to provide the possibility of organized collective action or security on a macro-level. The de-institutionalization of

12 On the closure of alternative futures, conceptualised under the idea of a 'consensual' logic attached to resilience, see also Laura Quintana's chapter in this volume.

life and the permanent state of crisis—natural in appearance, but concretely produced by the progressive disintegration of a specific economic system of capital accumulation—means that our contemporary society lives not in an order properly speaking, but in a 'disorder'. As a result, the burden of the organization of everyday life moves to the micro-level. The burden is upon particular individuals to put up with the current situation governed by insecurity and to search for the mechanisms allowing them to continue surviving in this context. Resilience is one of the cultural devices implemented by the contemporary capitalist establishment to cope with this mode of existence. Resilience does not seek to resist these changes, to question their causes or to destroy this state of affairs; but imposes instead, to every individual, that they should be able to adjust and adapt to this volatile and insecure age.

I am not in a position to comment on all aspects of Streeck's characterization of what according to him is the ending phase of capitalism. However, I want to highlight that the relationship between capitalism, in its current neoliberal phase, and the frame of insecurity and risk enveloping our age cannot be overlooked. The sources of this catastrophic framing of current everyday life certainly relate to the ecological crisis and devastation in the midst of which we live. But there is also a material organization of human society that mirrors this ecological crisis, whose sources are to be sought in the ideology present in neoliberal capitalism and in the state forms that accompany this capitalist agenda. Although Streeck talks about a post-capitalist interregnum to describe this historical period, this moment is still considered as a phase of capitalism itself.

Therefore, by tying up the discourse on insecurity, risk and catastrophe with the economic, social and political bases within which our culture currently lives, it is possible to uncover the societal *structural* elements that make that discourse possible. If the resilience approach and discourse has become more pervasive (and, according to their advocates, more necessary as well), this is due to the structural conditions that allow for this discourse and approach to grow. The resilience approach is inseparable from the material bases upon which our society lives. It is thus crucial to scrutinize why the language of adaptation has become so important to talk about resilience, not only as description of a state of affairs, but as a normative imperative with ethical and political consequences. The notion of adaptation has, of course, a history of its own, one that could not be summarized in this chapter. I am interested in pointing to other references linking up the notion of adaptation to neoliberalism, in order to complement Streeck's ideas.

In a significant recent contribution on the neoliberal ideology, Barbara Stigler has precisely established a relationship between the development of neoliberalism and the notion of adaptation. Her book titled *Il faut s'adapter. Sur un nouvel impératif politique* (*One Must Adapt: On a New Political*

Imperative) ties up two ideas I have been discussing thus far: adaptation and normativity. Stigler carefully studies the neoliberal line of thought developed by Walter Lippmann and the philosophical sources that nourished his writings. Although Stigler does not refer to the concept of resilience, her approach to the idea of adaptation also implies that the normative structure of neoliberalism—at least as developed by Lippmann—supposes an understanding of the human as a natural species that must adjust to the development of world economy. According to Lippmann, the speed at which the global capitalist economy has developed from the Industrial Revolution onwards (what he calls the 'Great Revolution') has opened up a gap between the evolution of the human species and the new global environment centred around the global market. Following Stigler's account, we encounter here, once again, the insecurity-and-risk paradigm (ever-present in the resilience approach and discourse), now as one of the bases of Lippmann's line of neoliberalism:

> For the first time in the evolution of life and living beings, a species, ours, finds itself in a situation of complete disadaptation to its new environment. For Lippmann, this situation can be explained by the difference in rhythm between the natural inclinations of the human species, inherited from a long evolutionary history that changed at the very slow pace of biological history, and the demands of our new environment imposed brutally by the Industrial Revolution. This fact provided the problematic for all of Lippmann's political work: how to readapt the human species to an unstable, constantly changing and completely open environment, while its entire evolutionary history has adapted it to a stable and relatively closed environment, from the rural community to the City-State theorised by the Greeks? How can its vital need for stability and enclosure be reconciled with the acceleration of all flows and the destruction of all borders by globalisation? At what rhythm must the human species be reformed to reconcile its slow evolutionary history with the new demands of the "great" Industrial Revolution?[13].

Lippmann's answers to these questions are based upon an understanding of the human as a passive and malleable being, with whom a specific neoliberal agenda may work in order to re-adapt the species to these new challenges: 'What legitimises the rupture and what inspires the agenda of new liberalism is based on the diagnosis of a "cultural lag" of the human species, which implies to produce a "readjustment" between the stasis of the habit and the flow of the new, and thus to increase an "adaptability"

13 Barbara Stigler, *Il faut s'adapter. Sur un nouvel impératif politique* (Paris: Gallimard, 2019), p. 14. All translations from Stigler are mine.

[*adaptabilité*], or a "flexibility," imposing itself as the new content of the educational act' (Stigler, *Il faut s'adapter*, p. 220). Using the language of resilience, we may say that, for Lippmann, human re-adaptation requires a process of 'bouncing back' that may allow to sync up human individuals and communities with this new reality[14]. We can therefore observe that the whole language of 'adaptation' is extrapolated from an understanding of nature and that this operation responds to a specific political-cum-economic agenda. This is not to say that the human is not a natural being; it is only to uncover the specific epistemic and political conditions under which the human is said and required to be 'adaptable'.

Stigler's argument about this specific genealogical thread of neoliberalism is further complexified through the linkage she establishes between the adaptation imperative and contemporary biopolitics. She argues that the specificity of Lippmann's new liberalism is to question a traditional liberal idea: that a paradigm of total *laissez-faire* would achieve the purpose of species re-adaptation. At this point, Stigler enters into a dialogue with Michel Foucault. Commenting on his lectures delivered at the end of the 1970s in Paris, Stigler points out that Foucault's coinage of the concepts of biopolitics and bio-power was inextricably linked to his understanding of the nascent field of liberalism in the eighteenth century and, subsequently, of neoliberalism.[15] Stigler points to passages of Foucault's 1977–8 lectures where he says that the new liberal paradigm of government (targeting what he calls 'population' and not simply 'individuals') implies a certain trust in the *nature reality* of human beings. Hence, the *laissez-faire* paradigm takes shape: 'The game of liberalism—not interfering, allowing free movement, letting things follow their course; *laisser faire, passer et aller*—basically and fundamentally means acting so that reality develops, goes its way, and follows its own course according to the laws, principles, and mechanisms of

14 It is important to stress that, according to Stigler's reading of Lippmann, this does not entail a return of a romanticised pre-capitalist past.

15 Foucault defines what he means by bio-power at the beginning of his 1977–8 lectures: 'By this I mean a number of phenomena that seem to me to be quite significant, namely, the set of mechanisms through which the basic biological features of the human species became the object of a political strategy, of a general strategy of power, or, in other words, how, starting from the eighteenth century, modem Western societies took on board the fundamental biological fact that human beings are a species. This is roughly what I have called bio-power.' Michel Foucault, *Security, Territory, Population: Lectures at the Collège de France, 1977–1978*, ed. Michel Senellart, trans. Graham Burchell (New York: Palgrave, 2007), p. 1. *Grosso modo*, it is safe to say that, at least during this phase of his work, Foucault characterises the age of bio-power also as that of 'biopolitics' and of 'security governance'.

reality itself' (Foucault, *Security*, p. 48). However, Stigler points to a crucial difference between this liberal *laissez-faire* attitude towards populations and the *neoliberal* approach. In this new liberalism, the trust in the nature of the human species is qualified through the idea that the human is *not naturally* able to adapt or re-adapt to the new conditions imposed by capitalism: 'With the new liberalism theorised by Lippmann, a new age of biopolitics is opened, based no longer on confidence in a good nature, but on the fact that the human species is radically deficient, linked to the inertia of its evolutionary history' (Stigler, *Il faut s'adapter*, p. 221).

The consequences of this dispute between Stigler and Foucault do not lie in the nature of biopolitics as the government of populations encroached upon their bodies. They rather lie in the idea that, in order to fully understand the biopolitical nature of the neoliberal agenda, it is not possible to separate bio-power from regimes of *disciplinary* power aiming at a specific individual. As Stigler correctly notes, Foucault hesitates on the relationship between these two regimes of power, bio-power and discipline. The issue is that there was ultimately a tendency in Foucault's lectures to separate these two regimes, *as if biopolitcs could do without disciplinary power*. Stigler wants to underline that, in order to understand Lippmaniannian neoliberalism, it is important to fully reintegrate disciplinary power into the study of biopolitics and bio-power. According to her, this new liberalism

> also places at the centre of its agenda the programme of a permanent adjustment [*redressement*] of behaviour by the disciplines, which takes up to the letter their objective of bringing the labour force into line with the demands of globalised capitalism. By extending public health policies with educational and cultural policies that reform [*redressent*] the human species and steer it in the right direction, Lippmannian biopolitics thus reinforces the disciplinary project instead of counterbalancing it. (Stigler, *Il faut s'adapter*, pp. 228–9)

Following Stigler, my view is that this how we should understand resilience: as a disciplinary device imposing the normative imperative of adaptation on individual human beings, within a biopolitical environment marked by a discourse of looming risk and catastrophe.

What would be the specificity of this disciplinary device of resilience? We may follow Stigler again in pointing out that the adaptation imperative relates to a series of neoliberal policies implemented in a top-down fashion and invading an individual's life in the areas of public health, education and labour. The goal of this Lippmannian agenda would be to redress or adjust the human population, so as to make it more adjustable to drastic changes. While I agree with this diagnosis, I would argue that the resilience approach and discourse should take into account a further consideration about the structures under which such a top-down agenda promoting adaptation operates. Considered as a disciplinary device, I will argue that resilience contributes to a *cognitive erasure* of the structures that constitute the conditions of possibility for generating or preventing (or least diminishing the risks of) catastrophe.

In order to develop this argument, let us go back to Foucault's lectures and establish how it would be possible to restore an analysis simultaneously involving bio-power and disciplinary power. While Stigler is right in that there is a tendency in the later Foucault to separate bio-power from disciplinarity, there are also moments in his work where we can observe how both modes of power may operate together.

Towards the end of his lecture of 18 January 1978, Foucault lists some differences between the regimes of discipline and 'security' (this latter corresponding to the emergent biopolitical mode of government). It is not my point to summarize these differences in detail. I would rather like to underline that Foucault also notes that, in the passage from one regime to the other, disciplines are not abolished. They are rather subsumed or reorganized within the new regime of biopolitical security:

> with the establishment of these mechanisms of security there is a considerable activation and propagation of the disciplinary corpus. For in order actually to guarantee this security one has to appeal, to take just one example, to a whole series of techniques for the surveillance of individuals, the diagnosis of what they are, the classification of their mental structure, of their specific pathology, and so on; in short one has to appeal to a whole disciplinary series that proliferates under mechanisms of security and is necessary to make them work. (Foucault, *Security*, pp. 7–8)

What happens, therefore, is that discipline devices, traditionally attached to the vigilance and control of a single bodily individual, are now reformulated within a security regime targeting the whole population. Therefore, disciplinary and juridical-legal techniques are reformulated in this new paradigm of governance. I believe Stigler is fruitfully updating this theory of securitarian governance when she says that neoliberalism (at least in its Lippmannian version) requires and implements a disciplinary biopolitics through mechanisms such as education, health and labour.

It would be most useful to understand how the disciplinary technics aiming at increasing the adaptability of individuals fit with the development of securitarian biopolitical strategies. This would lead us to better account for the regime of contemporary biopolitical discipline. A full account of this issue would require a whole study. However, in order to ground the argument that the resilience discourse and approach has become one of the disciplinary devices operating within a larger biopolitical paradigm, I would like to draw attention to one aspect of Foucault's characterization of the security paradigm.

When Foucault illustrated the differences between the disciplinary regime and the nascent security regime, he compared different ways of organizing cities (or plans to build cities) corresponding to each regime. The disciplinary mode aims at regimenting the city through a static model of space where everything needs to be built from scratch, in a site where the created city is envisaged as something fully completed and perfect. On the other hand, securitarian biopolitical governance breaks with the previous paradigm and conceives of space as a milieu within which a human liveable space may be built. This milieu is considered as dynamic space. 'Dynamic' here implies an ordering based on open series of individuals and things circulating through a territory. It is an order that can only be assured through the calculation of probabilities. This is why Foucault insists that the security regime factors in an ever-changing and totally uncertain future: 'security will try to plan a milieu in terms of events or series of events or possible elements, of series that will have to be regulated within a multivalent and transformable framework. The specific space of security refers then to a series of possible events; it refers to the temporal and the uncertain [*aléatoire*], which have to be inserted within a given space' (Foucault, *Security*, p. 22).

In this last formulation, space must conform to a regime of governance targeting the whole population. If we take seriously Foucault's idea that it is not possible to envisage this securitarian regimen without a reformulation of disciplinary measures, then we have to establish what specific disciplinary devices are required for this paradigm of governance full of unpredictability. Although Stigler attempts to supplement Foucault's analysis by insisting that the biopolitical paradigm of neoliberalism considers the nature of the human species somewhat differently from what Foucault had proposed, we can also understand how a disciplinary paradigm based on adaptability fits with this description of the securitarian regime. Indeed, if discipline has to be reformulated to fit within biopolitical security, the disciplinary technics would have to be based, just as the security paradigm, on adaptability to an unpredictable future.

Resilience is one (though certainly not the only) mechanism whereby this condition of 'fit' between biopolitics and discipline can be fulfilled. What I have discussed as a framing of the resilience-cum-adaptation imperative within a discourse of risk and catastrophe corresponds to the contemporary avatar of Foucault's characterization of the securitarian paradigm of governance. Resilience connects the unpredictability about the future with an insecurity on an individual level, thus forcing the individual to adapt to whatever change.

There is a further element that needs to be accounted for in this resilience imperative. Stigler notes that adaptation in neoliberalism required, according to Lippmann (and also to Foucault), a specific agenda on which it relied to carry out its disciplinary programme. My argument is that adaptation in the form of resilience accomplishes a further task, which is that of *hiding* the very existence of that agenda and of the structural conditions needed for that agenda to be carried out. To put this in a language that it most probably different to Foucault's: resilience contributes to hiding the very idea that there are certain structural conditions required for this security paradigm to eventuate. The result is that resilience—considered as a disciplinary mechanism—not only fits well within a security regime stressing unpredictability, catastrophe and risk, but it also contributes to diluting the possibility of challenging the very conditions that allow for the existence of that security paradigm.

One of the mechanisms whereby resilience operates in this way is by affecting another concept often associated with it: resistance.

III

I have proposed the previous discussion about the intersection between resilience, adaptation, discipline and neoliberalism to complement my characterization of resilience as a conservative concept. Defining the notion of resilience in this way is not only a matter of conceptual analysis, but also involves a political dimension. The imperative to resiliently adapt to a risky environment thus contributes to conserving and maintaining a specific structure that is inseparable from contemporary neoliberal capitalism.

Let us now go back to Streeck's definition of resilience, where he distinguishes it from resistance: 'resilience is not resistance but, more or less voluntarily, adaptive adjustment' (Streeck, *How Capitalism*, p. 40; see also Evans and Reid, *Resilient Life*, pp. 6–8). Although Streeck does not further develop the difference between these two concepts, it is an important insight that needs to be explored. It is not enough to establish that resilience is not resistance; it is also necessary to establish, via a critique of resilience, how the notion of resistance is affected by its assimilation or differentiation with resilience and what political consequences result from this conceptual comparison.

If we go back to Obama's speech about the United States' resilience after the Twin Tower attacks, we could say that his words have an implicit understanding of resistance as related to resilience: to resist is to maintain or to conserve something. Resisting a tragic event or shock would then suppose being able to reconstruct life (almost the same) as it was before the shock. This implicit assumption present in Obama's words is explicitly stated in the Oxford English Dictionary's definition of resilience. One of its entries of this term reads: 'the quality or fact of being able to recover quickly or easily from, or *resist* being affected by, a misfortune, shock, illness, etc.; robustness; adaptability' (my italics).

In this conservative use of the notion of resistance—assimilated with the conservative nature of the concept of resilience—resistance becomes emptied of any political positive meaning. Resilience does not seem capable of problematizing what is considered to be a 'normal' a way of life. Even more importantly, resilience seems to be a concept not suited to guide us towards a critique of the structural conditions under which the traumatic event first took place. Is there something problematic in the structure of the American Way of Life and its imperialistic ramifications that created the conditions, *in the first place*, for trauma and catastrophe to happen? Are we not simply recreating those same conditions when we try to bounce back into normality after trauma? If resilience focuses on the ability to conserve a relational structure after trauma, it does not seem conceptually appropriate to question that very structure of life—and particularly of social life—whose conditions made possible those traumatic events. Assimilated to this idea of resilience, resistance becomes purely reactive.

Obama is not a theoretician of resilience and we may deem the remarks in his speech only as a rhetorical tool. However, the mutual affectation of resilience and resistance is further attested in the literature. Zolli and Healy point out that some terms such as robustness, redundancy and recovery may well relate to resilience, but are not the same. One could have expect the same for the concept of resistance. Instead, at times they make resistance equivalent to resilience or at least to some forms resilience may take: 'Enhancing the resilience of an ecosystem, an economy, or a community can be achieved in two ways: by improving its ability to *resist* being pushed past these kinds of critical, sometimes permanently damaging thresholds, and by preserving and expanding the range of niches to which a system can healthily adapt if it is pushed past such thresholds' (Zolli and Healy, *Resilience*, p. 19, my italics). What happens here is that resistance is again only reduced to its ability to *not* be pushed back, thus maintaining the thresholds that conserve the structure within which an entity is located.

If this notion of resilience empties the concept of resistance by assimilating it as an equivalent term, the same results when resilience advocates seek to distinguish it from resistance. In an interview broadcast on 9 April 2020—in the midst of the first Paris lockdown due to COVID 19—one of the main resilience researchers in Europe, the psychologist Boris Cyrulnik, established a contrast between resistance and resilience, precisely by referring to the pandemic and traumatic moment. He said to the radio interviewer: 'We are not at the time of resilience; we are at the time of resistance; that is, we face a virus [...], we face the fear of going out; thus, we are not at the time of resilience, because the definition of resilience is the resumption [*reprise*] of a new development after the trauma. And we are not after the trauma; we are in the middle of it'. This distinction between resistance and resilience, traversed by a chronological consideration of the former coming *before* the latter, also supposes a reductive conception of resistance. Resistance is reduced to 'facing' the trauma and is limited to a moment of the trajectory of a person, whose *defensive* capacities are in place to reconstitute themselves, so that they may re-enter into a new trajectory. This new trajectory would correspond to the proper moment of resilience, where the person, having successfully faced a traumatic danger, bounces back into those reconstituted networks and relationships that define normal life.

Thus, through assimilation with or differentiation from resilience, resistance is reduced either to a submissive acceptance of normality (as in the Obama discourse or Zolli and Healy's work) or to a passing moment of the trajectory of the person who has undergone a trauma (as in Cyrulnik).

It is therefore important to recover a different line of thought about resistance. It is a line certainly operative in common language and social movements, but one that tends to be effaced when resistance is affected by resilience. I am referring to the consideration of resistance as an active instance of *negation* of a portion of reality. By negation in this context I mean the obliteration of (or the attempt to obliterate) the structural mechanisms that allow creatures to simply accept that they ought to resiliently adapt to a given unsecure form of reality. In this sense, I would argue that resistance should be understood, not merely as a passing and submissive moment, but as way of establishing critical and existentially concrete mechanisms that counter the structural aspects of life that make catastrophe and trauma possible.

IV

One of the most interesting and relevant texts in this tradition of resistance is *Análise de Alguns Tipos de Resistência* (*Analysis of Some Kinds of Resistance*), by the activist, politician and theoretician from Cape Verde, Amílcar Cabral. This book is a transcription of several radio allocutions and interviews given by Cabral in 1969, in the context of the struggle against Portuguese colonialism in Cape Verde and Guinea-Bissau. It is therefore a text that responds to a very specific context, but whose reflections on the nature of resistance may be expanded to establish certain core elements present in the idea of resistance.

Cabral defines resistance in the following way: resistance is 'to destroy something, in order construct something else'.[16] These two dimensions—destroying and constructing—are key to the concept and practice of resistance and Cabral very carefully delineates the relationship between them. In fact, we may say that resistance is constituted as a dialectical relationship between destruction and construction; both dimensions are entangled, to the point that one is not conceivable without the other. This dialectical relationship is linguistically marked by the formulation 'in order to' (one English translation of the preposition *para* in the original Portuguese). It designates that 'construction' is not possible under some specific context and state of affairs and therefore 'destruction' is a necessary condition of possibility for construction: without destruction, there is no construction. Destruction is required because something happens in a given situation that does not allow constructing. While construction points to a future and different state of affairs, destruction, in turn, signals present conditions which are 'rotten' and do not allow for the emergence of the new future dimension. Thus, the *para* in this formulation refers both to a break with current existing conditions and to a movement towards a new situation or context.

Insofar as resistance integrates the dimensions of destruction *and* construction, destruction for the sake of destruction does not respond to the demands of resistance. Destruction must be performed with a view to future construction, otherwise it is not proper resistance. Cabral's perspective about the inextricable entanglement of destruction and construction in the process of resistance emerges from a very specific practice: the struggle against Portuguese colonialism. Therefore, the conceptualization that we may extract from Cabral theorization of resistance is not something separable from the practice of resistance itself. He recognizes that resistance is something natural (Cabral, *Análise*, p. 9), but the observation of nature is not enough to understand what resistance is: it is rather the very experience of resistance that allows for a clear conceptualization of this notion. Resistance is thus an experientially situated concept in this line of thought. It emerges from a specific experience: the struggle against Portuguese rule. We understand that it is this experience that constitutes, as it were, the concrete reservoir to understand the dialectical dynamics between destruction and resistance. If destruction is an act to be accomplished with a view to construction, this is a practical and theoretical point that emerges from the concrete needs of the colonial struggle: there is no

16 'A resistência é o seguinte: destruir alguma coisa, para construer outra cosa.' Amílcar Cabral, *Análise de Alguns Tipos de Resistência* (Bolama: Imprenta Nacional, 1979), p. 9. All translations from Cabral are mine.

point in destroying Portuguese rule without a view to the construction of a future independent state.

What is the object of this act of destroying? What is to be destroyed? Is it reduced to the Portuguese state? Cabral is very careful to giving an answer to this question; to some extent, explaining this issue, in alignment with the action of future construction, is the whole purpose of these allocutions. As the title of the book states, it is an inquiry about *some* kinds or modes (*alguns tipos*) of resistance, so not all forms of resistance are included here. This perspective matches with a concretely and experientially situated conception of resistance, because other experiences may include other forms of resistance. Cabral divides the forms of resistance he is to review in four kinds: political, economic, cultural and armed resistance. Each of these forms of resistance constitutes a particular domain with specific purposes. Therefore, although it is possible to identify that the object of resistance is, in this case, the destruction of Portuguese colonial rule and the construction of a new independent state, the singularity of these objectives is, as it were, deflected into an array of specific tasks of destruction and construction corresponding to each of these domains.

By the same token, Cabral also recognizes that colonial rule constitutes a whole structure, in which all these domains are entangled. This is precisely what emerges, for example, from his words on economic domination: 'Colonialism is primarily economic domination. Colonialism or imperialist domination is to seek, in the first place, to dominate other peoples economically. To this it adds a political domination; it extends the forces of the imperialist or colonial state into the land it wants to dominate economically' (Cabral, *Análise*, p. 34). This gives us clues about what Cabral is considering as the object of destruction. As mentioned, this can be easily identified with Portuguese colonial rule. But what surfaces in this complex understanding of colonialism is a network of relations allowing for domination to take place. For example, in the specific domain of economic resistance, the target of destruction is not a single specific object. Cabral's analysis starts from the diagnosis that economic exploitation is based upon the Portuguese forcedly buying agricultural products at prices established by the colonial state. The specific labour system that this form of exploitation involves results in the constitution of a network of relations of exploitation between colonialists and the local population. Cabral's point about agricultural exploitation helps us to observe that the destructive dimension of resistance implies dismantling an operative *structure of relations*: 'Now this is what we want to destroy. We have to destroy this, we have to destroy these relations of economic exploitation [*exploração*] of the colonialists over our people' (Cabral, *Análise*, p. 36).

We can now come back to our previous discussion on resilience. While resilience considers catastrophe and trauma as unexpected events that may impact on a well-functioning system of relations, resistance considers catastrophe and exploitation as something that has already eventuated and is sustained by the structure of relations in place in a given community. For instance, in Cabral's contextualized ideas on resistance, catastrophe and trauma are not probable future events that may happen; they are rather rooted in the community, as a daily reality sustained by the structure of relations taking place in a colonial society.

Unlike resilience, those relations that sustain the structural conditions of a rotten and deteriorated reality are the target of resistance's destructive dimension. It is not about destroying randomly everything that exists. Destruction responds to a diagnosis about daily and seemly 'normal' living conditions that contain catastrophe. Resistance is therefore especially—though not exclusively—operative at times when the relationships that sustain a specific form of life are in place and appear to be working *as if* no catastrophe or disaster are taking place.

Resilience operates with a probabilistic idea that catastrophe *may* happen; and, once it happens, it aims at conserving the relationships sustaining life as it was, as best as possible. Resistance, on the contrary, operates by attempting to negate those very structural relations that allow for catastrophe to happen in the first place. Furthermore, resistance cannot be reduced to a nihilistic moment of random destruction or to a passive instance in the face of catastrophe. Cabral's idea of resistance as a process also involving construction implies that resistance holds an active and future dimension, wherein structural relations should be constituted anew.

As I previously did with resilience, I may now give a characterization of resistance. It is not a conservative concept, because it does not seek to keep or maintain a specific form of life already in place. Rather, resistance is a destructive concept, not because it seeks to violently annihilate everything that exists, but because it aims at negating portions of reality whose presence make violence, trauma, catastrophe or disaster possible in the first place. The destructive or negative dimension of resistance is therefore a condition of possibility for understanding how construction may happen, not as a separate process, but as part of the renewal of the structural conditions on which resistance operates. If resilience's contribution to human development is to accept a deteriorated and risky reality in order to lead an acceptable form of life within that order, resistance goes further: it exposes the rotten aspects of that deteriorated milieu and ultimately condemns it, so as to structurally transform it.

V

This comparison between resistance and resilience helps us to further understand my claim that it would be appropriate to consider resilience as a disciplinary device. In its application to human behaviour and, most especially, as a normative claim of how humans ought to face catastrophe and risk, resilience tends to 'privatize' the absorption of trauma. Such a privatization focuses almost exclusively on the resources a person, or eventually a community of individuals, may have to absorb trauma. This is why the normative element of adaptation is so important. For adaptation implies that on a private level people have to learn to cope and adjust to a hostile and deteriorated environment. This way of resiliently dealing with trauma and catastrophe contributes to hiding the fact that there is a whole set of relations at play that structurally allow insecurity to permeate almost every aspect of life. As a disciplinary device, resilience contributes to deflecting the resisting energies that may be destructively directed against the structure sustaining this whole set of relations that foster insecurity. Instead of critically targeting the whole structure, more or less atomized individuals absorb into themselves the destructive tendencies of reality, to the point that they have to adapt to those deteriorated conditions.

I am not saying that resilience, as a strategy of the self to cope with a deteriorated reality, is useless. It may indeed be the case that integrating the normative ought of 'having to adapt' is useful to survive or even to improve living conditions within a deteriorated context of perpetual risk and constant catastrophe. This is an important element in disciplinary devices: they are useful and serve their purpose. The point is that, precisely in being useful and achieving its purpose, resilience accomplishes an erasure of the structural conditions that, on a structural macro-level, do not contribute to fostering security. Resilience thus contributes to cognitively obliterating the very idea that those structural conditions do exist. It does as if the set relations that constitute certain structural conditions do not exist. Therefore, resilience is not only about private adaptation to an unexpected future and to a deteriorated reality; it is also a disciplinary device that aims at 'hiding' structural conditions to the point that they disappear as a target of critical destruction. The prescription to adapt to certain structural conditions renders inoperative any attempt to destroy those conditions.

Bibliography

Bacon, Francis, *Sylva Sylvarum*, in *The Works of Francis Bacon*, 4, ed. James Spedding, Robert Leslie Ellis, Douglas Denon Heath (Boston: Brown and Taggard, 1862).

Cabral, Amílcar, *Análise de Alguns Tipos de Resistência* (Bolama: Imprenta Nacional, 1979).

Evans, Brad, and Julian Reid, *Resilient Life: The Art of Living Dangerously* (Cambridge: Polity Press, 2014).

Foucault, Michel, *Security, Territory, Population: Lectures at the Collège de France, 1977–1978*, ed. Michel Senellart, transl. Graham Burchell (New York: Palgrave, 2007).

Graham, Linda, *Bouncing Back: Rewiring Your Brain for Maximum Resilience and Well-Being* (Novato: New World Library, 2013).

Leary, John Patrick, *Keywords: The New Language of Capitalism* (Chicago: Haymarket Books, 2018).

Mesa, Álex, 'Resistencia en vez de resiliencia. Plasticidad en vez de flexibilidad', *Papel máquina*, 20 (2024), 139–52.

Neocleous, Marc, 'Resisting Resilience', *Radical Philosophy*, 178 (2013), 2–7.

Shwaikh, Malaka, 'Beyond Expectations of Resilience: Towards a Language of Care', *Global Studies Quarterly*, 17 (2023), 1–13.

Spinoza, Benedictus de, '*Ethics*', in *The Collected Works of Spinoza*, ed. and transl. Edwin Curley, I (Princeton: Princeton University Press, 1985).

Stigler, Barbara, *Il faut s'adapter. Sur un nouvel impératif politique* (Paris: Gallimard, 2019).

Streeck, Wolfgang, *How Capitalism Will End: Essays on a Failing System* (London: Verso, 2016).

The next person who calls me resilient I'm gonna stab in the neck', Catfish for Lunch, https://catfishforlunch.wordpress.com/2012/08/31/the-next-person-who-talks-about-resilience-ill-gonna-stab-in-the-neck/ (accessed 8 December 2024).

Zolli, Andrew, and Marie Healy, *Resilience: Why Things Bounce Back* (New York: Free Press, 2012).

2

Countering Resilience and its Consensual Logic: Persistence, Resistance, Re-existence

Laura Quintana

In 2015, the United Nations Sustainable Development Summit endorsed a comprehensive set of 17 goals aimed at fostering ecological and social sustainability with the objective of transforming the world by 2030. These goals encompass a broad range of initiatives, including poverty alleviation, reducing global inequality, combating climate change and its impacts, and addressing land degradation, deforestation and biodiversity loss.[1] Disappointingly, the UN's annual reports indicate that progress towards these goals has been inadequate, falling short of the necessary and anticipated changes. They have become unfulfilled promises, repeatedly deferred over time. Astonishingly, despite the growing urgency and imperative for transformation, we appear to be drifting further away from their realisation. This discouraging trend is substantiated by the findings of the Oxfam Report for 2023, 'for the first time in 25 years extreme wealth and extreme poverty have sharply increased at the same time [...]. Meanwhile low- and middle-income countries are also facing the greatest harmful impacts of climate change, with the poorest people worst affected, despite the fact they have done least to cause it'.[2] Global inequality and environmental destruc-

1 The reader can easily review the Sustainable Development Goals (SDG) at: 'Sustainable Development Goals: 17 Goals to Transform our World', United Nations, https://www.un.org/en/exhibits/page/sdgs-17-goals-transform-world - :~:text=GOAL 1%3A No Poverty GOAL,10%3A Reduced Inequalities GOAL 11 (accessed 28 July 2023).

2 'False Economy: Financial Wizardry Won't Pay the Bill for a Fair and "Sustainable" Future', Oxfam International Media Briefing, https://

tion are inherently interconnected, as each influences and exacerbates the other. The repercussions of environmental degradation, primarily caused by wealthier nations,[3] disproportionately impact countries with lower incomes, further intensifying their social vulnerability. Furthermore, as posited by dependency theory in the past,[4] this relationship is intricately connected to economic dynamics characterised by extraction, expansion, surplus value and accumulation. Such dynamics have enriched certain nations situated at the centre, while perpetuating the exploitation of others confined to the periphery. These long-standing processes have involved persistent colonial relations that have been repeatedly actualised, shaping the ongoing interactions between the Global North and South.[5] However, it is important to note that these boundaries are not merely geographical and have become increasingly complex in present times.[6]

These initial observations highlight that the framework of sustainable development not only fails to effectively address social and environmental devastation but also indicates a worsening situation, despite the rhetoric of change so enmeshed in the sustainability discourse. And this should not come off as a surprise. Upon reviewing the 17 goals, it becomes apparent that several of them not only fail to challenge, but actually reinforce the premise that social development and environmental sustainability are dependent on economic

oi-files-d8-prod.s3.eu-west-2.amazonaws.com/s3fs-public/2023-04/Report%20%28English%29.pdf (accessed 28 July 2023).

3 According to Jason Hickel recent findings 'the USA was responsible for 40% of excess global CO_2 emissions. The European Union (EU-28) was responsible for 29%. The G8 nations (the USA, EU-28, Russia, Japan, and Canada) were together responsible for 85%'. See Jason Hickel, 'Quantifying National Responsibility for Climate Breakdown: An Equality-Based Attribution Approach for Carbon Dioxide Emissions in Excess of the Planetary Boundary', *The Lancet*, 4:9 (2020), 399–404 (p. 399), doi: https://doi.org/10.1016/S2542-5196(20)30196-0 (accessed 28 July 2023).

4 Developed by authors such as Raúl Prebisch, Andre Gunder Frank, Eduardo Galeano, Pablo González Casanova and Fernando Coronil.

5 As Hickel et al. have recently argued, 'advanced economies' of the Global North continue to rely 'on a large net appropriation of resources and labour from the Global South, extracted through price differentials in international trade'. See Jason Hickel et al., 'Imperialist Appropriation in the World Economy: Drain from the Global South through Unequal Exchange, 1990–2015', *Global Environmental Change*, 73 (2022), doi: 10.1016/j.gloenvcha.2022.102467 (accessed 28 July 2023).

6 Not only are there increasingly more places treated as peripheral in the Global North, but there are also locations within the Global South that have become part of the Global North. Moreover, countries such as China and India within the Global South have attained hegemonic status.

growth. Sustainable development heavily relies on the notion of transitioning to clean energy production, technological innovations and carbon capture and storage to mitigate CO_2 emissions. However, it often overlooks the critical need to reduce overall energy consumption and material flows, as well as the importance of redistributing existing wealth. The belief persists that by decoupling economic growth from fossil fuels, it is possible to continue expanding in an 'environmentally friendly' manner while simultaneously 'alleviating poverty' without adequately addressing the issue of social injustice. Nevertheless, empirical evidence fails to demonstrate that resource consumption can be sufficiently decoupled from carbon emissions at a rate fast enough to remain within the temperature limits of 1.5°C or 2°C.[7]

The overwhelming evidence regarding the irreversible damage to ecosystems[8] adds to the concern surrounding the continued emphasis on 'green growth' and the accompanying technological optimism as the prevailing response to this tangible destruction. Such approach fails to acknowledge and address the deep-rooted inequalities that economic growth has engendered. Instead, it tends to normalise and accept these disparities as natural outcomes. In fact, since its inception in the mid-twentieth century, the development discourse has depoliticised poverty by abstracting it from its historical and structural causes. It portrays poverty as a technical problem that can be resolved through institutional interventions, such as those promoted by the World Bank, the International Monetary Fund and other international organisations like the UN.[9] These interventions aim to modernise countries and integrate them into the global order of a growth-based economy. And, as we will see, the discourse on resilience proves to be crucial in achieving that integration.

7 See Jason Hickel and Giorgos Kallis, 'Is Green Growth Possible?', *New Political Economy*, 25:4 (2019), 469–86; Enno Schröder and Servaas Storm, 'Economic Growth and Carbon Emissions: The Road to "Hothouse Earth" Is Paved with Good Intentions', *International Journal of Political Economy*, 49:2 (2020), 153–73, doi:10.1080/08911916.2020.1778866 (accessed 19 November 2024).

8 According to the Intergovernmental Panel on Climate Change's Report on Impacts, Adaptation and Vulnerability, irreversible damage is already affecting ecosystems on earth, and will accelerate to an unparalleled scale and pace if global temperatures rise beyond 1.5°C. See: 'Climate Change 2022: Impacts, Adaptation and Vulnerability', IPCC, https://www.ipcc.ch/report/ar6/wg2/ (accessed 29 July 2023).

9 See Arturo Escobar, *Sentipensar con la tierra: Nuevas lecturas sobre desarrollo, territorio y diferencia* (Medellín: UNAULA, 2014), 1–184 (p. 29). See also Jason Hickel, 'The Development Delusion'. In *The Divide* (London: Penguin Random House, 2018), 11–32.

In the first part of this chapter, I argue in fact that the prevailing discourse on resilience, which is highly emphasised and widespread in various domains today, has played a role in normalising the growth-based development framework and depoliticising the detrimental consequences it has engendered. Furthermore, this discourse has sought to hinder the emergence of genuine alternatives to the dominant model, which has gained consensus. In the subsequent part of this chapter, I will emphasise the importance of adopting alternative political practices and vocabularies that challenge the resilience paradigm. At the same time, I explore diverse economic and political possibilities that go beyond the constraints of the growth economy and the consensus it has engendered. By adopting this perspective, I align myself with the approaches that have critically scrutinised the discourse of resilience. I argue that it operates within the securitarian logic of neoliberalism,[10] and perpetuates the precarisation and abandonment of certain lives, while simultaneously contributing to the depoliticisation of these effects.[11] However, as I consider some of the shifts that the notion of resilience has undergone, and the way it has been adopted within a framework committed to a logic of growth, I am interested in extending the critique to demonstrate, on the one hand, how it persists in discourses that are not necessarily recognised as neoliberal but can be broadly characterised as 'consensual'. On the other hand, I aim to make visible certain colonial distributions of power that these discourses entail. In contrast to some critical approaches, I explore alternatives that go beyond mere antagonistic visions of resistance. Instead, I advocate for approaches that acknowledge and grapple with the materiality of the harm inflicted by current systems. These alternatives emphasise the importance of transformative practices intended to remake and reshape life in the midst of what remains.

I Consensualist resilience

Consensualism is the prevailing logic in an economy fuelled by the pursuit of economic growth and the staunch conviction that there exist no alternatives outside of capitalism. This perspective entails the necessity of expanding markets, supply and purchasing power, driven by the imperative of

10 See, Mark Neocleous, 'Don't Be Scared, Be Prepared: Trauma-Anxiety-Resilience', *Alternatives: Global, Local, Political*, 37:3 (2012), 188–98, doi: 10.1177/0304375412449789 (accessed 29 July 2023).

11 See Brad Evans and Julian Reid, *Resilient Life: The Art of Living Dangerously* (Cambridge: Polity Press, 2014).

accumulation. As shown by Rancière,[12] consensual logic proclaims the existence of a rationality deemed suitable for the times, to which all reasonable individuals should align. This rationality is assumed to be oriented solely by technical criteria rather than ideological considerations, with the belief that it can resolve conflicts wherever they arise. Thus, consensualism aligns with the notion that a 'government of experts' should prevail: a technocracy that has the capacity to comprehend the intricate workings of economic systems and determine the most optimal approach to navigate within these systems. Based on this rationale, it is believed that there exists an inherent order in the world, operating at both national and global levels, governed by a complex system of evidence. Within this framework, various operations, such as the market, financial and governmental activities, are deemed necessary, even if their complexity is not entirely understood. Thus, this logic asserts the existence of a temporal order dictated by inevitable economic and social processes. It demarcates what is thinkable and unthinkable, possible and impossible, and viable and unviable in terms of projects, actions, capacities and bodies. Under this perspective, the present, past and future seamlessly merge as distinct phases of a unified global present: a time determined by the market, progress, development and the imperative of sustainable growth. Confronting this presumed global 'reality', the primary emphasis lies in grasping how to proficiently navigate it through expert knowledge (economic, technological, sociological, etc.) that enables our adaptation to its demands.

Resilience precisely encompasses this ability to adapt, making it a fundamental attribute within the framework of consensual logic. According to the UN, 'resilience is the ability of a system, community or society exposed to hazards to resist, absorb, accommodate to and recover from the effects of a hazard in a timely and efficient manner, including through the preservation and restoration of its essential basic structures and functions'.[13] It is, therefore, the capacity to adapt to a 'disturbance' that enables the preservation of the fundamental structures of an individual, system or community, while also allowing transformation in response to the disturbance itself. Before delving into the ethical and political implications of this concept and exploring some of its influential applications, let us take a moment to examine some of the notable transformations it has undergone.

12 Jacques Rancière, *La Mésentente* (Paris: Galilée, 1995).

13 See the report 'Disaster Risk and Resilience', UNISDR and WMO, https://www.un.org/en/development/desa/policy/untaskteam_undf/thinkpieces/3_disaster_risk_resilience.pdf (accessed 28 July 2023).

I.I Significant shifts

As evinced by various proposed genealogies of the notion of 'resilience',[14] the term itself originated from the Latin word *resiliens*, which is the present participle of *resilire*, meaning 'to rebound, recoil'.[15] The term was initially used in the nineteenth century to describe the physical ability of objects to bounce back and restore themselves to their original state after undergoing compression. In the 1970s, with the work of Crawford Holling, the term was introduced to allude to the capacity of an ecosystem 'to absorb changes of state variables, driving variables, and parameters, and still persist'.[16] From that juncture, the term began to be commonly employed in complexity theories to denote the ability of a system, whether ecosocial or psychoindividual, to adapt and reorganise itself following a disturbance or damage. As a result, the concept underwent a shift from primarily describing the physical behaviour of objects to encompassing processes within ecosystems, and subsequently extending to include the capacities of individuals and communities.

The framework of understanding through which this capability has been conceived has also experienced notable transformations. As emphasised by Béné et al., the shifts in the conceptual framework for resilience can be delineated through a progression from (i) mechanical resilience (or what Holling referred to as 'engineering resilience'), which emphasises efficiency, recovery and stable equilibrium; to (ii) ecosystemic and social resilience, which encompasses the notions of shock resistance, conservation of function, persistence, and robustness across multiple equilibria; and finally to (iii) socio-ecological resilience, characterised by the 'interplay of disturbance and re-organisation, sustaining and developing', fostering 'adaptive capacity' for transformation, 'learning' and 'innovation', within dynamic systems (Béné et al., 'Resilience, Poverty and Development', p. 600). These shifts in

14 See Filippa Lentzos and Nikolas Rose, 'Governing Insecurity: Contingency Planning, Protection, Resilience', *Economy and Society,* 38:2 (2009), 230–54, doi: 10.1080/03085140902786611 (accessed 29 July 2023); Christophe Béné et al. 'Resilience, Poverty and Development', *Journal of International Development,* 25 (2014), 598–623, doi: 10.1002/jid.2992 (accessed 29 July 2023); Melinda Cooper and Jeremy Walker, 'Genealogies of Resilience: From Systems Ecology to the Political Economy of Crisis Adaptation', *Security Dialogue,* 42:2 (2011), 143–60 (p.?), doi: 10.1177/0967010611399616 (accessed 29 July 2023).

15 See 'Resilience', Online Etymology Dictionary, https://www.etymonline.com/word/resilience (accessed 29 July 2023).

16 Stanley Crawford Holling, 'Resilience and Stability of Ecological Systems', *Annual Review of Ecology and Systematics,* 4 (1973), 1–23 (p. 17), doi: 10.1146/annurev.es.04.110173.000245 (accessed 29 July 2023).

understanding resilience reflect a progression towards a deeper recognition of complexity, transitioning from a focus on structural complexity to emergent complexity. In the first case (i), the emphasis is placed on the system's stability when facing disturbances. In the second case (ii), the emphasis shifts to the system's flexibility. Finally, in the third case (iii), the ability to transform is emphasised, where the disturbance is no longer seen as a problem but as an opportunity for learning and innovation (Béné et al., 'Resilience, Poverty and Development', p. 601). In this progression, resilience evolves from being a capacity associated with restoring equilibrium after a perturbation and preserving existing structures (in a linear system of fixed relationships). Instead, it becomes associated with the adaptive capacity to respond to perturbations in a dynamic system (with variable and nonlinear relationships) (Béné et al., 'Resilience, Poverty and Development', p. 600).

While I cannot delve into the intricate complexities of this displacement, I find it crucial to explore the ethical and political implications it carries and how they intersect with consensual logic. In this context, as highlighted by Cooper and Walker,[17] the rapid extrapolation of the concept of resilience, originally rooted in ecological systems, to other domains such as the market, security systems, various institutions and even individual psyche in the work of Holling, becomes pivotal. This line of thinking led to the notion that all ecosystems, including socio-ecological systems, can be conceptualised as dynamic systems that can adapt and undergo autopoiesis through perturbation, reorganisation and subsequent growth. The Resilience Alliance, established by Holling, even identified an 'adaptive cycle' consisting of four phases: 'successional growth', a 'conservation phase of stable equilibrium', 'collapse, and then a spontaneous reorganisation that leads to a new growth phase' (Cooper and Walker, 'Genealogies of resilience', p. 147). Indeed, from this standpoint, both the disturbance or crisis and the adaptation to it, as well as the tendency for growth, are naturalised even as moments of 'creative destruction', as Schumpeter would say. They are considered inevitable phases in life that one must adapt to and seize the opportunities they present, although a complete understanding may never be possible due to the complexity of ecosystemic relationships. Resilience then perceives damage as an opportunity for new growth and asserts that adaptation to this process is the only horizon of possibility, serving as an ontological framework—describing how things are—that demands unquestioned consensus. In doing so, it overlooks the power dynamics and social harms associated with ecological-social disturbances. Even these disruptions can be justified as necessary to uncover new opportunities for growth.

17 Melinda Cooper and Jeremy Walker, 'Genealogies of Resilience', 143–60 (p. 147), doi.org/10.1177/0967010611399 (accessed 29 July 2023).

In light of the above, it is essential to recognise the significant expansion of the concept of 'resilience' across influential global public policies, discourses and programmes in various domains such as environmental, humanitarian, financial and psychological contexts.[18] As discussed earlier, the term 'resilience' carries significant weight within the UN's sustainable development agenda, aligning with dominant security policies that prioritise economic growth.[19] It is also used in psychological discourse to depict an individual's capacity for 'adapting well in the face of adversity, trauma, tragedy, threats, or significant sources of stress', which 'involves "bouncing back" from these difficult experiences', but 'can also involve profound personal growth'.[20] There is also an abundance of self-improvement literature and manuals that encourage us to seize moments of crisis as opportunities for personal growth, exploring new aspirations and achieving self-realisation. However, these resources often fail to examine the social conditions that exacerbate vulnerability, the root causes of the experienced harm, or the role of social structures in reproducing such damage.

Hence, the concept of resilience operates at both descriptive and regulatory-normative levels. It functions as an explanatory framework for comprehending various behaviours (physical, ecological, psychological), while also prescribing desirable or appropriate behaviours based on psychological recommendations, public programmes and policies. At times, resilience is explicitly presented as an imperative, while in other instances, it is subtly implied. This imperative urges individuals and communities to derive lessons from crises, restructure themselves and explore new trajectories, all within

18 For example, in the 3,068 pages of the 2022 IPCC climate change report, the term 'resilience' appears 2,433 times (see 'Climate Change 2022: Impacts, Adaptation and Vulnerability'; in the 2023 Global Humanitarian Overview, the notion of resilience figures 46 times in its 184 pages (see 'Global Humanitarian Overview 2023', OCHA, https://reliefweb.int/report/world/global-humanitarian-overview-2023-enaresfr?_gl=1*1npus08*_ga*MTkxMzkzNzA1NS4xNjgyNDU1MzQx*_ga_E60ZNX2F68*MTY4MjQ1NTM0MS4xLjEuMTY4MjQ1NTM3NS4yNi4wLjA (accessed 29 July 2023).

19 For example, according to the US National Strategy for Homeland Security of 2022: 'The future of America's success in the world depends upon our strength and resilience at home—and especially the strength of our middle class, which is critical to our national security as an engine of economic growth and a key source of democratic vibrance and cohesion" (see 'National Security Strategy', The White House, https://www.whitehouse.gov/wp-content/uploads/2022/10/Biden-Harris-Administrations-National-Security-Strategy-10.2022.pdf) (accessed 29 July 2023).

20 See, 'Building your Resilience', American Psychological Association, https://www.apa.org/topics/resilience/building-your-resilience (accessed 28 July 2023).

the unquestioned horizon of 'growth'. However, this perspective often disregards power dynamics and inequalities that contribute to heightened vulnerability in specific regions and for certain individuals.

For example, the IMF designed a Resilience and Sustainability Trust (RST) to 'help low-income and vulnerable middle-income countries build resilience to external shocks and ensure sustainable growth, contributing to their longer-term balance of payments stability'.[21] These vulnerable economies, already burdened by substantial debt, are presented with new loans disguised as measures to foster resilience. These loans aim to ensure that these countries can fulfil their debt obligations, thereby perpetuating their state of vulnerability. It becomes apparent that resilience is considered a prerequisite for the most vulnerable countries to remain ensnared in the cycle of debt and economic growth. This framework has resulted in the enrichment of higher-income countries and the corporations that control the financial system, while further impoverishing lower-income countries and exacerbating their social vulnerability.

The notion of resilience serves to reinforce and perpetuate the existing framework and its presumed validity, guaranteeing its ongoing continuity. It promotes the idea that sustainable growth is a necessary pursuit to achieve social resilience. Simultaneously, it suggests that the capacity for resilience, be it at an individual, community or ecological level, facilitates economic growth. However, it is precisely the pursuit of economic growth that has led to heightened ecological and social vulnerability in certain regions and for specific groups, particularly in the Global South. These regions and individuals are now expected to be resilient in order to sustain growth. By functioning within this consensual framework, the concept of resilience not only normalises ecological and social harm but also depoliticises it. It effectively colonises the spectrum of possibilities and alternatives, impeding the emergence of alternative potential futures.

I.II Depoliticising harm and colonising the future

The fixation and naturalisation of vulnerability to certain places and populations conceal a profound and significant history that should not be disregarded. We often refer to certain regions as 'low-income countries' or 'poor countries', and label individuals as vulnerable, as if their circumstances were inherent and predetermined. Certainly, life, in its finitude, in its fragile and

21 See Resilience and Sustainability Trust, International Monetary Fund, International Monetary Fund, 'Resilience and Sustainability Trust', https://www.imf.org/en/Topics/Resilience-and-Sustainability-Trust (accessed 29 July 2023).

intricate webs, is susceptible to being harmed, to being wounded, and therefore, it is ontologically vulnerable. In the present era of extensive ecological destruction, we are aware of this more than ever. However, it is crucial to acknowledge that social mechanisms can exacerbate and unevenly distribute this ontological vulnerability, just as they can also alleviate it through public frameworks that promote conditions of care, equality and stability.[22]

Marxist and decolonial analyses have effectively revealed how the economic growth of Europe, particularly during the Industrial Revolution, was made possible through the extraction of raw materials from dispossessed and colonised lands. This growth relied on the utilisation of enslaved labour in the colonies and the exploitation of wage labourers in the metropolis, who had been stripped of their means of production, coerced into employment, compelled to sell their labour power and forced to purchase industrialised goods. Furthermore, recent studies like those by Hickel[23], and previously González Casanova[24] and Coronil,[25] have shed light on how the economic growth of the Global North was bolstered by unjust trade rules that undermined local manufacturing industries in various regions of the Global South. These regions were reduced to mere enclaves, serving as suppliers of easily extractable raw materials obtained at low costs, while being compelled to purchase manufactured goods from the Global North at higher prices. As Harvey[26] argues, the imperative of growth that propels capital accumulation and valorisation persists by relying on ongoing dispossession to expand production frontiers and extract value. This strategy aims to mitigate the recurrent crises inherent in the process of growth. Capital, as we know, devalues when it remains stagnant, which is why it relentlessly pursues opportunities for sustained growth.

These growth opportunities emerge, for example, when capital shifts to regions with lower labour costs to establish supply chains. This leads to significant profits for transnational corporations with minimal investment, while simultaneously intensifying the marginalisation and ecological degradation of the regions where raw materials are sourced and products are

22 See Athena Athanasiou and Judith Butler, *Dispossession: The Performative in the Political* (Cambridge: Polity Press, 2013).

23 Jason Hickel, *Less is More* (London: Penguin Random House, 2020), p. 55.

24 Pablo González Casanova, 'La explotación global', in *Globalidad: Una mirada alternativa,* ed. Miguel Ángel Porrúa (Mexico: Centro Latinoamericano de la Globalidad, 1999), pp. 69–95.

25 Fernando Coronil. 'Naturaleza del poscolonialismo: del eurocentrismo al globocentrismo', in *La colonialidad del saber: Eurocentrismo y ciencias sociales. Perspectivas latinoamericanas*, ed. Edgardo Lander (Buenos Aires: CLACSO, 2000), pp. 53–67.

26 David Harvey, *The New Imperialism* (Oxford: Oxford University Press, 2003).

manufactured. Similarly, one can think of heavily indebted countries that, under the mandate of financial institutions such as the World Bank or the IMF, have to adhere to 'structural adjustment programmes' and austerity measures as a condition for extending their credit. These measures lead to reductions in public resources and decreased investments in social welfare, along with the privatisation of state-owned enterprises and the expansion of precarious employment. Such measures further deepen social insecurity and inequality in the countries that execute them, as observed in the implementation of neoliberal programs, which were later extended to various regions in the Global North. As a result of dismantling social protections and turning them into profit-driven services that create growth opportunities for large corporations, vulnerability is exacerbated. This effect becomes even more evident with the escalation of environmental degradation, which has intensified since the second half of the nineteenth century, driven by the relentless pursuit of GDP growth during what is known as the 'great acceleration'. This degradation has led to the destruction of forests, depletion of soils, exploitation of mountains, contamination of rivers and seas, creation of dead zones in the ocean due to overfishing, accumulation of toxic waste and increased susceptibility to environmental disasters. These negative impacts have predominantly affected regions in the Global South, but have increasingly spread to the Global North and across the world.

It is at this juncture, marked by the heightened vulnerability of interconnected life, as was recently evident with the COVID-19 pandemic, that the discourse of resilience emerges and gains profound significance.[27] It normalises the occurrence of social and environmental disasters, while acknowledging that certain regions and lives are more susceptible to risk. In doing so, it obscures the colonial pattern of harm,[28] that has fuelled and perpetuated economic growth, while leaving the root structural conditions that contribute to such disasters largely unaddressed. As mentioned earlier, the discourse of resilience operates within a securitarian framework, aiming to

27 Actually, the exposure of life during the pandemic, exacerbated by neoliberal forms of organisation, coincided with the historical peak in the usage of the concept of resilience, as shown by this Google Trends search available at: 'Resilience', Google Trends, https://trends.google.com/trends/explore?date=all&q=resilience&hl=es-CO (accessed 29 July 2023).

28 As Hickel reminds us, in this direction, it is possible to speak of a process of 'atmospheric colonisation'. For a small number of high-income nations have appropriated the vast majority of the safe atmospheric commons, and have contributed the vast majority of emissions in excess of the planetary boundary [...] And ironically, despite having contributed virtually nothing to the climate crisis, the South bears the vast majority of the impact of climate breakdown' (Hickel, *Less is More*, p. 106).

maintain the functionality of the growth-oriented economy. Resilience is employed to anticipate disasters and focuses on mitigating the impacts that could jeopardise the long-term viability of growth. It highlights the importance of creating strategies to adapt to these impacts and utilises anticipatory technologies to regulate the future. Let us for a moment delve on the workings of this securitarian logic.

As elucidated by Foucault,[29] security mechanisms operate under the assumption that certain undesirable events, such as poverty, epidemics, criminality and environmental damage, are inevitable. However, they can be controlled and managed to minimise their impact on economic growth. This is achieved by calculating an 'average index' that determines when an event becomes dangerous, and efforts are focused on managing the associated risks by manipulating influential variables. In this context, the importance of anticipatory technologies becomes evident. According to Anderson,[30] these technologies can adopt a 'precaution' logic, aiming to prevent a threat from escalating into a catastrophic event.[31] They can also follow a 'pre-emption' logic, where certain conditions are interpreted as threatening and addressed before they materialise into concrete events.[32] Alternatively, they can employ a 'preparedness' logic, aimed at mitigating the most destructive consequences once an event has already been triggered.[33]

These logics of security share a common objective: the protection of a specific way of life, that of the privileged white subject in high-income countries, dedicated to capital accumulation. Their primary concern is to minimise 'negative surprises' that may disrupt this way of life, recognising the inherent

29 Michel Foucault, *Sécurité, territoire, population 1977–1978)* (Paris: EHSS, Gallimard, Le Seuil, 2004).

30 Ben Anderson, 'Preemption, Precaution, Preparedness: Anticipatory Action and Future Geographies', *Progress in Human Geography*, 34:6 (2010), 777–98, doi: 10.1177/030913251036260 (accessed 15 November 2023).

31 An illustrative example of this dynamic is the use of carbon offsets to address emissions-related processes. Carbon offsets assign a financial worth to greenhouse gas pollution and offset it by investing in projects, often located in the Global South, that promise environmental improvements. However, what has transpired is that the excessive emissions in the Global North have been compensated for by reductions in the Global South, while fossil fuel extraction persists. This approach relies on the belief that market forces will incentivize substantial emission reductions, enabling continued economic growth and capital accumulation (see Anderson, 'Preemption, Precaution, Preparedness', p. 789).

32 As Anderson points out, this logic was seen at work in the US pre-emptive war against terrorism (Anderson, 'Preemption, Precaution, Preparedness', p. 790).

33 Just as with infrastructure and programs designed to mitigate the impacts of a disaster.

uncertainty of complex systems and the limitations of making linear predictions. However, this protection often comes at the expense of other lives, as interventions and undesirable effects on marginalised communities are disregarded or even produced. At the same time, there is an underlying drive to profit from uncertainty by identifying new avenues for future growth. Examples of this include the sale of financial products such as derivatives, carbon credits, life insurance or loans designed to foster social resilience in countries where vulnerability can be exploited as a business opportunity.

Moreover, these anticipatory technologies tend to view disasters as extraordinary and isolated events, often overlooking the underlying social and institutional factors that contribute to increased vulnerability among certain populations, such as poverty and social insecurity. This approach conveniently avoids acknowledging the inherently political character of disasters. By disregarding the power dynamics and conflicts that contribute to the occurrence of disasters, these technologies effectively depoliticise them. The discourse of resilience further reinforces this depoliticisation by downplaying and negating any critical agency. Its underlying message is: 'in the face of risk, prepare yourself as best as possible and cultivate resilience to endure the damage when it occurs, so that you can overcome it and reinvent yourself'. It does not encourage individuals to identify the conditions that cause harm and to unite with others in the struggle against the forces reproducing these conditions. Instead, the message also implies a sense of victimisation, albeit with a touch of post-traumatic self-improvement:[34] 'you may suffer as a victim, but find ways to reconfigure the trauma and move forward. Psychological counselling, humanitarian aid, and resilience programs can eventually assist you'.[35] Indeed, as it stands, it fails to acknowledge the oppressive conditions that have rendered certain lives more vulnerable (racialised individuals, the poor, and those living in marginalised parts of

34 See, Michael Basseler, 'Stories of Dangerous Life in the Post-Trauma Age: Toward a Cultural Narratology of Resilience', in *Narrative in Culture*, ed. Astrid Erll et al. (Berlin, Boston: De Gruyter, 2019), pp. 15–36, doi: 10.1515/9783110654370-002 (accessed 15 November 2023).

35 I do not have the space here to fully explore the connection between the discourse of resilience and 'humanitarian reason' as discussed by Didier Fassin and Rachel Gomme, *Humanitarian Reason: A Moral History of the Present* (California: University of California Press, 2012). This discourse operates under a mode of governmentality that diminishes individuals to the status of victims, aiming to alleviate their suffering based on the belief that their lives are sacred. However, both resilience and humanitarian reason share the tendency to assume eventual victimisation, leading to a depoliticisation that overlooks the agency of those affected and fails to acknowledge the historical and social contexts of the harm they endure.

the Global South). It disregards their capacity to recognise these conditions, resist them and work towards constructing a more egalitarian world. Instead, it consigns them to a future devoid of opportunities, thereby perpetuating their role in sustaining future economic growth. The consensus-driven logic of economic growth precludes any alternative possibilities by default, as it demands and promotes adaptation to the existing order rather than genuine social transformation. Imagining the possibility of other futures requires, therefore, the creation of alternative vocabularies, practices and ways of thinking that consider the enduring power of bodies amid what remains.

II Beyond resilience: persisting, resisting, re-existing

> Re-existing indicates that there is something beyond development; capitalism is not the only way to exist on this planet. We must manage it differently so that future life has meaning and [...] there is more to life than merely accumulating and increasing wealth.[36]

Re-existence is claimed when a way of life has been devastated. In fact, the notion emerges to account for the long-lasting processes of harm that various indigenous communities in Latin America have endured since the conquest of America (Albán and Rosero, 'Colonialidad de la naturaleza', p. 39). This is assumed as the moment when the indigenous world suffered its destruction and had to confront how to exist again after the devastation.[37] Such destruction continues through contemporary forms of territorial enclosure and extraction practices, intensified by developmental programmes and neoliberal policies. Indeed, the concept of re-existence is mobilised intensively to denounce and resist practices of territorial dispossession through violent expulsion, illegal contracts, soil depletion, loss of biodiversity, accumulation

36 Adolfo Albán and José R. Rosero, 'Colonialidad de la naturaleza: ¿Imposición tecnológica y usurpación epistémica? Interculturalidad, desarrollo y re-existencia', *Nómadas,* 45 (2016), 27–41 (p. 38). My translation.

37 Some attribute the emergence of the term to indigenous Misak communities in Colombia, who speak of re-existence to allude to 'insurgent practices that crack modernisation/coloniality and make possible very different ways of being, thinking, knowing, feeling, existing, and living-with' (see G. Tunubalá-Velasco and J. Fayad-Sierra, 'Voces invisibilizadas, voces visibilizadas: Hacia un diálogo intercultural entre el saber misak y el conocimiento global', *Nodos y Nudos,* 7:50 (2021), 159–72 (p. 131), doi: 10.17227/nyn.vol7.num50-12610 (accessed 15 November 2023).

of toxic waste and forms of structural and slow violence.[38] These phenomena are often associated with development projects such as the construction of large-scale port complexes, hydroelectric plants, intensive mining, monoculture agriculture, livestock farming, seed privatisation and the utilisation of genetically modified seeds, among others. Thus the concept of re-existence has been shaped and embraced by communities in Latin America as a way to confront the lasting harms they have experienced, rebuild their lives, and persist in the face of challenging circumstances. From their perspective, to express it in the words of Misak, 'the world never ends, because it is like a thing that, as it moves, moves'.[39] There are always threads left behind, from which it is possible to weave again, gathering what survives, to braid new paths in the territory, drawing nourishment from those already travelled. Because 'history is in the territory and must be read in it, while also creating it [...] our territory speaks and has much to say' (Hurtado, Aranda and Vasco, *Guambianos, hijos del arcoiris*, p. 67).

Such persistence stands in stark contrast to the language of resilience that we examined earlier, and it directly challenges the development model upon which it relies. It recognises that this model has not only had devastating impacts on local communities, their territories, and their cultural identities, but it has also been imposed without their consent, completely disregarding their life aspirations and agency (Albán and Rosero, 'Colonialidad de la naturaleza', p. 38). Thus, re-existence is not about merely 'adapting' to these conditions; rather, it involves critically analysing how these conditions came to be and forging paths of dissident existence or 'resistance' in the face of what remains. Re-existence entails the creation of alternative ways of life that are situated, embedded, embodied and rooted in specific territories. It challenges the prevailing paradigms and aims to transform the existing world.

II.I To acknowledge the materiality of harm and its relational nature

In contrast to the discourse of resilience, the concept of re-existence acknowledges that the ecological and social harms experienced by a community are not abstract, random and unpredictable 'disturbances'. Instead, they are specific and localised damages that are intricately intertwined with power dynamics, which have eroded a particular way of life. It recognises the historical and geographical context of these impacts and how they have become

38 See Robert Nixon, *Slow Violence and the Environmentalism of the Poor* (Cambridge, MA: Harvard University Press, 2011).

39 Abelino Hurtado, Misael Aranda and Luis Guillermo Vasco, *Guambianos, hijos del arcoiris y del agua* (Bogotá: CEREC, 2015), p. 63. My translation.

embedded in the bodies, territories and relationships between humans and non-humans. Re-existence emphasises the importance of a situated approach, starting from the place where existence unfolds, understanding the territory as a living space. As expressed by social leader Francia Márquez, a member of the Afro-Colombian movement *Proceso de Comunidades Negras* (PCN) and currently serving as the Vice President of Colombia:

> A hegemonic vision of development has been forcefully imposed upon our territory, utilising armed violence, structural racism, and patriarchy. These systemic forms of violence have profoundly impacted both the land and its inhabitants, particularly marginalised communities who are predominantly Black, Indigenous, and peasant peoples. We have been subjected to racialisation, impoverishment, and continuous violations of our rights. Throughout vast areas of Colombia, our lived experiences with the land have tragically been defined by these imposed conditions of violence. These circumstances have stripped away our humanity and reduced the territory to a mere commodity within a market-driven logic, where development is measured solely by the accumulation of economic capital, disregarding principles of social redistribution and ecological preservation.[40]

The communities affected by the destructive consequences of the development framework, driven by economic growth, recognise its inherent bias towards the pursuit of capital accumulation and the privileging of a particular way of life associated with the dominance of white culture. This approach, driven by efficiency, functionality, and self-interest, has subjected previously marginalised territories and the lives of racialised bodies, unfairly perceived as ignorant and backward, to exploitation as mere resource and wealth sources. The consequences have been devastating for those categorised as 'appropriable nature'. It is clear that this framework has perpetuated an unequal distribution of prosperity and the subordination of certain lives through the establishment of persistent borders, stemming from colonialism, that separate the centre from the periphery, viable lives from non-viable lives, developed subjects (considered capable and active) from backward subjects (seen as incapable, impotent and passive), human capacities from exploitable nature, and qualified life from exploitable materiality. These boundaries, delineating areas of extraction and expansion, have served the interests of 'development' and the well-being of some at the expense of others, playing a central role in the accumulation of wealth.

40 Francia Márquez, 'El territorio es vida', in *Territorio* (Bogotá: Futuro en tránsito—Comisión de la verdad de Colombia), pp. 9–20 (p. 12). My translation.

By recognising the territorial dimension of damage, it becomes apparent that it has not only arisen from long-standing relationships but has also shaped geographies that impact both human bodies and landscapes, as well as the interconnected ecosystems involving humans and non-human entities. As emphasised by Jason Moore, these dynamics of economic growth operate through the appropriation of vital networks and their exploitation for maximum profit at minimal cost, a phenomenon he aptly terms 'cheapening nature'.[41] Accumulation, therefore, expands not only by exploiting labour forces and feminised practices associated with the reproduction of life, but also through the appropriation and commodification of intricate territorial processes.

In response to the commodification of life networks, the logic of re-existence recognises that these interactions are not mere mutable relations between independent entities. Instead, they are constitutive relations that shape both the agents involved and the worlds they inhabit. Entities do not exist as separate entities before their relationships; rather, they exist as interconnected and interdependent networks. The biotic realm relies on the abiotic, and through various practices, new interdependencies and new agents emerge. When we speak of *soils*, as emphasised by the *Vía Campesina* movement, we are not solely considering their capacity for carbon sequestration. We are also acknowledging the entire interconnected system that sustains life, including microorganisms, fungi, minerals, organic matter, water, sunlight and the agricultural practices that either strengthen or disrupt these relationships.[42]

A profound understanding of relationality is crucial in this context, distinguishing it from the perspective derived from systems theory and applied to both natural ecosystems and the social sphere when discussing resilience. It is crucial to acknowledge that the social realm cannot be reduced to a collection of ecosystems viewed solely through a biological lens, assessing them based only on their adaptive capabilities (which may imply a sort of social Darwinism).[43] It entails acknowledging the intricate entanglement of nature

41 Jason Moore, 'The Rise of Cheap Nature', in *Anthropocene or Capitalocene? Nature, History, and the Crisis of Capitalism*, ed. Jason Moore (Oakland: PM Press/Kairos), pp. 78–115.

42 'Engañados en el invernadero: Contra las soluciones falsas al cambio climático', La Vía Campesina, https://viacampesina.org/es/por-que-luchamos/soberania-alimentaria/8 (accessed 30 March 2023).

43 In fact, according to Stiegler, neoliberalism actually embraces a form of social Darwinism, approaching social structures through an evolutionary lens that emphasises adaptation, individualism and gradualism. See Barbara Stiegler, *Il faut s'adapter. Sur un nouvel impératif politique* (Paris: Gallimard, 2019), p. 14.

and culture and embracing the interconnected 'ecologies of life'[44] that they jointly construct. These interweavings manifest in various directions, producing diverse effects and rhythms that frequently result in conflicts due to the power dynamics at play within bodies and territories. Therefore, their dynamics cannot be reduced to gradualism or adaptationism alone. Instead, they require an understanding of power struggles, engaging with them from within, while also adopting a comprehensive notion of nurturing the interconnectedness of life's networks.[45] This highlights the significance of cultivating context-specific practices and knowledge that recognise their situatedness within these interdependencies and the consequential impact they have on the world.[46] Continuous attention must be devoted to understanding these effects: how and where they arise, whom they affect and which relationships are most profoundly impacted. As a result, the question of territory assumes a central role within this framework.

II.II Persisting by resisting

The concept of re-existence, accompanied by related notions like 'good living', 'dignified life', *vivir sabroso* (literally, 'living with flavour') or 'politics of life', allude to a capacity for persistence situated within the network of relationships that constitute existence. They constantly unfold as coexistence within a territory. This understanding acknowledges these relationships as a complex web of interdependence 'embodied senses' and perceptions

44 See Tim Ingold, 'Toward an Ecology of Materials', *Annual Review of Anthropology*, 41 (2012), 417–39, doi: 10.1146/annurev-anthro-081309-145920 (accessed 15 November 2023)

45 This relational sense of 'care' can be linked with the notion proposed by María Puig de la Bellacasa: 'Care is everything that is done (rather than everything that "we" do) to maintain, continue, and re-pair "the world" so that all (rather than "we") can live in it as well as possible. That world includes [...] all that we seek to interweave in a complex, life-sustaining web', María Puig de la Bellacasa, *Matters of Care* (Minneapolis: University of Minnesota, 2017), p. 161.

46 Hence, for the indigenous peoples of Colombia, 'to speak, give offerings and ask permission to Mother Earth, in *Wayuunaiki, Isashii*, the big house of the spirits, is to recognize a Vital Network, a web, a weave that not only finds place in the physical and evident, but that acquires meaning and life through the order given by the practices of struggles and by the knowledge of the spiritual and the situated knowledge', Centro Nacional de Memoria Histórica-Organización Nacional Indígena de Colombia, *Tiempos de vida y muerte* (Bogotá: CNMH-ONIC, 2019), p. 28.

manifested in our 'bodies, habits, and sensibilities'.[47] This framework takes shape and finds embodiment through economic, political, ritual and imaginative practices. It fosters the creation of affective connections, the generation and reconfiguration of what is considered valuable, and the formation of new networks of vital interconnections. The territory, encompassing both geographical and affective dimensions, as well as the realm of collective memory, remains in a constant state of transformation. It is perpetually being territorialised, entangled in conflicts and explorations, while simultaneously being inhabited and reclaimed. Therefore, from this understanding, living is the ability to compose, to come together within territorial frameworks, as emphasised precisely by the notion of 'buen vivir' (good living) and 'vida digna' (dignified life). The first concept, known as *sumak kawsay* in Kichwa and *suma qamaña* in Aymara, emerges from an intercultural dialogue that bridges indigenous and non-indigenous perspectives. It serves as a critical recognition of the detrimental impacts of extractive interventions on territories, grounded in a relational understanding of life rather than one rooted in harmonistic ideals. The second concept emphasises the performative aspect of dignity, encompassing economic practices that are conscientious of their consequences. It ensures the establishment of favourable conditions for food sovereignty, healthcare, education and the right to make crucial decisions regarding coexistence. Within this framework, defending the territory involves shedding light on the harms inflicted, politicising them and resisting practices that exploit and disrupt vital networks.

Indeed, within this framework, resistance goes beyond the mere act of bringing visibility to existing antagonisms through protests, land reclamations or legal actions, and demanding changes in social institutions. It often involves concrete processes of reshaping life within inhabited spaces. For instance, it comprises the creation of alternative economic practices, innovative approaches to land and water usage, waste management, relationships with animals and the materials necessary for sustaining life. These transformative actions take place even in circumstances where life has been severely damaged. A telling example can be found in the southern regions of Colombia, which have faced significant repercussions from chemical glyphosate spraying in the context of the so-called 'War on Drugs'. Glyphosate is a highly toxic pesticide that has had a devastating impact on the lives of peasants. It has caused severe damage to crops, contaminated animals and water sources, exacerbating the already precarious state of the local economy, already burdened by violence from armed groups, land dispossession,

47 See Daniel Ruiz-Serna, 'El territorio como víctima', *Revista Colombiana de Antropología*, 53:2 (2017), 85–113 (p. 95), doi:10.22380/2539472X.118 (accessed 15 November 2023).

low prices for agricultural products and lack of connectivity and essential services.[48] In the face of such destruction, some peasants have been compelled to abandon their lands, while others have taken legal recourse to expose the harm caused and seek compensation. Others still have formed collectives to resist a drug policy that has turned into a form of necropolitics, endangering peasant livelihoods.[49] Many individuals, having witnessed the ineffectiveness of conventional approaches, persevered in their territories, exploring regenerative agricultural practices instead. Their persistence not only showcased their resilience but, as demonstrated by Kristina Lyons (see Lyons, *Vital Decomposition*), led them to uncover alternative modes of production and foster new relationships with soils. They began to critically question monoculture agriculture and large-scale farming techniques. Recognising the unique qualities of Amazonian soil, they cultivated a newfound appreciation and forged a distinct connection with it. In doing so, they persevered in their endeavours despite the forces that aimed to marginalise them. While they may not have directly or openly confronted the sources of power that inflicted harm upon them, they resisted their effects and challenged the underlying logic that gave rise to those effects. Thus, in contrast to the adapt, learn and innovate of resilience, one finds here a 'delicate balance between opposing, enduring, and transforming [...] the very conditions that make some lives and ecologies flourish at the expense of making others endure' (Lyons, *Vital Decomposition*, p. 40).

Strategies of re-existence also include proposals of political antagonism, visibly challenging the conditions that cause harm, while presenting alternative approaches for reorganising and sustaining life. A notable example is the advocacy for 'food sovereignty' championed by the *Via Campesina*, a global movement comprising approximately 182 organisations from 81 countries worldwide, which despite geographical, historical and value-based differences, come together in their defence of a peasant way of life. Food sovereignty promotes small-scale agricultural practices that prioritise the utilisation of native seeds and local food production, emphasising affordability, nutrition and sustainability. It encompasses practices deeply rooted in understanding soils, climates, crop rotation, responsible consumption and the preservation of biodiversity. Moreover, it advocates for preventive healthcare approaches and distributive policies that effectively address malnutrition. Initiatives like *Via Campesina* aim to tackle the interconnected challenges

48 See Kristina Lyons, 'Chemical Warfare in Colombia, Evidentiary Ecologies and Senti-Actuando Practices of Justice', *Social Studies of Science*, 48:3 (2018), 414–37, access link: https://www.jstor.org/stable/48569082 (accessed 19 November 2024).

49 Kristina Lyons, *Vital Decomposition: Soil Practitioners and Life Politics* (Durham, NC and London: Duke University Press, 2020), p. 22.

of social precarity and ecological destruction. They strive to disrupt prevailing dynamics that devalue and cheapen life. Furthermore, their approach to addressing ecological and social devastation is grounded in concrete and relational terms. They advocate for an ecological economy that goes hand in hand with practices aimed at decommodifying land, housing and healthcare. The movement also calls for the dismantling of what they term as the 'military-industrial complex', designed to 'extract every last drop of fossil fuel from Mother Earth' (see 'Engañados en el invernadero').[50] They emphasise the crucial connection between equality, freedom and the environment, as reflected in the principles of 'environmental justice' and 'energy democracy' (see 'Engañados en el invernadero'). The concept of environmental justice underscores the stark inequality in the distribution of ecological damage, particularly its disproportionate occurrence in territories inhabited by marginalised and impoverished communities. It sheds light on the unjust pattern of these impacts being concentrated in specific regions, while the affected communities have limited meaningful participation in decisions that directly impact on their inhabited spaces.[51] The notion of 'energy democracy' emphasises the imperative to dismantle the 'imperial ways of life',[52] that have historically perpetuated the exploitation of so-called 'peripheral' regions to sustain the energy consumption of the 'centre'. It underlines the significance of democratic control over the appropriation of natural resources, including questions of who benefits from their exploitation and how they are utilised. Moreover, it challenges the assumption that a growth-driven economy is indispensable for achieving equitable redistribution.

*

In light of what has been presented in this chapter, we could say that resilience and re-existence propose two distinct orientations towards the future. Resilience focuses on anticipating and controlling the effects of disasters to shape a consensual future based on foreseeable circumstances. In contrast, strategies of re-existence challenge this colonisation of the future. They interrogate the underlying conditions that give rise to disasters, rebuild life in their aftermath, acknowledge both the damage and hidden possibilities that have been buried, reshape existence amidst what remains and generate dissenting potentialities that have not been eradicated by violence.

50 My translation.

51 See Bryant Bunyan and Paul Mohai, *Race and the Incidence of Environmental Hazards: A Time for Discourse* (Boulder, CO: Westview Press, 1992).

52 See Ulrich Brand and Markus Wissen, *The Limits to Capitalist Nature: Theorizing and Overcoming the Imperial Mode of Living* (Durham, NC: Rowman and Littlefield, 2018).

Such strategies teach us that we must look at the past ahead and embrace the future as something we cannot yet see, but that 'comes walking from behind' (Hurtado, Aranda and Vasco, *Guambianos, hijos del arcoiris*, p. 64) a formulation that resonates with various indigenous communities in South America.[53] So, we must carry with us the marks, the residues that our interventions have left on the world, embodying them in how we live, in order to build a more habitable world for the multitude of life forms that coexist with us. In the eloquent words of Ailton Krenak, it becomes a matter of 'reforesting the imagination' and allowing 'the forest to live in us as well',[54] as we acknowledge the undeniable debris, the tangible waste we have already generated.

Bibliography

Albán, Adolfo, and José R. Rosero, 'Colonialidad de la naturaleza: ¿Imposición tecnológica y usurpación epistémica? Interculturalidad, desarrollo y re-existencia'. *Nómadas*, 45 (2016), 27–41.

Anderson, Ben, 'Preemption, Precaution, Preparedness: Anticipatory Action and Future Geographies'. *Progress in Human Geography*, 34:6 (2010), 777–98, doi:10.1177/030913251036260 (accessed 15 November 2023).

Athanasiou, Athena, and Judith Butler, *Dispossession: The Performative in the Political* (Cambridge: Polity Press, 2013).

Basseler, Michael, 'Stories of Dangerous Life in the Post- Trauma Age: Toward a Cultural Narratology of Resilience', in *Narrative in Culture*, edited by Astrid Erll and Roy Sommer (Berlin: De Gruyter, 2019), pp. 15–36, doi:10.1515/9783110654370-002 (accessed 15 November 2023).

Béné, Christophe, Andrew Newsham, Mark Davies, Martina Ulrichs, and Rachel Godfrey-Wood, 'Resilience, Poverty and Development'. *Journal of International Development*, 25 (2014), 598–623, doi:10.1002/jid.2992 (accessed 29 July 2023).

Brand, Ulrich, and Markus Wissen, *The Limits to Capitalist Nature: Theorizing and Overcoming the Imperial Mode of Living* (Lanham, MD: Rowman and Littlefield, 2018).

Centro Nacional de Memoria Histórica-Organización Nacional Indígena de Colombia, *Tiempos de vida y muerte* (Bogotá: CNMH-ONIC, 2019).

53 For example, in Misak communities living in Colombia and in Aymara communities living in regions of Bolivia, Peru, and Chile.

54 Ailton Krenak, *Futuro Ancestral* (São Paulo: Companhia das Letras, 2022), pp. 34–6. My translation.

Cooper, Melinda, and Jeremy Walker, 'Genealogies of Resilience: From Systems Ecology to the Political Economy of Crisis Adaptation'. *Security Dialogue*, 42:2 (2011), 143–60, doi.org/10.1177/0967010611399 (accessed 29 July 2023).

Coronil, Fernando. 'Naturaleza del poscolonialismo: Del eurocentrismo al globocentrismo', in *La colonialidad del saber: eurocentrismo y ciencias sociales. Perspectivas latinoamericanas*, edited by Edgardo Lander (Buenos Aires: CLACSO, 2000), pp. 53–67.

Engañados en el invernadero: Contra las soluciones falsas al cambio climático', la vía campesina. https://viacampesina.org/es/por-que-luchamos/soberania-alimentaria/8 (accessed 30 March 2023).

Escobar, Arturo, *Sentipensar con la tierra: Nuevas lecturas sobre desarrollo, territorio y diferencia* (Medellín: UNAULA, 2014).

Evans, Brad, and Julian Reid, *Resilient Life: The Art of Living Dangerously* (Cambridge: Polity Press, 2014).

Fassin, Didier, and Rachel Gomme, *Humanitarian Reason: A Moral History of the Present* (California: University of California Press, 2012).

Foucault, Michel, *Sécurité, territoire, population (1977–1978)* (Paris: EHESS, Gallimard, Le Seuil, 2004).

González Casanova, Pablo, 'La explotación global', in *Globalidad: Una mirada alternativa,* edited by Miguel Ángel Porrúa (México: Centro Latinoamericano de la Globalidad, 1999), pp. 69–95.

Harvey, David, *The New Imperialism* (Oxford: Oxford University Press, 2003).

Hickel, Jason, 'The Development Delusion'. In *The Divide* (London: Penguin Random House, 2018), 11–32.

Hickel, Jason, *Less is More* (London: Penguin Random House, 2020).

Hickel, Jason, 'Quantifying National Responsibility for Climate Breakdown: An Equality-Based Attribution Approach for Carbon Dioxide Emissions in Excess of the Planetary Boundary'. *The Lancet*, 4:9 (2020), 399–404, https://doi.org/10.1016/S2542-5196(20)30196-0 (accessed 28 July 2023).

Hickel, Jason, Christian Dorninger, Hanspeter Wieland and Intan Suwandi, 'Imperialist Appropriation in the World Economy: Drain from the Global South through Unequal Exchange, 1990–2015'. *Global Environmental Change*, 73 (2022), doi:10.1016/j.gloenvcha.2022.102467 (accessed 28 July 2023).

Hickel, Jason, and Giorgos Kallis, 'Is Green Growth Possible?' *New Political Economy*, 25:4 (2019), 469–86, doi:10.1080/13563467.2019.1598964 (accessed 19 November 2024)

Holling, Stanley Crawford, 'Resilience and Stability of Ecological Systems'. *Annual Review of Ecology and Systematics*, 4 (1973), 1–23, doi:10.1146/annurev.es.04.110173.000245 (accessed 29 July 2023).

Hurtado, Abelino, Misael Aranda, and Luis G. Vasco, *Guambianos, hijos del arcoiris y del agua* (Bogotá: CEREC, 2015).

Ingold, Tim, 'Toward an Ecology of Materials'. *Annual Review of Anthropology*, 41 (2012), 417–39, doi:10.1146/annurev-anthro-081309-145920 (accessed 15 November 2023).

Krenak, Ailton, *Futuro Ancestral* (São Paulo: Companhia das Letras, 2022).

Lentzos, Filippa, and Nikolas Rose, 'Governing Insecurity: Contingency Planning, Protection, Resilience'. *Economy and Society*, 38:2 (2009), 230–54, doi:10.1080/03085140902786611 (accessed 29 July 2023).

Lyons, Kristina, 'Chemical Warfare in Colombia, Evidentiary Ecologies and Senti-Actuando Practices of Justice'. *Social Studies of Science*, 48:3 (2018), 414–37, https://www.jstor.org/stable/48569082 (accessed 19 November 2024).

Lyons, Kristina, *Vital Decomposition: Soil Practitioners and Life Politics* (Durham, NC and London: Duke University Press, 2020).

Márquez, Francia, 'El territorio es vida', in *Territorio*, edited by Francia Márquez, Tatiana Acevedo, and Álvaro Restrepo (Bogotá: Futuro en tránsito—Comisión de la verdad de Colombia).

Moore, Jason, 'The Rise of Cheap Nature', in *Anthropocene or Capitalocene? Nature, History, and the Crisis of Capitalism*, edited by Jason Moore (Oakland, CA: PM Press/Kairos), pp. 78–115.

Neocleous, Mark, 'Don't Be Scared, Be Prepared: Trauma-Anxiety-Resilience'. *Alternatives: Global, Local, Political*, 37:3 (2012), 188–98, doi:10.1177/0304375412449789 (accessed 29 July 2023).

Nixon, Robert, *Slow Violence and the Environmentalism of the Poor* (Cambridge, MA: Harvard University Press, 2011).

Puig de la Bellacasa, María, *Matters of Care* (Minneapolis: University of Minnesota, 2017).

Jacques Rancière, *La Mésentente* (Paris: Galilée, 1995).

'Resilience', Google Trends, https://trends.google.com/trends/explore?date=all&q=resilience&hl=es-CO (accessed 29 July 2023).

Ruiz-Serna, Daniel, 'El territorio como víctima'. *Revista colombiana de Antropología,* 53:2 (2017), 85–113, doi:.10.22380/2539472X.118 (accessed 15 November 2023).

Schröder, Enno, and Servaas Storm, 'Economic Growth and Carbon Emissions: The Road to "Hothouse Earth" Is Paved with Good Intentions. *International Journal of Political Economy*, 49:2 (2020), 153–73, doi:10.1080/08911916.2020.1778866 (accessed 19 November 2024).

Stiegler, Barbara, *Il faut s'adapter. Sur un nouvel impératif politique* (Paris: Gallimard, 2019).

Tunubalá-Velasco, Gerardo, and Javier A. Fayad-Sierra, 'Voces invisibilizadas, voces visibilizadas: Hacia un diálogo intercultural entre el saber misak y el conocimiento global'. *Nodos y Nudos*, 7:50 (2021), 159–72, doi:10.17227/nyn.vol7.num50-12610 (accessed 15 November 2023).

3

'How Each Particle, When It Bangs into Another, Either *Bounces Back* or Passes on a Part of Its Motion': On a Famous Spinozist Occurrence about the *Resilience* Problem, and Its Inadequacy

Vincent Legeay

In physics, the definition of resilience according to the Cambridge Dictionary is 'the ability of a substance to return to its usual shape after being bent, stretched, or pressed'.[1] Wikipedia mentions that 'in material science, resilience is the ability of a material to absorb energy when it is deformed elastically, and release that energy upon unloading'. Proof resilience is defined 'as the maximum energy that can be absorbed up to the elastic limit, without creating a permanent distortion'. In both definitions, it is clear that the notion is strongly co-dependent to that of the shape and form of the object or substance concerned. It is also associated with the notion of an *ability*.

1 The Cambridge Dictionary also gives this definition, that we shall study later: 'the ability to be happy, successful, etc. again after something difficult or bad has happened'.

These definitions raise the question of what is the *usual shape* or a *permanent distortion* pertaining to an object, thus triggering from the start a second question: what kind of observation defines the usual shape and the unusual distortion to an object? In short, resilience is not an attribute or a property of the thing, no more than a sheer impression or effect on the part of an observer. It is a relationship that an observer develops *in time* with a thing or an individual, being able to state its or their usual shapes and outlines.

In physics, the answer to the question of shape seems quite easy to give, since objects are as simple as possible. A physicist's choice is at the core of the definition of the studied object: a pool ball is chosen for its sphericity, wholeness and unity, an atom as the smallest particle of a chemical element for elementary combinations with others, a magnetic field is a series of vectors with aims, directions and influences. Their forms are often minimal; it is the complexification with other shaped objects that constitute the basis for experimentation. As Bachelard would put it, physics study 'phenomeno-technical'[2] objects, namely: sheer materializations of theories and conceptualizations, created in order to control all factors and reactions in experimentation. As such, these are rather 'noumenal objects' (Bachelard, *Le nouvel esprit scientifique*, p. 9) than given things surrounding us in reality. The observer creates the thing to be observed, logically mastering all aspects of its shape.

The notion of resilience then, when applied outside this realm of physics, could be tricky to use, since the observer is not the creator of the object. Biological individuals as complex organisms might be seen as resilient when the word is used according to the first kind of definition: if 'usual shape' is considered within a wide enough set of considerations and observations. The pool ball will remain a pool ball until it cannot be played with, but a dent will not entail its definition. An organism will remain one as long as the functions that are held necessary for its viability will prevail: respiration, nutritious mechanisms, nervous system, etc. The criteria of what constitutes a usual shape can be met according to multiple definitions of what *using* the object means.

But the observation of resilience will inevitably entail a contradiction within the bounds of the second definition, when explaining 'deformed elastically' becomes a central matter. Deformation and elasticity are relative properties: the pool ball will experience a deformation through the making of a dent, but will still keep its usual shape according to the first kind of definition. An organism can grow or decrease while still performing usual functions. In those cases, resilience might then just be misinterpreted for *hysteresis*: 'the lag in a variable property of a system with respect to the effect

2 Gaston Bachelard, *Le nouvel esprit scientifique* (Paris: PUF, 2020), p. 17.

producing it as this effect varies' (Collins Dictionnary). 'Hysteresis is the dependence of the state of a system on its history' (Wikipedia).

Worse, deformation and elasticity in daily life could be implied and necessitated by the normal and usual functioning, thus shaping, of those things. Deformation, that is, the pressing of the rotundity, is a normal thing that happens to a played *pool* ball, unless it is only a collection ball. Elasticity, that is the bending and stretching of arteries and veins, are usual requirements to an organism that needs its blood to circulate throughout different parts of its body.

It seems that the observation of resilience will vary according to what constitutes the unity of the object considered, and what constitutes mere parts required for the *functioning* of this object. Parts can be deformed and can perform some kind of elasticity, as long as the whole will not suffer a change that will transform it into something else. But this change can alter shape or function or even affective state, depending on the thing observed.

The correlation between the observation of deformation, stretching, bending, pressing, etc., and the mereological mechanics between parts and wholes is at the core of a Spinozian question concerning the concept of resilience, that he clearly states in a famous letter:

> Let us feign now, if you please, that there is a little worm living in the blood which is capable of distinguishing by sight the particles of the blood, of lymph, of chyle, etc., and capable of observing by reason how each particle, when it encounters another, *either bounces back, or communicates a part of its motion* , etc. Indeed, it would live in this blood as we do in this part of the universe, and *would consider* each particle of the blood *as a whole, not as a part* [*ut totum, non verò ut partem, consideraret*]. It could not know how all the parts of the blood are regulated by the universal nature of the blood, and *compelled to adapt themselves* [se accommodare coguntur] to one another, so that they agree with one another in a definite way.[3]

3 Baruch Spinoza, 'Letter 32', in *The Collected Works of Spinoza*, ed. and trans. Edwin Curley, I (Princeton: Princeton University Press, 2016). The complete Latin text reads as follows: Fingamus jam, si placet vermiculum in sanguine vivere, qui visu ad discernendas particulas sanguinis, lymphae, &c. valeret, & ratione ad observandum, quomodò unaquaeque particula ex alterius occursu, vel resilit, vel partem sui motûs communicat, &c. Ille quidem in hoc sanguine, ut nos in hâc parte universi, viveret, & unamquamque sanguinis particulam, ut totum, non verò ut partem, consideraret, nec scire posset, quomodò partes omnes ab universali naturâ sanguinis moderantur, & invicem, prout universalis natura sanguinis exigit, se accommodare coguntur, ut certâ ratione inter se consentiant. Our emphasis.

The first thing to be noted is that this occurrence of the term 'resilit' seems significant because in previous physical works,[4] where the term would be equally relevant, that is to say, when Spinoza is analysing Cartesian categories to describe the movements and interactions of two objects colliding, he uses mainly the verb *reflectere*, and not *resilire*, that could easily be translated by *bounce back* in English. We have noted around twenty occurrences of the verb reflectere. So significance of the term *resilit* in letter 32 could then indicate a reference to Bacon.[5] But we will not dig into this trail.

We would rather explore the possibility that Spinoza, as he often does, borrows a term to produce a new definition. This will be the main hypothesis of this chapter: we conjecture that the perception of resilience is a mutilated version of the adequate and rational perception of a scientific cognition. This does not preclude the Bacon hypothesis, and could in fact complement it, but we leave this issue aside on this occasion.

Why this hypothesis? Because in letter 32, Spinoza develops a theory of the epistemological *point of view* of an observer when perceiving physical laws of motion inside an organism. The reader is provided with a biological, ecological and physical reinterpretation of the types of knowledge (those disciplinary fields are mixed up in his mind, and do not need to be separated by epistemological predicaments). A first kind of perception, close to imagination, that does not consider the infinite composition of the parts into a whole, and a second kind of knowledge, that cannot be reduced to mere imagination, which considers the interactions as ecological parts into infinite interactions.

This has severe consequences that we aim to develop (I) from an epistemological point of view regarding biological and physical implications (this will be the main part of our *exposé*); and (II) regarding socio-ethical

4 Very notably in Baruch Spinoza, 'Descartes' Principles of Philosophy', *in The Collected Works of Spinoza*, ed. and trans. Edwin Curley, I (Princeton, NJ: Princeton University Press, 1988), as we shall see.

5 That Spinoza was aware of all the subtleties in the use of the notion of 'resilience' according to Bacon, we do not know. Now we have a (slight) clue of how he could criticize such a notion, mainly used by Bacon for physical matters in order to describe the bouncing of sound or light, in letter 2 to Oldenburg (Spinoza, *Collected Works I*, p. 167). He indeed declares that Bacon held the mistakes of the human mind as a bended mirror. The original analogy of resilience with the sheer observation of lights or sounds could indicate that Spinoza was suspecting the notion to concern only very simple objects in nature, not highly composed objects. But that is only a conjecture. Spinoza seems to be addressing only the *Novum Organum* (Oxford: Clarendon Press, 2004).

considerations, ethical being understood here both in the sense of Deleuze[6] regarding individuals as ethological modes and (III) in the sense of a separated field of research concerning ecosystemic-political human interactions.

I

Let us reconsider *in extenso* the passage we started with. Except for the excerpt quoted above, we indicate the Latin version when we see it fit regarding the relevance of what we want to demonstrate, namely, mostly concerning those aspects in relation to the issues of *accommodation*, *resilience* and epistemological notions like *adequation* and *contrariety* towards *environmental conditions*. The passage is long, but we think it is quite useful to have the full context, since it develops an entire epistemology to the notion of resilience.

By the coherence of parts, then, I understand nothing but that the laws *or* the nature of the one part *adapts* itself to the laws *or* the nature of the other part so that they are *opposed* to each other as little as possible [*quàm quòd leges, sive natura unius partis ità sese* accommodat *legibus, sive naturae alterius, ut quàm minimè sibi* contrarientur]. Concerning whole and parts, I consider things as parts of some whole to the extent that the nature of one *adapts* itself to that of the other so that they all *agree* with one another as far as possible. But insofar as they *disagree* with one another [*ut partes alicujus totius, quatenus earum natura invicem se* accommodat, *ut, quoad fieri potest, inter se* consentiant, *quatenus verò inter se* discrepant] to that extent each forms in our Mind an idea distinct from the others, and therefore it is considered as a whole and not as a part.

For example, when the motions of the particles of lymph, chyle, etc., so *adapt* themselves to one another, in relation to their size and shape, that they completely *agree* with one another [*ità se* accommodant, *ut planè inter se* consentiant] and they all constitute one fluid together, to that extent only the chyle, lymph, etc., are considered as parts of the blood. But insofar as we conceive the particles of lymph, by reason of their shape and motion, to differ from the particles of chyle, to that extent we consider them as a whole and not as a part.

Let us feign now, if you please, that there is a little worm living in the blood which is capable of distinguishing by sight the particles of the blood, of lymph, of chyle, etc., and capable of observing by reason how each particle, when it encounters another, *either bounces back* [resilit], or communicates

6 See, for instance, Gilles Deleuze, *Spinoza, Philosophie Pratique* (Paris: Éditions de Minuit, 2003), p. 40.

a part of its motion, etc. Indeed, it would live in this blood as we do in this part of the universe, and would consider each particle of the blood as a whole, not as a part. It could not know how all the parts of the blood are regulated by the universal nature of the blood, and *compelled to adapt themselves* [se accommodare coguntur] to one another, so that they agree with one another in a definite way.

For if we should feign that there are no causes outside the blood which would communicate new motions to the blood, and no space outside the blood, nor any other bodies to which the particles of blood could transfer their motion, it is certain that the blood would always remain in the same state, and its particles would undergo no variations other than those which can be conceived from the given relation of the motion of the blood to the lymph, chyle, etc. Thus the blood would always have to be considered as a whole and not as a part. But because there are a great many other causes which regulate the laws of the blood in a definite way, and which in turn are regulated by the blood, the result is that other motions and other variations arise in the particles of the blood which follow not simply from the relation of the motion of its parts to one another, but from the relation of the motion of the blood as a whole and of its external causes to one another. In this way the blood has the nature of a part and not of a whole. That is what I say concerning whole and part.

Now, all bodies in nature can and must be conceived as we have here conceived the blood, for all bodies are surrounded by others, and are determined by one another to existing and producing an effect in a fixed and determinate way, the same ratio of motion to rest always being preserved in all of them at once—i.e. in the whole universe—is always the same. From this it follows that every body, insofar as it exists modified in a definite way, must be considered as a part of the whole universe, must agree with its whole and must cohere with the remaining bodies. *And since the nature of the universe is not limited, as the nature of the blood is, but is absolutely infinite, its parts are regulated in infinite ways by this nature of the infinite power, and compelled to undergo infinitely many variations.* But in relation to substance, I conceive each part to have a closer union with its whole. [...] Since it is of the nature of a substance to be infinite, it follows that each part pertains to the nature of corporeal substance, and can neither be nor be conceived without it. You see, therefore, how and why I think that the human Body is a part of Nature. But as far as the human Mind is concerned, I think it is a part of Nature too. For I maintain that there is also in nature an infinite power of thinking, which, insofar as it is infinite, contains in itself objectively the whole of Nature, and whose thoughts proceed in the same way as Nature, its object, does. *Next, I maintain that the human Mind is this same power, not insofar as it is infinite and perceives the whole of Nature, but insofar as it is finite and perceives only the human body.* For this reason I maintain that the human Mind is a part of a certain infinite intellect.[7]

We would like to make several comments regarding this long text, since it bears multiple implications.

First, this could ring a Leibnizian bell to some of the readers. The infinite complexity of organisms and, most especially, the infinite composition of their parts could be an extract from the *Monadology*.[8] Now this bell still has another ring, for Spinoza suggests a different take on what should be considered an epistemological point of view in observation: it is always located in a finite perception that is both mental *and* physical. The physical perception of resilience is quite fundamental here for the very concept of resilience. Indeed, this perception occurs because we *lack* an element of context: the ecological element of an infinite causality that permanently requests the particles, and then incidentally the bouncing back seems to be an *unusual* modification and movement of those particles. Now, when taking this ecological context into account, each particle becomes a part, and it seems to be usual for them to suffer those changes. Infinite complexity could suspend the simplicity comprised in the concept of resilience.

Second, this finite perception has concrete implications in terms of *distortion* of the observed objects: the concrete network of determination always escapes our knowledge, and this determination involving ignorance of infinite causal connections forces a finite point of view to considering things as wholes, when they should actually be interpreted as parts. This mereological approach is a radical one: there is always an infinity of factors in a physical or biological interaction between two objects. The bouncing back of a thing is a perception of interaction between two wholes, one that is always on a multi-dimension scale that could also present them as two compatible parts of a superior organism. *Resilience* reveals the point of view of the *observer*. It discloses an attribute of a situated mind rather than a property of the thing itself. In Spinozian terms, resilience might state an inadequate and mutilated

7 Baruch Spinoza, 'Letter 32', in *The Collected Works of Spinoza*, II, ed. and trans. Edwin Curley (Princeton, NJ: Princeton University Press, 2016).

8 Leibniz, Gottfried Wilhelm, Monadology, in *The Philosophical Works of Leibnitz* (New Haven: Tuttle, Morehouse & Taylor, 1890), §64: 'Therefore every organic body of a living being is a kind of divine machine or natural automaton, infinitely surpassing all artificial automatons. Because a machine constructed by man's skill is not a machine in each of its parts; for instance, the teeth of a brass wheel have parts or bits which to us are not artificial products and contain nothing in themselves to show the use to which the wheel was destined in the machine. The machines of nature, however, that is to say, living bodies, are still machines in their smallest parts ad infinitum. Such is the difference between nature and art, that is to say, between divine art and ours.'

perception of the environment, where factors are too many to hide our ignorance of the processes involved.

Third, there is a confusion, if we follow this text, between *external* and *internal* processes in a physical interaction. Spinoza points to the finite and biased dimension of this notion describing a rebound, a bouncing back between *two* objects in *one* relation of impenetrability. On the contrary, an adequate kind of knowledge should understand objects as being determined by infinite factors (that is, by infinite other *objects*) within a superior relation (Spinoza calls this a *connection*).[9] To put it slightly differently, an adequate knowledge of two objects colliding and bouncing back should understand this relation as a second-hand interaction *inside* an infinite network, nature being the ultimate individual composed of an infinite number of interconnections. *Resilience* introduces a bias in perception: it separates things in the interaction, favouring external or disjunctive relationships. However, an adequate way of undestanding the bouncing back of two particles should describe these connections as conjunctive-disjunctive, leading to a relative and open field of observation.

Fourth and last remark: resilience, according to this text, relies on a simplistic and rigid idea of what is *contradiction*. Two objects experience contradictory directions and exchange *opposed* movements when colliding. This corresponds to the Cartesian view, roughly situated within a worm's perception or in our own. The Spinozian notion of *accommodation* stated in this text, on the contrary, proposes a plastic idea of *contradiction*: an object that is contradictory to another at a certain time and space can be transformed into an 'accommodating' object, since there is some common properties that can positively bind the individual and the circumstances. Let us take Spinoza's anecdote literally and consider an example from the field of immunology. Vaccination against a virus is a nice example of the potential plasticity of a contradiction: two types of particles (cells and viruses, for instance) are in opposition with one another *until* there is a common property making them compatible (antibodies, for example). Pasteur's intuition in his experience with chickens and pigs was nothing else: the scientist/observer has to make antigens vary enough with their environment until there is common ground vis-à-vis the usual processes of antibodies *inside* the whole system of an individual.[10]

9 See for example Baruch Spinoza, *Ethics*, II, proposition 7, in *The Collected Works of Spinoza,* vol. I, ed. and trans. Edwin Curley (Princeton: Princeton University Press, 1988): 'The order and connection of ideas is the same as the order and connection of things.'

10 See *Oeuvres de Pasteur*, vol. 6, ed. Pasteur Vallery-Radot (Paris: Masson et Cie, 1933). Navigation is also a good example: the first time a series of *sapiens* sees an ocean and dive in it; they do not master the art or swimming or floating

In a recent article written with Marc Daëron,[11] an immunologist from the Pasteur Institute in Paris, we used the same Spinozian conceptions linked to non-linearity[12] to efficiently criticize the notion of 'function'. We argued that Spinoza gives a good account both of:

1. the type of abstraction represented by a point of view on biological objects, as these are always accommodated in a higher whole, which is itself under the yoke of an infinity of modifications
2. the type of inversion present in natural observation that simplifies, linearly, cause and effect, while the partial causes of lymph and chyle can never have the same status as the accommodating effect produced by this lymph and chyle at another level, that of the blood, which itself is only a part of a larger body.

The elements of description are applied to an environment requiring the parts to accommodate to each other. Here, functioning can be perceived as 'good' or 'useful' at the higher level, that of the organism or highly composed individual. This description engages a cognitive critique of science.

Once the observation has been made in the synthesis of the scientific observation, a scientific practice recalls that causes and effects be separated artificially. At the time of observation and analysis, it would nevertheless have cut into its object's artificial parts affected in reality by an infinity of modifications. The latter are themselves impossible to extract from the environment in which they enter into operation, because this environment releases the effects perceived as adjuvant or good resulting from the functioning of the parts, without them ever acting to this purpose, but in their own usefulness.

Not only does Spinoza suggest an unprecedented conception of the biological environment as a set of indefinite circumstances, but above all, he links this understanding to accommodation as a general requirement of nature. Body and mind are immersed in an infinitely constraining universe

---

and sinking. Then they learn how to swim, and then combine physical laws of floating with carpentry, creating boats, and what was used to destroy mankind can be used to travel on the planet. This process cannot be described as resilience in the way Spinoza states it above, for it necessitates almost infinite different variables to be adjusted to reach that point of equilibrium. A simple bouncing back is completely excluded in such an example.

11 Marc Daëron and Vincent Legeay, 'La Fonction en biologie. Une critique spinoziste', *Cahiers Philosophiques*, 169:2 (2022), 9–22 (p. 10).

12 We will understand non-linearity here in the sheer sense of a process of infinite inputs constraining and addressed to a thing that can in return only answer to those inputs in a finite manner.

that imposes itself on finite mind and bodies, and resilience is an effect that has a causal structure that extends beyond concerned individuals.

Spinoza's mereological perspective, which destroys the linearity of the causal relationship by unravelling the simple implication of a cause for an effect, not only unmasks the process of abstraction necessary for any observation and point of view, but also sheds light on the possible aetiological inversions when considering a higher, systemic element. The Spinozist criticism is positive: it is not a judgment on observation, but an attempt to restore a double bias, necessary to any point of view concerning what appears to be simple objects in interaction.

This Spinozist analysis can be illustrated through a simple example, borrowed from today's medicine, that of a blood bag such as provided to hospitals by the French Blood Hospital Institution. The red blood cells contained in this bag are perfectly functional: the haemoglobin they contain fixes oxygen and carbon dioxide as it did before the sample was taken from a body. However, their donor function was lost. This function will be restored when the blood is transfused to a recipient: the haemoglobin will again bring oxygen to the organs and rid them of carbon dioxide. The function of red blood cells does not belong to them. The abstraction contained in the vocabulary of 'function' is here unmasked by a Spinozist type of mereological reasoning, applied to contemporary biology.

The same could apply to the notion of resilience: when used to describe the behaviour of one individual to make it responsible for this rebound, there is both a bias of etiological inversion and abstraction. The course of action of a physical object or the trajectory of a human individual are susceptible of the same inadequate perceptions.

II

An adequate knowledge must take into account that objects are not merely wholes colliding into one another, but constitute parts *accommodating* inside an environment that offers infinite variation to its constituents. We would be inclined to add: this is especially true when concerning human affects and emotions, that are even more complex. Indeed, the notion of resilience is often used positively to point that an individual has overcome sadness or emotional crisis. As noted above, the Cambridge Dictionary mentions a second definition for resilience: 'the ability to be happy, successful, etc. again after something difficult or bad has happened' as noted above. A Spinozian take on accommodation could debunk multiple aspects of this assumption. What does this mean exactly, and how can it give us some concrete elements for a positive *critique* of resilience?

The notion of *accommodation* in Spinoza's works is rather difficult. In English, it translates as *adaptation*. But this does not entirely fit what Spinoza means. The idea of accommodation relies on a non-linear intuition (Spinoza does not have this vocabulary but the idea is there): every mode, that is, every singular and finite modification in nature is an *ex-pression*, literally the result of infinite pression on all the parts of the thing considered; this expression is in itself a synthetic identity of composed ideas and bodies. Let us read another passage by Spinoza, now in the *Ethics*:

> So such an affect will always remain the same; and hence the affects that are contrary to it, and that are not encouraged by their external causes, will have to accommodate [*accomodare*] themselves to it more and more, until they are no longer contrary to it. To that extent an affect arising from reason is more powerful.[13]

And let us confront it with two other extracts from the Appendix of Part Four:

> It is impossible for man not to be a part of nature and not to follow the common order of nature. But if he lives among such individuals as agree with his nature, his power of acting will thereby be aided and encouraged On the other hand, if he is among such as do not agree at all with his nature, he will hardly be able to *accommodate* himself to them without greatly changing himself[14] [...] But human power is very limited, and infinitely surpassed by the power of external causes. So we do not have an absolute power to *adapt* things outside us to our use.[15]

The formulation using the infinitive *accommodare* in Chapter 7 is almost the same as the one in letter 32 quoted above. To overcome obstacles and constraints in our daily emotions is, in those passages, to *accommodate* the

13 'Quare talis affectus idem semper manet, et consequenter affectus, qui eidem sunt contrarii quique a suis causis externis non foventur, eidem magis magisque sese accomodare debebunt, donec non amplius sint contrarii, et eatenus affectus, qui ex ratione oritur, est potentior' (Spinoza, *Ethics*, V, proposition 7), our emphasis.

14 'Nec fieri potest, ut homo non sit naturae pars et communem ejus ordinem non sequatur; sed si inter talia individua versetur, quae cum ipsius hominis natura conveniunt, eo ipso hominis agendi potentia juvabitur et fovebitur. At si contra inter talia sit, quae cum ipsius natura minime conveniunt, vix absque magna ipsius mutatione iisdem sese accommodare poterit'.(Spinoza, *Ethics*, IV, appendix, chap. VII). Our emphasis.

15 'Sed humana potentia admodum limitata est et a potentia causarum externarum infinite superatur; atque adeo potestatem absolutam non habemus res, quae extra nos sunt, ad nostrum usum aptandi' (Spinoza, *Ethics*, IV, appendix, chap. XXXII). Our emphasis.

circumstantial and structural causality that affects us. This accommodation requires one to precisely not flee away or bounce back from those circumstances, but rather to vary with them and attend their daily courses. The infinite surpassing of affective variables summons individuals to be shaped (*accommodare debere*) by things rather than trying to shape them (*aptare*). The observer of human passions, as the physicist influenced by gravity or the biologist informed by immunity, must first recognize the humility of our condition and accept that we are *parts* of nature rather than mere wholes (or a 'kingdom within a kingdom' as Spinoza states in the Preface of *Ethics* III).

Nature summons us to accommodate with her rather than we summon her to accommodate with us. Adaptation is a structural and plastic process to which we are almost entirely subjected. There is no bouncing away from permanent affective solicitation that will not stop contradicting us, due to the infinite power external causes have. The key is thus to adopt practically an opposite version of resilience as the one depicted in Cartesian terms above.

This does not entail that we are mere toys or passive subjects in the hands of Nature. There is room enough for us to *direct* parts of the accommodation process. As Spinoza states, the affects that spring from reason are more powerful than the passions that drive us blind in the order of nature. Why? Because reason is a process based on the observation of *common* properties, that is the expression of how contrariety between objects (for instance, the immediate relations between us and destructive processes such as diseases or hostile environments) can be reduced and *used* to produce a positive outcome. Now, concerning the *quantity* of change we must undertake to face adversity, it is indeed determined by the common order of things and not by us.

An ethical formula that would sum things up and give a Spinozian version of pliancy, which is no resilience, can be found in the Corollary of Proposition 4 in Ethics IV:

> From this it follows, that man is necessarily subject to passions, that he follows and obeys the general order of nature, and *accommodates* himself to it as much as the nature of things demands.[16]

It is clear for Spinoza that the common order of nature (which is chaotic from *our* point of view, since we are only a part of nature and consequently observe it with partial eyes) dictates us the *quantity* of change that we must go through.

16 'Hinc sequitur hominem necessario passionibus esse semper obnoxium communemque naturae ordinem sequi et eidem parere seseque eidem, quantum rerum natura exigit, accommodare.' *Ethics*, IV, proposition 4, corollary. Our emphasis.

Now, due to non-linearity, our perseverance in being is finite, while circumstances are infinite. It seems that general balance contributes to our destruction.

Nevertheless, if indeed death is inexorable, as complex organisms, our *aptitude* at doing many actions or receiving many impressions at once[17] allows us to answer multiple solicitations with unique and composed affects. We are quite well equipped for facing infinite, unfavourable factors. Aptitude in Spinozian terms defines the rate of variation that we can undertake to create new patterns of understanding, based on interactions involving mostly contrariety.[18] As vaccination against multiple viruses or boats to navigate different seas, similar active affects can be developed to answer several different obstacles. In other words, it is possible to reduce emotional and affective 'noise' with a finite number of affective compositions. But the individual composition of those affects is in itself dependent on the political structure in which we are living. Accommodation, which is the Spinozian adequate equivalent of our current *resilience* concept, is particularly hinged on social interactions. What are the socio-political consequences of such a view?

III

We will now conclude this chapter on a Spinozian conception of resilience within the frame of the socio-ethical consequences of this epistemological critique.

It is first to be noticed that the epistemological critiques stated above can be transferred, from a Spinozian point of view to the observation of the social world. The 'resilience' of several individuals has to be interpreted as affective non-linear trajectories. Affective *trajectories* can be classified (this is one of the ambitions of Part IV of the *Ethics*), but are really every time built and adjusted on specific and singular local contexts, especially when social circumstances increase the number of solicitations, by adding educative processes, for instance.

This notion of an onto-sociological trajectory overcoming obstacles transforming negativity and contrariety into individual usefulness has recently been reinterpreted, in France, by Chantal Jaquet, who coined a new term: 'transclass'. This notion aims precisely at moving away from a linear interpretation of a trajectory and at including complex affective interactions that escape *typical* affective schemes. The overcoming of socio-affective negativity

17 See, Spinoza, *Ethics*, II, proposition 13, scholium.

18 An analysis of this mechanism goes beyond the scope of this chapter. For more on this subject, see Vincent Legeay, *Être apte chez Spinoza* (Paris: Garnier, 2020).

is construed within a bottom-up framework, where singularities in difficult affective encounters produce new general ideas of the environment that are paradoxically better fitted than those that, for example, the educational system gives.

In her work *Transclasses: A Theory of Social Non-reproduction*[19] Chantal Jaquet wants to show, by complementing the sociological analyses of Bourdieu,[20] that affective trajectories like those of the transclasses are 'the proof in action of the existence of a mobility and plasticity of beings, even in the most unfavourable conditions' which 'contradicts the essentialist as existentialist visions' (Jaquet, *Le transclasses,* p. 219, my translation). The social process of encountering obstacles is, since Bourdieu, defined as a reproduction of cognitive and affective advantages for dominant classes and of cognitive and affective drawbacks for dominated classes. Chantal Jaquet relies on a Spinozian framework concerning emotions to demonstrate that singularity, idiosyncrasy, namely, complexions present in infinite local situations are potentially inexhaustible to overcome social drawbacks in a society. Now, this cannot be described as *resilience*, but as affective structures that each time rely on a connection of affects presented by extraordinary situations.

As she puts it: 'this thought of complexion recaptures all the common and singular determinations that are forged in an individual, through his lived existence, his encounters, at the crossroads of his intimate history and collective history'(Jaquet, *Le transclasses,* pp. 219–20, my translation). It does not reject 'social habitus, it includes them in a larger and more complex combinatorics where childhood, family history, position in order of siblings, sexual orientation, emotional life, friendly and romantic relationships, are integrated into the examination of the trajectory' (Jaquet, *Le transclasses,* p. 220, my translation). Those crossroads are innumerable affective solicitations answered by *ingenii* of the individuals. What does this mean? *Ingenium* is the singular cognitive mark of an association made and composed by an individual to answer problems in her environment. It defines the cognitive and affective complexion of an individual based on her experience. Chantal Jaquet describes it as 'a composite of sedimented affects constituting an individual, her lifestyle, her judgments and her behaviour' (Jaquet, *Le transclasses,* p. 220, my translation).[21]

19 Chantal Jaquet, *Le transclasses ou la non-reproduction* (Paris: PUF, 2014).

20 See Pierre Bourdieu, *La Reproduction. Éléments d'une théorie du système d'enseignement* (Paris: Éditions de Minuit, 1970).

21 Chantal Jaquet, 'La mobilité sociale au prisme de Spinoza', in *Spinoza à l'œuvre : Composition des corps et force des idées* (Paris: Éditions de la Sorbonne, 2017).

The idiosyncratic determinations in the history and experience of a complex individual crystallise into a affective and cognitive associations. When forged in negativity and contrariety, these determinations sometimes lead to a heightened attention to accommodation processes and the imitation of affects. The dominated individual knows how to use contextual constraints to 'blend in' and 'adapt to' new environments and situations, and master the rules of different environments. Paradoxically enough, these determinations provide the individual with a dialectic power that individuals from ruling classes do not possess. This theory of the non-reproductive aspects of individuals' experiences that do not fit with their original social classes allow us some final comments.

Chantal Jaquet does not specifically target the notion of resilience, but surely takes the kind of singular and moral approach that makes the individual solely responsible for her linear trajectory. An individual cannot be considered as a rigid whole that experiences only impenetrability of thoughts and affections in the different shocks of daily life. The idea of school meritocracy, particularly strong in France, represents this type of comprehension. It propagates the myth of individuals who can earn the symbolic capital that diplomas and *curricula* offer, just by working intensely, where in fact children from the dominated class are statistically excluded from any real success in studies since they do not master the codes of learning. Resilience is an objective ally of such a system of interpretation, since it conceptualizes individuals as entities that could be absolutely separated and distinguished from the environment and can be held responsible for success (or failure) of their *curricula*, associated with the emotions fit for this purpose: happiness or shame.

An affective and social rebound or bouncing back can never be a *simple* shock of an entity versus another. It always constitutes a multidimensional phenomenon with different scales of interpretation. In those dimensions, Spinoza insists on one in particular: the irreducible psycho-physical unity of encounters. A rebound is never a mere physical *or* psychological process. The rebound interaction is always in some sense a *reflection* on an encounter. This is already included in the Cartesian physical concept of *resilience*.

In his commentary on Descartes' physics, the *Descartes' principles of Philosophy,* Spinoza uses the verb *reflectur* more than twenty times. Where Descartes in the *Principles of Philosophy* favours the French '*rebondir*', which is literally means 'bouncing back', Spinoza prefers the notion of 'reflection', which has the elegance of also agreeing to the laws of optics and refraction. Now, this conception of reflection within that treatise on physics involves traditionally two dimensions: *determination* and *movement.* When determinations (that is, directions) are in opposition/contradiction and collide, the objects must vary until they reach an equilibrium where a quantity of force (either determination, movement or both of them) *passes* from one object to another. In simple things, like the pool ball, the ideas that are associated to that process are also very simple and not *integrated*, if we may state it this way, in a complex network of ideas.

For complex organisms however this physical reflection entails a passive accommodation to the forces of determination and movement that can be transformed into active understanding of how those forces work so as to develop an idea of the common properties that unite those objects interacting. This idea, being submitted to new interactions, grows into a complex one, and *resilience* in this case consists in transforming new and surprising interactions in a sort of *redundancy*, where the same answer can satisfy different soliciting environments. Resilience as reflection then constitutes a finite psycho-physical response to an indefinite number of new solicitations. The positivity of resilience stems from an *aptitude* for experiencing singular passive variation and integrating it into a complex system of active understanding.

We can now return to the definitions we first considered and draw some conclusions. Resilience as 'the ability of a substance to return to its usual shape after being bent, stretched, or pressed' (Cambridge Dictionary) would not align with a Spinozian view. This is not because Spinoza is unsympathetic to the notion of resilience *per se*. After all, what is at stake here is a sheer question of definition and coining of a physical process, and Spinoza is an adept of redefining old terms with new properties. Rather, this definition would not align with Spinoza, because it is discrepant with what is for him an *ability* or *aptitude* of complex organisms.

Aptitudes follow incremental processes; any *stable shape* seems to be excluded since it is always varying with the circumstances, at least in its psycho-physical functioning within this environment. The concept of resilience relies on observation of simple objects (or rather observation simplifying objects, where it should be complexified, as Bachelard would claim,[22] because they are considered distinct wholes that can be recognized as such before and after an event. There is no such thing as *returning to a usual shape* in a Spinozian world, since any bending or stretching of pressure changes at least the shape of the *idea* (the *ex-pression* as Deleuze would claim)[23] that the individual construes within and about new circumstances.

As for the other definition, 'in material science, resilience is the ability of a material to absorb energy when it is deformed elastically, and release that energy upon unloading' (Wikipedia), it seems more appropriate, since the

22 Gaston Bachelard, *Le nouvel esprit scientifique* (PUF, Paris, 2020).

23 See Gilles Deleuze, *Spinoza et le problème de l'expression* (Paris: Éditions de Minuit, 1968).

notion of elasticity does not explicitly involve any *conservation* of a precedent or usual shape. Deleuze claimed precisely that the definition of 'the power to be affected' (very close in the Spinozian vocabulary to the notion of aptitude) entails some sort of elasticity.[24] Now this has been strongly debated,[25] since elasticity can be interpreted as a temporary state of growth or shrinking with the tendency to return to a previous state. If we set aside the notion of resilience, the closest contemporary notion with which Spinoza would agree could be that of *plasticity.*

But it might still be too poor a concept to match the one of accommodation, since plasticity does not include the three fundamental epistemological points listed above:

1. every individual is a *part* of nature and as such entails a *partial* observation,
2. every interaction is a non-linear process, which means there is always an infinity of variables in each encounter,
3. for a complex individual, the overcoming of affective and social contrarieties necessarily includes a psychophysiological deformation-reformation, which means the acquiring of new affects and ideas that are better fitted to the world (what we have called *reflection*).

Bibliography

Bachelard, Gaston, *Le nouvel esprit scientifique* (Paris: PUF, 2020).

Bacon, Francis, *Novum Organum* (Oxford: Clarendon Press, 2004).

Bourdieu, Pierre, *La Reproduction. Éléments d'une théorie du système d'enseignement* (Paris: Éditions de Minuit, 1970).

Curley, Edwin, ed. and trans., *The Collected Works of Spinoza, I* (Princeton, NJ: Princeton University Press, 1988).

24 See, 'En second lieu, il faut faire intervenir un autre niveau de variations possibles. Car le pouvoir d'être affecté ne reste pas constant toujours, ni sous tous les points de vue. En effet, Spinoza suggère que le rapport qui caractérise un mode existant dans son ensemble est doué d'une sorte d'élasticité" (Deleuze, *Spinoza et le problème de l'expression*, p. 204).

25 Catherine Malabou strongly criticizes Deleuze on this aspect. See the article by Nicolas Lema Habash on the matter: 'La plasticité des termes "force" et "vie" dans les Pensées métaphysiques de Spinoza', in *L'Essence plastique: Aptitudes et accommodements chez Spinoza*, ed. Vincent Legeay (Paris: Éditions de la Sorbonne, 2018).

Curley, Edwin, ed. and trans., *The Collected Works of Spinoza, II* (Princeton, NJ: Princeton University Press, 2016).

Daëron, Marc, and Vincent Legeay, 'La Fonction en biologie. Une critique spinoziste', *Cahiers philosophiques*, 169:2 (2022), 9–22.

Deleuze, Gilles, *Spinoza et le problème de l'expression* (Paris: Éditions de Minuit, 1968).

Deleuze, Gilles, *Spinoza, philosophie pratique* (Paris: Éditions de Minuit, 2003).

Jaquet, Chantal, *Spinoza à l'œuvre: Composition des corps et force des idées* (Paris: Éditions de la Sorbonne, 2017).

Jaquet, Chantal, *Le transclasses ou la non-reproduction* (Paris: PUF, 2014).

Leibniz, Gottfried Wilhelm, *Monadology*, in *The Philosophical Works of Leibnitz* (New Haven, CT: Tuttle, Morehouse & Taylor, 1890).

Lema Habash, Nicolas, 'La Plasticité des termes "force" et "vie" dans les Pensées métaphysiques de Spinoza', in *L'Essence plastique: Aptitudes et accommodements chez Spinoza*, ed. Vincent Legeay (Paris: Éditions de la Sorbonne, 2018).

Legeay, Vincent, *Être apte chez Spinoza* (Paris: Garnier, 2020).

Pasteur, Louis, *Oeuvres de Pasteur*, vol. 6, edited by Pasteur Vallery-Radot (Paris: Masson et cie, 1933).

4

Resilience and Sustainability as Complementary Concepts in Political Thought

Anna Wienhues

Abstract

Green political philosophy has paid a lot of attention to the notion of sustainability (often in the form of sustainable development). Against the background that sustainability and sustainable development have been subjected to a range of critiques, and alternative concepts—such as resilience—have been proposed in different disciplinary contexts, the aim of this chapter is to elaborate on why political theorists should not give up on the notion of sustainability too readily. It has a function in theories of justice and state legitimacy which is distinct from and complementary to the function attributed to the concept of resilience. The so far less considered concept of resilience, in turn, ought to receive more attention in political thought akin to the attention that has been given to sustainability in the literature. Accordingly, for the purposes of political theorising these constitute two complementary notions, which this chapter illustrates by highlighting some central similarities and differences.

Keywords: sustainability, resilience, political theory, political philosophy, justice, state legitimacy

1 Introduction

What is meant by the term 'sustainability' differs between different fields and areas of application. For example, compare the field of sustainable material cycles (where sustainability allows us to compare two consumer products with each other—claiming that one is 'more sustainable' than the other) with the field of green political philosophy (where sustainability takes the role of a moral ideal of global and intergenerational justice). Yet, a core normative notion remains: that it is desirable to 'sustain' certain goods, opportunities or processes in the long term. Beyond this core, sustainability is a contested concept. In essence, there are 'many "sustainabilities"'.[1] As Marcel Wissenburg nicely phrased it, 'sustainability is not just about ecological facts but also, primarily, about a normative choice for the society and environment that we deem worth living in' (Wissenburg, 'Sustainability, democracy and the value of freedom', p. 121).

Although several notions of sustainability that are either employed for different disciplinary purposes or that are based on different visions of the human-nature relationship can then plausibility coexist, mapping and integrating the relevant normativity of the notion of sustainability is a challenge for green political thought. That is particularly so because sustainability in the morally more substantive sense involves a range of internal tensions by often constituting the attempt to include several concerns of justice within its remit: global justice to current generations (i.e., intra-human justice), justice to future generations (i.e., intergenerational justice) and, as a more recent addition, interspecies justice (i.e., non-anthropocentric justice also known as multispecies or ecological justice).[2] As philosophical theories of justice fall within the remit of political philosophy, it is not surprising that a

1 Marcel Wissenburg, 'Sustainability, Democracy and the Value of Freedom'. In B. Bornemann, H. Knappe and P. Nanz, *The Routledge Handbook of Democracy and Sustainability* (London: Routledge, 2021), pp. 121–34 (p. 122). See also Walter Alfredo Salas-Zapata and Sara Milena Ortiz-Muñoz 'Analysis of Meanings of the Concept of Sustainability', *Sustainable Development* 27:1 (2019), pp. 153–61.

2 On non-anthropocentric sustainability see Anna Wienhues, *Ecological Justice and the Extinction Crisis: Giving Living Beings Their Due* (Bristol: Bristol University Press, 2020), pp. 1–244; Michel Bourban, 'Strong Sustainability Ethics', *Environmental Ethics* 43:4 (2021), pp. 291–314. On non-anthropocentric sustainable development see Livia Boscardin and Leonie Bossert 'Sustainable Development and Nonhuman Animals: Why Anthropocentric Concepts of Sustainability are Outdated and Need to be Extended'. In *Ethics of Science in the Research for Sustainable Development* (Baden-Baden: Nomos, 2015), pp. 323–52. This development changes the notion of sustainability

growing body of literature in environmental political thought has developed that tries to marry environmental concerns with the notion of justice via engagement with the concept of sustainability—or its more policy-focused variant: sustainable development, which in turn is exemplified by the United Nations *Sustainable Development Goals* (UN SDGs).

Accordingly, sustainability is frequently being portrayed as a comprehensive collective goal in political and moral philosophy and policy discourses. In those contexts, it is depicted as a moral ideal[3] that generates a collective responsibility to work towards its achievement as a political community which, in turn, is commonly understood as involving a range of justice concerns integral to its definition. That tendency is particularly present in policy discourses about sustainable development illustrated by its famous definition in the report *Our Common Future* presented by the World Commission on Environment and Development in 1987: 'Sustainable development is development that meets the needs of the present without compromising the ability of future generations to meet their own needs'.[4] Looking at this definition from the perspective of political thought, it clearly implies two main concerns of justice: global justice towards current (i.e., alleviating global poverty) and future generations (i.e., not precluding future generations the possibility of meeting their needs/living a good life). Thus, it comes as no surprise that the definition of sustainable development postulated in *Our Common Future* is also commonly found in philosophical writings about sustainability.

Against this background and a noteworthy body of multidisciplinary work critiquing—and dismissing—the notions of sustainability and/or sustainable development in favour of other approaches such as emphasising resilience, my aim in this chapter is to support the case for retaining sustainability as an important notion for central concerns within political philosophy.[5] For that purpose, I will explain why the related concept of resilience is not an

---

in several respects, removing nonhuman beings from the role of only being objects of sustainability (they are more than just 'capital').

3 Such as in Frank L. B. Meijboom and Frans W. A. Brom. 'Ethics and Sustainability: Guest or Guide? On Sustainability as a Moral Ideal', *Journal of Agricultural and Environmental Ethics* 25 (2012), pp. 117–21.

4 World Commission on Environment and Development. *Our Common Future.* (United Nations report: 1987), pp. 1–247 (p. 37). For a critical analysis of this definition of sustainable development see Lucas Seghezzo, 'The Five Dimensions of Sustainability', *Environmental Politics* 18 (2009), pp. 539–56.

5 For an overview of critiques aimed at the concept of sustainable development see John C. Dernbach and Federico Cheever, 'Sustainable Development and Its Discontents', *Transnational Environmental Law* 4:2 (2015), pp. 247–87. And for a critique that emphasises resilience see Neil W. Adger, 'Ecological and Social

appropriate replacement for the notion of sustainability, but rather constitutes a complementary concept for normative theorising. That is, in turn, particularly relevant against the background that green political philosophy had so far comparatively little to say about resilience. Thus, my second aim in this chapter is to suggest that more political philosophical research on resilience and its relationship to sustainability is needed. As this is a large field, I will exemplify this complementarity by focusing on their respective functions in theories of distributive justice and state legitimacy. That is, references to resilience do not have the same moral content as references to the notion of sustainability. Of course, that complementarity does not preclude other reasons justifying the rejection of either of these two notions to still apply. Yet, for the purposes of this chapter I will largely set these broader concerns aside.

In the next section I will briefly explain how sustainability has been engaged in political philosophy (section 2). Then I will introduce the notion of resilience, which has received less attention in political thought (section 3). In section 4 I will illustrate some of their similarities and differences as well as demonstrating a case of how they complement each other.

2 Sustainability

Let me begin with introducing two dimensions of definitional differences concerning the concept of sustainability to illuminate the extent of contestations about this notion. First, it is not obvious *what should be sustained*, which leads us to debates about substitution and compensation. In this regard, particularly the fields of economics and philosophy contributed to discussions about the differences and respective desirability of so-called 'weak' versus 'strong' sustainability. In a nutshell, against the background that the same level of human welfare[6] ought to be maintained, weak sustainability allows for 'natural capital' (apart from 'critical' natural capital) to be degraded if 'total capital' remains constant. In contrast, strong sustainability demands

Resilience'. In *Handbook of Sustainable Development*, edited by G. Atkinson et al. (Cheltenham and Northampton: Edward Elgar, 2007, pp. 78–90.

6 How such welfare should be understood and how it is related to sustainability is also a matter of debate. See Alan Holland, 'Sustainability: Should We Start from Here?' In *Fairness and Futurity: Essays on Environmental Sustainability and Social Justice,* edited by Andew Dobson. Online edition published 2003 (Oxford: Oxford University Press, 1999), pp. 1–20. Moreover, this is related to the broader issue of how to account for a broad variety of different worldviews, see Laÿna Droz, 'Redefining Sustainability: From Self-Determination to Environmental Autonomy', *Philosophies* 4:42 (2019), pp. 1–14.

sustaining overall natural capital irrespectively of the trajectory of other types of capital (while allowing for replacements within each capital stock). That is, 'total natural capital' needs to be sustained to sustain 'natural income'.[7] For example, these two perspectives would differ in their assessment of whether it would be legitimate—in terms of being sustainable—for future generations to be better off in 'human-made capital' terms (e.g., better off in terms of water desalination infrastructure etc.) while having less access to natural goods (e.g., clean ground water etc.) than current generations. Although that is partially a debate about conceptual and empirical viability, it is also a question of moral values and underlying ideas about a good human life.[8]

Second, separate from such debates about different kinds of 'capital', what is meant by sustainability also depends on what kind or *dimension(s) of sustainability* are highlighted, such as being ecologically, socially or economically sustainable. The combination of the three is frequently referred to as the three-pillar conception of sustainability.[9] Moreover, we can also differentiate between sustainability and sustainable development, which are either treated as distinct—and sometimes even antagonistic to each other—or synonymously in the literature.[10] Whether sustainability and sustainable development are antagonistic concepts to each other, partly depends how sustainable development is understood. One typical criticism concerns the 'development' part of sustainable development. Yet, it should be kept in mind that conceptually speaking as opposed to its treatment in different policy contexts from which the term originated, 'development' does not have to be equated with perpetual economic growth. On the contrary, sustainable development—in terms of improving human wellbeing—can also be understood as a critique of the latter. However, this charge can be reformulated in a potentially more worrying form, such as when Simon Lumsden notes that sustainable development—at least on some influential presentations of the term[11]—does not free itself *from* but operates *within* a human/nature

7 Robert Costanza and Herman Daly 'Natural Capital and Sustainable Development', *Conservation Biology*, 6:1 (1992), pp. 37–46 (p. 39).

8 See John O'Neill, 'Sustainability', in D. Moellendorf and H. Widdows (eds) *The Routledge Handbook of Global Ethics* (London: Routledge, 2015), pp. 401–15; John O'Neill, 'Ethics, Economics and Sustainability', *Philosophy* 97 (2022): 337–59.

9 See Ben Purvis, Yong Mao and Darren Robinson, 'Three Pillars of Sustainability: In Search of Conceptual Origins'. *Sustainability Science* 14:3 (2019), pp. 681–95.

10 For an example of the former more critical view, see Bourban, 'Strong Sustainability Ethics'.

11 As Lumsden attests to be exemplified by economist Jeffrey Sachs' manuscript on sustainable development. See Jeffrey Sachs, *The Age of Sustainable Development* (New York: Columbia University Press, 2015), pp. 1–543.

dualism.[12] In Lumsden's words, '[t]his modern narrative of freedom through liberation from the domination of nature is powerful. SD [i.e., sustainable development] does not contest this idea; it takes it to its extreme' (Lumsden, 'The Logic of Modernity and Ecological Crisis', p. 285).

And indeed, in so far as 'nature' is purely conceptualised as 'capital' and ecosystem 'services' needed as input and as waste dumping ground for human economic endeavours within an economic growth paradigm, then the notion of sustainable development seems unhelpful. In that case there would be little room for the human-nature relationship constituting anything other than that of 'rational' managerialism where 'nature' is reified and relegated to the role of a passive background that requires management and control. It seems plausible that, ironically, such widespread descriptions of sustainable development *as* continuous growth ultimately run counter to—as opposed to facilitate—sustainability. Thus, the takeaway at this point should be that it matters a great deal—not just for conceptual clarity but also for the concepts' normative content and implicit outlook on the world—how sustainability and sustainable development are presented and how they differ.

To explain, sustainability and sustainable development are in several respects distinct notions. For example, one relevant difference is that sustainable development constitutes a contextual application of the broader notion of sustainability—namely, the sustainability of development. That, in turn, implies a second crucial difference because sustainable development is inherently goal-directed, while sustainability simpliciter—as a kind of stability concept—is not (which should not be confused with it describing anything static). Moreover, most commonly with respect to environmental philosophy, sustainability simpliciter primarily refers to some understanding of ecological or environmental sustainability. Yet, also in this regard we can differentiate, for instance, between two types of sustainability. First, what Randall Curren and Ellen Metzger call throughput/environmental sustainability, which constitutes 'supply-side throughput sustainability … [which] pertains more widely to the flows of energy and matter on which human activity depends', and secondly ecological sustainability with concerns 'exclusively … the health of ecosystems and preserving their biocapacity' and, thus, can be understood in terms of 'waste-side throughput sustainability'.[13] In essence, we can differentiate between an upstream and a downstream aspect of sustainability from a human society perspective. Upstream concerns the reliance

12 Simon Lumsden, 'The Logic of Modernity and Ecological Crisis', *Environmental Values* 30:3 (2021), pp. 277–96.

13 Randall Curren and Ellen Metzger, 'What Sustainability Is and Why it Matters'. In *Living Well Now and in the Future: Why Sustainability Matters*m edited by Randall Curren and Ellen Metzger (Cambridge, MA: MIT Press, Online edition, 2017), pp. 1–27 (p. 5).

on a continuous supply of natural resources, such as oil, gas and fresh water (supply side); and downstream refers to the impact of human activities on the continuous functioning of ecological systems, such as concerning the absorption capacity of emitted CO_2 (waste side).

Notwithstanding these questions pertaining how sustainability should be understood, a further question is in how far sustainability matters regarding how to theorise good political institutions und underlying norms about social and political life. To merely provide one example of a theme in this extensive field of discussion, consider the interrelated notions of sufficiency and ecological limits, the latter of which will become relevant later.[14] For instance, sustainable development has been frequently interpreted as combining liberal sufficientarian theories of justice that illustrate a minimum threshold that needs to be achieved in terms of human welfare with the idea that there is a maximum threshold (Earth's carrying capacity) that should not be surpassed.[15] The basic idea is that there is a space between a lower and maximum threshold in which humanity can live sustainably and that sufficiency lies at the core of theorising sustainability.[16] More broadly, the notion of limits is integral to sustainability theorising in which different descriptions of maximum thresholds imply different notions of so-called 'descriptive' ecological limits—what Fergus Green sub-divides into resource and system limits; which are reminiscent of the above-mentioned supply- and waste-side aspects of sustainability—[17] and which in turn lead to different 'normative' limits proposed in the literature, such as found in different theories of justice.

14 Additional notable topics in the literature concern sustainability's relationship to interspecies justice (see footnote #2), its relationship with democracy (see Wissenburg, 'Sustainability, Democracy and the Value of Freedom') and different relational approaches to sustainability. On the latter see Simon L. West, Simon, Jamila Haider, Sanna Stålhammar and Stephen Woroniecki 'A Relational Turn for Sustainability Science? Relational Thinking, Leverage Points and Transformations', *Ecosystems and People* 16:1 (2020), pp. 304–25.

15 E.g., Laura Spengler, 'Two Types of "Enough": Sufficiency as Minimum and Maximum', *Environmental Politics* 25 (2016), pp. 921–40; Rita Oliveira Vasconcellos, 'Irreplaceable Goods: Bridging Sustainability and Intergenerational Sufficientarianism', *Ethics, Policy & Environment* 26:3 (2023), pp. 438–54.

16 For an opposing perspective that highlights the different ideals of the good life involved in these two types of sufficiency see Philipp Kanschik, 'Eco-Sufficiency and Distributive Sufficientarianism—Friends or Foes?' *Environmental Values* 25 (2016), pp. 553–71.

17 Fergus Green, 'Ecological Limits: Science, Justice, Policy, and the Good Life', *Philosophy Compass* (2021), 16e12740.

3 Resilience

The concept of resilience is also discussed in a variety of different disciplines. Although also examined within the humanities—as this volume demonstrates—it can be found primarily within research in the social and natural sciences, broadly under the headings of resilience theory or resilience thinking. C. S. Holling is credited as introducing the concept to ecology in 1973 and from then onwards its relevance for human-nature relations spread into many other disciplines, such as notably sustainability science.[18] Accordingly, while resilience is an established concept in several disciplines, the question that now poses itself for political thought is in how far this notion simply constitutes an additional buzzword in policy spheres, or whether it introduces genuine unique normative considerations beyond sustainability that need to be accounted for in political theorising.

Although definitions of resilience are heterogeneous and contested, the notion of resilience implies in most general terms the ability to withstand shocks of different kinds. Akin to sustainability, resilience has social and ecological aspects, which in turn are related to other notions such as social and ecological vulnerability. Social resilience can be understood as 'the ability of communities to withstand external shocks to their social infrastructure'[19], while ecological resilience can be ascribed to ecosystems in the light of disturbances.[20] Also akin to sustainability, resilience is inherently conservative as it involves normative ideas about stability being desirable which, in turn, is only desirable in cases in which the persistence of a particular system is desirable in itself. Yet, it is important to locate the target of such conservativism correctly. Concerning ecological resilience, for instance, it 'relates to the functioning of the system, rather than the stability of its component populations, or even the ability to maintain a steady ecological state'(Adger, 'Social and Ecological Resilience', p. 349). Thus, resilience is more about maintaining the functioning of systems rather than being critical of system change as such. On the contrary, the ability to change and adapt to a degree is usually a prerequisite to respond to shocks to the system.

18 C. S. Holling, 'Resilience and Stability of Ecological Systems'. *Annual Review of Ecology and Systematics* 4:1 (1973), pp. 1–23. For a historical overview see Henrik Thorén, 'Resilience'. In *Situating Sustainability: A Handbook of Contexts and Concepts*, edited by C. Parker Krieg and Reetta Toivanen (Helsinki: Helsinki University Press (2021), pp. 79–90.

19 Neil W. Adger, 'Social and Ecological Resilience: Are They Related?' *Progress in Human Geography* 24:3 (2000), pp. 347–64 (p. 361).

20 For a more detailed description see Vasilis Dakos and Sonia Kéfi. 'Ecological Resilience: What to Measure and How', *Environmental Research Letters* 17:4 (2022), 043003.

While the relationship between social and ecological resilience has been subject of analysis,[21] the use of the compound term social-ecological resilience[22] or speaking of the resilience of socioecological systems[23] have become commonplace. This literature starts from the premise that humans are part of 'nature' (whatever that might mean, Lumsden's earlier-mentioned critique of sustainability resurfaces here), which makes it apt to speak of social-ecological systems.[24] Social-ecological resilience thereby is broadly understood as the capacity of a particular system to persist, adapt or transform to deal with shocks and stresses to the system in the light of environmental change.[25] In this context, a shock or stressor can be something like climate change, large-scale biodiversity loss, an 'invasive' species, a financial crisis and so on. So, resilience thinking is applicable, on the one hand, to more long-term stressors like climate change that can lead to regime shifts when tipping points are surpassed, which reintroduces the above-mentioned system limits. On the other hand, social-ecological resilience is also applied to how human communities cope with particular events such as natural hazards. In this context, resilience is understood as 'the capacity of linked social-ecological systems to absorb recurrent disturbances such as hurricanes or floods so as to retain essential structures, processes, and feedbacks' (Adger et al., 'Social-Ecological Resilience', p. 1036).

Like sustainability, resilience has been the subject of critique. Complaints range from social-ecological resilience being instrumentalised in support of neoliberal agendas, to concerns about power and inequality not being central enough in resilience scholarship. As Raven Cretney highlights, the resilience discourse has arisen out of a particular context of threats of different kinds (social, environmental and economic) and the simultaneous dominance of neoliberalism at the same time.[26] Thus, while the politics of resilience—

21 See, Adger, 'Social and Ecological Resilience'.

22 E.g., Neil W. Adger, Terry P. Hughes, Carl Folke, Stephen R. Carpenter and Johan Rockström. 'Social-Ecological Resilience to Coastal Disasters'. *Science* 309:5737 (2005), pp. 1036–9.

23 E.g., Steve Carpenter, Brian Walker, J. Marty Anderies and Nick Abel. 'From Metaphor to Measurement: Resilience of What to What?' *Ecosystems* 4:8 (2001), pp. 765–81.

24 'What is Resilience?' [website] *Stockholm Resilience Centre* (2015), https://www.stockholmresilience.org/research/research-news/2015-02-19-what-is-resilience.html (accessed 15 February 2023).

25 Steve Lade, 'What is Social-ecological Resilience?' *Stockholm Resilience Centre TV* (2020). Video available at: https://www.youtube.com/watch?v=k_KQCqcb7EQ (accessed 16 February 2023).

26 Raven Cretney, 'Resilience for Whom? Emerging Critical Geographies of Socio-Ecological Resilience: Resilience of What, for Whom?' *Geography*

such as it being instrumentalised in support of a neoliberal agenda—need more consideration, this highlights again that the normativity of resilience demands attention.

While I am neither arguing for nor against the importance or adequacy of the concept more generally, there are two points worth noting concerning these two critiques. First, as Avery Kolers pertinently comments on this issue,

> the moral objectionable resilience that critics challenge arises from a shift in the conception of "resilience of what to what"; it is in this objectionable sense something more like "resilience *of* individuals and communities *to* unjust assaults and disasters wrought by capitalism". *If* resilience is to be endorsed, it is essential that the liberal state be able to resist such a shift.[27]

And second, recently Earth system science—a field contributing to resilience thinking—has turned towards integrating justice concerns more explicitly within their remit. That includes assessing what would constitute a '*safe and just corridor* for human development on Earth'[28] (indicating the close links with sustainable development) and the increased engagement with what has been termed 'planetary justice'.[29] This later term is also already part of discussions in political thought.[30] Thus, while it can be argued that this

---

Compass 8:2 (2014), pp. 627–40; For further concerns see Brendan Gleeson, 'Resilience and Its Discontents'. Research Paper No. 1, *Melbourne Sustainable Society Institute* (2013), pp. 1–20.

27 Avery Kolers, 'Resilience as a Political Ideal', *Ethics, Policy & Environment* 19:1 (2016), pp. 91–107 (p. 93, italics in original). Here I am setting aside that Kolers has also emphasised the notion of sustainability in previous work. See Avery Kolers, *Land, Conflict and Justice* (Cambridge: Cambridge University Press, 2009), pp. 1–238; see that being discussed in Alejandra Mancilla, 'Review Article: The Environmental Turn in Territorial Rights', *Critical Review of International Social and Political Philosophy* 19:2 (2016), pp. 221–41).

28 Johan Rockström, Joyeeta Gupta, Timothy M. Lenton, Dahe Qin, Steven J. Lade, Jesse F. Abrams, Lisa Jacobson et al., 'Identifying a Safe and Just Corridor for People and the Planet', *Earth's Future* 9:4 (2021), pp. 1–7 (p. 2, italics in original).

29 E.g., Prakash Kashwan, Frank Biermann, Aarti Gupta and Chukwumerije Okereke. 'Planetary Justice: Prioritizing the Poor in Earth System Governance', *Earth System Governance* 6: December (2020), 100075.

30 See John S. Dryzek and Jonathan Pickering. *The Politics of the Anthropocene* (Oxford: Oxford University Press, 2019), pp. 1–196; Colin Hickey and Ingrid Robeyns, 'Planetary Justice: What Can We Learn from Ethics and Political Philosophy?' *Earth System Governance*, March (2020), 100045.

development is still lacking, it is notable that justice concerns have seeped into this scientific field.

Thus, all in all it matters what is meant by resilience, how it is engaged (and for what purpose) and how its normativity is interpreted. Although this concept has received comparatively little attention in political theory, there are exceptions. Let me illustrate two proposals that discuss resilience as a matter of justice: Kolers' proposal to understand resilience as a political ideal and Teea Kortetmäki's suggestion to understand resilience as an ecosystem capability.[31] While Kolers argues that resilience shapes how the content and methodology of intra-human justice should be theorised, Kortetmäki presents an argument in favour of making resilience an essential feature of interspecies justice.

Starting with Kolers, he understands the resilience of social-ecological systems as a political ideal that is 'a compulsory goal of liberal political institutions. It must be given a place within liberal theories of justice and legitimacy' (Kolers, 'Resilience', p. 92). Because resilience in itself is not necessary desirable (e.g., harmful systems should not be resilient), Kolers specifies what resilience as a goal of liberal institutions is supposed to mean. That is the 'resilience *of* high-HDI [Human Development Index] democratic societies to natural disasters, infrastructure failures, and economic collapse' (Kolers, 'Resilience', p. 95, italics in original)[32]. Kolers' argument in favour of such resilience is twofold. On the one hand, we care about people being able to live good lives and being able to pursue their projects, but a lack of community resilience can lead to a considerable amount of human suffering. On the other hand, Kolers conceptualises resilience as a public good. If a community is resilient, this will be beneficial for all its members, but its members cannot create this public good on their own. Thus, it is the state's responsibility—as a matter of its legitimacy—to provide this morally important public good.

In contrast, Kortetmäki takes a different angle on the notion of resilience, focusing primarily on ecological resilience as an aspect of overall social-ecological resilience.[33] Yet, she also takes an interest in theories of justice, focusing on Martha Nussbaum's version of the capabilities approach,

31 Kolers, 'Resilience'; Teea Kortetmäki, 'Applying the Capabilities Approach to Ecosystems: Resilience as Ecosystem Capability', *Environmental Ethics* 39:Spring (2017), pp. 39–56.

32 Kolers' definition is a form of 'specified resilience' as opposed to 'general resilience'. On this distinction see John M. Anderies, Carl Folke, Brian Walker and Elinor Ostrom, 'Aligning Key Concepts for Global Change Policy: Robustness, Resilience, and Sustainability', *Ecology and Society* 18:2 (2013), 8.

33 Kortetmäki, 'Applying the Capabilities Approach to Ecosystems'.

which constitutes one version of a liberal theory of justice.[34] Against the background that several authors have argued for expanding the capabilities approach towards also including (some) nonhuman beings—including Nussbaum herself—and that some of these authors have even argued for including ecosystems into the remit of justice, Kortetmäki enquires into the specifics of how to integrate ecological systems into the capabilities approach.

One central aspect of the capabilities approach is the claim that humans and in this case also nonhuman entities ought to have the opportunity to fulfil a range of central capabilities,[35] which are important for their wellbeing. So, if ecosystems are supposed to be included as entities that matter in their own right into the capabilities approach as proposed by David Schlosberg,[36] then we need an account of the ecosystem's capabilities. Such an account of one ecosystem capability—out of several potential capabilities—is what Kortetmäki aims to provide.

She then argues that ecosystem flourishing (in essence, its 'wellbeing') should be understood as 'a condition in which the ecosystem can perform and maintain the functions characteristic of it, and exhibit and sustain its quality and diversity' (Kortetmäki, 'Applying the Capabilities Approach to Ecosystems', p. 46). This definition of what it means for an ecosystem to flourish clearly has connotations of how resilience is usually understood. Thus, non-surprisingly this is how Kortetmäki spells out the respective ecosystem capability as ecosystem resilience that needs to be promoted (or at least not impeded) as a matter of justice: 'Having the capability of ecosystem resilience means being able to absorb disturbances so that the essential features and functionings characteristic of that ecosystem persist and continue to support flourishing of the system' (Kortetmäki, 'Applying the Capabilities Approach to Ecosystems', p. 50, italics removed from original).

34 Martha C. Nussbaum, *Frontiers of Justice: Disability, Nationality, Species Membership.* (Cambridge, MA and London: Belknap Press, 2006), pp. 1–487; Martha C. Nussbaum, *Creating Capabilities* (Cambridge, MA: Harvard University Press, 2011), pp. 1–237.

35 Nussbaum's famous list of central human capabilities includes: (1) life, (2) bodily health, (3) bodily integrity, (4) sense, imagination and thought, (5) emotions, (6) practical reason, (7) affiliation, (8) other species, (9) play and (10) control over one's environment in political and material terms. See, Nussbaum, *Frontiers of Justice*, pp. 76–7.

36 David Schlosberg, *Defining Environmental Justice: Theories, Movements, and Nature* (Oxford: Oxford University Press, 2007), pp. 1–238.

4 How Sustainability and Resilience Complement Each Other

To take stock, sustainability and resilience are both contested and partially overlapping concepts. Yet, they diverge enough conceptually for also their theoretical scope and normative functions in political thought to differ. In the remainder of this chapter, I will elaborate on a few non-exhaustive ways in which they are similar (i–ix) and differ (I–II). For that purpose, I will omit—and remain neutral on—a set of broader relevant questions. For example, I take it as given that both notions are relevant for political philosophy, but it might as well be that neither is a fruitful way of (re)imagining the human-nature relationship. Moreover, how sustainability and resilience are related to theorising justice partly depends on how they are conceptualised, and I will not provide an argument for a specific version of either notion.[37] Rather assuming that there are ultimately good arguments for considering and integrating both—resilience and sustainability—into political theorising and particularly theories of justice, I will outline a proposal for how these two concepts overlap, differ and dovetail into each other, on a level of analysis that does not presuppose a particular narrow definition for either of these two concepts.

Returning to some earlier-mentioned themes, there are several similarities between sustainability and resilience in so far as they are relevant for political philosophy. Most broadly, (i) they both pertain to the human-nature relationship and (ii) both function on large collective scales that go beyond the individual and that necessitate collective action. Moreover, (iii) both are normative in a conservative way, in that they highlight the desirability of the persistence or stability of a particular system or process. Because they constitute (iv) qualities of such systems neither of them is desirable in itself, as they derive their desirability from the value of the system (e.g., democracy, an ecosystem) or process (e.g., development) to which they are attributed. Most fundamentally, they ultimately receive their moral relevance from their instrumental importance for the possibility and further continuation of human and nonhuman life, wellbeing and any value found in nature

37 For instance, concerning sustainability one can look in this regard at Dobson's typology of three types of environmental sustainability and their relationship to distributive justice theorising (Andrew Dobson, *Justice and the Environment: Conceptions of Environmental Sustainability and Theories of Distributive Justice*, Oxford: Oxford University Press, 1998, pp. 1–280). Moreover, I am also not discussing here whether justice should be included in the definition of sustainability or constitutes a separate concern. Rather, here I am looking into the *implications* of including sustainability into justice theorising.

beyond these. This circumstance in combination with the necessity of collective action makes it, in turn, (v) possible to describe both as political ideals. Yet, (vi) that is not their only function in political thought as both are also engaged as empirical measurable properties of systems or processes that shape the content of political theorising, such as the principles of justice.

Furthermore, (vii) while not constituting a similarity as such, sustainability and resilience clearly overlap and have effects on each other as they are commonly described as constituting necessary (but not sufficient) conditions for each other. For example, on the one hand, some writers on resilience claim that 'resilience, in both its social and ecological manifestations, is an important aspect of the sustainability of development' (Adger, 'Social and ecological resilience', p. 357). On the other hand, we can also see writers on sustainability providing descriptions of sustainability that seem to make resilience one of its necessary components, such as exemplified by Laÿna Droz's statement that 'sustainability is the process of maintaining self-robust ecosystems according to the precautionary principle' (Droz, 'Redefining Sustainability', p. 10).

Finally, both have been described as necessary (but not sufficient) conditions for (viii) distributive justice and (ix) state legitimacy.[38] Yet, from these last two similarities spring also the two central differences. Beginning with (I) justice, different conceptions of sustainability (e.g., weak vs. strong sustainability) have direct relevance for the core question of distributive justice: 'Who gets what?' To answer this question, it can be broken down into three sub-questions which all are relevant for sustainability. First, what constitutes the 'what' and 'how much' is there of it? Different conceptions of sustainability will highlight in this regard the potential scarcity of different currencies of distribution (say, natural resources). Such scarcity might be materially present (e.g., there is simply no more fossil oil available anymore) or it is conceptually superimposed by the notion of sustainability by setting limits to human environmental impacts by reference to abstract limits of the Earth's carrying capacity as is, in essence, the function of visualisations of (un) sustainability like the 'planetary boundaries model' that set limits to what counts as a 'safe operating space' for humans on Earth.[39]

38 By looking at *state* legitimacy, I put alternatives forms of governance aside. In this chapter this is employed as an example for different themes in political thought and not meant as a defence as the typical nation state model as such. Similarly, as a matter of simplicity I only discuss a few relevant aspects regarding *distributive* justice instead of more wide-ranging justice concerns.

39 Johan Rockström, Will Steffen, Kevin Noone, Åsa Persson, F. Stuart Chapin, Eric F. Lambin, Timothy M. Lenton, Marten Scheffer, Carl Folke and Hans Joachim Schellnhuber, 'A Safe Operating Space for Humanity', *Nature* 461:7263 (2009), pp. 472–5.

Moreover, with respect to waste-side and supply-side sustainability scarcity might look different, in that we have two dimensions relevant for theorising distributive justice where different levels of scarcity might be present: ecological capacity at the wasteside and natural resources at the supply side. Different theories of justice and sustainability, in turn, will emphasise these two dimensions differently. An accent on the supply side hilghlights, for instance, the necessary conditions in terms of material consumption needs to support human wellbeing, and thus, intra-human justice. In contrast, an emphasis on the waste side involves—among other things—a more direct reflection on the human-nature relationship and related environmental values, which are not only relevant for interspecies justice but also for the material and non-material aspects of human wellbeing. That, in turn, feeds back to the supply side and shows how these two dimensions are related but not reducible to each other.

Second, sustainability also speaks to the 'how to distribute it?' sub-question, as different accounts of sustainability not only point towards different normative grounds that should guide such distribution (e.g., needs or opportunities), but also provide guidance on what patterns of distribution are possible depending on their stance on matters like substitutability. And third, different accounts of sustainability also speak to the 'to whom?' question of distributive justice by evoking (one or several) relevant dimensions of distribution such as global, intergenerational and interspecies justice. From this follows that different accounts of sustainability have direct implications for how distributive justice is theorised.

In contrast, resilience says comparatively little about the scope, content and shape of justice theorising in terms of the 'who gets what?' question of distribution. That does not make resilience less important for political thought than sustainability (there is no reason to think that it would be), but rather this highlights how the normative scope of the two concepts differs. Rather, resilience concerns the reduction of risk of harm now and in the future, which makes it relevant to justice by primarily providing a background against which a fair distribution can be upheld and remains meaningful. Yet, it also has some more direct implications for justice theorising. For instance, if one draws on an account of sustainability that relies on the notion of 'critical natural capital' (relevant in turn for 'what' gets distributed), then resilience can be a relevant aspect for determining what constitutes such 'critical' capital which, in turn, makes resilience relevant for the debates surrounding different interpretations of sufficiency. Moreover, Kortetmäki's account of ecosystem resilience as a capability is an example of a perspective on resilience that makes the maintenance of resilient ecosystems a matter of justice, not by merely being conducive to justice but by constituting a demand of justice in itself. Nonetheless, the capabilities approach that Kortetmäki draws on emphasises opportunities and freedoms as opposed to the material goods that are needed to bring these about.

Accordingly, while both concepts are frequently declared to be necessary for justice, they differ in how that necessity arises as well as which aspects of distributive justice they address. Regarding the latter, while intra-human global justice, in the short term at least, might rely less on (waste- or supply-side) sustainability, sustainability becomes central to theorising interspecies and intergenerational justice. Accordingly, sustainability needs to be integrated into theories of intra-human global justice not only due to the synchronic short-term demands of global justice itself, but to achieve compatibility with accounts of intergenerational (future humans impacted by lacking natural resources and ecological capacity) and interspecies justice (as nonhuman beings also rely on ecosystem functioning and a range of physical resources).

In comparison, community resilience matters to intra-human global and intergenerational justice by reducing the risk of harm. Because it is a concern of justice that people can live good lives and are being able to pursue their projects, as exemplified by the account presented by Kolers, it also matters to people currently whether they can expect these projects to remain relevant in the future. However, the resilience of human communities is not directly necessary for achieving interspecies justice (at least if limited to wild nonhuman beings only). In that regard ecosystem resilience needs to be foregrounded; either because ecosystems matter in themselves, as argued by Kortetmäki, or because their persistence is important for the morally considerable individual beings that live within them. Whether ecosystems are resilient is, in turn, partly determined by the waste-side sustainability of human practices.

Against this background, we can see why a range of political theorists have claimed that sustainability or resilience should be qualifiers for a state's legitimacy and/or sovereignty.[40] Yet, (II) that brings me to a further difference between these two concepts concerning ideal and non-ideal circumstances. Putting larger debates about ideal/non-ideal theory in political thought aside, it seems that (different versions of) sustainability and resilience take different functions in these two contexts.

For one, sustainability is a matter of an ideal theory of justice, that is, how a just society is envisaged. Simply put, a just society will also be a sustainable society, if intergenerational and interspecies justice are considered to matter. Yet, in current non-ideal and, thus, unsustainable conditions we need non-ideal theories of 'just sustainability transition' to indicate a path towards such

40 Kolers' earlier-introduced account of resilience is an example of the former, while the latter is exemplified pertaining sustainability in Alfonso Donoso, 'New Politics: Sovereignty, Representation, and the Nonhuman'. In *Global Changes*, edited by L. Valera and J. C. Castilla (Cham: Springer, 2020).

a sustainable society while also addressing the negative effects on current human and nonhuman generations potentially caused by that transition. So, in these two contexts those two theories will likely provide different principles of justice as it is not obviously the case that, for example, an ideally just distribution constitutes also the fairest and most transition-conducing approach towards achieving sustainability in non-ideal conditions.

In contrast to sustainability, whereas resilience also seems to be relevant for both ideal and non-ideal theorising, it relates to these differently. For example, Kolers' theory only pertains to the resilience of high-HDI democratic societies. In that way, it only applies to fairly ideal circumstances (high-HDI, democracy) while at the same time it is trying to address—by being resilient to—less ideal environmental circumstances, such as natural hazards. So, neither the resilience of non-democratic nor less-developed states is desirable in itself, if one would follow Kolers' account. However, because human welfare also matters in these cases it seems reasonable to propose that we need at least two different non-ideal theories of 'just resilience transition'—one pertaining to non-resilient high-HDI democracies like theorising just sustainability transitions and one pertaining to non-resilient non-democratic and/or less-developed states. In the latter case, aiming for developed democratic institutions and high human welfare, we are essentially looking for a version of how a theory of sustainable development is usually understood. However, that requires some more contextualisation for at least two reasons. First, the underlying assumption that resilience of so-called less-developed states is not desirable ought to be questioned. And relatedly, sustainable development—and, thus, 'development'—might be taken to mean quite different aims, as we saw earlier. From these two concerns follow at least two observations with respect to how to theorise just resilience transitions.

First, looking at resilience itself, it seems straightforward to claim that non-resilient states—regardless of how wealthy they are—need to develop their resilience capacities if socio-ecological resilience is deemed of moral relevance, irrespective of what its citizens deem important for a good life. Thus, under non-ideal conditions a resilience transition is needed for all non-resilient communities, but this might take many forms.

Second, because of a plurality of local contexts, it seems warranted to look beyond the high-HDI democratic societies that Kolers is primarily interested in as ideal cases. This is the more controversial aspect, as it leads us back to into the territory of controversies about sustainability development. For example, depending on the local conditions on the ground, one might find—more or less—resilient and democratic albeit less-developed states. That is, states that are less developed according to the Kolers' employed high-HDI criterium of development. In some of these cases, aiming for more (sustainable) development might be neither locally wanted nor needed, while it might be in other cases. There is certainly not a one-fits-all solution such as a numerical HDI benchmark value that can be applied in all circumstances to assess state legitimacy. For instance, while the HDI involves aspects such as life expectancy and education which are arguably less controversial while still imperfect markers of human wellbeing, it also involves gross national income per capita as a rather limited measure of a decent standard of living. Accordingly, while the HDI was introduced as an improvement to previous reliance on economic growth measures to account for development, also the United Nations Development Programme articulates itself that '[t]he HDI simplifies and captures only part of what human development entails. It does not reflect on inequalities, poverty, human security, empowerment, etc.'[41] Ultimately, as some commentators have pointed out, there are comparability issues across different social and cultural contexts suffered by global development indicators more generally and also the HDI in particular, which are all situated against the historical background that 'measurement was central to the many forms of colonial control'.[42] Thus, to take stock, whether and in what way sustainable *development* is needed depends on the local context.

Setting such complexities aside, it is currently difficult to find any real-world state that would simultaneously satisfy sustainability and resilience criteria in a manner that would fulfil the demands of theories that make these a prerequisite for its legitimacy and/or sovereignty, if both are necessary but not sufficient on their own (in addition to other plausible necessary requirements that I am setting aside here, such as the protection of human rights). Consequently, one might conclude that the legitimacy of real-world states would be qualified or even entirely lacking. However, on an alternative view a state's legitimacy in non-ideal circumstances should be judged by its commitment to the demands of respective non-ideal theories of just transition towards sustainability and resilience rather than being based on more demanding ideal theories (that is, not expecting them to be already sustainable or resilient). Important seems to be whether states can be seen to implement policies—to a relevant degree—that are supportive of and compatible with transitions to sustainability, resilience and, in the case of some states, potentially sustainable development. These may or may not be

41 United Nations Development Programme 'Human Development Index (HDI)'. *Human Development Reports* (2024). Available at https://hdr.undp.org/data-center/human-development-index#/indicies/HDI (accessed 23 February 2024]. See also Jeni Klugman, Francisco Rodríguez, and Hyung-Jin Choi 'The HDI 2010: New Controversies, Old Critiques', *The Journal of Economic Inequality* 9:2 (2011), pp. 249–88.

42 Morag Goodwin, 'The Poverty of Numbers: Reflections on the Legitimacy of Global Development Indicators', *International Journal of Law in Context* 13:4 (2017), pp. 485–97 (p. 486).

compatible with what might be required to maintain sustainability and resilience *simpliciter*.

This difference is also relevant for the compatibility of resilience and sustainability when judging real-world states. Taking Kolers' emphasis concerning a high-HDI democratic society with respect to resilience as an example, then taking this difference seriously requires one to judge that state's sustainability-qualified legitimacy based on its implementation of a non-ideal theory of just sustainability transition rather than on whether it already is sustainable. That emphasis on a non-ideal theory of transition is needed to avoid the requirements of sustainability to be potentially in tension with the prospective resilience of that society. Consider this hypothetical case of an *unsustainable although resilient society*:

> A democratic society has high degree of community resilience due to diversified and adaptive institutions that are trusted and democratically legitimated by its citizens. However, this high-HDI society also still has a high level of consumption and environmental impact which cannot be sustained in the long run, and this has effects well beyond its borders. Recognising the injustices involved in using more than their 'fair share' of resources and ecosystem capacity, this society has started to seriously implement policies to reduce its environmental impact but is still far off from reaching its targets.

Now, if one would judge this state's legitimacy on an ideal-theoretical expectation of sustainability (as it is not sustainable yet, which negatively impacts human and nonhuman beings within and beyond its borders), then one would have to conclude that this state's legitimacy would be impaired. Yet, judged on a non-ideal account of just transition this society seems to be on a good path and let us assume that this is the case in this hypothetical scenario. Accordingly, declaring limited legitimacy on ideal sustainability-grounds would seem to get it wrong in this case, because it would come at the cost of undermining instead of promoting the legitimacy of a democratically organised and resilient society that is fulfilling the demands of justice in non-ideal circumstances. Thus, this provides an initial case to regard sustainability and resilience to be *interacting variables* for accounts of legitimacy (and sovereignty etc.) that, in turn, rely on these concepts as opposed to sustainability and resilience simpliciter constituting necessary conditions independently from each other. That is, they might be both necessary conditions, but the content of the sustainability condition in specific cases is dependent on the content of resilience condition, and vice versa.

5 Conclusion

To summarise, I suggested that both—ecological sustainability and socio-ecological resilience—are necessary—but not sufficient—interacting conditions for justice and state legitimacy. While sustainability is directly relevant for a range of central questions of distributive justice, resilience rather functions as a necessary background against which a fair distribution can be upheld and remains meaningful. They also differ in ideal and non-ideal circumstances. However, as it is currently difficult to identify any real-world states that are simultaneously sustainable and resilient, non-ideal theorising becomes particularly pertinent, such as in the form of theories of just sustainability transition, accounts of just resilience transition and, in some cases, theories of sustainable development.

Ultimately, if one takes sustainability and resilience to be important concepts describing a desirable human-nature relationship (which is controversial in itself in addition to both concepts being contested), then I have proposed that these two notions are not substitutes but rather complementary by taking different functions in political thought on a general level of analysis that does not presuppose any particular version of either concept.[43] Yet a range of open questions remains. For example, despite being complementary and interacting it is not obvious that the demands of sustainability (transition) and resilience (transition) are mutually reinforcing or even compatible in all cases. Thus, more systematic analysis on the relationship between these two concepts in political theory is welcome.

Bibliography

Adger, Neil W. 'Social and Ecological Resilience: Are They Related?' *Progress in Human Geography* 24:3 (2000), pp. 347–64.

Adger, Neil W. 'Ecological and Social Resilience'. In *Handbook of Sustainable Development,* edited by G. Atkinson and et al. Cheltenham and Northampton: Edward Elgar (2007), pp. 78–90.

Adger, W. Neil, Terry P. Hughes, Carl Folke, Stephen R. Carpenter and Johan Rockström. 'Social-Ecological Resilience to Coastal Disasters'. *Science* 309:5737(2005), pp. 1036–9.

43 That is in line with calls in other disciplines for simultaneously combining and keeping 'sustainability science' and 'resilience theory' separate. See Charles L. Redman, 'Should Sustainability and Resilience be Combined or Remain Distinct Pursuits?' *Ecology and Society* 19:2 (2014), 37.

Anderies, John M., Carl Folke, Brian Walker and Elinor Ostrom. 'Aligning Key Concepts for Global Change Policy: Robustness, Resilience, and Sustainability'. *Ecology and Society* 18:2 (2013), 8.

Boscardin, Livia, and Leonie Bossert 'Sustainable Development and Nonhuman Animals: Why Anthropocentric Concepts of Sustainability are Outdated and Need To Be Extended'. In *Ethics of Science in the Research for Sustainable Development* edited by Simon Meisch, Johannes Lundershausen, Leonie Bossert and Marcus Rockoff. Baden-Baden: Nomos (2015), pp. 323–52.

Bourban, Michel. 'Strong Sustainability Ethics'. *Environmental Ethics* 43:4 (2021), pp. 291–314.

Carpenter, Steve, Brian Walker, J. Marty Anderies and Nick Abel. 'From Metaphor to Measurement: Resilience of What to What?' *Ecosystems* 4:8 (2001), pp. 765–81.

Costanza, Robert, and Herman Daly. 'Natural Capital and Sustainable Development'. *Conservation Biology*, 6:1 (1992), pp. 37–46.

Cretney, Raven. 'Resilience for Whom? Emerging Critical Geographies of Socio-Ecological Resilience: Resilience of What, for Whom?' *Geography Compass* 8:2 (2014), pp. 627–40.

Curren, Randall, and Ellen Metzger. 'What Sustainability Is and Why it Matters' in *Living Well Now and in the Future: Why Sustainability Matters* (Cambridge, MA: MIT Press, Online edition, 2017), pp. 1–27.

Dakos, Vasilis, and Sonia Kéfi. 'Ecological Resilience: What to Measure and How'. *Environmental Research Letters* 17:4 (2022), 043003.

Dernbach, John C., and Federico Cheever. 'Sustainable Development and Its Discontents'. *Transnational Environmental Law* 4:2 (2015), pp. 247–87.

Dobson, Andrew. *Justice and the Environment: Conceptions of Environmental Sustainability and Theories of Distributive Justice* (Oxford: Oxford University Press, 1998), pp. 1–280.

Donoso, Alfonso, 'New Politics: Sovereignty, Representation, and the Nonhuman'. In *Global Changes*, edited by L. Valera and J. C. Castilla (Cham: Springer, 2020), 45–55.

Droz, Laÿna, 'Redefining Sustainability: From Self-Determination to Environmental Autonomy'. *Philosophies* 4:42 (2019), pp. 1–14.

Dryzek, John S., and Jonathan Pickering. *The Politics of the Anthropocene* (Oxford: Oxford University Press, 2019), pp. 1–196.

Gleeson, Brendan, 'Resilience and Its Discontents'. Research Paper No. 1, *Melbourne Sustainable Society Institute* (2013), pp. 1–20.

Goodwin, Morag. 'The Poverty of Numbers: Reflections on the Legitimacy of Global Development Indicators'. *International Journal of Law in Context* 13:4 (2017), pp. 485–97.

Green, Fergus. 'Ecological Limits: Science, Justice, Policy, and the Good Life'. *Philosophy Compass* (2021), 16e12740.

Hickey, Colin, and Ingrid Robeyns. 'Planetary Justice: What Can We Learn from Ethics and Political Philosophy?' *Earth System Governance*, March (2020), 100045.

Holland, Alan. 'Sustainability: Should We Start from Here?' In *Fairness and Futurity: Essays on Environmental Sustainability and Social Justice,* edited by Andew Dobson. Online edition published 2003 (Oxford: Oxford University Press, 1999), pp. 1–20.

Holling, C. S. 'Resilience and Stability of Ecological Systems'. *Annual Review of Ecology and Systematics* 4:1 (1973), pp. 1–23.

Kanschik, Philipp. 'Eco-Sufficiency and Distributive Sufficientarianism—Friends or Foes?' *Environmental Values* 25 (2016), pp. 553–71.

Kashwan, Prakash, Frank Biermann, Aarti Gupta and Chukwumerije Okereke. 'Planetary Justice: Prioritizing the Poor in Earth System Governance'. *Earth System Governance* 6:December (2020), 100075.

Klugman, Jeni, Francisco Rodríguez and Hyung-Jin Choi. 'The HDI 2010: New Controversies, Old Critiques'. *The Journal of Economic Inequality* 9:2 (2011), pp. 249–88.

Kolers, Avery. *Land, Conflict and Justice* (Cambridge: Cambridge University Press, 2009), pp. 1–238.

Kolers, Avery. 'Resilience as a Political Ideal'. *Ethics, Policy & Environment* 19:1 (2016), pp. 91–107.

Kortetmäki, Teea. 'Applying the Capabilities Approach to Ecosystems: Resilience as Ecosystem Capability'. *Environmental Ethics* 39: Spring (2017), pp. 39–56.

Lade, Steve. 'What is Social-ecological Resilience?' *Stockholm Resilience Centre TV* (2020). Video available at https://www.youtube.com/watch?v=k_KQC-qcb7EQ (accessed 16 February 2023).

Lumsden, Simon. 'The Logic of Modernity and Ecological Crisis,' *Environmental Values* 30:3 (2021), pp. 277–96.

Mancilla, Alejandra. 'Review Article: The Environmental Turn in Territorial Rights'. *Critical Review of International Social and Political Philosophy* 19:2 (2016), pp. 221–41.

Meadows, Donella. H. et al. *The Limits to Growth.* (London: Earth Island Ltd, A Potomac Associates Book, 1972), pp. 1–205.

Meijboom, Frank L. B., and Frans W. A. Brom. 'Ethics and Sustainability: Guest or Guide? On Sustainability as a Moral Ideal'. *Journal of Agricultural and Environmental Ethics* 25 (2012): 117–21.

Nussbaum, Martha C. *Frontiers of Justice: Disability, Nationality, Species Membership.* (Cambridge, MA and London: Belknap Press, 2006), pp. 1–487.

Nussbaum, Martha C. *Creating Capabilities* (Cambridge, MA: Harvard University Press, 2011), pp. 1–237.

Oliveira Vasconcellos, Rita. 'Irreplaceable Goods: Bridging Sustainability and Intergenerational Sufficientarianism'. *Ethics, Policy & Environment* 26:3 (2023), pp. 438–54.

O'Neill, John. 'Sustainability', in D. Moellendorf and H. Widdows (eds) *The Routledge Handbook of Global Ethics* (London: Routledge, 2015), pp. 401–15.

O'Neill, John. 'Ethics, Economics and Sustainability'. *Philosophy* 97 (2022): 337–59.

Purvis, Ben, Yong Mao and Darren Robinson. 'Three Pillars of Sustainability: In Search of Conceptual Origins'. *Sustainability Science* 14:3 (2019), pp. 681–95.

Redman, Charles L. 'Should Sustainability and Resilience be Combined or Remain Distinct Pursuits?' *Ecology and Society* 19:2 (2014), 37.

Rockström, Johan, Will Steffen, Kevin Noone, Åsa Persson, F. Stuart Chapin, Eric F. Lambin, Timothy M. Lenton, Marten Scheffer, Carl Folke and Hans Joachim Schellnhuber. 'A Safe Operating Space for Humanity'. *Nature* 461:7263 (2009), pp. 472–5.

Rockström, Johan, Joyeeta Gupta, Timothy M. Lenton, Dahe Qin, Steven J. Lade, Jesse F. Abrams Lisa Jacobson et al. 'Identifying a Safe and Just Corridor for People and the Planet'. *Earth's Future* 9:4 (2021), pp. 1–7.

Sachs, Jeffrey. *The Age of Sustainable Development* (New York: Columbia University Press, 2015), pp. 1–543.

Salas-Zapata, Walter Alfredo and Sara Milena Ortiz-Muñoz 'Analysis of Meanings of the Concept of Sustainability'. *Sustainable Development* 27:1 (2019), pp. 153–61.

Schlosberg, David. *Defining Environmental Justice: Theories, Movements, and Nature* (Oxford: Oxford University Press, 2007), pp. 1–238.

Seghezzo, Lucas 'The Five Dimensions of Sustainability'. *Environmental Politics* 18 (2009), pp. 539–56.

Spengler, Laura. 'Two Types of "Enough": Sufficiency as Minimum and Maximum'. *Environmental Politics* 25 (2016), pp. 921–40.

Stockholm Resilience Centre. 'What is Resilience?' [website] (2015), https://www.stockholmresilience.org/research/research-news/2015-02-19-what-is-resilience.html (accessed 15 February 2023).

Thorén, Henrik 'Resilience'. In *Situating Sustainability: A Handbook of Contexts and Concepts*, edited by C. Parker Krieg and Reetta Toivanen. Helsinki: Helsinki University Press (2021), pp. 79–90.

United Nations Development Programme 'Human Development Index (HDI)'. *Human Development Reports* (2024). Available at: https://hdr.undp.org/data-center/human-development-index#/indicies/HDI. [Accessed 23 February 2024].

West, Simon, L. Jamila Haider, Sanna Stålhammar and Stephen Woroniecki. 'A Relational Turn for Sustainability Science? Relational Thinking, Leverage Points and Transformations'. *Ecosystems and People* 16:1 (2020), pp. 304–25.

Wienhues, Anna. *Ecological Justice and the Extinction Crisis: Giving Living Beings Their Due* (Bristol: Bristol University Press, 2020), pp. 1–244.

Wissenburg, Marcel 'Sustainability, Democracy and the Value of Freedom'. In B. Bornemann, H. Knappe and P. Nanz, *The Routledge Handbook of Democracy and Sustainability* (London: Routledge, 2021), pp. 121–34.

World Commission on Environment and Development. *Our Common Future.* (United Nations Report, 1987), pp. 1–247.

5

Resilience, Ecosystems and Places: Can Resilience Delineate Dynamic Entities?

Patrik Baard

Abstract

While resilience is often taken to be a measurable quality of ecosystems—frequently understood as the capacity to absorb disturbances or adapt to changes in a way that retains functioning—I will in this chapter investigate whether resilience is a quality by which to define and delimit ecosystems. Resilience in the environmental context includes qualities such as long-term identity and persistence. A characteristic of an ecosystem, such as resilience, could reduce contingent factors when defining and delimiting ecosystems in favour of a less agent-relative quality. A challenge to most holistic accounts of environmental ethics is to define and delimit what it is that has value, often requiring consideration of entities having vague boundaries and being dynamic systems. Thus, resilience has much to potentially offer environmental ethics. Objections will be considered to resilience as offering a non-contingent way of delineating places and ecosystems.

Keywords: resilience; environmental ethics; boundary objects; vagueness
Acknowledgements: This chapter has received funding from the European Research Council (ERC) under the European Union's Horizon 2020 research and innovation programme (grant agreement No 948964, project 'Dynamic Territory')

I Introduction

Many environmental ethicists provide reasons for accepting the view that nature has value. However, nature is a vague term making it unclear what it is that has value. This unclarity makes the axiological view difficult to uphold and to practically implement. One possible response is that it is *all* of nature, and all interconnected ecosystems have value. While this may be true, possibilities for ranking would have to be provided to make this a practically useful and theoretically credible standpoint. Another approach is to state that ecosystems are valuable or that we have duties towards biotic communities.[1] A shortcoming of such views is that the observer-independence of delimiting ecosystems and biotic communities is disputed. If delimitating ecosystems is fully observer-dependent,[2] then the viewpoint that ecosystems are valuable or that we have duties towards biotic communities become problematic. Two observers with the same axiological commitments may differ in their delimitation of that which is valued.

In this chapter I will investigate the extent to which resilience is a characteristic of ecological systems that reduces observer dependency. This will support the overall aim of this chapter, which is to investigate whether there can be a non-contingent or observer-independent way of delimiting ecosystems in a normatively relevant manner. That is, a quality by which two observers can delimit ecosystems in the same manner.

If successful, one upshot of the argument is that environmental ethics is offered a reliable way of delimiting what is valued. Resilience enables a way of clearly specifying what it is that has this value, and towards what we have duties. The reasons for this are that resilience ideally refers to a quality of ecological systems that is not observer-dependent, and to notions of identity and persistence.[3] That is, 'for *S* to be resilient with respect to disturbance *D* it has to be *the same system* through a disturbance' (Thorén, 'Against general resilience', p. 28). Moreover, resilience is instructive in what the potential duties towards ecological systems consist of, by formulating a baseline identity of those systems which should persist through time. These reasons would greatly benefit an ecologically informed ethic.

1 Holmes Rolston, *A New Environmental Ethics: The Next Millennium for Life on Earth* (London and New York: Routledge, 2012).

2 Kurt Jax, *Ecosystem Functioning* (Cambridge: Cambridge University Press, 2010), p. 83.

3 Henrik Thorén, 'Against General Resilience', in *The Routledge Handbook of Urban Resilience,* ed. Michael A. Burayidi et al. (London and New York: Routledge, 2019), pp. 26–34; Brian Walker and David Salt, *Resilience Practice* (Washington, DC: Island Press, 2012).

Such an ethics is here understood as placing moral standing on ecosystems. The view is not limited to individual entities as it includes species and ecosystems as morally relevant holistic entities. A unique challenge for ecocentric ethics compared to other ethics where moral standing refers to persons or animals, is that it is not as clear *what* the entity is that has moral standing, as the borders between species and ecosystems are not always clear and may differ between different conceptualizations. In contrast, though not uncontroversially, individual entities are easier to delimit, and it is easier for different observers to agree on their borders; namely, that it is *this* animal or *this* person that has moral standing. The concept of resilience has potential of addressing this problem in the case of ecosystems having vague borders and being dynamic systems, since resilience ideally refers to long-term identity and persistence.

Following this introduction, I will first discuss the relation between environmental ethics and ecology, and the central role that the latter has to ethics. Second, I will address the central issue of this chapter, being the extent to which resilience provides a characteristic that can reduce observer dependency in defining ecosystems. Consequently, I will assume rather than show that there are normative reasons to commit to ecocentric axiologies but that it must be specified in a reasonable manner *what* the entity is that has moral standing. Following that, I will consider objections to the main argument. The chapter will end with a short summary.

II What can resilience bring to environmental ethics?

This chapter will be limited to discussing 'ecocentric' environmental ethics. Such ethical theories have in common that they place an ethical relevance on holistic entities, meaning entities made up of several individual components forming a whole. As the aim of this chapter does not concern whether ecocentric ethics is reasonable axiologically or principally, the focus will be on the entities that ecocentric ethics suggests have moral relevance. That is, if there are reasons to adopt the axiological commitment that X ought to be preserved, what is X?

II.I Environmental ethics and ecology: disputed ecosystems

Many of us may have the intuition that species and ecosystems are valuable for reasons that exceed their instrumental value and usefulness for humans. But the intuition also grants moral standing to holistic entities. It is not necessarily *this* particular and individual bird that matters, but rather the species to which it belongs. It is not *this* particular and individual tree that we want to conserve, but the ecosystem to which it belongs. Ecocentric ethics provides reasons for why that attitude should be adopted. But to account for what an ecosystem is, such an ethic must be ecologically informed. While this section cannot fully account for the relation between environmental ethics and ecology, a few words must be said to motivate the potential need for resilience as a characteristic by which to identify that which has value.

We can start at the other end, by assuming an ecologically uninformed ethics. Such an ethic risks ascribing value and duties to entities that do not exist (Rolston, *A New Environmental Ethics,* p. 166). Environmental philosopher Holmes Rolston correctly suggests that ethicists risk facing this challenge, as 'ecosystems can seem little more than stochastic processes' and 'it can seem as if an ecosystem is too low a level of organization to be the direct focus of moral concern' (Rolston, *A New Environmental Ethics,* p. 166). Environmental ethicist Callicott notes that 'nature is dynamic' and 'chaotic, changing unpredictably, and disturbance [...] by wind, fire, pestilence, not freedom from such disruptions, is nature's normal state'.[4] So what are the entities that an ecocentric environmental ethic is committed to preserving, and how can it be ecologically informed?

From an ecological perspective, the notion of 'ecosystem' is not straightforward. To ecologist Kurt Jax, ecosystems are not 'naturally delimited objects, but are strongly dependent on the perspective of the observer' (Jax, *Ecosystem Functioning,* p. 83). Jax suggests that 'the most accepted meaning of "ecosystem" is that of an assemblage of (interacting) organisms with their abiotic environment' (Jax, *Ecosystem Functioning,* p. 83). He notes that while this definition of ecosystem is broadly applicable, it is not of much use in assessing ecosystem functions and provides no way to count ecosystems in an area. If true, it follows from Jax's claim that two observers may delimit and define ecosystems differently. This entails that two observers with similar axiological commitments may delimit differently that towards which they have duties. This could, at the very worst, lead to conflicting policies and conservation policies, despite identical axiological ecocentric commitments. More precision is required to make such an ethic intelligible and credible.

Before we move on to the issue of the different views on ecosystems, a brief reflection on observer dependency is in order despite it being a wide topic in the philosophy of science, to say the least. John Searle[5] illustrates the differences between claims about reality by the distinction between

4 J. Baird Callicott, 'Do Deconstructive Ecology and Sociobiology Undermine Leopold's Land Ethic?', *Environmental Ethics,* 18:4 (1996), 353–72 (p. 355), doi:10.5840/enviroethics19961843 (accessed 14 November 2023).

5 John Searle, 'The Basic Reality and the Human Reality', in *Thinking About the Real World,* ed. Dirk Franken et al. (Frankfurt: Ontos Verlag, 2010), pp. 19–46.

observer-dependent and observer-independent features of the world. He writes that 'most of reality exists independently of what anybody thinks', and that 'mountains, molecules, and tectonic plates are all observer-independent' (Searle, 'The Basic Reality', p. 27). In contrast, things such as nation states, ethical systems, and private property, are what he calls observer-relative. The distinction is related to, but not equivalent with, the distinction between the objective and subjective (Searle, 'The Basic Reality', p. 27). Related to this distinction is the question of having knowledge. Commonly, a person S has knowledge about proposition p, p referring to some feature of reality, if and only if S believes p, S is justified in believing p, and p is true,[6] being three classical, though not unproblematic, conditions of knowledge. Thus, the classical picture of knowledge assumes that (parts of) the world we seek to understand exists independently of us and our beliefs about it, and evidence provides justification for which beliefs about that world we should adopt (Boghossian, *Fear of Knowledge*, p. 22). In contrast, social constructivism about knowledge disputes that the features of the world that we seek to understand exist independently of us and social context (Boghossian, *Fear of Knowledge*, p. 22).

But do ecosystems belong to the observer-independent or the observer-relative realm? The views on ecological communities have ranged from viewing them as ephemeral collections of individual entities, to 'superorganisms' with tight causal interrelations. The distinction goes back to the early days of ecology, and the different views of Frederic Clements and Henry Gleason.[7] While Clements argued that plant communities reveal specific stages upon disturbance (Odenbaugh, 'Seeing', p. 629), to Gleason any assemblage of plants 'was nothing more than a coincidental assembly of individual plants sharing an area arbitrarily defined by an ecologist at a particular instant of time' (Woods, *Rethinking*, p. 162). To Justus, although assumptions about 'balance' in nature have 'been supplanted with a recognition that nonequilibrium models with complex dynamics such as chaos, limit cycles, and so-called strange attractors may best represent many types of ecological systems' (Justus, *The Philosophy of Ecology*, p. 60), the idea about a balance of nature

6 Paul A. Boghossian, *Fear of Knowledge: Against Relativism and Constructivism* (Oxford: Oxford University Press, 2006), p. 15.

7 James Justus, *The Philosophy of Ecology* (Cambridge: Cambridge University Press, 2021), pp. 1–224; Laura Landen, 'Biotic Community—Real or Unreal: A Philosophical Dilemma', *Worldviews*, 7 (2003), 58–79, doi:10.1163/156853503321916219 (accessed 14 November 2023); Jay Odenbaugh, 'Seeing the Forest and the Trees: Realism about Communities and Ecosystems', *Philosophy of Science*, 74:5 (2007), 628–41, doi:10.1086/525609 (accessed 14 November 2023); Mark Woods, *Rethinking Wilderness* (Peterborough, ON: Broadview Press, 2017).

persists. Similarly, to Woods, 'ecologists have not jettisoned equilibrium and stability ideas in their research' (Woods, *Rethinking*, p. 174).

It is not uncommon to hear charges that 'ecological systems are too complex to admit laws: they are simply too complicated, chaotic, and/or random to exhibit lawful regularities' (Justus, *The Philosophy of Ecology*, p. 39), but factors such as complication, chaos and stochastics do not necessitate the conclusion that there are no ecological laws, especially considering the advancements in other areas of high complexity (Justus, *The Philosophy of Ecology*). Closely related are ecology's predictive failures (Justus, *The Philosophy of Ecology*, p. 40ff.). Most candidates for laws in ecology 'are based on models and theories that are *highly* idealized' (Justus, *The Philosophy of Ecology*, p. 43).

If ecosystems are observer-relative, where to set the boundaries of an ecosystem will depend on the observer. Similarly, if there is no equilibrium or 'balance' towards which ecosystems strive, the desirable state of an ecosystem will be observer-relative. It will be a property that an observer ascribes to an ecosystem, but which is not there without the observer. This provides some challenges to holistic ecocentric environmental ethics, and a charge of carelessly using disputed concepts as a way of being ecologically informed lay close at hand. As suggested by Mark Woods, 'if wilderness is really nothing more than changing disturbances in flux, wilderness preservation [...] seems to necessitate holding the disturbances in place' (Woods, *Rethinking*, p. 167). Landen suggests that ecology 'has impact well outside its own borders', and that 'although ecologists differ about the nature, and even the reality, of biotic community, in the popular arena the expression is widely, albeit sometimes uncritically, accepted' (Landen, 'Biotic', p. 58). To Cooper, 'there is a disturbing tendency in the environmental ethics literature to rely on metaphysically rich, but scientifically controversial, ideas from the sciences of ecology and ethology'.[8] To Justus, ecology has 'uniquely epistemic authority vis-à-vis environmental ethics' (Justus, *The Philosophy of Ecology*, p. 5). This is because ecology provides 'scientific facts that ethicists must recognize and respond to', and because environmental ethics 'often trades in concepts and claims that have both normative and descriptive content' (Justus, *The Philosophy of Ecology*, p. 5).

But if there are disputes amongst ecologists regarding what an ecosystem is, what is it then that holistic environmental ethicists are committed to preserve? Do ecosystems exist in an 'objective' and observer-independent manner, so that holistic environmental ethicists can reasonably and meaningfully

8 Gregory Cooper, 'Teleology and Environmental Ethics', *American Philosophical Quarterly*, 35:2 (1998), 195–207 (p. 195), access link: http://www.jstor.org/stable/20009930 (accessed 14 November 2023).

refer to them by for instance specific sequences after disturbance, as Clements suggested? If ecosystems are fully observer-relative and 'subjective', being mere coincidental rather than following any identifiable or systematic progressions, then there are high degrees of contingency regarding what it is that has value.

In the following sub-section, I will investigate whether 'resilience' has the possibility of offering a way out of the impasse regarding what it is that has value in a way that informs environmental ethics.

II.II The possibilities of resilience

What will be investigated here is the extent to which resilience may be a characteristic of ecosystems that enables delimiting ecosystems in a way that is not fully contingent. If successful, this would provide a characteristic of ecosystems that is 'objective', or at the very least that reduces observer dependency.[9] That is, resilience provides a characteristic that two or more observers agree is meaningful to delimit an entity towards which they ascribe value and have conservation duties.

The main reasons for why 'resilience' can have this function that is relevant for normative claims is that it is a property of ecosystems or biological communities that has scientific relevance, and that it refers to stability as identity through time. Interestingly, resilience has also been gestured at as a criterion relevant for statehood.[10] Thus, Kolers draws a link between resilience, sustainability and statehood, as a form of place-based and ecologically informed notion of persistent long-term sovereignty (Kolers, *Land, Conflict, and Justice*, p. 76ff.). Indeed, 'resilience as a concept makes little sense without some notion of persistence' (Thorén, 'Against general resilience', p. 28). Consequently, resilience is a concept that sustainability can be construed to,[11] and to that extent entails a conceptual specification of a leading concept in planning and relating to nature based on long-term identity despite disruptions. Thus, if it is a challenge to ecocentric holistic ethics that the objects of value are dynamic and changing, and resilience is a property that refers to persistence throughout time, then resilience becomes

9 In this article I will not take sides regarding the extent to which any fully observer-independent factual claims are possible.

10 Avery Kolers, *Land, Conflict, and Justice: A Political Theory of Territory* (Cambridge: Cambridge University Press, 2009), p. 74.

11 Henrik Thorén, and Johannes Persson, 'Resilience: Some Philosophical Remarks on Ostensively and Stipulatively Defined Concepts', *Sustainability: Science, Practice and Policy*, 11 (2015), 64–74, doi:10.1080/15487733.2015.11908140 (accessed 24 July 2023).

a property by which to refer both to the entities that an ecocentric holistic ethic is committed to preserve, as well as provide a baseline regarding what state that entity is to be in.

According to Justus, resilience 'is the rate at which a system returns to *R* following perturbation' (Justus, *The Philosophy of Ecology*, p. 68),[12] *R* being 'a reference state or dynamic (R) of that system against which stability is assessed' (Justus, *The Philosophy of Ecology*, p. 62). While identifying considerable semantic diversity, Thorén[13] suggests that two conceptualizations have special significance: first, denoting the 'returning to the reference state (or dynamic) after a temporary disturbance';[14] second, 'resilience is not about returning to a reference state, but rather a kind of buffer within a system' telling us, by measurable magnitude, 'how large a disturbance a system can withstand without being pushed on to a trajectory where the system will, through its own dynamics, become extinct' (Thorén, 'Resilience', p. 306). While the first definition largely coheres with Justus' characterization above, this second understanding of resilience has gained traction outside of ecology, being relevant both to archaeology, sociology, community psychology and social medicine. Thorén provides the following definition of this second form: 'The ability of *S* to absorb disturbance *D* and maintain *I*' (Thorén, 'Resilience', p. 312), where *I* denotes a property of the system *S* that is maintained during the disturbance, 'ordinarily associated with the identity or persistence of the system' ('Resilience', p. 310).

Stating that the concept is 'one of the most important research topics in the context of achieving sustainability',[15] Brand and Jax list a typology of resilience with varying balance between descriptive and normative content, including 'hybrid' definitions of resilience that includes elements from both sides of the descriptive–normative divide. They distinguish between resilience as 'a clearly specified concept [...] that is merely used in ecology' and 'a vague and malleable concept of resilience that is used as a communication

12 See also Sven Ove Hansson and Gert Helgesson, 'What is Stability?', *Synthese*, 136:2 (2003), 219–35, doi: 10.1023/A:1024733424521 (accessed 14 November 2023).

13 Henrik Thorén, 'Resilience as a Unifying Concept', *International Studies in the Philosophy of Science,* 28:3 (2014), 303–24, doi: 10.1080/02698595.2014.953343 (accessed 24 July 2023).

14 Volker Grimm and Christian Wissel, 'Babel, or the Ecological Stability Discussions: An Inventory and Analysis of Terminology and a Guide for Avoiding Confusion', *Oecologia,* 109:3 (1997), p. 325, doi:10.1007/s004420050090 (accessed 14 November 2023).

15 Fridolin Simon Brand and Kurt Jax, 'Focusing the Meaning(s) of Resilience: Resilience as a Descriptive Concept and a Boundary Object', *Ecology and Society,* 12 (2007), https://www.jstor.org/stable/26267855 (accessed 24 July 2023).

tool across different scientific disciplines and between science and practice' (Brand and Jax, 'Focusing the Meaning(s)'). They suggest that resilience is increasingly viewed in the second manner. This is somewhat consistent with changes to the concept identified by others, such as Folke[16] who views resilience as having moved from a focus on the robustness of ecological systems, towards social-ecological resilience. Indeed, they write that 'resilience is increasingly interpreted in a broader meaning across disciplines as a way of thinking, a perspective or even a paradigm for analysing social-ecological systems' (Brand and Jax 'Focusing the Meaning(s)').

The purely descriptive account of resilience is one that, ideally, excludes normative content, and gives rise to quantitative approaches. This requires specifying the possible disturbances to an ecosystem, as well as what it is that is to be resilient, or identify 'the specific regime that is meant to be resilient to the identified disturbance regime' (Brand and Jax, 'Focusing the Meaning(s)'). To answer this, Brand and Jax suggest a process. First, one must assess the ecosystem services and processes that are of primary concern and, second, explicate the identity of the selected regime including 'explicating the precise boundary of the regime, the set of variables of interest, and the expected internal degree of relationships' (Brand and Jax, 'Focusing the Meaning(s)'). They concede that these two steps are contingent upon societal values or normative judgments and therefore must include participative deliberations. Third, one must specify what mechanisms 'control the specific position of an ecosystem' (Brand and Jax, 'Focusing the Meaning(s)'). As a concept 'resilience can be a clearly specified and delimited stability concept', and thus 'represents a quantitative and measurable concept that can be used for achieving progress in ecological science' (Brand and Jax, 'Focusing the Meaning(s)'). This despite the involvement of societal values or normative judgments in the first two steps which are, assumedly, primarily at a descriptive level to the extent that different delimitations and normative statements are surveyed and recognized rather than assessed and scrutinized as ethical statements. Nevertheless, the property 'resilience' becomes defined and stipulated by such a process. Here, such a process as described by Brand and Jax would define the object towards which an ecocentric holistic environmental ethics has duties, and what those duties consists of.

If the process that Brand and Jax portray has wide application, is the resulting ecosystem with different degrees of resilience observer-dependent or observer-independent? Is resilience a property belonging to the ecosystems, or a property that is ascribed to it? When used in a descriptive manner

16 Carl Folke, 'Resilience: The Emergence of A Perspective for Social-ecological System Analyses', *Global Environmental Change,* 16:3 (2006), 253–67, doi:10.1016/j.gloenvcha.2006.04.002 (accessed 14 November 2023).

resilience seems clearly intended to relate to an observer-independent property. The ability of a system to absorb disturbance and maintain an identity through time seems like a property of that system which is not dependent on observers and is thus observer-independent.[17] However, with the first two steps of Brand and Jax's model, and the identity of a system, more contingency is involved.

The above discussion relates to the main topic of this chapter in the following way. What is searched for here is whether there is a way to tackle the contingency when delimiting ecosystems. Resilience can potentially offer such a concept. However, as seen above, even descriptive accounts of resilience invite some contingency. In the first two steps provided by Brand and Jax, different observers may delimit and set a baseline for an ecosystem in different manners. Stated differently, the delimitation and baseline of the resilience of an ecosystem will depend on the presence and recognition of observer perspectives.

Yet, by introducing characteristics that relate to ecosystems, the contingency is reduced, even if not absolved. That is, the capacity of that which has been delimited to either return to a prior state, or to withstand disturbances, is a property of that ecosystems. While the delimitation of the ecosystem, as well as establishing the state it is to be in, are observer-dependent, the resilient capacity is not. Establishing what state it is to be in will depend on contingent factors such as the ecosystem services it provides, as well as its possible cultural meaning and historical states it has been in. Thus, it seems as if resilience fulfils the *desiderata* sought here, and provides the ground for an ecologically informed environmental ethics, where resilience plays a central role to delimit and identify the bearers of value.

III Objections

In this section I will pose and respond to objections to the arguments above. Conjunctly, the objections risk establishing that resilience does not meet the aim of this chapter in identifying a property of ecosystems that allows for delimitation and normatively establishing what state an ecosystem is to be in, in a non-contingent manner. That is, identifying a property that is not observer-relative, and which enables two or more observers to converge on a similar delimitation and identity of an ecosystem.

17 Of course, observers can intervene and affect the resilience of a system. But that is not what is meant here. Even if they modify the resilience of a system, the property of resilience will, to a purely descriptive account, depend on mechanisms and interrelations that work *regardless* of their modifications.

III.I Resilience is observer-dependent

A first objection is to challenge the extent to which resilience is an observer-independent property of ecosystems. If the process that Brand and Jax introduces is a general enough model, the first two steps introduced contingency—to assess the ecosystem processes and services that are of primary concern on spatial and temporal scales, and to explicate the identity of the selected regime. Brand and Jax suggest that these steps 'are dependent on societal values or normative judgments' (Brand and Jax, 'Focusing the Meaning(s)'). It is only in the third step that mechanisms of the ecosystems are established in a measurable way.

But does not such a process make resilience based on contingent components in which different observers will delimit the spatial area and the scales differently, as well as the ecosystem functions? Is there an observer-independent way of clarifying ecosystems? According to Odenbaugh, there have been roughly three main ways of conceiving of ecological communities, corresponding to the distinction between Clements and Gleason. Odenbaugh distinguishes between aggregates, wholes and individuals: *Aggregates* occur when the parts 'bear insignificant causal relations to one another at a time and over time'; a *whole* is when 'certain causal relations exist between its parts such that it is causally structured at a time and through time'; and an *individual* refers to when the parts 'bear causal relations to one another such that the object is highly structured and integrated' (Odenbaugh, 'Seeing the Forest', p. 630).

Though there are some ecosystems that show a high degree of persistence and identity throughout time, most ecosystems are dynamic entities and change over long enough time periods. Or rather, the entities that are found in them and their interactions transform throughout time; very few ecosystems qualify as 'individual' or 'wholes' and those that do are often limited in both spatial scale and permanence. If resilience is interpreted as requiring conservation of a specific set of species and interactions between them, then resilience seems as a non-starter considering the dynamic entities that ecosystems are. Furthermore, defining what level of equilibrium is desirable is a normative question and must be accepted by the group to whom resilience—not limited to ecosystems—matters.[18] To Ochoa Espejo, resilience as a normative conception denotes equilibrium specific to a group and is not a 'decision-independent criterion' (Ochoa Espejo, *On Borders*, p. 117).

But we should perhaps not let the dynamic character of ecosystems provide a full charge to the argument here. Mark Woods argues that there are at

18 Paulina Ochoa Espejo, *On Borders: Territories, Legitimacy, and the Rights of Place* (Oxford: Oxford University Press, 2020), p. 116.

least three ways of responding to the charge that ecosystems are in total flux. That is, responses to the objection that establishing a static character for ecosystems to be in requires ascribing a quality to ecosystems that are foreign to them. In other words, to ascribe too much static to something that is inherently ever-changing and dynamic. In response, Woods (Woods, *Rethinking*, p. 168) argues (1) that not all disturbances are equal and the flux of nature can be ordered; (2) the 'paradigm shift' from a nature in balance view to a nature in flux view is not clear and; (3) wilderness preservation has not historically relied on the 'balance-of-nature' paradigm in ecology. Even if all ecosystems are dynamic, there are different levels of such dynamics. Regarding the second point, Woods argues that 'no ecologist has held the view that nature is static and completely unchanging' (Woods, *Rethinking*, p. 171), while some have suggested that ecosystems have a *tendency* to resist change. The 'equilibrium' of which ecologists such as Clements speak is not a simplistic 'everything stays the same'—stability (Woods, *Rethinking*, p. 171). Lastly, discussing Aldo Leopold's land ethic, Woods suggests that wilderness conservation has not regarded nature as static and that it stays the same when left alone (Woods, *Rethinking*, p. 175).

It suffices here to note that much conservation has embraced disturbances and encompassed dynamics of the entities that they aim to preserve without this causing trouble or giving one reason to reject conservation per se. The objection that resilience is an observer-relative property that can therefore not fulfil the *desiderata* sought here need not be devastating. The reason is that most views that have historically underpinned conservation did not rely on a simplistic perspective of stability, but rather encompassed the dynamic character of ecosystems. Fully observer-independent accounts of ecosystems that includes both its delimitation and which state it is to be in are far-fetched. There will most likely always be components that require human judgments when determining resilience. But once established in a systemic, reasonable and meaningful manner, the relation between the components of an ecosystem that provides resilience are less observer-relative. Thus, using resilience as a descriptive and normative concept at the very least reduces observer-relative components, even if not abolishing them. That is, two different observers can meaningfully identify the same ecosystem by non-arbitrarily chosen criteria.

III.II What is resilience, really? Resilience as a vague object, and as a boundary object

Brand and Jax emphasize that resilience has transformed from a descriptive concept into a vague and malleable concept. They stress that in some variants, resilience is lacking a workable definition. More explicitly, Thorén states the following about resilience:

> The concept is famously a mess of different definitions, and there are wildly different ideas about what the concept does, and should do, and what is significant about it. Is it a useful metaphor not to be taken too seriously, a powerful way to conceptualize sustainability, or a framework that gives scientific legitimacy to a political agenda? (Thorén, 'Against General Resilience', p. 26)

But is vagueness and the multiple definitions of resilience a problem? Brand and Jax suggest that the 'increased vagueness and malleability of resilience is highly valuable' (Brand and Jax, 'Focusing the Meaning(s)'). That the vagueness and malleability of the property of resilience should be a strength may seem intuitively odd given that preciseness, clarity and vagueness-avoidance are *desiderata* for scientific concepts.[19] Why would not such *desiderata* hold also for resilience? Brand and Jax consider the increasing use of resilience as a boundary object having the potential to cross disciplinary boundaries and coordinate different groups. Concepts that function as boundary objects have three features: flexibility and 'adaptation to local needs', rigidity as in 'maintenance of identity across sites', and the possibility to enable 'communication between different cultures that could not otherwise communicate' (Thorén 'Resilience', p. 315). This makes resilience relevant and applicable to a wide range of instances and groups.

But boundary objects also have drawbacks. Brand and Jax exemplify this with the concept of sustainability, stating that the term has become highly diluted and unclear and has 'been reduced to a listing of any societal objectives that agents happen to think important' (Brand and Jax, 'Focusing the Meaning(s)'). The vagueness gives rise to more problematic outcomes, as vague concepts can be used by different 'scientific disciplines or socials groups to justify their particular interest' (Brand and Jax, 'Focusing the Meaning(s)') hiding power relations when different speakers agree on the desirability of the same concept, despite the concept having different extensions to the speakers.

Acknowledging the function of resilience as a boundary object, Thorén suggests that there are usually two different resilience concepts in play which he dubs 'local' and 'global', depending on whether it concerns a single domain of a specific system or is considered a property of the system as a whole (Thorén, 'Resilience as a Unifying Concept', p. 310). Thorén

19 Sven Ove Hansson, 'How to Define – A Tutorial', *Princípios*, 19: 13 (2006), 5–30, https://periodicos.ufrn.br/principios/article/view/508 (accessed 14 November 2023).

investigates how the use of resilience in various disciplinary contexts are closely related, but also that highly abstract versions of the concept tend to be preferred by those who make explanatory use of it. High levels of abstraction lead to context insensitivity, but this comes at a high price 'since the unification that ensues is often relatively weak' (Thorén, 'Resilience as a Unifying Concept', p. 304). That is, the more abstract the concept is, the more applicable it becomes to a wide diversity of fields, but with weak interdisciplinary links as a result (Thorén, 'Resilience as a Unifying Concept', p. 317). Thorén suggests that this may explain why there has been no more intellectual exchange despite similar resilience concepts being used in different fields.

Brand and Jax do not seem unaware of this issue of vagueness and ultimately consider it a strength of resilience. Thorén can also be interpreted in that manner when stating that the highly abstract character of resilience is an overlooked and important feature pertaining to it, even if coming at a price (Thorén, 'Resilience as a Unifying Concept', p. 304). To Brand and Jax the strength of the concept resides in how it 'is able to foster communication across disciplines and between science and practice' (Brand and Jax, 'Focusing the Meaning(s)'). However, they suggest a balance: when resilience is conceived as a descriptive concept, it should be clear, well defined and specified to allow for operationalization and application in ecology, whereas, in contrast, when it is conceived as a boundary object it 'should be designed in a manner to foster interdisciplinary work' (Brand and Jax, 'Focusing the Meaning(s)'). In that manner, the degree of specification that the concept requires will depend on context and usage.

On a more general level, definitions of central concepts ought not always strive for more specification and preciseness than is necessary. There is for instance a difference between vagueness-preserving and vagueness-resolving definitions (Hansson, 'How to Define', pp. 23ff.). To some multi-dimensional concepts, meaning concepts that do not refer to a single well-defined (one-dimensional) scale, it may be impossible to transform all the different properties of a concept to single one-dimensional measures (Hansson, 'How to Define', p. 25). Assuming that resilience is a multi-dimensional concept it may very well be challenging, if not impossible, to specify all its components. While resilience may be defined by the property of returning back to a defined state after disturbances, or the ability to absorb disturbances and maintain desired state of affairs, operationalizing that metric requires taking multiple dimensions into account. Justus describes the importance of modelling the ecological system that is to be stable, which in ecological modelling often entails including variables that represent system parts (such as species of a community), namely, parameters that influence those variables but are not influenced by them and model equations to describe system dynamics

(Justus, *The Philosophy of Ecology*, p. 62). While this obviously requires some work, both on the conceptual but also the normative level, it is not impossible, and resilience as a boundary object promotes interdisciplinary communication. However, that it is a boundary object should only signal the start of such communication, not the end of it, as much work needs to be done to further specify resilience in both descriptive and normative ways. At the very least, the concept allows for meaningful communication.

III.III Resilience is only one aspect of long-term persistence and identity of ecosystems

One final objection is that it is not resilience per se that enables one to delimit and value an ecosystem. Rather, it is persistence and identity, usually measured through resilience, that is valuable. We may for instance value a forest area that has existed for a very long time, due to the mere fact of its longevity. But 'some systems persist as a consequence of being resilient, others because they are not disturbed' (Thorén, 'Resilience as a Unifying Concept', p. 319). High degrees of resilience work as well as to promote identity through time as lack of disturbance. We may value an environmental area due to its persistence and identity over time, but the level of resilience may be a poor fit for assessing that longevity. Rather, it may be a lack of disturbing events that give rise to the persistence and longevity of the ecosystem. If true, this means that it is not resilience that we value, but rather resilience working as a proxy for what we really value, such as ecosystems that have existed for a long time. However, it seems unlikely that long-term ecosystems have not been required to face disturbances. Discussing Kolers' use of resilience and relating it to sustainability and statehood, Ochoa Espejo argues that there are several different possible equilibria for ecosystems and that 'an ecosystem may be more resilient when there are periodic or constant disturbances than when there are only few changes' (Ochoa Espejo, *On Borders*, p. 118). The extent to which ecosystems with low levels of resilience can last a long time due to lack of disturbance is an empirical issue, but it does raise the question of how resilience relates to long-term identity and persistence, the last two being characteristics that makes it possible to delimit and identify specific ecosystems.

The final objection that will only be sketched here is that an undesirable ecosystem may be resilient in a descriptive sense. Brand and Jax observe that 'a degraded savannah or a polluted lake can be highly resilient but at the same time undesirable from an anthropocentric perspective' (Brand and Jax 'Focusing the Meaning(s)'). But if resilience is the concept by which an ecosystem is deemed normatively valuable in the sense that it enables delimiting the ecosystem and identifying a property that makes it valuable, then the degraded savannah or polluted lake are entities that a holistic ecocentric environmental ethics is committed to preserve or conserve. This is contradictory with the ambitions of such an ethic.

Taken jointly, what the objections show is that resilience cannot in isolation settle the issue of what the identity of an ecosystem is, or whether its persistence is of the normatively relevant kind. Other factors are required to make such a conclusion reasonable. These factors include for instance what meaning an environmental area has, what forms of ecosystems that are desirable, and the reasons for why they have existed for a long time. To reiterate, the mere fact that an ecosystem has existed for a long time does not necessitate concluding that it is resilient. Conversely, resilience does not necessitate concluding that an ecosystem is valuable, as also destructive or undesirable ecosystems can be resilient.

IV Summary

In this chapter I have sought to address whether resilience provides a characteristic of ecosystems that makes it possible to clearly delimit them throughout time. If possible, this would contribute to ecocentric environmental ethics by clearly pointing towards that which they are committed to preserve and towards we have duties. This would make such an ethic ecologically informed by using a central concept in ecology to address one central problem.

It was found that while resilience refers to a characteristic of ecosystems, it suffers from vagueness and does not exclude contingency and observer dependency. Even as a descriptive concept, resilience requires introducing values and judgments. However, vagueness may be a strength of the concept of resilience. First, due to its level of abstraction the concept has the potential of being implemented in a wide array of contexts. Second, if resilience is a multi-dimensional concept, it should not be more specific than necessary, even if it must be defined in context for relevant usage. Lastly, resilience may only be one dimension of an ecosystem referring to its continuance throughout time, despite disturbances; it is only one aspect, as we would for instance not value a degraded savannah or a polluted lake, even if they are resilient.

While resilience does not fully refer to an observer-independent characteristic of ecosystems that allows for clear delimitation of the entities that an ecologically informed holistic ecocentric environmental ethic is committed to preserve, resilience has the potential to both delimit an entity and allow for communication about it. It provides a meaningful concept that two or more different observers with the same axiological commitments can use for starting a discussion on what exactly they wish to preserve. Resilience is a central concept of such discussions, but does not by any means provide the final word.

Bibliography

Boghossian, Paul A., *Fear of Knowledge: Against Relativism and Constructivism.* (Oxford: Oxford University Press, 2006).

Brand, Fridolin S., and Kurt Jax, 'Focusing the Meaning(s) of Resilience: Resilience as a Descriptive Concept and a Boundary Object', *Ecology and Society* 12 (2007). https://www.jstor.org/stable/26267855 (accessed 24 July 2023).

Callicott, J. Baird, 'Do Deconstructive Ecology and Sociobiology undermine Leopold's Land Ethic?', *Environmental Ethics,* 18:4 (1996), 353–72, doi: 10.5840/enviroethics19961843 (accessed 14 November 2023).

Cooper, Gregory, 'Teleology and Environmental Ethics', *American Philosophical Quarterly* 35 (1998), 195–207, http://www.jstor.org/stable/20009930. Accessed 13 Nov. 2023 (accessed 14 November 2023).

Folke, Carl, 'Resilience: The Emergence of A Perspective for Social-ecological System Analyses', *Global Environmental Change* 16:3 (2006), 253–67, doi:10.1016/j.gloenvcha.2006.04.002 (accessed 14 November 2023).

Grimm, Volker, and Christian Wissel, 'Babel, or the Ecological Stability Discussion: An Inventory and Analysis of Terminology and a Guide for Avoiding Confusion', *Oecologica,* 109:3 (1997), 232–4, doi:10.1007/s004420050090 (accessed 14 November 2023).

Hansson, Sven Ove, 'How to Define—A Tutorial', *Princípios, 19:* 13 (2006), 5–30, access link: https://periodicos.ufrn.br/principios/article/view/508 (accessed 14 November 2023).

Hansson, Sven Ove, and Gert Helgesson,. 'What is Stability?', *Synthese* 136:2 (2003), 219–35, doi:10.1023/A:1024733424521 (accessed 14 November 2023).

Jax, Kurt, *Ecosystem Functioning* (Cambridge: Cambridge University Press, 2010).

Justus, James, *The Philosophy of Ecology* (Cambridge: Cambridge University Press, 2021).

Kolers, Avery, *Land, Conflict, and Justice: A Political Theory of Territory* (Cambridge: Cambridge University Press, 2009).

Landen, Laura, 'Biotic Community—Real or Unreal: A Philosophical Dilemma', *Worldviews* 7 (2003), 58–79, doi:10.1163/156853503321916219 (accessed 14 November 2023).

Ochoa Espejo, Paulina, *On Borders: Territories, Legitimacy, and the Rights of Place* (Oxford: Oxford University Press, 2020).

Odenbaugh, Jay, Seeing the Forest and the Trees: Realism about Communities and Ecosystems, *Philosophy of Science,* 74 (2007), 628–41, doi:10.1086/525609 (accessed 14 November 2023).

Rolston, Holmes, *New Environmental Ethics: The Next Millennium for Life on Earth*, (London and New York: Routledge, 2012).

Searle, John, 'The Basic Reality and the Human Reality', in *Thinking About the Real World,* edited by Dirk Franken, Attila Karakus and Jan G. Michel (Frankfurt: Ontos Verlag, 2010), pp. 19–46.

Thorén, Henrik, 'Against General Resilience', in *The Routledge Handbook of Urban Resilience*, edited by M. A Burayidi, A. Allen, J. Twigg and C. Wamsler (London and New York: Routledge, 2019), pp. 26–34.

Thorén, Henrik, 'Resilience as a Unifying Concept', *International Studies in the Philosophy of Science,* 28:3 (2014), 303–24, doi:10.1080/02698595.2014.953343 (accessed 24 July 2023)

Thorén, Henrik, and Johannes Persson, 'Resilience: Some Philosophical Remarks on Ostensively and Stipulatively Defined Concepts', *Sustainability: Science, Practice and Policy,* 11 (2015), 64–74, doi:10.1080/15487733.2015.11908140 (accessed 24 July 2023).

Walker, Brian, and David Salt. *Resilience Practice* (Washington, DC: Island Press, 2012).

Woods, Mark, *Rethinking Wilderness* (Peterborough, ON: Broadview Press, 2017).

6

Adapt Creatively or Perish: How Resilience Dug the Grave of Strong Sustainability

Andrea Lehner

I Introduction

This chapter critically examines the political implications of resilience thinking's promotion of flexible adaptive capacities in response to events such as disruptions, disasters and crises. According to resilience thinking, flexibility and adaptability are the most *pragmatic* and *realistic* approach that managers, policymakers, communities and individuals can uphold in a turbulent and uncertain world. The argument I put forth is that this adaptive stance has led to the ongoing postponement of substantial, transformative and environmentally just actions needed to effectively address the pressing climate and ecological emergency we face today. By conveniently adopting a specific approach to global crises, founded on an ontology of complex systems and an epistemology of limited knowledge, resilience thinking has diverted attention away from the most evident causes that have brought us to what can be termed an age of catastrophe.[1] By focusing on responding

1 In his book *The New Age of Catastrophe* Marxist thinker Alexis Callinicos examines how the permanent state of emergency that characterizes our contemporary world allows for this new way of naming our present era and for declaring catastrophe as a benchmark for understanding our present. In the contemporary world, catastrophe, understood as 'some sequence of events that disrupts established routines of life and inflicts suffering or death to many' (William H. McNeill, cited in Alexis Callinicos, *The New Age of Catastrophe* (Cambridge: Polity Press, 2023), p. 2) is no longer sporadic nor exceptional but has become the new normal. Drawing on Adorno's definition of the

to symptoms rather than addressing causes, it has failed to bring about transformative change and has well served the interests of those who want to delay environmental action.

The chapter is divided into three sections. The first section delves into the origins of resilience, tracing how it grew out of the field of ecology in the 1970s and was afterwards adopted as a management and governance agenda in the post-Cold War decades, becoming pervasive after the 9/11 securitarian turn. The second section examines critical scholarship around resilience and shows how resilience tends to fit intuitively with certain forms of governance which benefit from the current world configuration resulting in feeble measures to address the current global crises. The third section questions whether resilience can be leveraged for real transformative change or whether we must resist it since its way of functioning is preventing us from envisioning and making tangible a different kind of future.

II The Emergence of Resilience in the Field of Ecology

As is typically acknowledged in the literature, there is no agreed definition of resilience. The term takes on distinct meanings in the fields of psychology, engineering and ecology. While we recognize resilience's polysemic nature, we will primarily focus on its initial usage within the field of ecology and how it eventually began informing not only natural resource management and ecology, but also sustainable development policy, disaster management, securitarian discourses, international development agendas and other forms of governance.

In the field of ecology, the term 'resilience' gained popularity through C. S. Holling's groundbreaking 1973 article, 'Resilience and Stability of Ecological Systems'.[2] Holling juxtaposes two distinct approaches to natural resource management: the traditional *stability approach* deeply rooted in

---

world-spirit of capitalism as a permanent catastrophe in *Negative Dialectics*, Callinicos states that the main driver of such a catastrophe is the blind process of capital accumulation that destroys the natural world, of which humans are dependent. In his words: 'capitalism, having overstayed its welcome, has become a 'permanent catastrophe' (Callinicos, *The New Age of Catastrophe*, p. 5). Catastrophe is immanent to the system that has created it, and arises from its internal logic, demonstrating that the system has hit the buffers (Callinicos, *The New Age of Catastrophe*, p. 7). Chief among the multidimensional nature of catastrophic destruction is climate change. See Alexis Callinicos, *The New Age of Catastrophe*.

2 C. S. Holling, 'Resilience and Stability of Ecological Systems', *Annual Review of Ecology and Systematics*, 4 (1973), 1–23.

environmental science and his innovative *resilience approach*, which heralded a new era in ecology. The *stability approach*, which he later[3] dubbed 'engineering resilience', aligns with the type of resilience pursued by engineers. This perspective conceives ecological systems through the lens of linear dynamics, operating under the assumption that ecosystems are predictable and tend to gravitate towards equilibrium. This approach understands resilience as 'the ability of a system to return to an equilibrium state after a temporary disturbance; the more rapidly it returns and the less it fluctuates, the more stable it [is considered to] be' (Holling, 'Resilience and Stability', p. 14). In this case, resilience is determined by how swiftly a system can resume and return to equilibrium following a shock or disturbance.

While this understanding, or 'view of the world' as he calls it, offers a manageable and simplistic view of systems, which is useful when dealing with systems with limited or controlled exposure to external conditions, Holling finds it *unrealistic* for the kind of systems natural resource management deals with. The simple causal models it relies on fail to accurately represent the complexity of real-world ecological systems (Holling, 'Resilience and Stability', p. 15). For instance, it erroneously assumes that an outcome can be expected to recur with *near certainty* if it has happened repeatedly over time, and naively believes that natural systems can be kept near equilibrium through management. This leads to a type of natural resource management which attempts to transform an unpredictable system, considered inefficient in terms of the constancy of its yields, into one that yields products in a predictable and 'efficient' manner. Holling and Meffe later termed this approach 'command and control',[4] one which aims to control nature in a way that allows it to 'harvest its products, reduce its threats, and establish *highly predictable outcomes* for the short-term benefit of humanity' (Meffe and Holling, 'Command and control', p. 329, emphasis added). Command and control management replaces natural ecological controls, which are highly complex and variable, with engineered constructs and manipulations that on the surface seem entirely within human control (Meffe and Holling, 'Command and control' pp. 329–30). Examples of command of control management are resumed in the following quote:

> We control agricultural pests through herbicides and pesticides; we convert natural, multi-species, variable-aged forests into monoculture, single-aged

3 C. S. Holling, 'Engineering Resilience versus Ecological Resilience', in *Engineering Within Ecological Constraints*, ed. Peter C. Schulze (Washington, DC: The National Academy Press, 1996), p. 33.

4 Gary K. Meffe and C. S. Holling, 'Command and Control and the Pathology of Natural Resource Management', *Conservation Biology*, 10:2 (1996), pp. 328–37.

> plantations; we hunt and kill predators to produce a larger, more reliable supply of game species; we suppress fires and pest outbreaks in forests to ensure a steady lumber supply; we clear forests for pasture development and steady cattle production, and so forth. (Meffe and Holling, 'Command and Control', p. 330)

Their main contention is that even if "command and control" management achieves short-term success in stabilizing yields, it eventually leads to long-term surprises and unintended consequences. For instance, in seeking to control fish stock by concentrating on only one single variable, the system's variability and diversity are reduced. Over time, this leads to a pathology in which shocks and disturbances that were previously absorbed by the ecological system eventually overwhelm its capacity. The paradoxical nature of this pathology is that the desire to increase a complex system's efficiency leads to a reduction of its resilience, which means sudden and unexpected alterations of the whole system can arise and cause it to flip to another domain of attraction (causing a regime shift). As a result, the system no longer behaves as it used to and ceases to provide the goods and services that human communities depend on. When a system's resilience suddenly breaks down, it becomes more vulnerable and less capable of dealing with change, hindering its persistence or what Holling later termed 'long-term sustainability'.

In his 1973 article, Holling advocates for a resilience-based approach to resource management and makes a case for shifting the focus from 'constancy of behaviour' to 'persistence of the relationships'. Said persistence is what allows the system to function and absorb external disruptions without being dramatically altered. In other words, it makes it resilient, a term he defines as follows: 'But there is a property, termed resilience, that is a measure of the persistence of systems and their ability to absorb change and disturbance and still maintain the same relationships between populations or state variables' (Holling, 'Resilience and Stability of Ecological Systems', p. 14). Resilience, therefore, 'determines the *persistence* of relationships within a system and is a measure of the ability of these systems to absorb changes of state variables, driving variables and parameters and still *persist*' (Holling, 'Resilience and Stability of Ecological Systems', p. 17, emphasis added).

Holling's innovative approach can thus be summarized as follows. Systems do not need to be stable to be resilient. Highly unstable systems, such as those in regions with extreme climatic conditions, tend to be more resilient due to their frequent exposure to disruptions and high fluctuation of key variables. High resilience allows for persistence whereas low resilience increases the likelihood of collapse or catastrophic change. Ecological resilience is thus what makes a system less vulnerable and more capable of absorbing disturbances under changing conditions. Moreover, aiming at maximizing efficiency in resource management is counterproductive in the long run, as it tends to decrease a system's resilience.

By the late 1970s, Holling refined his approach, advocating for what he called adaptive management—a more realistic and pragmatic alternative to the stability approach. Adaptive management emerged as the best way to flexibly manage ecological systems and natural resources amid increasingly frequent unexpected events, driven by humanity's growing pressure and reliance on ecosystem services. Holling displayed a growing sense that 'traditional' and 'narrow view' approaches exacerbated management problems. He and his colleagues emphasized the complexity of the world and the impossibility of having complete knowledge or predicting outcomes with certainty. They argued that surprises were inevitable due to the ever-evolving nature of ecosystems and even claimed it was *hubristic* to try to predict the future. Once complexity and unpredictability became accepted as inevitable, adaptive management surfaced as the soundest approach to managing under uncertainty, as it does not require detailed prediction. Instead, decisions are made based on the best available information, and the approach is flexible enough to accommodate changing conditions as new information becomes available.

Lance Gunderson summarizes the differences between old resource management and the new adaptive management promoted by Holling and his colleagues:

> [The former] focuses on parts of the system and deals with experiments that *narrow uncertainty* to the point of acceptance by peers, it is *conservative and unambiguous* by being *incomplete and fragmentary*. The other view [i.e. adaptive management] is integral and holistic, searching for simple structures and relationships that explain much of nature's complexity. The latter view provides the underpinning for an approach to dealing with resources called adaptive environmental assessment and management (Holling, *Adaptive Environmental Assessment and Management*; Walters, *Adaptive Environmental Assessment and Management*), which assumes that *surprises are inevitable*, that *knowledge will always be incomplete*, and that human interaction with ecosystems will *always be evolving*.[5]

Notice the terminology used to describe the old resource management approach: it aims at controlling and narrowing uncertainty, tends to be conservative in the sense that it is averse to change and wants to keep the system's behaviour stable and near equilibrium. Moreover, it is also reductionist and

5 Lance H. Gunderson, 'Adaptive Dancing: Interactions Between Social Resilience and Ecological Crises', in *Navigating Social-Ecological Systems: Building Resilience for Complexity and Change*, ed. Fikret Berkes, Johan Colding and Carl Folke (Cambridge: Cambridge University Press, 2002), pp. 33–52, at p. 40 (emphasis added).

holds a fragmentary and incomplete view of systems, ignoring emergent properties which cannot be anticipated. Adaptive management, on the other hand, insists that unexpected behaviour and ecological surprises are the rule. An ecological surprise is defined as 'a qualitative disagreement between ecosystem behavior and *a priori* expectations—and environmental cognitive dissonance' (Gunderson, 'Adaptive Dancing', p. 34). For resilience approaches being *realistic* means accepting the fact that ecological surprises are normal, and that one must increment a system's capacity to cope with these constant disruptions.

Furthermore, Holling and his peers recognized that ecosystems are deeply intertwined with social systems and cannot be studied in isolation. They coined the term socio-ecological systems (SES) to better convey this interconnectedness. Along the way, they sophisticated their understanding of system dynamics, modelling how SES function through adaptive cycles, alternating between phases of relative stability and phases of reorganization and renewal. This adaptive cycle perspective redefined resilience, shifting the focus from what merely allowed a system's relationships to persist, to emphasizing the capacity to cope with disturbance while undergoing systemic reorganization to respond to changes. In essence, resilience became about how well a system can cope with disturbances by transforming adaptively in response to new conditions.

What interests us for our purposes is how this more refined approach introduced a new term to the equation: adaptive capacity. SES came to be framed as adaptive systems that cycle through four phases (i.e. the adaptive cycle): rapid growth, conservation, release (or 'creative destruction'), and reorganization.[6] During the first two phases, known as the 'fore loop', connectedness and stability increase, and the system goes through a period of accumulation (for example, of nutrients and biomass). During this loop, the system's resilience tends to decline as it becomes rigid, stable and dependent on existing structures and processes, thereby becoming 'increasingly vulnerable to disturbance'.[7] A disturbance that exceeds the system's resilience triggers a shift to the subsequent two phases, known as the 'back loop, which begins with a collapse of the previous organization in which the system loses the previous structure, and enters the release phase (or omega phase, Ω)'. In this chaotic phase, 'linkages are broken, and natural, social and economic capital leaks out of the system [...] the dynamics are chaotic [...] *uncertainty rules; all options are open*' (Walker and Salt, *Resilience Thinking*, pp. 77–8,

6 See Carl J. Walters, *Adaptive Environmental Assessment and Management* (New York: Macmillan, 1986); Lance Gunderson and C. S. Holling, *Panarchy: Understanding Transformations in Human and Natural Systems* (Washington, DC: Island Press, 2002).

7 Brian Walker and David Salt, *Resilience Thinking: Sustaining Ecosystems and People in a Changing World* (Washington, DC: Island Press, 2006), p. 77.

emphasis added). A brief phase of 'creative destruction', a term borrowed from the economist Joseph Schumpeter, initiates, and a new phase of reorganization and renewal follows. In the last phase of the cycle, the reorganization phase (alpha phase, α), 'novelty can thrive [...] small, chance events have the opportunity to powerfully shape the future. Invention, experimentation, and reassortment are the order of the day' (Walker and Salt, *Resilience Thinking*, p. 78). Walker and Salt describe the transition from the release to the reorganization phase as follows:

> in systems terms, the release phase is chaotic—there is no stable equilibrium, no attractor, no basin of attraction. The reorganization phase begins to sort out the players and to constrain the dynamics [...]. Early in the renewal, *the future is up for grabs.* This phase of the cycle may lead to a simple repetition of the previous cycle, or the initiation of a novel pattern of accumulation, or it may precipitate a collapse into a degraded state (in social systems, a poverty trap). (Walker and Salt, *Resilience Thinking*, p. 78, emphasis added)

The adaptive cycle framework reframes system stability, once heralded as a strength, as a marker of rigidity and inflexibility, indicating low resilience. In other words, stability now renders socio-ecological systems less resilient and more vulnerable. The opportunity to shape the future differently arises during brief bursts of chaos and destruction triggered by disturbances. One might assume, then, that resilience is all about transformative change and challenging the status quo, allowing pioneers to envision novel ways of shaping the future through experimentation and reassortment. Thus, resilience sells itself as the antithesis of conservatism, by calling for a more flexible and less controlling behaviour on the part of managers. It is not about maintaining stasis, but about letting systems cycle through stability and instability, fostering transformation and renewal. These disturbances are no longer seen as anomalies but as regular occurrences that intersperse phases of stability and instability. The best response to constant unrest is the capacity to adapt and renew, rather than resist change.

Rapid change and disruptions are accepted as inevitable, and there is not a lot of emphasis placed on wanting to make the current state of affairs less turbulent. For instance, they include reflections like the following from their book *Panarchy:*

> The world is now moving through a period of extraordinary turbulence, reflecting the genesis and intensification of deep economic, social, political, and cultural changes associated with the current technologic-economic revolution. In addition, the speed and magnitude of global change, the increasing connectedness of the social and natural systems at the planetary level, and the growing complexity of societies and their impacts upon

> the biosphere result in a high level of uncertainty and unpredictability. These changes pose *new threats* but also *new opportunities* for humankind. (Gunderson and Holling, *Panarchy*, p. 361, emphasis added)

> Considering the speed, magnitude and pervasiveness of the changes in our times and the fast increase in connectedness and complexity, as discussed before, the *only certainty* may be that things will indeed change very much and that the future world trajectory will not be a projection from past trends. The increase in complexity and connectedness (especially *non-evolved* and *nonplanned* connectedness) might lead, as a number of results from different areas suggest, to *decreased stability*, increased vulnerability, and sharp increase in the cost of errors. (Gunderson and Holling, *Panarchy*, p. 371, emphasis added)

The *only certainty* is that rapid global change leads to more instability due to the excessive connectedness and growing complexity of the technologic-economic revolution. Instead of attempting to revert this human-induced instability, and striving to re-establish stability, the focus has shifted to enhancing systems' ability to adapt as the unexpected arises. Thus, adaptive capacity becomes the hallmark of resilience. Turbulence and intensified change are not only accepted as givens but are reframed as opportunities for renewal. Current times inevitably create crises, but we can benefit from them by being pioneers and seizing these moments as opportunities for renewal.

Albeit their talk about 'extraordinary turbulence' resulting in high levels of uncertainty and unpredictability, they seem to trick us into believing that this uncertainty is now an inescapable fate. They easily (or realistically?) surrender to the idea that the future will be unavoidably unstable, leading us into deep uncertainty. What is particularly daunting is how, by promoting resilience as the paramount adaptive strategy to rapidly shifting global conditions, and by branding this approach as 'realistic', they are, in fact, envisioning the future in a very specific manner. They assert that this future, which they deem 'up for grabs' in the late phase of the adaptive cycle, will be inherently turbulent, emphasizing adaptation as the primary means to navigate this new normal. Instead of addressing the often-elusive socio-ecological and economic-political dynamics that are the true culprits behind this manufactured and escalating complexity—complexity which complicates management from the outset—they advocate for a pragmatic acceptance of these evolving conditions. Herein lies the true tragedy: a squandered opportunity to rethink and redirect the global development trajectory to avert future catastrophic scenarios. Instead of adopting a planned strategy to transform the world away from an inevitable catastrophic future, there is an acceptance of a future that will become more and more uncertain and unstable. By being less politically challenging and quicker to implement, resilience was thus adopted as a more palatable strategy for addressing the rapidly increasing challenges of the last decades of the twentieth century. As we will see in the next sections, instead of actually being a transformative approach, resilience has managed to leave the *status quo* that began in the 1970s fairly unchallenged.

III Governing Turbulence: Resilience as a Key Term to Twenty-First Century Governmentality

Somewhere between the 1980s and the 2000s resilience shifted from being a desired property of social-ecological systems to becoming a widely adopted strategy for tackling the monumental global challenges of the twenty-first century. Originally, Holling's ecological resilience was not intended to inform governance. However, it was soon 'plucked from the ecology literature and used in a fairly instrumental way to justify particular forms of governance'.[8] It swiftly became the go-to solution for a myriad of issues, including climate change, disaster response, national and international security, economic crises, and international development interventions. This section delves into why resilience became so appealing as a governance strategy and examines critical perspectives that challenge its effectiveness in addressing the 'great unraveling'[9] currently happening. It questions resilience's potential to induce structural, transformative change like the one needed to deal with the current climate and ecological emergency.

8 Jonathan Joseph, 'Resilience as Embedded Neoliberalism: A Governmentality Approach', *Resilience: International Policies, Practices and Discourses*, 1:1 (2013), 38–52 (p. 40).

9 The 'Great Unravelling' is a term coined by Joanna Macy and adopted by Asher Miller and Richard Heinberg in their book *Welcome to the Great Unravelling: Navigating the Polycrisis of Environmental and Social Breakdown* (Corvallis, OR: Post Carbon Institute, 2023). It describes the current period marked by compounding environmental and social crises that threaten the stability of global ecosystems and industrial societies. Unlike the 'Great Acceleration', which refers to the rapid industrial and economic growth driven by fossil fuels and technological advancements since the mid-twentieth century, the Great Unravelling highlights the inevitable consequences of this unsustainable growth. The Great Unravelling emphasizes the interconnectedness of multiple crises—such as climate change, biodiversity loss, and social inequality—that are now converging and intensifying, leading to a systemic breakdown. This period requires new ways of thinking and acting to address the root causes of these crises and to build resilience at all levels of society.

i Resilience as a Response to the Elusive Promise of Security

To begin with, it is crucial to reflect on what prompted the adoption of resilience as the soundest governance response to global challenges in our century. Scholars attribute its growing importance to a pervasive sense of radical uncertainty, spurred by numerous unforeseen events in the early 2000s, such as the 9/11 terrorist attacks, the 2007/2008 financial crisis, and increasingly frequent climate disasters. Claudia Aradau identifies the core problem as the rising recurrence of surprising events, marked by a fourfold 'un-ness': unexpected, unknowable, unpredictable, unmanageable.[10] This 'un-ness' fostered a governance approach more attuned to uncertainty, which abandoned the pretence that it was possible to prevent surprises and protect civilians against them, marking a new way of framing and managing the unknown.

In the early days, security strategies focused on calculating risks and understanding cause-effect relations to control outcomes and reduce vulnerabilities by trying to *know more*. However, as uncertainty grew, there was a growing awareness that unknowable risks could show up, which could lead to catastrophic events. This shift prompted a 'full recognition of the unknowability of the future effects of our current activities'.[11] For instance, Mikkel V. Rasmussen points out that since the end of the Cold War, Western governments have become 'much less certain of whether and when they are secure'.[12] The promise of security that once underpinned governance was subtly rephrased to acknowledge it may no longer be possible to protect people from potentially catastrophic events such as global warming, terrorist attacks, or pandemics. As Evans and Reid claim, the 'dream of lasting security [was] seconded by a catastrophic imaginary that promotes insecurity by design'.[13]

This new logic fostered alternative ways of thinking about security and governance. Instead of trying to reduce the unknown and unexpected to what is predictable, a new limit to security emerged: the *unknown unknowns*. In security studies, the unknown is often divided into *known unknowns* (risks) and *unknown unknowns* (uncertainty). Aradau and Von Munster (Aradau and Van Munster, *Politics of Catastrophe*, p. 21) highlight how

10 Claudia Aradau, 'The Promise of Security: Resilience, Surprise and Epistemic Politics', *Resilience: International Policies, Practices and Discourses*, 5:1 (2017), 73–7 (p. 82).

11 John G. Glenn, *Foucault and Post-Financial Crises: Governmentality, Discipline and Resistance* (Cham: Palgrave Macmillan, 2019), p. 87.

12 Mikkel V. Rasmussen, 2004, quoted in Claudia Aradau and Rens Van Munster, *Politics of Catastrophe: Genealogies of the Unknown* (London: Routledge, 2011), p. 18.

13 Brad Evans and Julian Reid, *Resilient Life: The Art of Living Dangerously* (Cambridge: Polity Press, 2014), p. 1.

twenty-first-century governance witnessed a strategic shift from ***known unknowns*** to ***unknown unknowns***. This shift emphasizes the inability to control the uncontrollable and an acceptance that we live in a society defined by uncontrollable dangers that push us 'beyond rational calculation into the realm of unpredictable turbulence'.[14] Post-9/11, the security discourse leaned towards uncertainty, thus redefining how governance conceptualized and came to terms with the unknown unknowns.

A clear example is found in the 2021–2 UNDP's Human Development report, 'Uncertain times, unsettled lives',[15] which strongly delivers a sense of mounting uncertainty. The report's forward by Achim Steiner begins with:

> We are living in uncertain times. The Covid-19 pandemic, now in its third year, continues to spin off new variants. The war in Ukraine reverberates throughout the world, causing immense human suffering, including a cost-of-living crisis. Climate and ecological disasters threaten the world daily. [...] Layers of uncertainty are stacking up and interacting to unsettle our lives in unprecedented ways. People have faced [...] disruptions before. But the confluence of destabilizing planetary pressures with growing inequalities, sweeping societal transformations to ease those pressures and widespread polarization present new, complex, interacting sources of uncertainty for the world and everyone in it.

Despite admitting that uncertainty has always existed, it introduces a new kind of uncertainty, that has emerged in the last decades, labelled the 'uncertainty complex':

> Global crises have piled up: the global financial crisis, the ongoing global climate crisis and Covid19 pandemic, a looming global food crisis. There is a nagging sense that whatever control we have over our lives is slipping away, that the norms and institutions we used to rely on for stability and prosperity are not up to the task of ***today's uncertainty complex***. Feelings of insecurity are on the rise nearly everywhere, a trend that is at least a decade in the making and that well precedes the Covid-19 pandemic [...] One of the frustrating ironies of the Anthropocene is that while we have more power to influence our future, we do not necessarily have any more control over it. From the climate crisis to far-reaching technological changes, other important forces—many of our own making—are expanding the set of possible outcomes, some unknowable, of any given action. For many, getting

14 Ulrich Beck, *Risk Society: Towards a New Modernity* (London: Sage Publications, 2002), p. 43.

15 UNDP (United Nations Development Programme), *Human Development Report 2021–22: Uncertain Times, Unsettled Lives: Shaping our Future in a Transforming World* (New York: UNDP, 2022), p. iii.

> from point A to point B in their lives and in their communities feels unclear, unsure, hard. (UNDP, *Human Development Report*, p. 4)

This report shows that governance strategies have very well incorporated the view not only of the world as radically uncertain and unpredictable, but of a type of uncertainty that magnifies the unknown unknowns. This uncertainty results from the piling or stacking of multiple crises, making the set of possible outcomes more unpredictable than ever and incrementing people's feeling of insecurity.

It was precisely when faith in security waned and the acceptance of radical uncertainty grew that resilience rose to prominence as the best security response. As a report from the UK's Department for International Development (DFID) put it back in 2009, 'we may not be able to protect people from stresses, shocks and catastrophic events, but we can help them withstand disasters, recover and adapt'.[16] Aradau notes that resilience is precisely the answer to the 'implicit realisation that security is [no longer] possible in a complex world eliciting surprises, while its promise remains desirable for individuals' (Aradau, 'The Promise of Security', p. 82). Evans and Reid echo this sentiment, stating that 'the liberal discourse of resilience functions to convince peoples and individuals that the dream of lasting security is impossible' (Evans and Reid, *Living Dangerously*, p. 68). Thus, as has been signalled by many critical scholars, resilience became an important tool in the governance arsenal when states could no longer guarantee security or protection for their citizens.

ii The Troubling Dimensions of Resilience as a Governance Tool

Promoting resilience as a governance strategy encompassing most fields which address security issues (understood in the broadest possible sense ranging from terrorism, financial, climate to pandemic security) in place of traditional security measures, has sparked significant criticism. This criticism generally falls into three main areas. First, resilience fosters an unquestioning acceptance of turbulence as a constitutive feature of the world, leading to a *depoliticization* of disasters, crises, and catastrophes. Second, by personalizing security and *shifting the responsibility* onto individuals and communities, it places the burden of protection on their adaptive capacities, thereby exempting the state from its role as a protector. In Mark Duffield's words: 'rather than try to make major cities disaster-proof, some security advisers

16 Camilla Toulmin, *Building Resilience for an Interdependent World: Why the Environment Matters and What DFID Should Do About It* (London: IIED, 2009), quoted in Aradau, 'The Promise of Security, p. 82.

argue it is better to accept that they are "built to be vulnerable"—the proviso being to stop demanding protection and just learn to adapt'.[17] This extends to international development, where the most vulnerable and least responsible regions for disasters and crises are expected to enhance their adaptive capacities and rely less on international aid. Finally, these arguments converge into a broader critique that aligns resilience thinking with neoliberal principles. Resilience is thus seen as a palatable approach to keep the practices of late capitalism unchallenged, since it deflects attention away from structural reforms. In what follows, I will cover these critics to better understand why resilience as governance instigates so much suspicion.

iii Depoliticizing Effects of Resilience

Concerning the first point, Wendy Brown (2006)[18] defines depoliticization as follows:

> Depoliticization involves construing inequality, subordination, marginalization, and social conflict, which all require political analysis and political solutions, as individual and personal, on the one hand, or as natural, religious, and cultural on the other. [...] Depoliticization involves removing a political phenomenon from comprehension of its *historical* emergence and from a recognition of the *powers* that produce and contour it. No matter its particular form and mechanics, depoliticization always eschews power and history in the representation of its subject. (Brown, *Regulating Aversion*, p. 15)

Resilience aligns with both vectors of depoliticization identified by Brown. By framing uncertainty as a constitutive feature of the world which becomes more pronounced over time, it naturalizes turbulence as an inevitable destiny we must uphold. As Frédéric Neyrat argues, this uncertainty has become the 'new hidden god, the *deus absconditus* of the risk society' (Neyrat, *The Unconstructable Earth,* p. 11), compelling everything and everyone to adapt to his destiny by becoming resilient (Neyrat, *The Unconstructable Earth,* p. 78). This naturalization of uncertainty prevents scrutiny of the power dynamics and history that have shaped and produced it. It also shifts focus away from the political-economic histories of exclusion and exploitation that render certain regions, communities and individuals more vulnerable to the *unknown unknowns* in the first place, thereby necessitating reliance on their resilient capacities.

17 Mark Duffield, 'How Did We Become Unprepared? Emergency and Resilience in an Uncertain World', *British Academy Review*, 21 (2013), 55–8 (p. 56).

18 Wendy Brown, *Regulating Aversion: Tolerance in the Age of Empire and Identity* (Princeton: Princeton University Press, 2006).

Michael J. Watts[19] argues that resilience thinking often overlooks the insights of critical political ecology, which examines vulnerability and marginality in both ecological and socio-economic contexts. According to Watts, vulnerability is '***produced*** by particular sorts of social and economic exposure rooted in the circuits of capital' (Watts, 'Political Ecology', p. 34). He critiques resilience thinking for framing vulnerability in a simplistic manner, focusing primarily on the capacity of systems to adapt and recover without addressing the deeper, structural causes of vulnerability. Watts points out that resilience thinking often uses the language of political ecology without critically engaging with the power dynamics and political inequalities that shape these concepts. This approach, he argues, tends to depoliticize vulnerability by treating it as a technical problem to be managed rather than a symptom of broader socio-economic and political issues: 'it is incapable of addressing the radical asymmetries of power which make some autopoietic systems function well for a few but badly for many others' (Watts, 'Political Ecology', pp. 39–40). Instead, what is on offer according to Watts is 'a bland and bloodless shopping list of "conditions" for adaptive governance, including "policy will", "coordination of stakeholders", "science", "common goals", and "creativity"' (Watts, 'Political Ecology', p. 38). The same holds for accounts of the principles of resilient systems: typically enlisted are 'diversity, institutions, community, preparedness, equity, learning, social structure, non-equilibrium dynamics, and cross-scalar perspective as defining properties' (Watts, 'Now and Then', p. 38). These indicators of resilience, which allegedly make communities less vulnerable when exposed to disruptions, obscure the political agency that is crucial to understand human and social systems. Watts concludes that resilience thinking works at the 'expense of the careful political economy that was the hallmark of political ecology from the outset' (Watts, 'Now and Then', p. 38).

In a similar vein, Muriel Cote and Andrea J. Nightingale[20] argue that resilience thinking, by problematically assuming that social and ecological system dynamics are similar and by neglecting critical social science literature on the human dimensions of environmental change, repeats the weaknesses of earlier approaches in risk and hazard science. These earlier approaches overemphasized the role of physical shocks and undertheorized the political-economic factors in conceptualizing vulnerability. It overlooked the importance of

19 Michael J. Watts, 'Political Ecology: Now and Then: The Origins of Political Ecology and the Rebirth of Adaptation as a Form of Thought', in *Routledge Handbook of Political Ecology*, ed. Tom Perreault et al. (London: Routledge, 2015), pp. 19–38.

20 Murel Cote and Andrea J. Nightingale, 'Resilience Thinking Meets Social Theory: Situating Social Change in Socio-ecological Systems (SES) Research', *Progress in Human Geography*, 36 (2012), 475–89 (p. 479).

power relations, cultural values, and historical contexts in shaping adaptive capacities. By focusing on the functionality of institutions and adaptive governance, resilience thinking often ignores the deeper, normative questions of 'resilience for whom' and 'to what end' (Cote and Nightingale, 'Resilience Thinking', p. 479). By overemphasizing very generic qualities of self-organizing systems and their adaptive cycles and understanding them as constitutive features of ecosystems and social systems without establishing differences, they end up losing sight of important differences that matter. The authors call for an epistemological shift that integrates social theory into resilience research, highlighting the need to address issues of equity, justice, and power to fully grasp the dynamics of socio-ecological systems. The reliance on ecological principles to analyse social dynamics has led to a kind of social analysis that hides the possibility of asking important questions about the role of power and culture in adaptive capacity. The authors warn that 'the slippage from descriptive to prescriptive domains in social resilience analyses, particularly in research on governance, is risky if its treatment in social action is flawed' (Cote and Nightingale, 'Resilience Thinking', p. 479).

In general, the depoliticizing effects of naturalizing turbulence and blurring the boundary between the social and the natural imply that vulnerability is framed through a lens which loses sight of many critical factors like power, agency, struggles over access and control of property, labour and the disposition of surpluses. If the root causes of vulnerability are not addressed and framed within a political perspective, the unequal appropriation of nature will continue to create more vulnerability. As stated by Duffield: 'if politics can be defined as the ability to solve root problems, post-security landscapes [which call for resilience and adaptiveness] are […] post-political. Rather than solve root problems, taking our lead from nature and the behaviour of non-human species, [with resilience] we must now endlessly and uncritically adapt to survive' (Duffield, 'How Did We Become Unprepared?', p. 56).

iv Devolution of Responsibility in Resilience Driven Approaches

Resilience thinking not only naturalizes uncertainty and vulnerability, assuming them as unchangeable features of the world, but it also personalizes solutions, aligning with Wendy Brown's second depoliticization strategy. By emphasizing the enhancement of adaptive capacities of individuals and communities, resilience thinking shifts the focus from structural changes aimed at addressing the underlying causes of turbulence to a strategy based on enhancing a population's adaptive capacities to manage the effects of said turbulence and the disasters it creates when it meets vulnerability. This approach shifts the responsibility for security from the state to populations (individuals and communities). As Jonathan Joseph states, to survive the uncertainty of our complex world, populations are expected to 'show their own initiative as active and reflective agents capable of adaptive behavior' (Joseph, *Varieties of Resilience,* p. 18). Resilience's ***modus operandi*** is to shift the focus from what are the causes of uncertainty to promoting 'strategies of learning and adaptation that shift responsibility on to populations so that they are better able to govern themselves.'[21] Its usefulness and appeal as a governance tool derives precisely from the way it can govern or manage 'populations from a distance, through the conduct of conduct' (Joseph, *Varieties of Resilience,* p. 16).

Nevertheless, despite its reliance on an allegedly active subject, who is expected to continuously adapt, self-manage, and remain vigilant in the face of constant risk and uncertainty, resilient subjects end up having a passive relation to their wider context. This is due to the implicit fatalism of how resilience constructs the world as one beyond our control and comprehension: 'resilience resigns us to the view that the increasingly complex bigger picture is beyond both our control and compression, that the human-centered project of modernity is an illusion and that we must instead pay attention to our place within the system' (Joseph, *Varieties of Resilience,* p. 20). The type of social ontology resilience fits well with one that urges us to turn from a concern with controlling or trying to change the outside world to a concern with our 'own subjectivity, our adaptability, our reflexive understanding our knowledge acquisition, our decision-making, our life-choices and our risk assessments' (Joseph, *Varieties of Resilience,* p. 20). In other words, a social ontology which shifts the emphasis onto our micro-sphere of control and makes us renounce all pretence of being able to intervene in the wider social context, which is deemed too complex to control. Thus, the best way to navigate the mounting uncertainty is not trying to question what induces it, but through greater awareness of our own behaviour in relation to it. The fatalism that arises from naturalizing turbulence means that there is little we can do in the face of catastrophic threats it creates.

Thus, as a governance tool, resilience fosters a form of subjectivity that embraces servitude as though it were liberation, leading to a lack of political imagination for transforming the world for the better. As Brad Evans and Julian Reid highlight, resilience encourages individuals to abandon the dream of achieving security and embrace danger as a condition of possibility for life in the future:

> the resilient subject is not a political subject who on its own terms conceives of changing the world, its structure and conditions of possibility. The re-

21 Jonathan Joseph, *Varieties of Resilience: Studies in Governmentality* (Cambridge: Cambridge University Press, 2018), p. 16.

> silient subject is required to accept the dangerousness of the world it lives in as a condition for partaking of that world and accept the necessity of the injunction to change itself in correspondence with threats now presupposed as endemic and unavoidable [...]. Building resilient subjects involves the deliberate disabling of the political habits, tendencies and capacities of peoples and replacing them with adaptive ones. (Evans and Reid, *Resilient Life*, p. 42)

By personalizing solutions, resilience allows resilient subjects to become active participants in their own depoliticization, promoting adaptability and self-reliance at the expense of collective political action and systemic change.

Furthermore, the devolution of responsibility also happens from the Global North to the Global South. In international development, it became a strategy to promote resilience rather than addressing the historical root causes of underdevelopment. This shift replaces the field of political transformation with an agenda that substitutes the possibility of addressing inequality and violent exclusion. The Global South in particular has become 'the testing ground for a vision of security and care in which life is nothing more than a permanent readiness and flexible adaptiveness [...]. Building resilient peasants and resilient communities in say the West African Sahel or north India turns on an unleashing their self-organizing potential by welding together indigenous capabilities and knowledge with the powers of the self-organizing market' (Watts "Political Ecology", p. 41). Furthermore, the aim of developing self-reliance in the Global South through an international development agenda as Mark Duffield has argued is a strategy to contain 'the ripple effects of poverty, environmental collapse, civil conflict or health crises' (Duffield, *Development, Security and Unending War*, p. 1) which do not respect geographical boundaries. Otherwise, they threaten to inundate and destabilize Western society. Resilience is seen as one of the tools with which development 'reflects a neoliberal political agenda that shifts the burden of supporting life from states to people (Duffield, *Development, Security and Unending War*, p. 69). It attempts to reconfigure populations by bettering their individual and collective self-reliance. It is a 'security technology that attempts to contain the circulatory effects of non-insured surplus life by putting the onus on potential migrants to adjust their expectations while improving their resilience through reliance *in situ*' (Duffield, *Development, Security and Unending War*, p. 69).

The devolution of responsibility has significant implications for political agency and imagination. By framing vulnerability and risk as natural and inevitable parts of life, resilience thinking depoliticizes these issues. Individuals and communities are encouraged to focus on personal and local adaptive strategies rather than challenging the broader political and economic structures that create and perpetuate vulnerabilities. This shift from prevention to preparedness, as Juliane Prade-Weiss notes, anticipates future losses as a given and promotes a mindset of proleptic mourning, where individuals are resigned to managing rather than preventing disasters.[22] Resilient subjects and communities are expected to be non-lamenting, and go beyond the victim/blaming mode, and stop placing responsibility on others for making their lives better. The depoliticization that takes place embraces a 'there is no alternative' conception of turbulence, adopting a neutrality and objectivity that depoliticizes the possibility of politically intervening to make the world less turbulent.

To counter the depoliticization effects of resilience, we must establish an analytical framework which denaturalizes turbulence as a constitutive feature of the world. This framework should challenge the notion of humans as an immensely adaptable 'weed species' which 'adapt[s] continually to the changing topographies of the dangers they encounter' (Evans and Reid, *Resilient Life,* p. 63). According to Neyrat, politicizing what the 'new uncertainty complex' has depoliticized requires creating a sense of distance or detachment within it: 'a *distance* within the world without which no politics whatsoever is possible' (Neyrat, *The Unconstructable Earth,* p. 72).

It is crucial to differentiate between the ways complexity sciences embrace turbulence and uncertainty, proposing an ontology of unpredictability, and the techniques of government and economic-political management that address the uncertainty of chaotic systems (Neyrat, *The Unconstructable Earth,* p. 74). While ecologists focus on managing for resilience, the challenge for politics is to stabilize turbulence so that we do not have to constantly adapt to increasing complexity. Neyrat criticizes resilience thinking for leaving untouched the causes of turbulence and only managing the consequences: 'under the pretext of a turbulent world, full of "surprises"', those who make a case for resilience-based approaches 'leave causes in the hands of industry and take as their responsibility the administration of consequences' (Neyrat, *The Unconstructable Earth,* p. 127).

If we conflate these problems and fail to make distinctions, turbulence will be seen as an unavoidable feature rather than a result of global unbridled capitalism. It will be perceived as to be managed rather than prevented. By critically examining the dimensions of resilience, we can identify a political position whose aim would be 'to *provide room for distinguishing* between what we want and what we don't want' (Neyrat, *The Unconstructable Earth,* p. 124), instead of resigning to the notion that 'there is no alternative'.

22 Juliane Prade-Weiss, 'Anticipatory Anxiety, Proleptic Mourning: Grieving Pandemic and Ecological', *Philosophy World Democracy*, 21 (2022).

v Resilience's Intuitive Fit with Neoliberal Governance

Many scholars have highlighted resilience's alignment with neoliberal forms of governmentality and with neoliberalism's approach to managing the risks and crises it perpetually generates.[23] By naturalizing turbulence and devolving responsibility to individuals' resilience fits intuitively[24] with neoliberal principles.

Neoliberalism, in this context, is understood not merely as an economic doctrine but also a socio-political order which emerged after the 1970s crisis of Keynesianism. Its principles include the rollback of the welfare state, minimalist social policies, the privatization of profits while socializing losses, reliance on market mechanisms for allocating essential goods and services, deregulation, weak environmental regulations, and the promotion of individual self-reliance and responsibility. Critical scholars often frame the link between governmentality and neoliberalism through a Foucauldian lens. Michel Foucault[25] argued that neoliberalism is not just a market-based economic system but an active form of governance.[26] This governance maintains the functioning of competitive markets via a complex set of processes and dispersed mechanisms of power, which aim to control human social and personal behaviour and actively govern populations at a distance.

Resilience is an optimal tool for such forms of governmentality because it encourages individual responsibility, self-reliance and adaptability to a crises-ridden global configuration. Unlike earlier liberal forms of governance, which focused on protecting population from dangers, neoliberalism shifts the responsibility for managing risks and uncertainties from the state to individuals and communities, absolving those in power from accountability.

23 See, for example, Brad Evans and Julian Reid, 'Dangerously Exposed: The Life and Death of the Resilient Subject', *Resilience: International Policies, Practices and Discourses*, 2:1 (2013), 83–98, doi:10.1080/21693293.2013.770703 (accessed 11 December 2024); and Jonathan Joseph, 'Resilience as Embedded Neoliberalism: A Governmentality Approach', *Resilience: International Policies, Practices and Discourses*, 1:1 (2013), 38–52, doi:10.1080/21693293.2013.765741 (accessed 11 December 2024).

24 Jeremy Walker and Melinda Cooper, 'Genealogies of Resilience: From Systems Ecology to the Political Economy of Crisis Adaptation', *Security Dialogue*, 42:2 (2011), 143–60.

25 See Michel Foucault, *The Birth of Biopolitics: Lectures at the Collège de France, 1978–1979*, ed. Michel Senellart, trans. Graham Burchell (New York: Picador, 2010).

26 On the relationship between Foucault, neoliberalism and resilience, see also Nicolas Lema Habash's chapter in this volume.

Resilience also aligns well with neoliberal environmentalism. Critical scholars argue that resilience's intuitive fit with neoliberal forms of governance secures the *status quo* and benefits those interested in addressing global risks through weak protective measures. Melinda Cooper and Jeremy Walker claim that the science of complex adaptive systems, as a theoretical reference point for the full spectrum of contemporary risk, has 'neutralized critical inquiry into the disastrous consequences of neoliberal approaches to financial regulation, urban planning and crisis response, environmental policy and development' (Walker and Cooper, 'Genealogies of Resilience', p. 144).

Critics find resilience suspicious because, while it advocates for minimal state intervention by promoting the self-reliance of individuals and communities, it ultimately allows the market to operate as the creator of spontaneous order. The market's self-ordering and auto-poietic renewal become the dominant force, overshadowing all other forms of political organization and future planning. The so-called ontological turbulence is merely a façade for the chaos generated by the current economic system, which resilience encourages us to accommodate rather than resist. As Neyrat wryly observes, the pretext that the world has become so convoluted that it can no longer follow a straight path only serves to favour the one path 'imposed upon it by the democracy of the economy and its geo-capitalism' (Neyrat, *The Unconstructable Earth,* p.81).

Resilience thinking is also critiqued for its role in the marketization and commodification of nature and social relations. By promoting resilience, policies and practices often prioritize market-based solutions (like voluntary carbon markets) and economic growth over environmental sustainability and social justice. This approach, Watts argues, reinforces existing inequalities and power imbalances, as it favours those who can afford to adapt and thrive through turbulence. Nevertheless, adaptability has limits. Regeneration and renewal cannot be always rebooted. Those limits are experienced first by the marginalized and vulnerable.

While resilience thinking offers a pragmatic approach to managing crises, it ultimately falls short by failing to address the underlying causes of our current ecological and social challenges. It has been instrumental for weak protective measures, emphasizing adaptation over mitigation, allowing destructive neoliberal capitalism to be resilient and reboot like a chameleon taking new forms after each crisis. This paradoxically pushes even further planetary limits and social vulnerability, making them in the end in need of building more resilience.

In other words, resilience thinking, remains remarkably timid in addressing the obvious causes of disasters and crises that converge toward the current destructive arrangement led by global capitalism. Despite critical voices highlighting for decades how capitalism's internal logics not only endemically creates disasters but also ingeniously turns them into opportunities for further economic expansion[27]. As stated by Mark Neocleus (2013: 4) resilience has come to be 'a fundamental mechanism for policing the political imagination, nothing less than the attempted colonization of the political imagination by the state'.[28]

IV Resilience as a Strategy for Weak Environmentalism

Jeremy Walker and Melinda Cooper in their article 'Genealogies of Resilience' and Walker's book *More Heat than Life*,[29] illustrate how two visions of the global future emerged in the 1970s in the United States, as the energy and economic crisis hit the Western world. One vision stemmed from ecosystems ecology, while the other was promoted by economists of the Chicago School. These two perspectives—the ecological and the economical—were in sharp political conflict throughout the decade.

Ecologists warned of an impending environmental catastrophe, advocating for dramatic socio-economic transformations to halt pollution, resource depletion and overheating caused by unchecked industrialization and limitless growth. This position was clearly articulated in the 1972 *Limits to Growth*[30] report, which argued for a steady-state economy to prevent catastrophic transgression of biophysical limits. The report advocated for regulating industrial economies to achieve a global equilibrium, defined as a state where 'population and capital are essentially stable, with the forces tending to increase or decrease them kept in a tightly controlled balance' (Meadows et al., *Limits to Growth*, p. 189).

Public concern for the environment was evident, as seen in the first Earth Day on 222 April 1970, which involved 20 million US citizens. The first United Nations Conference on the Human Environment in June 1972 further highlighted environmental issues, noting 'growing evidence of man-made harm' and 'major and undesirable disturbances of the ecological

27 See Naomi Klein, *The Shock Doctrine: The Rise of Disaster Capitalism* (New York: Metropolitan Books, 2007).

28 Mark Neocleous, 'Resisting Resilience', *Radical Philosophy*, 178 (2013), 2–7 (p. 4).

29 Jeremy Walker, *More Heat than Life: The Tangled Roots of Ecology, Energy, and Economics* (Singapore: Palgrave Macmillan, 2020).

30 Donella H. Meadows et al., *Limits to Growth: A Report for the Club of Rome's Project on the Predicament of Mankind* (New York: Universe Books, 1972).

balance'.[31] Principle 14 calls for 'rational planning' to balance the needs of development and environmental protection (United Nations, *Declaration and Action Plan*, pp. 5), while Principle 17 calls for the entrustment of national institutions in the 'task of planning, managing or controlling the environmental resources of States with a view to enhancing environmental quality' (United Nations, *Declaration and Action Plan*, p. 5).

The time was ripe to set an environmental agenda which placed a strong emphasis on regulation, rational planning to avert the tendency of resource depletion, pollution and undesirable disturbances. Nevertheless, despite public concern and international declarations, and dire warnings, little effective environmental action was actually taken, and what has reigned ever since is political inertia and inaction. This inaction can be partly attributed to the aggressive neoliberal countermovement in the 1970s, which opposed the calls for limits to growth and ecological equilibrium. Mainstream economists like Milton Friedman and Friedrich Hayek, along with the business establishment, viewed environmental protection efforts as threats to the American free enterprise system. They launched a neoliberal counter-revolution, advocating for the liberation of individuals and businesses from government intervention to unleash market forces and entrepreneurial innovation (Walker, *More Heat Than Life*, p. 4).

Milton Friedman, in his famous 1970 *New York Times* article,[32] argued that the sole purpose of businesses was to generate profit for shareholders, dismissing social responsibilities like providing employment, eliminating discrimination and avoiding pollution as 'preaching pure and unadulterated socialism' (Friedman, 'Social Responsibility', p. 33). He deemed expenditures for social objectives beyond legal requirements as acceptance of the socialist view that political mechanisms, not market mechanisms, were the appropriate way to allocate scarce resources.

Friedrich Hayek's 1978 Nobel prize speech, 'The Pretence to Knowledge'[33], critiqued the *Limits to Growth* report, characterizing attempts to set limits to growth as hubristic and arguing that it was impossible to predict future resource scarcity with certainty. Chicago School economists emphasized that untrammelled markets were the most efficient mechanisms

31 United Nations, *Declaration and Action Plan of the United Nations Conference on the Human Environment* (Stockholm: United Nations, 1972), p. 3.

32 Milton Friedman, 'The Social Responsibility of Business is to Increase Profits', *New York Times Magazine*, 13 September 1970, https://www.nytimes.com/1970/09/13/archives/a-friedman-doctrine-the-social-responsibility-of-business-is-to.html (accessed 11 December 2024).

33 See Friedrich A. Hayek, 'The Pretence to Knowledge', Nobel Prize Lecture, 11 December 1974, https://www.nobelprize.org/prizes/economic-sciences/1974/hayek/lecture/ (accessed 5 July 2024).

for managing an unpredictable future, which scientific reason was unable to foresee or predict, and that any government intervention was seen as futile or damaging to 'the economy' (Walker, *More Heat than Life*, p. 20).

As the last 50 years of environmental (in)action has shown, the struggle initiated between these two versions of the future was more successfully managed by the growth optimists than by the proponents of ecological limits to growth. The former's faith in market mechanism and better technologies to ensure efficiency and deal with resource depletion eventually became the preferred approach to deal with ecological problems in the upcoming decades.

In a similar vein, a strand of ecologists shifted their focus from the critical and radical conclusions regarding limits and ended up subordinate to less radical and allegedly more realistic and pragmatic solutions.[34] Resilience was one such solution. According to Walker and Cooper's hypothesis, it was precisely through their way of understanding complexity that the by then estranged twin sciences of the *oikos* (economy and ecology), despite them having diametrically opposed views of limits, equilibrium, and growth, managed to neutralize their sharp contradictions and found a great intuitive fit in their ways of calling for a new approach to complex socio-ecological systems (Walker, *More Heat than Life*, p. 5).

Hayek and Holling shared a view that rejected near-equilibrium models in favour of a second-wave cybernetics approach to complex dynamic systems, which are far from equilibrium. Hayek's hostility towards the Keynesian welfare state and government planning stemmed from his belief that planners could never have complete information, leading to inefficiency or, worse, dictatorship (Cooper and Walker, 'Genealogies of Resilience', p. 149). He argued that 'planning leads to dictatorship because dictatorship is the most effective instrument of coercion and the enforcement of ideals, and, as such, essential if central planning on a large scale is to be possible.'[35]

Hayek's vision coincides with Holling's. In the late 1970s, Holling criticized ecologists for behaving like 'latter-day prophets', and 'functioning in a fashion reminiscent of the Delphic oracle',[36] without sufficient qualifications, which often led to discrediting the scientific method when those predictions failed. In his 1978 volume *Adaptive Environmental Assessment and Management,* Holling aimed to 'sweep away some of the exaggerations of popular ecology', (Holling, *Adaptive Environmental Assessment,* p. x) such

34 Nowadays, we have plenty of them: voluntary carbon markets, 'ecosystem services', techno-utopian geoengineering or carbon capture projects.

35 Friedrich A. Hayek, *The Road to Serfdom* (Chicago: University of Chicago Press, 1944), p. 67.

36 C. S. Holling, ed., *Adaptive Environmental Assessment and Management* (Chichester: John Wiley & Sons, 1978), p. x.

as' the belief that ecosystems are universally fragile and that all environmental components must be studied before evaluating the impact of a development project' (Holling, *Adaptive Environmental Assessment,* p. x). Contrary to the 'fragility of nature' thesis, Holling argues that ecosystems are resilient and in a state of dynamic equilibrium: 'they have evolved in such a manner as to be able to withstand considerable stress before their structure and integrity are damaged' (Holling, *Adaptive Environmental Assessment,* p. x). He even suggests that 'controlled stress' can actually 'enhance the useful productivity of some systems' (Holling, *Adaptive Environmental Assessment,* p. x).

Holling calls for an end to 'reactive' assessments and management alternatives that focus on environmental protection and regulation.[37] He views this reactive response, sparked by a sudden shift of public awareness concerning environmental problems in industrialized nations, as 'arbitrary, inflexible, and unfocused' (Holling, *Adaptive Environmental Assessment,* p. 6). With advancements in ecology and system sciences, new techniques allow us to handle uncertain information, mobilize available data on partially known processes, and formulate objectives less sensitive to the unexpected. These techniques lie at the heart of developing policies that recognize and benefit from both economic and environmental realities (Holling, *Adaptive Environmental Assessment,* p. 6).

Holling argues that management alternatives should not attempt to eliminate uncertainty and the unknown, as global stability is impossible: 'however much we may be sure of the stability landscape of a physical system, we *will rarely know* the societal or ecological stability landscape *in any detail.* Policies often attempt to *reduce variability* within these *partially known* systems, either as a goal in itself or as an effort to meet standards of safety, health, or environmental quality' (Holling, *Adaptive Environmental Assessment,* p.11, emphasis added). However, such policies can lead to 'tighter monitoring, regulation, and control based upon *an illusory assumption of sufficient knowledge*' (Holling, *Adaptive Environmental Assessment,* p. 11). Therefore, adaptive assessment and management are better suited to managing uncertainty and benefiting from the unexpected. Nature must be viewed as resilient instead of fragile and stable, where resilience is defined 'as the property that allows a system to absorb and *utilize* (or even benefit from) change' (Holling, *Adaptive Environmental Assessment,* p. 11).

The parallels with Hayek's and Holling's view of how to let the market mechanism tackle social phenomena are astonishing. Both mainstream

37 It might be worth remembering the context in the 1970s, in which several environmental laws were enacted for environmental protection in the United States, including the National Environmental Policy Act (1969), the Clean Air Act (1970), the Endangered Species Act (1973), the National Forest Management Act (1976), the Resource Conservation and Recovery Act (1976).

economists and ecologists began to portray complexity as an epistemological limitation for predicting outcomes with certainty and as an ontological feature of the world. They critiqued attempts to control and manage as potentially pathological. Both argued against reducing emerging complexity and keeping systems in a near-equilibrium state, advocating instead for *working with* instead of *against* complexity. They view regulation, control, protective measures as potentially worse than the problems they aimed to solve.

This approach has worked marvellously for market-based solutions, as the market was seen as the best mechanism to deal with complexity. This led to a form of environmentalism more palatable for the American enterprise and the new liberals, which became locked-in.

A more transformative approach was needed thirty years ago to achieve true environmental sustainability with social justice. Adopting resilience as the go-to strategy in ecology and governance was a major key to delaying the structural reforms needed to avert a catastrophic future. As crises continue to pile up in 2024, it might be time, as Neyrat says, to distance ourselves from the hidden god of turbulence and uncertainty and introduce discernment into the equation. While the causes of increased turbulence are multiscalar and multidimensional, there are pretty straightforward causes to the increased turbulence: the intensive carbon lifestyles of the developed world and the global elites, an economy based on growth and the unequal development between the North and the South which made it possible. Resilience's mystique of complexity and uncertainty allowed weak environmentalism to sidestep core issues and critical intervention points. The main turbulence inducers cannot be addressed primarily by market-based solutions, which often create new problems. As Audre Lorde famously claimed: 'the master's tools will not dismantle the masters house',[38] and resilience is one such tool.

Bibliography

Aradau, Claudia, and Rens Van Munster, *Politics of Catastrophe: Genealogies of the Unknown* (London: Routledge, 2011).

Aradau, Claudia, 'The Promise of Security: Resilience, Surprise and Epistemic Politics', *Resilience: International Policies, Practices and Discourses*, 5:1 (2014), 73–87.

Beck, Ulrich, *Risk Society: Towards a New Modernity* (London: Sage Publications, 2002).

38 Audre Lorde, 'The Master's Tools Will Never Dismantle the Master's House', in *Sister Outsider: Essays and Speeches*, ed. Nancy K. Bereano (Berkeley, CA: Crossing Press, 1984), pp. 110–14.

Brown, Wendy, *Regulating Aversion: Tolerance in the Age of Empire and Identity* (Princeton: Princeton University Press, 2006).

Callinicos, Alexis. *The New Age of Catastrophe* (Cambridge: Polity Press, 2023).

Cote, Muriel, and Andrea J. Nightingale, 'Resilience Thinking Meets Social Theory: Situating Social Change in Socio-ecological Systems (SES) Research', *Progress in Human Geography,* 36 (2012), 475–89.

Duffield, Mark, 'How Did We Become Unprepared? Emergency and Resilience in an Uncertain World', *British Academy Review*, 21 (2013), 55–8.

Evans, Brad, and Julian Reid, 'Dangerously Exposed: The Life and Death of the Resilient Subject', *Resilience: International Policies, Practices and Discourses,* 2:1 (2013), 83–98, doi:10.1080/21693293.2013.770703 (accessed 11 December 2024).

Evans, Brad, and Julian Reid, *Resilient Life: The Art of Living Dangerously* (Cambridge: Polity Press, 2014).

Foucault, Michel, *The Birth of Biopolitics: Lectures at the Collège de France, 1978–1979,* ed. Michel Senellart, trans. Graham Burchell (New York: Picador, 2010).

Friedman, Milton, 'The Social Responsibility of Business is to Increase Profits', *New York Times Magazine,* 13 September 1970, https://www.nytimes.com/1970/09/13/archives/a-friedman-doctrine-the-social-responsibility-of-business-is-to.html (accessed 11 December 2024).

Glenn, John G. *Foucault and Post-Financial Crises: Governmentality, Discipline and Resistance* (Cham: Palgrave Macmillan, 2019).

Gunderson, Lance H., and C. S. Holling, *Panarchy: Understanding Transformations in Human and Natural Systems* (Washington, DC: Island Press, 2002).

Gunderson, Lance H., 'Adaptive Dancing: Interactions Between Social Resilience and Ecological Crises', in *Navigating Social-Ecological Systems: Building Resilience for Complexity and Change*, edited by Fikret Berkes, Johan Colding and Carl Folke (Cambridge: Cambridge University Press, 2002), pp. 33–52.

Hayek, Friedrich A. *The Road to Serfdom* (Chicago: University of Chicago Press, 1944).

Hayek, Friedrich A. 'The Pretence to Knowledge', *Nobel Prize Lecture*, 11 December 1974, https://www.nobelprize.org/prizes/economic-sciences/1974/hayek/lecture/ (accessed 5 July 2024).

Holling, C. S., 'Engineering Resilience versus Ecological Resilience', in *Engineering Within Ecological Constraints,* edited by Peter C. Schulze (Washington, DC: The National Academy Press, 1996), pp. 31–44.

Holling, C. S., 'Resilience and Stability of Ecological Systems', *Annual Review of Ecology and Systematics*, 4 (1973), 1–23.

Holling, C. S., ed., *Adaptive Environmental Assessment and Management* (Chichester: John Wiley & Sons, 1978).

Joseph, Jonathan, 'Resilience as Embedded Neoliberalism: A Governmentality Approach', *Resilience: International Policies, Practices and Discourses*, 1:1 (2013), 38–52, doi:10.1080/21693293.2013.765741 (accessed 11 December 2024).

Joseph, Jonathan, *Varieties of Resilience: Studies in Governmentality* (Cambridge: Cambridge University Press, 2018).

Klein, Naomi, *The Shock Doctrine: The Rise of Disaster Capitalism* (New York: Metropolitan Books, 2007).

Lorde, Audre, 'The Master's Tools Will Never Dismantle the Master's House', in *Sister Outsider: Essays and Speeches*, ed. Nancy K. Bereano (Berkeley, CA: Crossing Press, 1984), pp. 110–14.

Meadows, Donella H., Jørgen Randers and William W. Behrens III, *The Limits to Growth: A Report for the Club of Rome's Project on the Predicament of Mankind* (New York: Universe Books, 1972).

Meffe, Gary K., and C. S. Holling, 'Command and Control and the Pathology of Natural Resource Management', *Conservation Biology*, 10:2 (1996), 328–37.

Miller, Asher, and Richard Heinberg, *Welcome to the Great Unravelling: Navigating the Polycrisis of Environmental and Social Breakdown* (Corvallis, OR: Post Carbon Institute, 2023).

Neocleous, Mark, 'Resisting Resilience', *Radical Philosophy*, 178 (2013), 2–7.

Powell, Lewis F. Jr., 'Attack on American Free Enterprise System', Memorandum, 23 August 1971, https://scholarlycommons.law.wlu.edu/powellmemo/1 (accessed 5 July 2024).

Prade-Weiss, Juliane, 'Anticipatory Anxiety, Proleptic Mourning: Grieving Pandemic and Ecological Losses', *Philosophy World Democracy*, 21 (2022).

Toulmin, Camila, *Building Resilience for an Interdependent World: Why the Environment Matters and What DFID Should Do About It* (London: IIED, 2009).

UNDP (United Nations Development Programme), *Human Development Report 2021–22: Uncertain Times, Unsettled Lives: Shaping our Future in a Transforming World* (New York: UNDP, 2022).

United Nations, *Declaration and Action Plan of the United Nations Conference on the Human Environment* (Stockholm: United Nations, 1972).

Walker, Brian, and David Salt. *Resilience Thinking: Sustaining Ecosystems and People in a Changing World* (Washington, DC: Island Press, 2006).

Walker, Jeremy, *More Heat than Life: The Tangled Roots of Ecology, Energy, and Economics* (Singapore: Palgrave Macmillan, 2020).

Walker, Jeremy, and Melinda Cooper, 'Genealogies of Resilience: From Systems Ecology to the Political Economy of Crisis Adaptation', *Security Dialogue*, 42:2 (2011), 143–60.

Walters, Carl J, *Adaptive Environmental Assessment and Management* (New York: Macmillan, 1986)

Watts, Michael J, 'Political Ecology: Now and Then: The Origins of Political Ecology and the Rebirth of Adaptation as a Form of Thought', in *Routledge Handbook of Political Ecology*, edited by Tom Perreault, Gavin Bridge and James McCarthy (London: Routledge, 2015), pp. 19–38.

Part II
Application

7

Resilience and Race in the Hagiographic Tradition of St Martin of Porres

Celia Cussen

A certain member of the order, without cause or occasion offered by said venerable Martin of Porres, because he never offered one, spoke violently to him, calling him a mulatto dog that ought to be [an enslaved rower] in a galley ship, and other insults of this type … and Friar Martin, with a joyful and smiling face, knelt before this friar and bent to the floor to kiss his feet, saying he deserved this and worse for his wickedness.[1]

[En una ocasión vio este testigo que cierto religioso de la dicha Orden, sin causa ni ocasión que diese el dicho venerable hermano fray Martin de Porras, porque nunca las daba, le trató mal de palabra, diciéndole que era un perro mulato y que merecía estar en una galera, y otros oprobios desta calidad, [y] fray Martín, con el rostro alegre y risueño, se hincó de rodillas delante del dicho religioso y se echó en el suelo a vesarle los pies, diciendo que mucho más merecía por sus maldades.]

I Introduction

In 1660 a Dominican friar stood before an assembly of ecclesiastical judges in Lima and gave his testimony in the canonization case of the Afroperuvian professed lay nurse, Martin of Porres (1579–1639). Rough words such as

1 Secretariado 'Martín de Porres', *Proceso de beatificación de fray Martín de Porres* (Palencia, Spain: Secretariado 'Martín de Porres', 1906), p. 303.

those this witness claims were directed at Martin were not unexpected in the rigidly hierarchical society. In addition to eliciting the occasional contemptuous epithets, those of enslaved African descent, like Martin, faced concrete limitations in colonial Lima; he could never aspire to the priesthood, for example. The early canonization testimonies contain only a few episodes of racial slurs, but these and other signs of racism were invariably included in the historiographies of subsequent generations as a reminder to readers of the racialized hierarchies that characterized colonial Peru and the Americas in general. His endurance of discrimination undoubtedly underlay John XXIII's decision to elevate Martin to the altars of sainthood in 1962 as the patron saint of racial justice.

Current research on Martin of Porres has focused on the racialized ill treatment directed at him, as well as his ability to absorb the pain of these attacks with patience and humility. They see this as evidence of a presumably racist tradition of the Catholic Church. In this reading, the Church constructed and promoted the life story of this saintly Black man as a model of the accepting victim of abject conditions. For these critics, Martin of Porres is a symbol of a colonized Catholic who bowed his head under the yoke of structural racism. One scholar, for example, has recently contended that his sainthood 'has helped to promote, sanction, and excuse white mastership'.[2] One might remind these critics that notions of difference in Spanish America were based on a complex and fluid set of factors that included skin colour, economic position, social capital, and even a demonstrated adherence to Spanish culture. Colonial ethnoracial categories did not adhere to strict biological definitions, nor were they dependent on observable physical traits. Even the meanings of terms that would seem to denote African ancestry, such as *mulato*, could shift over time and from place to place in ways that rendered them multilayered, fluid categories of identity.[3] Unlike their Anglo American counterparts, subjects of the Spanish Empire could move

2 Katie Walker Grimes, *Fugitive Saints: Catholicism and the Politics of Slavery* (Minneapolis: Augsburg Fortress Press, 2017), p. 75. For a review of writing that traces the history of this assertion among black theologians see Ronald L. Sharps, 'Black Catholic Gifts of Faith', *U.S. Catholic Historian*, 15 (1997), pp. 29–55, access link: https://www.jstor.org/stable/i25154598 (accessed 13 December 2023).

3 Joanne Rappaport, *The Disappearing Mestizo: Configuring Difference in the Colonial New Kingdom of Granada* (Durham, NC: Duke University Press, 2014), p. 173; Ben Vinson III, *Before Mestizaje: The Frontiers of Race and Caste in Colonial Mexico* (New York: Cambridge University Press, 2017), p. xiii; María Elena Martinez, *Genealogical Fictions: Limpieza de Sangre, Religion, and Gender in Colonial Mexico* (Stanford, CA: Stanford University Press, 2008), p. 7; Ruth Hill, *Hierarchy, Commerce and Fraud in Bourbon Spanish*

horizontally and even vertically within the complex social structure, passing between social categories by means of an advantageous marriage, for example, or as the result of a successful career as an artisan. As scholars of Latin America Catholicism have noted, in the colonial period, sainthood for African-descended people was often interpreted to be a sign of the universalism of the faith and a metaphor of the light of baptism overcoming the 'dark' circumstances of one's birth.[4]

What are we to make, then, of the references to race-based discrimination in the early versions of Martin's life story that were underscored and expanded in later hagiographies directed toward twentieth-century Catholics throughout Africa, Asia, Europe and Latin America? Perhaps beyond condemning them as evidence of a structural racism of colonial Catholicism, we might ask how Martín's reaction to these affronts resonated with his biographers and, presumably, his devotees. In this more nuanced view, one might consider Martin of Porres' social and racial condition and the suffering it brought him as forces that fortified a wisdom gained from pain, and a sturdiness from adversity. His story becomes one of resilience, the ability to adapt to hardship and overcome it as a form of resistance and strengthening.

This chapter seeks to analyse how, beginning in the nineteenth century, the hagiographic tradition propelling Martin of Porres' devotion increasingly underscored his ability to transform the difficult circumstances of his birth into opportunities for charitable actions and spiritual growth. Although his early biographers understood that the hardships of Martin's birth and his response to racial attack and the customary discrimination prevalent in the colonial world were essential elements of his story, they did not envision them to be the heart of his appeal, which dwelt on episodes of healing and his mystical proximity to Christ. Yet, as we shall see, the focus on his birth and early childhood became more pronounced in nineteenth-century Peru. These writers described his as a life of resilience, a model that was adopted by missionaries among African Americans in the United States and elsewhere, when the campaign to recognize Martin as a saint of the Catholic Church was striving toward its goal. The colour of his skin, his African features and

---

America: A Postal Inspector's Expose (Nashville, KY: Vanderbilt University Press, 2005), pp. 197–238.

4 On the life and colonial hagiographies of Martin of Porres and the meaning of Spanish colonial Black saintliness see Celia Cussen, *Black Saint of the Americas* (London and New York: Cambridge University Press, 2014); Erin Kathleen Rowe, 'After Death, Her Face Turned White: Blackness, Whiteness, and Sanctity in the Early Modern Hispanic World', *American Historical Review*, 121 (2016), pp. 726–54; and Larissa Brewer-García, *Beyond Babel: Translations of Blackness in Colonial Peru and New Granada* (New York and London: Cambridge University Press, 2020), pp. 493–4.

the enslaved past of Martin's mother took on increasing prominence in the versions of the story written by Dominican friars in the United States for the edification of their white and black parishioners, for example. There, the story of Martin enriched the message to black Catholics, who suffered the systematic discrimination of the Jim Crow era, that their suffering echoed the Biblical strife of the Israelites and the passion of Christ.

Resilience is a concept that has entered the general vocabulary to denote the ability to adapt to adversity in a positive and enduring way. Scholars of religion have employed the term to speak of the spiritual growth gained from the trials wrought upon God's chosen people in the Bible.[5] Theologian David Carr argues that suffering and its survival were virtually 'written into' into the Old Testament, which he describes as a 'deposit of centuries of survival of suffering, communal resilience'. As a part of the broad story of redemption, he writes, the Israelites were subjected to great episodes of displacement and disasters, even slavery, but God carried them through the suffering to greater knowledge (Carr, *Holy Resilience,* pp. 3, 6). The New Testament continues the narrative of injustice and pain, offering Christ as the model of resilience in the face of persecution, including for those who follow him. 'If the world hates you, know that it has hated me before you. … If they persecuted me, they will persecute you' (John 15:18–20) (Carr, *Holy Resilience,* 3, 6). Andrew Byers elaborates on the idea that, for Christians, suffering, social exclusion and even death at the hands of darkness is inevitable, and he agrees with the notion that Christianity offers modes of resilience, especially the ability to emulate Christ's adaptation to overwhelming adversity. Thus, Christians, following the example of Christ, are called to transform suffering into glory. Nevertheless, he adds, the ability to grow from pain is more than a human challenge; ultimately it is 'a divine gift' (Byers, 'Abide', pp. 74–80). Christianity is helpful for thinking about the portrayal of Martin of Porres' response to the insults and other forms of rejection he suffered, an issue that conceivably would have meaning for descendants of enslaved Africans throughout the Americas.

The infant Martin of Porres was baptized in Lima in the spring of 1579, as the son of an unknown father who was later revealed to be Juan de Porras, a Spaniard with business and family connections in Ecuador. His mother Ana Velásquez was a formerly enslaved woman of African descent. In a sign of his public, if not formal, recognition of his offspring, Martin's father

5 Andrew J. Byers, 'Abide in Me: A Johannine Theology of Resilience', in *Biblical and Theological Visions of Resilience: Pastoral and Clinical Insights*, ed. Nathan H. White and Christopher C. H. Cook (London and New York: Routledge, 2020), pp. 70–83, doi:10.4324/9780429001185 (accessed 13 December 2023); and David McLain Carr, *Holy Resilience: The Bible's Traumatic Origins* (New Haven, CT: Yale University Press, 2014).

travelled with him and his sister, Juana, to Guayaquil, Ecuador when they were children. Sometime later he sent the boy back to the care of his mother, a household servant in Lima. At age fifteen Martin entered the populous Dominican convent as a voluntary lay friar, *donado*, where he gradually took on the duties of barber and nurse in the monastery's infirmary. For over forty years Martin of Porres swept the ward, changed the linen, snipped hair, sutured wounds and relieved as best he could the fevers and other illnesses that afflicted the order's friars, servants, and slaves in the convent in central Lima as well as in the Dominican hacienda several miles to the south.

To the residents of the erstwhile capital of the Viceroyalty of Peru, a city that glittered with symbols and manifestations of the divine, Martin was a modest but captivating servant of the Dominican order who exemplified the Catholic virtues of obedience, humility and charity. He was also known as a prodigious miracle-worker, whose fingertips could expertly bind a wound or chase off a fever. His kindness extended to individuals of all walks of life, from elite Hispanic clergymen to the Indian villagers and Black slaves who laboured in the countryside outside Lima. The witnesses to Martin's life, convoked by the local bishop and the Vatican, detailed a series of episodes that attested to his human qualities and divine gifts, including the reputed ability to heal the sick in China or console captive Christians on the Barbary Coast without leaving the convent walls in Lima. After his death, a series of individuals came forward to attest to the miracles worked by God through their appeal to the holy mulatto. Although they were eager to see their local hero added to the rolls of Catholic saints, his case crept through the various stages of official recognition over the next three hundred years.

II The Peruvian hagiographies

Writing several decades after Martin of Porres' death, his first biographer, the Dominican friar Bernardo de Medina, does not mention the baptismal certificate that attests to his father's initial reluctance to acknowledge his son, but rather insists that Juan de Porras, in a gesture unusual in a noble, recognized the boy by taking him to Guayaquil, Ecuador. There his father introduced Martin to his relatives, effectively acknowledging his paternity.[6] Martin's facial features, hair, and skin colour are likewise not subjects of much discussion in this early version of his life story, except to say that he was 'brown, not white [*blanco*] in color', although he was indeed 'blanco'

6 Bernardo de Medina, OP, *Vida prodigiosa del venerable siervo de Dios Fr. Martín de Porras, natural de Lima, de la tercera orden de N.P. Santo Domingo* (Madrid: Domingo García Morras, 1673), pp. 25–8.

(target) of generalized admiration. His mother was of lowly status ('bajeza') as a formerly enslaved servant, but her skin colour and that of his father were portents of Martin's vocation in the Dominican convent, where friars donned robes of black and white. In another reference to his ancestry, Medina remarks that Martin stood out among other boys of his age and colour who 'are carried away by vices' ['se dejan llevar ordinariamente de los vicios'] (Medina, *Vida,* pp. 25–8).

While living in the convent, Martin was vilified and insulted, writes Medina. He includes in his narrative the testimony of a Dominican who, as will be recalled, reportedly referred to the convent healer as a 'mulatto dog'. Like the protomartyr, St Stephen, Martin had prostrated himself at the feet of the offender, and claimed that he deserved those words and much more 'for his wickedness' (Medina, *Vida,* p. 35). He was often the object of insults from his superiors, adds Medina, but his reaction to these attacks is overwhelming evidence of Martin's patience and humility, cardinal virtues of the faith. Finally, Medina states that when the convent was short of cash, the prior sent Martin out to beg, at which point Martin suggested that to relieve its financial distress, the convent should 'sell this mulatto dog, who is a slave of the order' ['venda aeste perro mulato, pues es de la Religión esclavo']. Naturally, the prior objected to this proposal, arguing that the convent needed Martin (Medina, *Vida,* p. 42).

This early biography conforms to the hagiographic tradition of the time that sets up the saintly individual as a paragon of the universal virtues all Christians are called on to demonstrate. Nonetheless, the account indicates a correlation between his colour, his suffering, and his proximity to Christ. This is particularly evident in Martin's repeated acts of penance when he scourged himself severely to induce a mystical state, and elevated in rapture before the life size cross in the convent chapter room, his blood mingled with that of the crucified Christ (Cussen, *Black Saint*, pp. 170–9).

A second, very successful version of Martin of Porres' life story was published in 1839 by José Manuel Valdez, Lima's chief medical authority and an Afroperuvian who, by his own reckoning, shared the same 'lowly class and humble birth' ['ínfima clase y humilde nacimiento'] as Martin, for Valdez was also the son of an formerly enslaved Afroperuvian woman and an unknown father.[7] He writes that Martin's father refused to sign the parish baptismal certificate out of shame. The reprehensible custom of refusing to recognize children born 'criminally in persons of lower class', writes Valdez, 'continues to this day'. (Valdez, p. 16.) Valdez repeats the story that Martin

7 José Manuel Valdez, *Vida admirable del bienaventurado Fray Martín de Porres* [1839] (Lima: Huerta, 1863), p. 16.

was called a 'mulatto dog' by an aspiring member of the order, among others, to which the convent healer responded that he was indeed 'a mulatto dog and a great sinner', due to the fact, as the friar knew, 'my mother was black'. ['soy un perro mulato, gran pecador, pues conoció a mi madre que era negra'.) (Valdez, p. 92). In this way, in Valdez's telling, Martin links his abject status to his mother's origins, in a place and time where 'negra' denoted her former condition of enslavement.

The definitive Peruvian twentieth-century edition of Martin of Porres' life is that published in 1949 by the Jesuit Rubén Vargas Ugarte. In his work, Vargas cites and recognizes Valdez's important biography of a century earlier, but also sustains that there was a need for a new, shorter version, one adapted to 'modern taste' ['gusto moderno'] and, if possible, closer to the historical truth.[8] He is aware of the American biographies that had begun to circulate, including the immensely popular summary of Martin's life by Norbert Georges, which we will turn to shortly. Nevertheless, he appears to differ from the American approach to the story, and even the original Medina version, as he omits a mention of Martin's colour and his father's rejection of his child at birth. Rather, he claims that when the elder Porres took Martin and his sister Juana to Guayaquil where he resided, the older man confessed to his relatives without hesitation ['sin turbar'] that he was the father of the two 'mulatillos', and he was therefore obligated to provide for them. Where Vargas Ugarte does mention colour, it is in connection with the quality of Martin's soul: 'the innocence of his soul shown through his brown and delicate face' ['en su rostro mate y delicado se transparentaba la Inocencia de su alma'] (Vargas Ugarte, *Vida*, p. 17). Furthermore, he claims that the child's life had taken place in peace and safety, whether in the hands of his mother or the home of one of his relatives' ['había deslizado tranquila y segura, ya al amparo de su madre, ya en el hogar de uno de sus deudos'] (Vargas Ugarte, *Vida*, p. 17). Vargas Ugarte omits mentions of racial epithets, and paints a consistent portrait of Martin of Porres as a devout, serious man of medicine who was widely respected and admired by all.

Despite the popularity of the Peruvian narratives that aimed to sustain the local devotion to Martin of Porres as model and intercessor, progress toward canonization moved slowly. The pope elevated Martin to the status of *beatus* in 1837, almost two centuries after his death, after which the case for canonization seemed to lose momentum. Things were to pick up again in the twentieth century, however, when the devotion to San Martin de Porres acquired a relevance and resonance in various parts of the world, especially in the United States. The first known evidence of this American interest in

8 Rubén Vargas Ugarte, *Vida de San Martín de Porras* (Buenos Aires: Imprenta López, 1963), p. 9.

the cause comes from the African American congregants of St Matthew's Parish in Washington, DC who, in 1864, chose Martin as the patron of the city's first chapel and school for free Blacks, forerunners of what would later become St Augustine Parish (Cussen, *Black Saint,* p. 188). This devotion to the Afroperuvian healer would be linked to an emerging hagiography with a modern bent, one that focused on Martin's enslaved African origins, the suffering he endured as a result, and his ability to overcome and grow from this injustice, a sign of resilience in the face of racism.

III American narratives

In the American hagiographic tradition, St Martin of Porres' race and the ability to endure and grow from discrimination is central. One of the first of the brief life stories, and one that would prove to be immensely popular, was Norbert Georges, OP, *Meet Brother Martin!* (1935).[9] Written in 1935, the short history gives a harsh view of Martin's early years, especially with regard to his relationship with his father: 'It wounded [Juan de Porras'] dignity as a conqueror to have a son and daughter who resembled the conquered, and pride touched to the quick, drove him to crush within himself the tender emotion of a father and to turn haughtily from children who came only to humiliate him. He shamefully left mother and children to take care of themselves' (Georges, *Meet,* p. 8). But Georges presents degradation as a springboard to resilience, saying that '[Martin] was reared amidst circumstances that ordinarily have a hardening effect on character, but which, for Martin, were the occasion of self-improvement and supernaturalization'. His experiences of humble beginnings and the immersion in a highly unjust world gave him an appreciation for human suffering that would characterize him throughout his life (Georges, *Meet,* p. 9).

Months later, another Dominican, Edward Hughes, would address his radio audience with the news that Martin was increasingly recognized by Catholics as a man who had 'trumpeted down the barriers and terrific prejudices of three hundred years ... a gallant religious hero ... the glorious symbol of man's triumph over self and the deceits of life'.[10] Hughes told his listeners that Martin's father, Juan, out of 'parental resentment' deserted

9 Norbert Georges, OP, *Meet Brother Martin!* (New York: The Torch, 1935). This text went through twenty-one editions before 1962. Cussen, *Black Saint,* pp. 191–4.

10 This radio address was delivered on 28 June, 1936. It was later published: Edward Hughes, OP, 'Rome May Soon Canonize an American Negro', *The Colored Harvest* (1936), pp. 5–7.

the boy, his sister, and their mother, who were stigmatized by 'color and birth.. amidst the sordid conditions of a destitute and oppressed people'. Nonetheless, Hughes continued, the boy never succumbed to the 'malicious cynicism that such would quite naturally create'. Rather, he exhibited a 'goodness of character, sturdiness of soul, an unusually amiable disposition and an extraordinary compassion for the suffering and unfortunate [that] exalted him above the teeming populace of Lima' (Hughes, 'Rome May Soon', p. 6). His strength of character allowed him to confront the difficulties of the times and engage in 'practical Christianity', devoting himself, says Hughes, to building a hospital, an orphanage and a school, and inaugurating a 'social security program proper to the time in reforestation and the cultivation of the soil' (Hughes, 'Rome May Soon', p. 8). [11]

The following year Father John Chrysostom Kearns published another biography of saintly Martin of Porres, one in which race comes to the forefront once again, as well as the ability to overcome the humiliation of rejection by his own parents. Kearn writes, 'The child [Martin] definitely inherited the dark skin and features of his mother's race. This heritage quickly displeased the Spanish cavalier [his father], and as with the passage of time the infant more and more clearly evidenced the physical characteristics of a race that was then held in bondage, the proud father felt that the dignity of his family had been impaired and he lost much of the affection that he had entertained for the child's mother'.[12] His mother, Ana, was also painfully aware of the child's colour, says Kearns, remarking that 'she could not but feel that her social status would have greatly improved had her little son more closely resembled his Castilian father' (Kearns, *The Life,* p. 12). In the Kearns story, despite the humiliation to which he was subjected by his father and others who insulted him. 'With all the ardor of his soul he strove to set aside the barriers of racial prejudice and injustice … But since humility and sweetness are a sure way to disarm insult and injury, Martin has given us heroic examples not merely of practising meekness, but even of eagerly seeking out opportunities for his own personal humiliation' (Kearns, *The Life,* p. 12). The degradation was taken with humility, but it did nothing to crush his spirit nor did it diminish his capacity to elicit the admiration of a city that constantly required his healing hands. Kearns shows him working so many cures among the merchants and priests of the city, as well as the poor Indians and Blacks, that he acquired a reputation and fame 'from which in his modesty he naturally shrank' (Kearns, *The Life,* p. 17).

11 These actions are not part of the colonial record.

12 John Chrysostom Kearns, OP, *The Life of Blessed Martín de Porres: Saintly American Negro and Patron of Social Justice* (New York: P. J. Kennedy, 1937), pp. 12–17.

As a result of worldwide attention, the case for Martin of Porres' canonization advanced over the ensuing years throughout the world. His life of overcoming racial hardship was taken up again in 1962 in an article by the Jesuit priest, Richard M. McKeon, in the midst of rumours of the impending canonization of Martin de Porres.[13] Writing in the *Interracial Review*, McKeon focused on what he called the 'contradiction' of Martin's life: 'Rejected by his father while still a helpless babe, not too well loved by his mother, who would dare expect a saint-to-be to spring from such a pitiful origins? Martin's life was in close imitation of Our Lord, who 'went about doing good yet ever subject to cruel misunderstanding'. Martin had put into action the ideals of social justice, insists McKeon, because from his own cruel experience he knew what hunger meant and was aware of the 'social evils crushing men's bodies and souls' (McKeon, 'Saint Martin', pp. 116–17). From a man of abject origins, he concludes, Martin of Porres became a model of interracial action.

IV Conclusion

The case of Saint Martin of Porres demonstrates how the notion of resilience was increasingly, though implicitly, embodied in the hagiographic tradition elaborated in Peru and, most especially, in the United States. The hard face of racial discrimination was a daily presence in the lives of Black men and women of the Jim Crow era in the United States, which became the site of the greatest campaign for Martin's canonization. These devotional biographies made him a relatable figure, a spiritual guide, and a brother to the Black Americans that the Dominican friars were hoping to attract to the Church. The diminished life chances for a person of enslaved African ancestry in colonial Lima, compounded by a lack of paternal recognition, were overcome by Martin through his absorbing commitment to healing and consoling the sick of all social standings. The clerical authors who penned versions of his life story emphasized the abuse to which he was subjected, including from his own parents, and made it the background to Martin's humble acceptance of his condition which gave way to acts of compassion. His ability to withstand scorn and transform it into a deeper engagement with the suffering of Christ, as well as a strong propensity to serve others, made Martin of Porres an example of resilience for Catholics.

The devotion to Martin of Porres extended across the Catholic world in the decades surrounding his canonization in 1962. Images, parishes and social centres were created under his patronage not only in the United States

13 Richard M. McKeon, 'Saint Martin—A Sign and a Contradiction', *Interracial Review*, 35 (1962), pp. 116–18.

and Peru but elsewhere in Latin America, Africa, Asia and Europe. His life story of rejection and social abjection echoed among men and women of diverse conditions, including those who had no connection to enslaved ancestry. Given evidence of its popularity, the devotion resonated among those who had suffered social degradation, and who understood that Martin of Porres offered a model for overcoming these obstacles to lead meaningful, even extraordinary, lives of service.

Bibliography

Primary sources

The Colored Harvest

Georges, Norbert, OP. *Meet Brother Martin!* (S/F: 1935).

Kearns, John Chrysostom, OP. *The Life of Blessed Martín de Porres: Saintly American Negro and Patron of Social Justice* (New York: PJ Kennedy, 1937).

McKeon, Richard M., 'Saint Martin—A Sign and a contradiction', *Interracial Review*, 35 (1962), pp. 116–18.

Medina, Bernardo de, OP, *Vida prodigiosa del venerable siervo de Dios Fr. Martín de Porras, natural de Lima, de la tercera orden de N.P. Santo Domingo* (Madrid: Domingo García Morras, 1675).

Secretariado 'Martín de Porres', *Proceso de Beatificación de fray Martín de Porres* (Palencia, Spain: Secretariado 'Martín de Porres', 1906), p. 303.

Valdez, José Manuel, *Vida admirable del bienaventurado Fray Martín de Porres* [1839] (Lima: Huerta, 1863).

Vargas Ugarte, Rubén, *Vida de San Martín de Porras* [1949] (Buenos Aires: Imprenta Lopez, 1963).

Secondary sources

Brewer-García, Larissa, *Beyond Babel: Translations of Blackness in Colonial Peru and New Granada* (New York and London: Cambridge University Press, 2020).

Byers, Andrew, 'Abide In Me: A Johannine Theology of Resilience', in *Biblical and Theological Visions of Resilience: Pastoral and Clinical Insights*, edited by Nathan H. White and Christopher C. H. Cook (London and New York: Routledge, 2020), pp. 70–83, doi:10.4324/9780429001185 (accessed 13 December 2023).

Carr, David McLain, *Holy Resilience: The Bible's Traumatic Origins* (New Haven, CN: Yale University Press, 2014).

Cussen, Celia, *Black Saint of the Americas: The Life and Afterlife of Martín de Porres* (New York and London: Cambridge University Press, 2014).

Grimes, Katie Walker. *Fugitive Saints: Catholicism and the Politics of Slavery.* (Minneapolis, MN: Augsburg Fortress Press, 2017).

Hill, Ruth, *Hierarchy, Commerce and Fraud in Bourbon Spanish America: A Postal Inspector's Exposé* (Nashville, TN: Vanderbilt University Press, 2005).

Martínez, María Elena, *Genealogical Fictions: Limpieza de Sangre, Religion, and Gender in Colonial Mexico* (Stanford, CA: Stanford University Press, 2008).

Rappaport, Joanne, *The Disappearing Mestizo: Configuring Difference in the Colonial New Kingdom of Granada* (Durham, NC: Duke University Press, 2014).

Rowe, Erin Kathleen, 'After Death, Her Face Turned White: Blackness, Whiteness, and Sanctity in the Early Modern Hispanic World,' *American Historical Review*, 121 (2016), pp. 726–54.

Sharps, Ronald L, 'Black Catholic Gifts of Faith', *U.S. Catholic Historian*, 15 (1997), pp. 29–55, https://www.jstor.org/stable/i25154598 (accessed 13 December 2023).

Vinson III, Ben, *Before Mestizaje: The Frontiers of Race and Caste in Colonial Mexico* (New York and London: Cambridge University Press, 2017).

8

Resilience in Gabriel García Márquez's *One Hundred Years of Solitude*

Stephen M. Hart

In this chapter I will be arguing that Gabriel García Márquez's novel, *Cien años de soledad* (One Hundred Years of Solitude, 1967) is the archetypal story of Latin American resilience. It provides a narrative—through the guise of the story of the vicissitudes experienced by the five generations of a Latin American family—about the birth of Latin America followed by the story of its struggle to achieve political and then economic independence. The characters in the novel fight for the ideals they believe in against what seem to be almost impossible odds. The enormity of those challenges is underlined by the finale of the novel which describes how the final scion of the Latin American family succumbs to his apocalyptic destiny 'because races condemned to one hundred years of solitude did not have a second opportunity on earth'.[1] Why should we see García Márquez's story as one of resilience and not, for example, as one of tragedy? If we were to focus on the ending in the final chapter of *One Hundred Years of Solitude* as the matrix hieroglyph through which to survey the novel, it is likely that we would see the novel as an unrelenting description of an inevitable disaster or as a tragedy. But if we see the banana strike in Chapter 15 of the novel, as Gerald Martin has done, as 'the central shaping episode of the entire novel',[2] then we are more likely to see the novel as a story of Latin American resilience. The

1 *One Hundred Years of Solitude*, trans. Gregory Rabassa (Harmondsworth: Penguin, 1973), p. 422.

2 Gerald Martin, *Journeys through the Labyrinth: Latin American Fiction in the Twentieth Century* (London: Verso, 1989), p. 229.

events of December 1928 in Colombia were highly significant for the direction that the country would later take. It was during the eruption caused by the collision of the Right and the Left at that precise time that Colombia's 'pueblo' stepped forward into the limelight of world history. It is, as I hope to show, a story of resilience rather than simply a modern-day version of Aristotelian tragedy.

The Meanings of Resilience

Resilience, of course, is an elusive term. The Oxford Languages dictionary definition of 'resilience' offers 'the capacity to withstand or to recover quickly from difficulties; toughness' as well as 'the ability of a substance or object to spring back into shape; elasticity'.[3] These two definitions—the first of which refers to the human world, the second to the phenomenal world—already alert us to some of the problems underpinning the word. For the cognate words offered for the two separate definitions—'toughness' vs. 'elasticity'—pull the original word 'resilience' in different direction, each persuading us to think of something that is 'hard' (i.e. tough) yet also 'soft' (elastic).

Based on this, we could be forgiven for trying our luck with etymology. The original meaning of the term grew out of the idea of the ability to 'bounce back'; thus, resilience can be traced back to the Latin word 'resalire' which translates as 'walking or leaping back'. In many disciplines, resilience denotes the capacity to rebound or recover after a shock or an event.[4] As Lance Gunderson points out, 'some scholars use the term to describe the amount of time needed to recover following an external force or perturbation'.[5] Initially, it provided an important hermeneutic tool for the physical sciences where it was viewed through the lens of a positivist epistemology about how the human habitat could be strengthened against natural disasters—often this took the form of engineers trying to produce sturdier materials with which to make bridges. From the 1970s onwards the concept of resilience spread to the social sciences where a constructivist approach was favoured, that is, one in which the notion of resilience—rather than being an objective given—depends on the subjective world of human perception, values, cultures, agency and ontologies.[6] Nowadays

3 https://www.cppe.ac.uk/support/resilience/ (consulted on 18 August 2025).

4 Lance Gunderson, 'Ecological and Human Community Resilience in Response to Natural Disasters', *Ecology and Society*, 15.2 (June 2010), 18 (online).

5 Gunderson, 'Ecological and Human Community', p. 2.

6 See Fiona Miller et al., 'Resilience and Vulnerability: Complementary or Conflicting Concepts?', *Ecology and Society*, 15.3 (September 2010).

resilience seems to be a panacea for all sorts of problems in fields ranging from economics (Brunnermeir's *The Resilient Society*) to behavioural psychology (Neenan's *Developing Resilience*).[7]

For a number of modern commentators, indeed, resilience is the 'new' miracle. Michael Hopkin, a neuroscientist, has written about how a 'Miracle Recovery' shows the brain's 'resilience'.[8] Arielle Essex, a self-help guru, uses a similar metaphor; she writes about *Practical Miracles*, and the journalist Elenor P. Ratcliff works with a number of stories of people who refused to give up on their dreams in her book, *You are a Champion: A Memoir of Miracles and Pure Resilience in Crisis*.[9] The list of ways in which resilience has been used to throw light on new areas of knowledge is astounding. These include resilience and empire building,[10] climate resilience,[11] resilience and food sovereignty,[12] resilience and human health,[13] and resilience and the arts,[14] to name but a few. To these developments we should add the discoveries advanced by contemporary ecological-biophysical research that studies the connectedness between human, animal, vegetal and elemental

7 Markus K. Brunnermeir, *The Resilient Society* (Princeton, NJ: Princeton University Press, 2021); Michael Neenan, *Developing Resilience: A Cogntive-Behavioural Approach* (London: Routledge, 2009).

8 '"Miracle recovery" shows brain's resilience', *Nature*, 3 July 2006.

9 Arielle Essex, *Practical Miracles: Choices that Heal and Build Resilience* (London: Hay House, 2013); Elenor P. Ratcliff, *You are a Champion: A Memoir of Miracles and Pure Resilience in Crisis* (Austin, TX: Lnoirs Fidelity Publishing, 2020).

10 Abraham Carmel and Gideon D. Markman, 'Capture, Governance and Resilience: Strategy Implications from the History of Rome', *Strategic Management Journal*, 32.3 (March 2011), 322–41.

11 Lisa Dale, 'Anticipate, Absorb, Reshape (A2R) A Baseline Study of Climate Resilience in Developing Countries', *Consilience*, 19 (2018), 36–57.

12 Marygold Walsh-Dilley, Wendy Wolford and James McCarthy, 'Rights for Resilience: food Sovereignty, Power and Resilience in Development Practice', *Ecology and Society*, 21.1 (March 2016).

13 Alastair Dobbin, 'Memory Matters: How Recall can Build Resilience', *British Journal of General Practice*, 68.669 (April 2018), 198–9; Sylvie Nail, 'Memory and Resilience: A Two-pronged Ppproach to Natural Spaces in Colombia's Transition to a Peaceful Society', *Urban Forestry & Urban Greening* (10 February 2018).

14 Paula Thorrington Cronovich, 'Out of the Blackout and into the Light: How the Arts Survived Pinochet's Dictatorship', *Iberoamericana*, 13.5 (September 2013), 119–37; Pilar Valenzuela Rettig, 'Literatura antropológica en Chile: Una manifestación de literatura intercultural', *Revista Chilena de Literatura*, 96 (November 2017), 333–49.

worlds. Agency is not restricted to the human mind,[15] trees think and can heal,[16] horses can whisper to us,[17] elephants have 'cultures',[18] and humans and plants share an 'ontological relationality' (Alain).[19] This connectedness can often operate as an almost invisible type of resilience, which is expressed as a type of agency. We might be forced to conclude that we see this resilience in the world around us—in the natural world and in the animal kingdom—but we do not fully understand where it comes from.

Resilience, Invisibility and Cultural Agency

In this chapter I intend to draw on the notion of the invisibility of resilience—as adumbrated in ecological-biophysical systems—and assess whether it can lead us to edge towards more nuanced readings of literary texts, particularly those that express political structures of feeling. Gabriel García Márquez's *One Hundred Years of Solitude*, I shall be arguing, is a particularly fruitful text to analyse in terms of its articulation of the concept of invisible, or not-as-yet-visible, resilience.

The first point to make is that García Márquez's text works in terms of what might be called invisible cultural agencies. *One Hundred Years of Solitude* is often seen as the originator of the global literary movement of magical realism, and the Colombian writer once wrote that he learned the tricks of the trade from his grandmother: 'The tone that I eventually used in *One Hundred Years of Solitude* was based on the way my grandmother used to tell stories. She told things that sounded supernatural and fantastic, but she told them with complete naturalness.'[20] But Tranquilina Iguarán was not his only source. In fact, she could be more readily described as the vehicle, since the real source are those beliefs buried in popular culture, that is,

15 Richard Healey and Angie Pepper, 'Interspecies Justice: Agency, Self-determination and Assent', *Philosophical Studies*, 178.4 (2021), 1223–43.

16 Suzanne Simard, *Finding the Mother Tree: Uncovering the Wisdom and Intelligence of the Forest* (Harmondsworth: Penguin, 2014).

17 Karin Bronkhorst, 'The Psychotherapeutic Worth of Horse Whispering for the Aggressive Child', MA dissertation, University of South Africa (June 2006).

18 G. A. Bradshaw, *Elephants on the Edge: What Animals Teach us about Humanity* (New Haven, CT: Yale University Press, 2010).

19 Hubert Alain, 'Vagabond: The Trans-species Ecologies of Plant/Human Encounters', http://www.greenhumanities.org/archives/vol02/; last consulted on 22 November 2024.

20 http://www.themodernworld.com/gabo/gabo_mr.html

what Florencia Mallon calls the 'buried treasures of popular imaginings'.[21] García Márquez suggested that the Caribbean gave him the ability to see the magical side of life: 'In the Caribbean, to which I belong, the unbridled imagination of the black African slaves got mixed up with the beliefs of the pre-Columbian natives and then with the fantasy of the Andalusian.'[22] A cursory reading of the autobiography of a runaway slave, *Biografía de un cimarrón* (1966) by Esteban Montejo, and edited by Miguel Barnet, would tend to confirm García Márquez's view. Montejo was interviewed in 1963 at the age of 103, and spoke of the details of his life as a runaway slave in Cuba in the second half of the nineteenth century. He regales his reader with tales of headless horsemen, witchcraft, zombies, mischievous ghosts, unexplained lights over cemeteries, witches who can take their skin off at will, leaving it hanging up on a hook behind the door, and then fly from the Canary Islands to Cuba. His account, indeed, does not present any of these events as if they were anything particularly unusual about them. Here is a brief example:

> The witches were one of those weird things. In Ariosa I saw them catch one. They caught her with sesame seeds and mustard, and she was trapped to the spot. As long as there's a little sesame on the floor, they can't move. The witches used to leave their skins behind, and then they could fly off, just wearing their bare flesh (...). All of them were from the [Canary] Islands. I've never seen any Cuban witches. They would fly here in Havana every night from the Canary Islands in just a few seconds. Even nowadays, when people aren't so scared, they still leave a light on in the house where there are small children, just so the witches don't come along interfering with them. If they did that would be the end of them, because witches are very partial to little children.[23]

Certainly, some of these popular imaginings seem to have found their way into García Márquez's inkwell and, with this in mind, I want to turn to one of the most famous supernatural beings to appear in the Colombian novelist's fiction, that is, José Arcadio Segundo's ghost who appears in Chapter 15 of *One Hundred Years of Solitude*. The backdrop to José Arcadio Segundo's apparition in the novel is an event—the wilful assassination of banana plantation workers—that allegedly occurred in real life in a coastal city in Colombia, Ciénaga, on 6 December 1928 on the orders of General

21 Florencia Mallon, *Peasant and Nation: The Making of Postcolonial Mexico and Peru* (Berkeley, CA: University of California Press, 1995), p. 329.

22 Quoted in Stephen Hart, *Crónica de una muerte anunciada: Critical guide* (London: Grant & Cutler, 1994), p. 12.

23 Miguel Barnet, *Biografía de un cimarrón* (Barcelona: Siruela, 1998), pp. 125–6; author's translation.

Carlos Cortés Vargas. We must draw out the contours of this event before we turn our attention to García Márquez's—as we shall see—resilient ghost.

The Banana Massacre, Ciénaga, Colombia, 6 December 1928

What happened at 1.30am on 6 December 1928 in the main square in Ciénaga—given the enormous disparity characterising the different accounts—will probably never be conclusively known. What *is* known is that trouble had been brewing for a while between the management of the U.S.-owned United Fruit Company that ran the banana plantation in Ciénaga (and, indeed, other plantations along the Caribbean coast) and the plantation workers.[24] In November 1928 the workers collectively demanded better pay, a shorter workday and better conditions, all of which were summarily rejected by the UFC management.[25] The banana strike broke out on 12 November 1928. The authorities found it difficult to contain the workers and they drafted in the Army.[26] The military officer in command of the Army at the time, General Carlos Cortés Vargas, received news of the decree which gave him state of siege powers on the night of 5 December 1928. He prepared his troops to face the crowd that had assembled in the main square of Ciénaga. The troops had rifles and three machine guns. At 1.30am, early in the morning of 6 December 1928, he initially gave the crowd five minutes

24 There were suspicions during this period about the tactics used by the United Fruit Company to control the land of the Banana Zone in a number of countries of the Caribbean. Antonio Saldaña, King of the Bribri people in Talamanca, Costa Rica, as a result of his opposition to the expansion of the United Fruit Company, was suspected of having been poisoned by agents working on behalf of the UFC. He died on 3 January 1910. It is alleged that he died as a result of being tricked into ingesting iodine tincture. His nephew, José, heir to the Kingdom of Talamanca, also died in suspiciously similar circumstances on the same day. There was no successor, and the UFC subsequently extended their operations in this territory; see Javier Gómez Jiménez, 'Antonio Saldaña', *Revista del Archivo Nacional* [San José, Costa Rica], 83 (December 2019), 1–2; file:///C:/Users/uclssth/OneDrive%20-%20University%20College%20London/Downloads/mherrera,+2019_01_Editorial+RAN+2019.pdf.

25 Gerald Martin, *Gabriel García Márquez: A Life* (London: Bloomsbury, 2008), p. 40.

26 Eduardo Posada-Carbó, 'Fiction as History: The Bananeras and Gabriel García Márquez's *One Hundred Years of Solitude*', *Journal of Latin American Studies*, 30.2 (1998), 395–414 (pp. 401–2).

to disperse. When they refused to do so, he gave them one more minute, after which—according to his own account—General Cortés Vargas gave the order to fire.[27] What happened next is very difficult to establish, especially in terms of how many people perished that night. As Gerald Martin suggests:

> How many people died? Forty years later, in *One Hundred Years of Solitude*, García Márquez would invent a figure of three thousand, a total which many of his readers would take at face value. On 19 May 1929 *El Espectador* of Bogotá said that there were 'more than a thousand dead'. (...) The statistics are still discussed and bitterly disputed to this day.[28]

Cortés Vargas admitted to killing thirteen (eight found dead in the square, and five more found dead in the vicinity of the square), while historians have proposed many different numbers, ranging from 60 to 75, 100, 400, 800, 1,000, 1,500 and 2,000.[29] None of the numbers suggested by historians reach García Márquez's figure of 3,000, which has led a number of historians to criticise the Colombian novelist for exaggerating the facts. Posada-Carbó, in particular, takes direct aim at García Márquez's work, suggesting that the use of the number of 3,000 dead in his novel

> does raise serious questions about the extent to which the novel can be used as a piece of historical evidence—as a source, in particular, to interpret the complex events of the 1928 strike and its aftermath. 'Nos complacemos en el ensueño de que la historia no se parezca a la Colombia en que vivimos, sino que Colombia termine por parecerse a su historia escrita', García Márquez observed in one of his recurrent indictments against a supposedly 'official story' of the country. The paradox here is that, since the publication of *One Hundred Years of Solitude* in 1967, Colombians' perception of the bananeras started to resemble not the 'Colombia en que vivimos' but the 'historia escrita' by the novelist.[30]

Posada-Carbó makes a very interesting point here when he refers to the complex relationship between the 'official story'—normally understood as a reference to the Colombian Government's whitewashing of the massacre—and the 'written story' (normally ascribed to García Márquez's unmasking

27 Carlos Cortés Vargas, *Los sucesos de las bananeras (historia de los acontecimientos que se desarrollaron en la zona bananera de Departamento de Magdaena—13 de noviembre de 1928 al 15 de marzo de 1929)* (Bogotá: Editorial Desarrollo, 1929), pp. 87–90.

28 *Gabriel García Márquez: A Life*, p. 42.

29 Stephen M. Hart, *Gabriel García Márquez* (London: Reaktion, 2010), p. 198, n32.

30 Posada-Carbó, 'Fiction as History', p. 414.

of the historical truth 'disappeared' by the government), and suggests that the roles have been reversed, and that the novelist's version has become the 'official' version. Whether one agrees with this is not as important as the implication underpinning this statement, for it draws attention to just how slippery versions of the past can be, whether they be historical or literary. In his autobiography García Márquez refers to these discrepancies, and suggests that—initially—his own version of the events was provided as a counterweight to his own mother's very conservative estimate of how many people died during the uprising:

> My mother's version had such meager numbers and a setting so abject for the imposing drama I had imagined that it caused a sense of frustration in me. Later, I spoke with survivors and witnesses and searched through newspaper archives and official documents, and I realized that the truth did not lie anywhere. Conformists said, in effect, that there had been no deaths. Those at the other extreme affirmed without a quaver in their voices that there had been more than a hundred, that they had been seen bleeding to death in the square, and that they were carried away in a freight train to be tossed into the ocean like rejected bananas. And so my version was lost forever at some improbable point between the two extremes. But it was so persistent that in one of my novels I referred to the massacre with all the precision and horror that I had brought for years to its incubation in my imagination. This was why I kept the number of dead at three thousand, in order to preserve the epic proportions of the drama, and in the end real life did me justice: not long ago, on one of the anniversaries of the tragedy, the speaker of the moment in the Senate asked for a minute of silence in memory of the three thousand anonymous martyrs sacrificed by the forces of law and order.[31]

As this statement suggests, the Colombian novelist *did* carry out some historical research, by consulting newspaper archives as well as official documents, and interviewing survivors and witnesses. But—and here is where the literary focus of his endeavours comes into focus—he decided that, in order to capture some of the epic drama of what occurred as well as its horror (the wounded being left to bleed slowly to death during the night, and then their bodies thrown into the sea like rotten bananas), he needed to use a higher number than that accepted and promoted by the conformists. Some might argue that García Márquez used the empiric fact that 'the truth did not lie anywhere' in order to justify his inflated and politically motivated number of dead. This may be true to some degree but we should bear in mind that García Márquez, in creating his text, may have been responding to those

31 García Márquez, *Living to Tell the Tale*, translated by Edith Grossman (London: Jonathan Cape, 2003), pp. 62–3.

factors that are used by lawyers and judges when calibrating the gravity of a crime. No trial occurred nor did any judicial mechanism take place to assess the gravity of the events that occurred on 6 December 1928, but, if one were to review the factors that are often used in criminal cases of this type—such as the seriousness of the offence, the harm caused to the victim, the offender's level of blame, and including aggravating as well as mitigating circumstances—these would have been likely to point to the heinousness of the crime, whatever the number of victims listed.[32] In this particular case the evidence provided by the witnesses consulted by García Márquez, particularly relating to victims who were left bleeding to death in the square during the night and the subsequent disposal of the victims' bodies ('tossed into the ocean like rejected bananas') speaks volumes relating to the factor of 'harm caused to the victim'. Since the individuals in the square were unarmed, the use of machine-guns as well as bayonets underlines the 'seriousness of the offence' as well as 'the offender's level of blame'. It is likely, furthermore, that all of these details would be seen as aggravating rather than mitigating circumstances. García Márquez, we might conclude, decided to keep the number of 3,000 dead for reasons of poetic rather than empiric justice.

The Banana Massacre in *One Hundred Years of Solitude*

Let us look now more closely at what García Márquez does with the 'empiric' facts of what occurred on 6 December 1928 in his novel. By analysing carefully the techniques he uses to describe the horror and epic power of the massacre, we shall see that he manages to bring a multi-layered depth to the events, allowing them to retain the 'complexity' that Posada-Carbó suggests they possessed (see above), though a portrayal of the agency of the 'pueblo' which thereby becomes an expression of resilience against all the odds. At the risk of over-simplifying the issue, I shall be suggesting that García Márquez, in his portrayal of the banana massacre, drew on three rhetorical features, which were: (i) the 3,000 dead; (ii) a striking metaphor; and (iii) a ghost. All three features of his account led to the enhancement of the 'epic proportions of the drama' as the Colombian novelist called it in his autobiography (see above), as well, as I shall be arguing, to the portrayal of the mysterious agency of resilience. Let's look at these three factors separately.

32 https://www.sentencingcouncil.org.uk/sentencing-and-the-council/how-sentencing-works/ (consulted on 18 August 2025).

The 3,000 Dead

On two occasions *One Hundred Years of Solitude* refers clearly to the number of 3,000 casualties in the main square of the city where the striking banana plantation workers were assembled. The first thing that José Arcadio Segundo says when he escapes from the train carrying the corpses to the sea, and arrives in Macondo is as follows:

> 'There must have been three thousand of them,' he murmured.
>
> 'What?'
>
> 'The dead', he clarified. 'It must have been all of the people who were at the station.'
>
> The woman measured him with a pitying look. 'There haven't been any dead here', she said. 'Since the time of your uncle, the colonel, nothing has happened in Macondo.' (García Márquez, *One Hundred Years of Solitude*, pp. 313–14)

The idea is repeated at the conclusion of Chapter 15:

> There were more than three thousand of them', was all that José Arcadio Segundo said. 'I'm sure now that they were everybody who had been at the station. (García Márquez, *One Hundred Years of Solitude*, p. 319)

By the time he wrote *One Hundred Years of Solitude* García Márquez was already aware of how contentious the figure of 3,000 dead had become. He allows the disparity between numbers to emerge in his novel when he chooses to portray the first gainsayer of that figure as an anonymous individual, simply called 'the woman'. It is true that, later on in the chapter, there is a more politically focused conflict portrayed as occurring between the Army and the people:

> At night, after taps, they [the soldiers] knocked doors down with their rifle butts, hauled suspects out of their beds, and took them off on trips from which there was no return. The search for and extermination of the hoodlums, murderers, arsonists, and rebels of Decree No. 4 was still going on, but the military denied it even to the relatives of the victims who crowded the commandants' offices in search of news. 'You must have been dreaming,' the officers insisted. 'Nothing has happened in Macondo, nothing has every happened, and nothing ever will happen. This is a happy town.' In that way they were able to wipe out the union members. (García Márquez, *One Hundred Years of Solitude*, pp. 315–16)

This description of an organised campaign of assassination in the work of a Colombian novelist can only be interpreted as a direct attack on the government. But the fact that the chapter ends with José Arcadio Segundo's mumbled words underlines the fact that the evidence provided by García Márquez's novel is nothing more than the mumbled ruminations of a ghost—a ghost who is, furthermore, not visible or audible to all and sundry. Hardly the kind of evidence that would stand up in a court of law! This is an important feature of García Márquez's novel, and suggests that the political message of his novel is not as black-and-white as some would have us believe.[33] This point will become clearer when we discuss the multi-layered role played by the ghost in García Márquez's fiction below.

Metaphor in Chapter 15, *One Hundred Years of Solitude*

The most striking use of metaphor in Chapter 15 of *One Hundred Years of Solitude* occurs in the very place that the reader would least expect it to appear. It is the metaphor of the dragon's tail combined with the onion cutter that is used to describe the impact of the machine guns used by the Army:

> The child's privileged position allowed him to see at that moment that the wild mass starting to get to the corner and the row of machine guns opened fire. Several voices shouted at the same time:
>
> 'Get down! Get down!'
>
> The people in front had already done so, swept down by the wave of bullets. The survivors, instead of getting down, tried to go back to the small square, and the panic became a dragon's tail in the street across the way, where the machine guns were also firing without cease. They were penned in, swirling about in a gigantic whirlwind that little by little was being reduced to its epicenter as the edges were systematically being cut off all around like an onion being peeled by the insatiable and methodical shears of the machine guns. (García Márquez, *One Hundred Years of Solitude*, p. 311)

It is extraordinary that, even though he knew that his portrayal of the banana massacre would be questioned in terms of its veracity, García Márquez decided very deliberately to incorporate an extravagant metaphor (the people are like a dragon's tail being cut to pieces by an onion cutter) that is so convoluted that the reader is likely to forget that we are witnessing a mass execution. Once more García Márquez is signalling to us very clearly that

33 For further discussion of this point, see the carefully worded discussion in Posada-Carbó, 'Fiction as History'.

his work is not to be understood as an example of a clinically legal account of an historic event. It flaunts its 'littérarité'. This leads us naturally to, perhaps, the most significant ingredient that the Colombian writer includes in his portrayal of the banana massacre, José Arcadio Segundo's ghost.

The Ghost of José Arcadio Segundo

Where did García Márquez get his ghosts from? The answer to this question must be: his childhood. As Gerald Martin's biography suggests, the house in which he lived with his grandparents during his childhood in Aracataca was filled to the brim with ghosts:

> Daytime (…) brought a vivid, varied, ever-changing world; sometimes violent, sometimes magical. Night-time was always the same, and it was terrifying. He recalled: 'That house was full of mysteries. My grandmother was very nervous; many things appeared to her which she would tell me about at night. When she talked about the souls of the dead she would say "they are always whistling out there, I hear them all the time". In each corner there were dead people and memories and after six o' clock in the evening you just couldn't move around in there. They would sit me in a corner and there I would stay, just like the boy in *Leaf Storm*.' Little wonder the child saw dead men in the bath and in the kitchen; once he even saw the devil at his window. (*Gabriel García Márquez: A Life*, p. 34)

The important point is not to establish whether or not García Márquez believed in ghosts but what he did with these popular beliefs in his fiction. As we shall see, he chose to use the ghost as a vehicle with which to express the trauma experienced by the 'pueblo' as well as their resilience in continuing to fight against social injustice, even if that meant doing so beyond the grave. I will be using the word 'ghost' in this chapter not according to its dictionary definition ('the disembodied spirit of a dead person, supposed to haunt the living'),[34] but rather in the sense of 'a projection within an ideologically riven nation of a subaltern forced to 'disappear' as a result of lying (in both sense of the term) on the wrong side of the political, gender or race line'.[35] I have mentioned above that the ghost is an extremely important leitmotif in Chapter 15 because—as we have seen—he is presented as the most important witness of the methodical extermination that occurred in

34 *Collins Paperback English Dictionary* (Glasgow: HarperCollins, 2003), p. 335.

35 Stephen M. Hart, 'Magical Realism in the Americas: Politicised Ghosts in *One Hundred Years of Solitude*, *The House of the Spirits*, and *Beloved*', *Journal of Iberian and Latin American Studies*, 9.2 (2003), 115–23, doi:10.1080/1470184032000171759

Ciénaga on 6 December 1928. Surely, we should read this as an ironic, if not tongue-in-cheek, act of poking fun at the military. García Márquez knows that they will say they never saw a thing, so he allows us to see this happening when a military officer arrives at the house in order to conduct a search for subversives:

> 'No one has lived in that room for a century,' she [Santa Sofía de la Piedad] said. The officer had it opened and flashed the beam of the lantern over it, and Aureliano Segundo and Santa Sofía de la Piedad saw the Arab eyes of José Arcadio Segundo at the moment when the ray of light passed over his face and they understood that it was the end of one anxiety and the beginning of another which would find relief only in resignation. But the officer continued examining the room with the lantern and showed no sign of interest until he discovered the seventy-two chamberpots piled up in the cupboards. (García Márquez, *One Hundred Years of Solitude*, p. 317)

Even when Aureliano Segundo and Santa Sofía de la Piedad actually reveal that José Arcadio Segundo is there, the military officer still doesn't get it:

> 'How many people live in this house?' he asked.
>
> 'Five.'
>
> The officer obviously did not understand. He paused with his glance on the space where Aureliano Segundo and Santa Sofía de la Piedad were still seeing José Arcadio Segundo and the latter also realised that the soldier was looking at him without seeing him. Then he turned out the light and closed the door. When he spoke to the soldiers, Aureliano Seguno understood that the young officer had seen the room with the same eyes as Colonel Aureliano Buendía.
>
> 'It's obvious that no one has been in that room for at least a hundred years,' the officer said to the soldiers. 'There must even be snakes in there.' (García Márquez, *One Hundred Years of Solitude*, p. 318)

García Márquez is cocking a snoop at the Army. Their officers are not only blind to individuals who do not see the world as they do (i.e. they cannot even see José Arcadio Segundo), they cannot tell the difference between human beings and snakes. But—the cruellest jibe of them all—García Márquez reveals that the military cannot even count. When Aureliano Segundo and Santa Sofía de la Piedad reveal that there are five people in the house, they are admitting that José Arcadio Segundo is there, but the military officer is none the wiser. If this is the case—García Márquez seems to be saying to us—how can we take seriously the numbers of dead provided by General Carlos Cortés

Vargas in his report? Is it really possible that just eight casualties were found dead in the town square of Ciénaga on 6 December 1928?

There is a detail in the account of the non-discovery of José Arcadio Segundo's ghost that needs to be underlined since it highlights the presence of the pueblo's resilience. When Aureliano Segundo and Santa Sofía de la Piedad believe that José Arcadio Segundo is about to be discovered the text tells us that they believed that 'it was the end of one anxiety and the beginning of another which would find relief only in resignation'. What is meant by this phrase? The first anxiety, clearly, relates to the fear that one of their family members would be discovered and taken away for execution. The second anxiety is the knowledge that this would lead to a struggle with the authorities which, it suggests, could only end in 'resignation', that is, being resigned to the acceptance of state-led murder, corruption and impunity. But, as *One Hundred Years of Solitude* suggests, this does not occur. The ghost was not discovered and political resignation did not occur. The ghost of the story of Colombia's disappeared in the banana massacre of 6 December 1928 escaped the long arm of the authorities and lived on. Perhaps the most crucial detail of all, the ghost lived on in the guise of the 'destructive storms', the 'hurricanes' and the 'redoubled rain' that lasted for 'four years, eleven months, and two years' (García Márquez, *One Hundred Years of Solitude*, p. 320). José Arcadio Segundo's ghost is a manifestation of the resilient and often invisible connectedness between human and elemental worlds explored in ecological-biophysical research (see above), a latter-day version of the perhaps unjustifiably discredited pathetic fallacy of the Romantics.

Most important of all, the continuing life of the ghost alludes symbolically to the continuation of the pueblo's political struggle. Though this story is not told directly as a narrative representation in *One Hundred Years of Solitude*, the banana massacre was the trigger that led to a tectonic shift in Colombian politics. The events of December 1928 in Colombia, as one historian has pointed out, were highly significant 'for the history of the country. They helped to bring down the Conservative Hegemony, a regime that dominated Colombian politics from 1886 to 1930. They marked the rise of the career of Jorge Eliécer Gaitán—a Liberal who became the outstanding Colombian populist, a leading protagonist in the politics of the country until his death in 1948. They provided the labour movement, and later the Communist Party, with symbols and martyrs in their struggle against capitalism and imperialism. They came to weigh heavily on the country's perception of the Army and of the role of foreign capital. And they inspired García Márquez's masterpiece.'[36] This story is, as it were, the pregnant underbelly of *One Hundred Years of Solitude*, alluded to synecdochically by the ghost's

36 Posada-Carbó, 'Fiction as History', p. 400.

continuing presence. We can, thus, call José Arcadio Segundo a politicised ghost since he epitomises the 'vigencia' of the Left's proposed solution to Colombia's political problems, its continuing struggle and its resilience even in the face of certain death.

Conclusion

García Márquez's *One Hundred Years of Solitude* is a book with many levels. It is as little a history book as it is a political pamphlet. It tells the story of the bravery and resilience of those people who stood up against the military in the town square of Ciénaga in December 1928, even in the face of enormous odds. The newspaper reports in *El Espectador* prove that there were about 3,000 people in that square on that day and—even if not all of them died—their bravery was demonstrated by the fact that they were unarmed. There are no reports in the historical documents of the workers firing back. García Márquez chose to use the figure of the ghost because it is a multilayered symbol. He used it to demonstrate the blindness and stupidity of the military in the scene of the non-discovery of José Arcadio Segundo in the Buendía residence. Ultimately, the ghost also operates in his fiction as a cipher of the enduring nature of the rights of the resilient workers who fought for social justice along the Caribbean coast in the 1920s and beyond. García Márquez's ghost was always predestined to bounce back.

Bibliography

Alain, Hubert, 'Vagabond: The Trans-species Ecologies of Plant/Human Encounters', http://www.greenhumanities.org/archives/vol02/; last consulted on 22 November 2024.

Barnet, Miguel, *Biografía de un cimarrón* (Barcelona: Siruela, 1998).

Bradshaw, G. A., *Elephants on the Edge: What Animals Teach us about Humanity* (Yale: Yale University Press, 2010).

Bronkhorst, Karin, 'The Psychotherapeutic Worth of Horse Whispering for the Aggressive Child', MA dissertation, University of South Africa (June 2006).

Brunnermeir, Markus K., *The Resilient Society* (Princeton: Princeton University Press, 2021).

Carmel, Abraham, and Gideon D. Markman, 'Capture, Governance and Resilience: Strategy Implications from the History of Rome', *Strategic Management Journal*, 32.3 (March 2011), 322–41.

Collins Paperback English Dictionary (Glasgow: HarperCollins, 2003), p. 335.

Cortés Vargas, Carlos, *Los sucesos de las bananeras (Historia de los acontecimientos que se desarrollaron en la zona bananera de Departamento de Magdaena—13 de noviembre de 1928 al 15 de marzo de 1929)* (Bogotá: Editorial Desarrollo, 1929).

Dale, Lisa, 'Anticipate, Absorb, Reshape (A2R): A Baseline Study of Climate Resilience in Developing Countries', *Consilience*, 19 (2018), 36–57.

Dobbin, Alastair, 'Memory Matters: How Recall can Build Resilience', *British Journal of General Practice*, 68.669 (April 2018), 198–9.

Essex, Arielle, *Practical Miracles: Choices that Heal and Build Resilience* (London: Hay House, 2013).

García Márquez, Gabriel, *One Hundred Years of Solitude*, trans. Gregory Rabassa (Harmondsworth: Penguin, 1973).

García Márquez, Gabriel, *Living to Tell the Tale*, translated by Edith Grossman (London: Jonathan Cape, 2003).

Gómez Jiménez, Javier, 'Antonio Saldaña', *Revista del Archivo Nacional* [San José, Costa Rica], 83 (December 2019), 1–2; file:///C:/Users/uclssth/OneDrive%20-%20University%20College%20London/Downloads/mherrera,+2019_01_Editorial+RAN+2019.pdf.

Gunderson, Lance, 'Ecological and Human Community Resilience in Response to Natural Disasters', *Ecology and Society*, 15.2 (Jun 2010), 18 (online).

Hart, Stephen, *Crónica de una muerte anunciada: Critical Guide* (London: Grant & Cutler, 1994).

Hart, Stephen M., *Gabriel García Márquez* (London: Reaktion, 2010).

Hart, Stephen M., 'Magical Realism in the Americas: Politicised Ghosts in *One Hundred Years of Solitude*, *The House of the Spirits*, and *Beloved*', *Journal of Iberian and Latin American Studies*, 9.2 (2003), 115–23; doi:10.1080/1470184032000171759

Healey, Richard, and Angie Pepper, 'Interspecies Justice: Agency, Self-determination and Assent', *Philosophical Studies*, 178.4 (2021), 1223–43.

Mallon, Florencia, *Peasant and Nation: The Making of Postcolonial Mexico and Peru* (Berkeley, CA: University of California Press, 1995).

Martin, Gerald, *Journeys through the Labyrinth: Latin American Fiction in the Twentieth Century* (London: Verso, 1989).

Martin, Gerald, *Gabriel García Márquez: A Life* (London: Bloomsbury, 2008).

Miller Fiona et al., 'Resilience and Vulnerability: Complementary or Conflicting Concepts?', *Ecology and Society*, 15.3 (September 2010). Online issue. Article 11.

Neenan, Michael, *Developing Resilience: A Cognitive-Behavioural Approach* (London: Routledge, 2009).

Nail, Sylvie, 'Memory and Resilience: A Two-pronged Approach to Natural Spaces in Colombia's Transition to a Peaceful Society', *Urban Forestry & Urban Greening* (10 February 2018).

Posada-Carbó, Eduardo, 'Fiction as History: The Bananeras and Gabriel García Márquez's *One Hundred Years of Solitude*', *Journal of Latin American Studies*, 30.2 (1998), 395–414.

Ratcliff, Elenor P., *You are a Champion: A Memoir of Miracles and Pure Resilience in Crisis* (Austin, TX: Lnoirs Fidelity Publishing, 2020).

Simard, Suzanne, *Finding the Mother Tree: Uncovering the Wisdom and Intelligence of the Forest* (Harmondsworth: Penguin, 2014).

Thorrington Cronovich, Paula, 'Out of the Blackout and into the Light: How the Arts Survived Pinochet's Dictatorship', *Iberoamericana*, 13.5 (September 2013), 119–37.

Valenzuela Rettig, Pilar, 'Literatura antropológica en Chile: Una manifestación de literatura intercultural', *Revista Chilena de Literatura*, 96 (November 2017), 333–49.

Walsh-Dilley, Marygol, Wendy Wolford and James McCarthy, 'Rights for Resilience: Food Sovereignty, Power and Resilience in Development Practice', *Ecology and Society*, 21.1 (March 2016).

9

Discovering Women's Resilience: The Development Film since the 1970s

Molly Geidel

The 2013 documentary *Girl Rising* reenacts the life stories of nine girls in the Global South. Scripted by women writers from around the world in collaboration with the girls, the stories are narrated by A-list celebrities from Meryl Streep to Selena Gomez to Kerry Washington. Directed by Richard E. Robbins, who had previously made the Oscar-nominated tale of US soldiers in Iraq and Afghanistan *Operation Homecoming*, *Girl Rising* opens on a Cambodian preteen, later identified as Sokha, performing a graceful, slow Apsara dance in a bright yellow gown against a black background. As Sokha dances, gazing into the camera with a confident smile, the narration by Alicia Keys, written by Cambodian American activist Loung Ung, begins. 'This is a simple story', says Keys, her voice taking on the cadence of performance poetry, 'and it did not begin here. This thing of beauty, a joy forever, rising. This warm glow in darkness like a harvest moon.' The scene shifts to an enormous garbage dump, the camera panning over the rubble as Keys continues: 'she was a child of the dump, a place where smoke blackened sun and moon, and eyes seldom looked up from a world of things tossed aside. An orphan, discarded, learning lessons no school would teach'. The bleak landscape of the dump is depicted first by closeups of the limbs of people picking garbage, then by an extreme long shot of two tiny girls in the rubble. Keys reinforces the point the camera has made, explaining that the dump is 'a place where a girl is simply one more thing the world has thrown away'. The scene dissolves back into the Apsara dance, as Keys confirms that the story has a happy ending:

> But when they found her, when this girl's dreams came true, she had not dreamed of gold, she had not wished for beauty. Hers was a simple dream: the bright white shirt of a school uniform, the crisp pleats of a skirt, shelves full of books. The dream of school. Now she dances behind a contented smile, because she knows this is no longer a simple story. Now this is her story to write. She is the author. And this is not the end. It is just the beginning.[1]

Through the juxtaposition between the desperate, gray-toned chaos of the dump and the regal bright order of Sokha's dance, *Girl Rising* stages education as a miraculous transformation, which, although 'she did not wish for beauty', has nonetheless beautified Sokha. But by combining the dance performance with performance poetry, the film takes this assertion a step further, reading the dance and the education that has made it possible not as a difficult feat of discipline but as the pure expression of the interiority of the 'author'/dancer/girl, even though she does not speak to confirm this. The film extends this argument about the power of education in interludes narrated by Liam Neeson, in which girls move around an open field, in order to explicate the film's central thesis, by 2013 ubiquitous in development circles: that educating girls 'may be the highest-return investment available in the developing world'. Neeson here reiterates almost verbatim Lawrence Summers' prognostication at the World Bank more than two decades earlier, that untold generational ripple effects would follow even minor investments in girls' education.[2] 'These girls hold our future in their hands', Neeson pronounces. 'If they and others like them succeed in getting the kind of education they need, incredible things will happen, for them, for their families, for their community, for their country, for all of us.'

At first glance, *Girl Rising* seems to hew to a story of its girls as victims who need saving, from Keys' initial narration of Sokha's salvation from the

1 *Girl Rising*, dir. by Richard E. Robbins (The Documentary Group, 2013). After the film's release, Girl Rising launched as a nonprofit, and made several follow-up documentaries about the girls featured in the original film. See https://www.girlrising.org/.

2 Summers' quote is: 'educating girls yields a higher rate of return than any other investment available in the developing world'. Lawrence H. Summers, 'Investing in All the People: Educating Women in Developing Countries,' EDI Seminar Paper 45 [originally delivered at the 1992 Annual Meeting of The World Bank] (Washington DC: World Bank, 1994). For an incisive account of this data and finance-driven biopolitical logic that posits girls primarily as investments, see Michelle Murphy, *The Economization of Life* (Durham, NC: Duke University Press, 2017). I build here on Murphy's work by considering the affective/sentimental tactics through which development media celebrates resilience and 'investability'.

dump to Neeson's assertion early in the film that 'It's a simple fact: there is no one more vulnerable than a girl.' However, despite Neeson's pedigree as a rescuer of kidnapped girls in previous films, the stories in *Girl Rising* self-consciously differentiate themselves from narratives of victimhood, abjection, and rescue.[3] The stories do not generally narrate girls being saved by others (or at least, as in Sokha's story, they do not dwell on the part when the girls are saved by others) but rather depict girls saving themselves. From Haitian eight-year-old Wadley (voiced by Cate Blanchett), whose home was destroyed by the 2010 earthquake but who insists on staying in school despite not being able to pay the fees, to Suma in Nepal (voiced by Kerry Washington), a bonded labourer who escapes and campaigns to free other girls; to Yasmine in Egypt (voiced by Chloe Grace Moretz), who fights back against and escapes the man who abducts her, the girls reenact stories of achieving their own salvation. This is not to say that the film conveys much of a sense of the girls as individuals: both the celebrity voiceovers and their nearly identical wishes for schooling flatten them. But by the end of each harrowing tale, its girl-protagonist looks hopeful and defiant: she has saved herself, she is rising, she will use her voice, she will save others. The conclusion of the film makes this clear, featuring closeups of face after face of determined-looking Afghan girls, who then clamber up a hill, a rainbow shining behind them. The final, composite girl, voiced by Anne Hathaway, takes a defiant stand:

> Change is coming. I will read, I will learn, I will study, I will return to school. I dare you to tell me it's a waste of time. If you try to stop me, I will just try harder. Put me in a pit, I will climb out. If you kill me, there will be other girls who rise up and take my place. I find a way to endure, to prevail. The future of man lies in me.[...]Do you doubt me? Do you underestimate my will? Look into my eyes. Do you see it now? I am change.

Here and throughout the film, harm is constructed not as something from which girls must be protected, but rather as something over which they must triumph, and emerge smiling. And the audience in the Global North is addressed not as saviours, but as witnesses to the girls' incredible resilience.

Resilience of the form *Girl Rising* depicts is often celebrated in neoliberalism. As John Pat Leary explains, resilience is one of the new 'keywords for the age of austerity'. Leary observes the prevalence of resilience as a goal in wellness and business literature, where it encourages workers to adapt to high-pressure work environments, as well as in humanitarian, disaster relief, and development discourses, in which 'a people's "resilience to crisis" is

3 See *Taken,* dir. by Pierre Morel (EuropaCorp, 2008); *Taken 2,* dir. by Olivier Megaton (EuropaCorp 2012).

thought to be proactive preparation for disaster'.[4] In all these situations, Leary shows, the commentators and technicians preaching resilience not only abandon the possibility of workers or victims resisting the structures that exploit or endanger them, but also disavow their own relationship to the conditions that cause those hardships. This point is powerfully made in a quote Leary cites by lawyer and activist Tracie L. Washington, emblazoned on posters around New Orleans on the eve of the tenth anniversary of Hurricane Katrina: 'Stop calling me resilient, because every time you say "oh they're resilient", it means you can do something else to me' (Leary, *Keywords*, p. 121).

The role of resilience discourse in films such as *Girl Rising,* however, suggests that resilience is not only neoliberal but also gendered; it serves as the missing piece between the assertions that the girl 'is the most vulnerable person in the world' and that she is 'the highest-return investment'. The film's implicit assertion that resilience is gendered female is supported by the work of Robin James, who identifies resilience as the central feminine norm and virtue in neoliberalism. James argues that femininity shifted, after second-wave feminism, from an ideal of passivity and weakness to a postfeminist ideal of resilience. This resilience ideal manifests through visible performances of overcoming damage, one accompanied by the implicit utterance, 'look, I overcame!'[5] James associates this formulation with pop singers from Kelly Clarkson to Beyoncé to Lady Gaga, whose songs not only tell of recycling pain into success, but also musically enact that recycling. For James, the performance of feminine resilience—characterised by a visible overcoming of the damage wrought by patriarchal, capitalist, white supremacist systems—normalises and bolsters those damaging systems by figuring them as necessary to self-development.

James argues that this feminine norm of resilience is a Global North phenomenon; Global South women, in her account, are envisioned only as objects of imperialist feminist rescue (James, *Resilience and Melancholy*, p. 80). This idea that Western and global governance forces construct women and girls as victims without agency continues to be a common assumption in recent critical scholarship across disciplines on women and girls, particularly in the Muslim world.[6] However, as *Girl Rising* and many other post-1990s

4 John Patrick Leary, *Keywords: The New Language of Capitalism* (Chicago: Haymarket Books, 2018), 120–1.

5 Robin James, *Resilience and Melancholy: Pop Music, Feminism, Neoliberalism* (Oxford: John Hunt Publishing, 2015).

6 See the important anthologies *Feminist Surveillance Studies*, ed. Rachel E. Dubrofsky and Shoshana Amielle Magnet (Durham, NC: Duke University Press, 2015), and *The Cunning of Gender Violence*, ed. by Lila Abu-Lughod, et al (Durham, NC: Duke University Press, 2023).

cultural and humanitarian projects demonstrate, far from being figured in the dominant imaginary as passive victims, women and girls in the Global South are often now constructed as hyper-resilient subjects: they pay back their loans, they bounce back from trauma and loss, they make do with deprivation, they make something from nothing, they lift up their communities and economies. These resilient qualities are in fact what make them such good investments: they are perfect subjects for development in the age of austerity.

Part of this glorification of agency and resilience in the least powerful people in the world comes from an absorption and distortion of the critique of the imperialist feminist project of saving women. The critique of Westerners 'saving' women in the Global South, which has been around at least since Frantz Fanon but came to prominence in the 1980s with the postcolonial feminist work of Gayatri Spivak and Chandra Mohanty, has become mainstream common sense.[7] As Kalpana Wilson has argued, these critiques were incorporated into neoliberal development narratives by recentring the voice and agency of women and girls while avoiding structural change.[8] However, even before this critique of imperialist feminism became pervasive in the popular Western imaginary, Third World women were already being constructed in Western visual culture not only as objects of rescue but also as models of resilience. In this chapter, I trace a genealogy of the ideal of Latin American women's resilience in particular. Considering development documentaries from the 1970s and 1980s, I argue that the 'Women in Development' imaginary is an important location where we can trace the beginnings of the glorification of girls' resilience found in *Girl Rising*. I focus on Helena Solberg and the International Women's Film Collective's pathbreaking 1975 film *The Double Day* and to a lesser degree the 1986 World Bank television episode 'Global Links: Women in the Third World', demonstrating how these works use similar visual strategies to centre Global South women's resilience, even as they register shifts over time from ideals of redistributive feminism to those of women's empowerment through financialisation and education.

7 See Frantz Fanon, 'Algeria Unveiled', in *A Dying Colonialism* (New York: Grove Press, 1965), pp. 38–68; Chandra Mohanty, 'Under Western Eyes: Feminist Scholarship and Colonial Discourses', *boundary 2*, 12:13 (Spring–Autumn 1984), 333–58; Gayatri Chakravorty Spivak, 'Can the Subaltern Speak?', *Marxism and the Interpretation of Culture*, ed. Cary Nelson and Lawrence Grossberg (Chicago: University of Illinois Press, 1988), pp. 271–316.

8 Kalpana Wilson, *Race, Racism and Development: Interrogating History, Discourse, and Practice* (London: Zed Books, 2012). I also demonstrate this shift in Molly Geidel, 'Building the Counterinsurgent Girl', *Feminist Studies*, 44:3 (2018), 635–65.

I *The Double Day*: The Development Film Meets Global Feminism

In the heyday of modernisation theory and practice, beginning after World War II and continuing through the mid-1960s, modernising theories and programmes focused on how to make men's work more productive. When women were mentioned at all by theorists and practitioners of capitalist development in those years, they were usually figured either as stubborn guardians of tradition or as insufficiently feminine overexploited obstacles to the development enterprise. In documentary films made by development agencies in this period, shots of dirty, dishevelled women and children—in doorways, at stoves, at the market—become shorthand for underdevelopment and the meaningless life that accompanies it.[9] Over and over, they represent the 'before' of a 'before/after' narrative that hinges on development intervention.

In the early 1970s women came into view as important subjects of international development in their own right, as workers rather than just as reproductive vessels. Development planners' new emphasis on women as the ideal subjects of development emerged in concert with global second-wave feminism, but also in conjunction with the leftward and then rightward lurches of the international development world. It seemed for a few years that the radical, redistributive vision of the New International Economic Order, officially adopted in 1974—a programme, driven by the insights of dependency theory, that aimed to provide countries in the Global South with more favourable trade terms—might reshape the international development world. However, this order was soon crushed, and development agencies and organisations, without much trouble, adopted neoliberal logics that negated even these modest trade reforms.[10] From the beginning, Women in Development initiatives were based on the idea that women's capacity for what experts called 'productive labour' was being insufficiently exploited in development projects; rather than finding ways to lessen or collectivise the outsized portion of household labour done by women, the new Women in Development imperatives imagined women's 'productive' labour as undercapitalised.[11]

9 Molly Geidel, *The Development Film in the Americas* (Oakland: University of California Press, 2025). This discussion of The Double Day adapts material from my book, with permission from UC Press.

10 Joanne Meyerowitz, *A War on Global Poverty: The Lost Promise of Redistribution and the Rise of Microcredit* (Princeton: Princeton University Press, 2021).

11 Ester Boserup, *Women's Role in Economic Development* (1970; London: Earthscan, 2011), p. xxvii.

Helena Solberg's 1975 film *The Double Day* is a key text for understanding how Women in Development ideas and funding sources, along with new feminist documentary aesthetics, shaped a narrative that positioned individual Third World women's resilience as the limit of feminist transformation. *The Double Day* is generally considered to be the first Latin American feminist documentary; it also establishes Bolivian labour activist Domitila Barrios de Chungara as an international symbol of both Third World women's radicalism and the burgeoning testimonial form. Through footage of women's labour and intimate interviews with working-class women in Bolivia, Mexico, and Argentina, the film compiles stories of women's oppression over various parts of the continent. However, rather than juxtaposing these stories in a way that moves towards analysis of the structural causes of women's oppression or offering possible visions of women's liberation, the film stays with the stories, emphasising individual women's perseverance in both enduring and voicing their experiences of this oppression and injustice. It concludes by highlighting the resistant capacity of Chungara, whose discovery of her voice in response to the government's brutal attacks on her mining community becomes the solution both offered and further facilitated by the film.

Solberg grew up in Brazil. In the 1960s, she began making films in Rio de Janeiro with her friends, some of whom went on to form the second wave of the country's radical Cinema Novo movement, a movement in which scholars sometimes place her.[12] However, Solberg was also influenced by US documentary culture. During her stays in the United States, first in Cambridge, Massachusetts from 1961 to 1963 (accompanying her first husband) and then in her longer stay in Washington DC beginning in 1970, Solberg became involved in the burgeoning documentary scene. She mused in a 2020 interview, 'I always thought that if I'd stayed in Brazil, I might have gone straight to working with fiction, but in the United States the documentary was so strong, direct cinema was so alive and so important.'[13]

While in the United States, Solberg was also drawn to feminism. With a group of historians and artists, she founded a film collective in 1974, soon to be called International Women's Film Project. That collective drew on their historical knowledge to make *The Emerging Woman,* a thoroughly researched and stylistically straightforward narrative account of the history

12 While most scholars associate Solberg with Cinema Novo, Marina Calvalcanti Tedesco questions her affiliation with the movement. See Marina Cavalcanti Tedesco, 'The Women's Film Project: an international collective in the career of Helena Solberg', *Jump Cut*, 61 (Fall 2022).

13 Helena Solberg, 'Helena Solberg Interview las 460/560', online video recording, YouTube, 17 September 2018, https://www.youtube.com/watch?v=W3HXmWzz2-c&ab_channel=UACenterforLatinAmericanStudies (accessed 29 June 2023).

of US feminism. One of the first films to piece together the story of US women's rights and feminism, *The Emerging Woman* was selected as an official film of the American Bicentennial Commission and, Solberg recalls, 'purchased by nearly all libraries in the US'. It earned Solberg attention and more filmmaking opportunities as a 'Latina' and Latin America expert in the United States.[14]

The success of *The Emerging Woman* marked Solberg's arrival on the scene of the US feminist documentary movement. Feminist documentary filmmakers like Solberg together created a recognisable feminist documentary aesthetic characterised by the 'talking head' giving personal testimony. This style, which featured women in closeup shots talking about their lives, has often been likened by scholars to consciousness-raising.[15] Yet this interview form, as Julia Lesage already noted in 1978, sometimes constrained the political imaginations of these feminist documentaries. She writes: 'the films' very strength, the emphasis on the experiential, can sometimes be a political limitation, especially when the film limits itself to the individual and offers little or no analysis or sense of collective process leading to social change'.[16]

The Double Day, the film Solberg and the International Women's Film Project (IWFP_ made after *The Emerging Woman*, embodies the experiential focus of United States 1970s feminist documentary culture, but is also inflected by the productivist aims of the new 'Women in Development' regime; it is the combined power of these two sensibilities that produces the film's turn to individual resilience as an answer to discrimination, overwork, and violence. The film was mainly funded by the US government's Interamerican Foundation, a development agency created by the Nixon administration that departed from previous development agencies in its emphasis on private-public partnerships. In preparation for *The Double Day,* Solberg attended a two-week workshop in Cuernavaca, Mexico run by Marxist feminist anthropologist Helen Safa; there she met women from around Latin America and began to formulate the film, which she would characterise as 'Marxist in method, not ideology' (Ribeiro Tavares, "Helena Solberg…", p. 29). After the workshop, Solberg and the IWFP crew travelled for three months, filming women in Argentina, Bolivia, Mexico, and

14 Mariana Ribeiro Tavares, 'Helena Solberg [an Interview]: Latin American Films Made in USA', *Post Script Essays in Film and the Humanities*, 40, 2/3 (Winter/Spring and Summer 2021), 28.

15 Barbara Halpern Martineau, 'Talking about our Lives and Experiences: Some Thoughts about Feminism, Documentary, and "Talking Heads"', in *Show us Life: Towards a History and Aesthetics of the Committed Documentary,* ed. Thomas Waugh (Metuchen: Scarecrow Press, 1984), p. 258.

16 Julia Lesage, 'The Political Aesthetics of the Feminist Documentary Film', *Quarterly Review of Film Studies*, 3:4 (1978), 509.

Venezuela; they attempted to film in Brazil but the military government confiscated their equipment.

The Double Day offers a range of intimate interviews with working-class and indigenous women, compiling stories of their exploitation and oppression. In each geographical location, the film alternates between scenes of women talking, mainly in groups, filmed in closeup, and scenes of women labouring in factories or fields. In the closeup scenes the women reflect on their work lives and the various difficulties and forms of discrimination they face. The film emphasises similarities in the women's experiences across regions, cutting between the groups being interviewed with eyeline-match shots that encourage viewers to see similarities in the scenes and to imagine that the women in different places are talking to one another.

After depicting the difficult work women across Latin America undertake, the film begins to articulate this as a problem rooted in class hierarchy. Towards the end of the film Solberg interviews some managerial types, who give accounts of their exploitation of women that are both callous and ridiculous. An Argentine factory manager, for example, explains that he gives women the most tedious jobs because 'in general, men are more restless than women, and this type of work tires and bores them easily'.[17] Likewise a school official gives an incoherent account of why he must separate children by gender for lunch and sports activities. Speaking over the children who squirm in their separate queues, he explains to Solberg the necessity of separating older from younger children for the differently sized lunch tables. Solberg pushes him further to explain the gendered separations—'but this is by sex, not by size'—until he gets confused. 'I don't understand', he says, and her retort of 'neither do I' is a perfect revelation of the senselessness of the gendering process.

But if the film effectively makes these points about the cluelessness of managers who enforce both gender and class regimes, it doesn't build a feminist analysis from them. The film gets its name from a scene in which a Bolivian woman remarks, 'We work a double day, and we're not happy about it.' Solberg notes that this phrase—*doble jornada* in Spanish—was not heard much before the film to the point where producers questioned her choice of title, but is now widely used in Latin America to describe the plight of working women.[18] However, despite the power of the phrase and the complaint it implies, and despite the babies and small children clinging to many of the women as the camera tracks them performing often-gruelling household and

17 *The Double Day*, dir. Helena Solberg Ladd (International Women's Film Project, 1975).

18 Julianne Burton, *Cinema and Social Change in Latin America* (Austin, TX: University of Texas Press, 1986), p. 89.

agricultural tasks, the film is not framed as critique of women as overworked labourers. Instead, following the logic of Women in Development, *Double Day* laments that women are barred from so-called 'productive' work. The opening moments of the film, for example, depict not women working but rather women looking for work; standing in a disorganised throng, frustrated, they explain that they've 'gone from factory to factory' in Buenos Aires without success. A group of nearby men contradicts them, saying there are plenty of jobs in factories. This condition of being barred from 'productive' factory work becomes a consistent through line for the film. Meanwhile the issue of housework, the other half of the double day, is rarely explicitly addressed.

In its advocacy for women to become more 'involved in production', *The Double Day* also ignores historical and contemporary attempts at gender equality, even in Latin America. In her review of *Double Day*, Helen Safa, on whose feminist anthropological work Solberg drew when formulating the film, critiques the film for its elision of Cuba, which had just passed its first Family Code granting women equal rights within the home. Safa notes that Cuba is the one place in Latin America 'where the organization of women has been consciously undertaken by the state'. Safa also worries in the review that despite 'the articulateness and even militancy of the Latin American women in this film', the film neither depicts solutions nor develops 'the link between sexual oppression, class oppression, and capitalism'.[19]

The result is that anti-capitalist feminist visions of social transformation, and particularly, any idea or programme of alleviating women's outsized share of the housework burden—the very double day that gives the film its name—are absent from the film. Rather than building a line of feminist analysis or presenting alternative ways of organising gender and labour, the film instead showcases the personal testimony of individual women. And although some of Solberg's interlocutors in *Double Day* are quite incisive, the film does not mobilise their testimony in a way that helps viewers understand the structural causes of women's oppression; nor does it offer visions of women's liberation. Instead, the film draws on this testimony to produce an ethos and ethics of resilience. This is made evident in one reviewer's glowing response: Nora Jacquez Wieser was impressed with how the film lets 'poor and working-class women in Latin America speak for themselves about their lives. Their style is not one of declamation or proclamation. They simply talk and the viewer is left with a positive respect for the strength and

19 Helen Safa, *The Double Day*, 1975. Produced by the International Women's Film Project. Directed by Helena Solberg-Ladd', *American Anthropologist* (September 1977), 746.

endurance which has meant these women's survival throughout history.'[20] As this review suggests, *Double Day*'s use of experiential testimony to cultivate audiences' 'positive respect' for Third World women's survival in the face of adversity limits the film's or its viewers' ability to understand why and how that adversity came to be.

In crafting this idealisation of Third World women's resilience, Solberg draws on the singular presence of Chungara, using her powerful testimony of trauma and resilience to fill the analytical gaps in the film. While she is unnamed, Chungara is the film's star and focal point: she is the only subject whose interview recurs throughout the film, and the only woman-worker subject interviewed alone, with no one else in the frame. Unlike many of the other women, many of whom are interviewed seated and who appear shy or contemplative or sometimes angry, Chungara stands confidently, shoulders back in three-quarter profile to the camera, well-lit and sturdy and smiling and gesturing as she speaks. Over the course of the film, she discusses women in mining communities as disrespected rather than esteemed by men—'why don't they get respect in their own homes?'; she then describes how, through 'getting organised', she and her comrades earned the men's trust and confidence: 'Now we speak and the men listen.'

In her final scene that also comprises the ending of *Double Day*, Chungara speaks for a long stretch, giving an extended graphic account of the 1967 San Juan massacre, when the Bolivian military attacked her mining community on a festival night. Standing tall, a small smile on her face, she tells the story of discovering the mutilated bodies of women and children without expressing overt shock or sadness at the details. Surviving the massacre, in her words, pushed her, finally, to speak in public and denounce the military: 'for the first time I got up and spoke what I really thought', she says. 'We had picked up so many dead that I felt courage and rage.' As Chungara recounts these events, Solberg prods her to elaborate on her feelings, asking 'was this the first time you'd spoken in public?' and 'weren't you scared?' in stark contrast with her analytical approach to her middle-class subjects like the school administrator. For its part, the camera zooms in on Chungara's face, moving closer over the course of her testimony. Chungara's monologue ends with her narrating, in her cheery and dynamic way, her harrowing tale of being jailed four times, losing a pregnancy, and being called, along with her fellow women activists, 'agitators, conspirators, everything'. At this point, her testimony abruptly stops and the final credits montage begins.

Chungara's testimony, here and throughout *The Double Day,* depicts women in collective struggle. Chungara is insistent on returning to the

20 Nora Jacquez Wieser, '*The Double Day*: simplemente Jenny', *Hispania,* 63:2 (May, 1980), p. 453 https://doi.org/10.2307/340318

collective voice even as Solberg prompts her towards an account of her individual courage and fear, and her confrontations with the militarised state are positioned as models that the rest of the women might be able to follow. At the same time, her final speech is undeniably a narrative of resilience. Chungara has experienced horrific oppression and come out stronger: she has used her anger at the murder of her comrades, at the murder of children, at the physical violence she's experienced to become a fearless, smiling leader who can finally stand up to the militarised state, no matter how many times she is imprisoned. Chungara's resistance and resilience, the immediacy of her struggle, ultimately stand in for both coherent analysis of women's oppression and any vision of a feminist future.

II 'Women in the Third World': Capitalising on Women's Resilience in the Lost Decade

Chungara's collective struggle—against the state, against capitalism—drops out of both development and its media representations over the next decade, while the iconography and rhetoric of resilience is absorbed by a more solidly neoliberal Women in Development endeavour, as well as by the transnational left. With regards to the latter, *Double Day* had a significant role in the construction of the *testimonio* boom, and ultimately Global North audiences' equation of left radicalism with a lone subaltern woman speaking and enduring. *Double Day* was screened at the 1975 Mexico City International Women's Year conference and was also the impetus for Chungara's presence there: Solberg told her about the conference and helped her travel to Mexico. At the conference, Chungara was a memorable presence, engaging in a famous confrontation with bourgeois feminist activists that is often remembered incorrectly as a confrontation with Betty Friedan.[21] In 1977 Chungara, in collaboration with Brazilian sociologist Moema Vizzier, published the testimonial memoir *Si me permiten hablar*, translated into English as *Let me Speak!*, which became the most widely translated and distributed Bolivian book of all time.[22] *The Double Day* played a key role in making iconic Chungara and her testimonial style, paving the way for the even greater success of Guatemalan Mayan activist Rigoberta Menchú's

21 Jocelyn Olcott, *International Women's Year: The Greatest Consciousness-Raising Event in History* (Oxford: Oxford University Press, 2017).

22 'Si me permiten hablar: El libro boliviano más traducido y difundido', Agencia de Noticias Fides, https://www.noticiasfides.com/nacional/sociedad/si-me-permiten-hablar-el-libro-boliviano-mas-traducido-y-difundido-183884 (accessed 29 June 2023).

subsequent testimonial memoir *I, Rigoberta Menchú*, as well as a wave of other testimonial novels and memoirs from Latin American revolutionary and activist women.[23] But the *testimonio* boom Chungara inspired, in retrospect, produced an odd effect: if the subjects of *testimonio* were always speaking for a collective, their positioning in texts like *Double Day* produced the acts of witnessing, telling, and individual overcoming as the end points of political action.

The loss of the redistributive and resistant ethos at the heart of Chungara's politics, and its replacement with a narrow ideal of resilience, was even more pronounced in Women-in-Development initiatives and the media that accompanied them. One representative example of this shift is the 1986 television documentary 'Women in the Third World', an episode in the *Global Links* series coproduced by the World Bank and Washington DC Public Television, prominently sponsored by Merrill-Lynch, and broadcast around the world.[24] 'Women in the Third World', which depicts Global South women in the years when the Western academy's critique of imperialist feminism was strongest, neglects entirely the harm done to these women by the patriarchal societies in which they are presumed to live. Less surprisingly, it also elides the economic harm done to women during Latin America's decade of debt crisis. Rather than constructing Third World women as victims who need saving, the film positions them as resilient undercapitalised resources in the national and global project of financialised development. The film also begins to link its depiction of resilient women to the ideal of girls' education, arguing that education will allow girls and women to understand the value to the global economy of their own labour, and their own resilience.

The 30-minute film opens on Malian women athletically grinding grain. The host, Jaime Martín-Escobal, intones in a voiceover that 'women do two thirds of the world's work while receiving only one tenth of the pay and own less than one percent of the world's property'.[25] Such sequences of women enthusiastically, resiliently working recur throughout the film. Despite its visual recording of women's constant, back-breaking physical labour, 'Women in the Third World' does not contain the critique of that

23 Doris Sommer, '"Not Just a Personal Story": Women's Testimonios and the Plural Self', in *Life/Lines: Theorizing Women's Autobiography*, ed. Bella Brodzki et al.(Ithaca: Cornell University Press, 1989), p. 122.

24 The thirteen half-hour documentaries produced for *Global Links* were broadcast in twenty-six countries. See Padma M. Karunaratne, 'An Interim Evaluation of the Global Links Documentary Program', World Bank Institute Evaluation Studies, No. ES99-39 (Washington DC: World Bank, 2000).

25 'Women in the Third World', dir. Jaime Martín-Escobal, *Global Links* (World Bank/WETA, 1986).

labour found in *Double Day*'s title and occasionally in its scenes. The film does assert repeatedly that Global South women are undervalued but, also in contrast with *Double Day,* it never identifies or attempts to confront those who undervalue them. Instead, the film exhorts governments, economies, and development agencies to capitalise on women's predicament, as when Martín-Escobal declares that, 'In the Third World, most of the work women do is not remunerated with money. It does not appear in the statistics and is often ignored by the economic planners. As a result, the economies of these countries suffer.' Incredibly, here, the sufferer is not the women working without compensation, but rather the economies of their countries; the visual construction of the women's good-natured resilience allows viewers to avoid the question of their exploitation and possible suffering.

Like *Double Day,* 'Women in the Third World' focuses on Bolivian Altiplano women, emphasising their resilient strength and endurance; the camera lingers on the hard labour they perform and the physical burdens they carry. However, the logic of 'Women in the Third World's' appreciation of Bolivian women's resilience differs significantly from that of *Double Day.* Here Andean women are not model revolutionary subjects, but rather examples of women's financialisation that women in other regions might be able to emulate. 'In the Bolivian highlands', Martín-Escobal notes over a long shot of a bustling market scene, 'Women have traditionally been and continue to be the driving force in the marketing of goods and agricultural products grown in the area.' As the camera tracks market women selling vegetables, in constant motion, Martín-Escobal comments that while some are only at the market to sell surplus produce, 'others are professional traders, with excellent business abilities that have been developed for generations.' A montage ensues of women around the world carrying heavy burdens, while the voiceover proclaims their centrality in 'bringing produce to market'.

In the final minutes of the film Martín-Escobal appears before a statue of a seated Andean woman, admiring it then admonishing the viewer that 'recognition should not stop at building monuments. Unless women are fully integrated into the economic systems of their nations, the chances for progress are very slim.' The film cuts abruptly to an Andean woman in silhouette, breaking up the soil with a pickaxe, pointing to women's near-infinite capacity for absorbing trauma, for arduous labour, for the double day, as an economic opportunity. The imperative to capitalise on women's resilience is made even clearer in the film's final shot of a woman leading her llama across the Altiplano, walking ceaselessly and resolutely, as Martín-Escobal intones that 'ignoring women is overlooking half the human resources, and no country can afford the luxury of wasting its resources'. The image and voiceover together convey how women's perseverance and in fact their very survival in the face of hyperexploitation is beginning to be presented as a resource that might strengthen national economies.

Even as the film refines *Double Day*'s iconography of Latin American women's resilience, linking it the growth of financialised economies, 'Women in the Third World' also prefigures the argument about the value of resilient educated girls made by Summers in his landmark World Bank speech, and repeated as a truism in *Girl Rising*. Over and over the film insists that educating girls and women constitutes a solution to the undervaluation of their work. Martín-Escobal first makes this claim over a scene of a woman weaving, meticulously but forcefully. 'The education and awareness of women in these areas can affect the health condition of the entire country. But the women must themselves be taught, so their contribution can be most productive.' In stark contrast with *Double Day*'s interrogation of the specifics of an education system that genders children, the film insists that the education of women (though the curriculum for that education remains unspecified) will lead to their greater economic productivity and social influence. Later, the episode extends this argument to encompass girls. Over a montage of small girls in school around the world, Martín-Escobal asserts that 'educating girls is one of the best investments a country can make in its economic growth and welfare, even if the girls never enter the labour market. Most girls eventually become mothers and their influence will be extended through their children for generations to come'. The education envisioned here has no pretentions to bringing about gender equality; in fact, for it to pay off best as an investment, girls must grow up into women who bear children and continue to perform the bulk of childcare duties, thereby extending their influence.

In 'Women in the Third World', this insistence that 'investment' in girls' and women's education will help countries' economic growth and general 'health condition' is only occasionally connected with the betterment of girls' and women's own lives. The one scene where the film depicts women in an improved situation does not seem to involve education or development assistance at all. Rather, it is a sequence in Kenya where women, walking and chatting excitedly, carry hoes and pickaxes down the road to a patch of farmland. These women, it turns out, have collectively bought a farm and are working the land together. Over a scene of the women energetically breaking up the land and singing, Martín-Escobal asserts that 'Women can improve their situation by pulling together their potential, their inventiveness, their creativity, and their resources.' This moment of energetic collective labour recalls feminist and anticolonial collectivities, but also anticipates the neoliberal focus on both 'creativity' and resilience: nothing is demanded of the powerful hoarders of land and resources, but the least powerful are encouraged, over and over, to creatively make something out of nothing.

III Conclusion

The Double Day bears the imprint of the radicalism of its moment. The scene of Solberg's insistent questioning of the school official, in particular, exemplifies second-wave feminist attempts to interrogate the entire process of gendering and how it is instilled in school. The contrast between this scene and the general push in 'Women in the Third World' and *Girl Rising* to 'educate girls' without a thought to the content of that education, could not be starker. In other ways, however, *Double Day* already contains the seeds of the neoliberal preoccupation with resilience. At the end, Solberg's camera zooms in on Chungara rather than taking aim at the state that brutalises and imprisons her, and Solberg asks about Chungara's feelings rather than about the militant programme of the Bolivian miners whose long history of Trotskyist political education and general radicalism she narrates in *Let Me Speak!* This political context, already absent but hinted-at in *Double Day,* completely disappears from later Women-in-Development media like 'Women in the Third World' and *Girl Rising*; the iconic shots of labouring women and the 'talking heads' intimately narrating their resilient survival of overwork and violence are all that remain.

This erasure of the militant traditions of mining communities and mining women can be seen in *Girl Rising's* story of fourteen-year-old Senna from Peru. Senna lives in La Rinconada, a perpetually snowy mining area; emphasising its bleakness, her story is the only one told in black and white. La Rinconada is notoriously dangerous: mining there is largely unregulated and unwaged.[26] Rather than implicate mine owners in the brutal conditions that killed Senna's father, the narration (written by Peruvian American writer Marie Arana, narrated by Salma Hayek) curses the mountain: 'This mountain, she will trample the fiercest spirit, shatter the strongest back.' Named for Xena Warrior Princess because her father hopes she will fight tirelessly for the poor, Senna instead falls in love with poetry. After struggling in school, Senna finds her voice as a poet. Her vignette ends with a scene of her giving a reading at school, while Hayek intones: 'In time I saw that my father had been right all along. I was a fighter, brave, and words made for mighty weapons … I know now that the fortune my father sought so haplessly was always buried in me. It was just a matter of finding it.' This metaphor seems apt for the condition of girls' resilient testimony when the social struggle that prompted testimonial modes of address falls away: Senna has found the treasure, the voice, the resilience buried in herself, and she, unlike her hapless

26 See 'Tears of the Sun: the Gold Rush at the Top of the World', The New Yorker, https://www.newyorker.com/magazine/2015/04/20/tears-of-the-sun (accessed 27 November 2023).

father, will mine it successfully. But the voice Senna extracts from inside herself does not so much liberate her as it props up the larger system of extraction that impoverishes mining communities like hers, as illustrated by the fact that the multinational corporation Intel, which relies on the dangerous and arduous mining of gold and many other metals, is *Girl Rising*'s main sponsor. Senna may be a 'girl rising' from the bottom of the power structure, but the neoliberal development industry capitalises upon her resilient ascent to lend said power structure credibility and force.

Bibliography

Boserup, Ester, *Women's Role in Economic Development* (1970; London, Earthscan, 2011).

Burton, Julianne, *Cinema and Social Change in Latin America* (Austin, TX: University of Texas Press, 1986).

Cavalcanti Tedesco, Marina, 'The Women's Film Project: An international Collective in the Career of Helena Solberg', *Jump Cut*, 61 (Fall 2022).

Fanon, Frantz. 'Algeria Unveiled', in *A Dying Colonialism* (New York: Grove Press, 1965), pp. 38–68.

Geidel, Molly, 'Building the Counterinsurgent Girl', *Feminist Studies*, 44:3 (2018), 635–65, doi:10.15767/feministstudies.44.3.0635 (accessed 27 November 2023).

Geidel, Molly, *The Development Film in the Americas* (Oakland: University of California Press, 2025).

Jacquez Wieser, Nora, '*The Double Day*; *Simplemente Jenny*', *Hispania*, 63:2 (May, 1980), 453.

James, Robin, *Resilience and Melancholy: Pop Music, Feminism, Neoliberalism* (Oxford: John Hunt Publishing, 2015).

Karunaratne, Padma M., 'An Interim Evaluation of the Global Links Documentary Program', World Bank Institute Evaluation Studies, No. ES99-39 (Washington DC: World Bank, 2000).

Leary, John Patrick, *Keywords: The New Language of Capitalism* (Chicago: Haymarket Books, 2018).

Lesage, Julia, 'The Political Aesthetics of the Feminist Documentary Film', *Quarterly Review of Film Studies*, 3:4 (1978), 507–23.

Martineau, Barbara Halpern, 'Talking about Our Lives and Experiences: Some Thoughts about Feminism, Documentary, and "Talking Heads"', in *Show us Life: Towards a History and Aesthetics of the Committed Documentary*, edited by Thomas Waugh (Metuchen, NJ: Scarecrow Press, 1984), pp. 252–73.

Martín-Escobal, Jaime, dir., 'Women in the Third World', *Global Links* (World Bank/WETA, 1986).

Megaton, Olivier, dir., *Taken 2* (EuropaCorp, 2012).

Meyerowitz, Joanne, *A War on Global Poverty: The Lost Promise of Redistribution and the Rise of Microcredit* (Princeton: Princeton University Press, 2021).

Mohanty, Chandra. 'Under Western Eyes: Feminist Scholarship and Colonial Discourses', *Boundary 2*, 12:13 (Spring–Autumn 1984), 333–58.

Morel, Pierre, dir., *Taken* (EuropaCorp, 2008).

Olcott, Jocelyn, *International Women's Year: The Greatest Consciousness-Raising Event in History* (Oxford: Oxford University Press, 2017).

Ribeiro Tavares, Mariana, 'Helena Solberg [an Interview]: Latin American Films Made in USA', *Post Script Essays in Film and the Humanities*, 40. 2/3 (Winter/Spring and Summer 2021), 27–37.

Robbins, Richard, dir., *Girl Rising* (The Documentary Group, 2013).

Robbins, Richard 'Si me permiten hablar: el libro boliviano más traducido y difundido', Agencia de Noticias Fides, https://www.noticiasfides.com/nacional/sociedad/si-me-permiten-hablar-el-libro-boliviano-mas-traducido-y difundido-183884 (accessed 29 June 2023).

Solberg, Helena. 'Helena Solberg Interview las 460/560,' online video recording, YouTube, 17 September 2018 https://www.youtube.com/watch?v=W3HXmWzz2-c&ab_channel=UACenterforLatinAmericanStudies [accessed 29 June 2023]

Solberg Ladd, Helena, dir., *The Double Day* (International Women's Film Project, 1975).

Sommer, Doris, '"Not Just a Personal Story": Women's Testimonios and the Plural Self', in *Life/Lines: Theorizing Women's Autobiography*, edited by Bella Brodzki and Celeste Schenck (Ithaca, NY: Cornell University Press, 1989), pp. 107– 30.

Spivak, Gayatri Chakravorty, 'Can the Subaltern Speak?' in *Marxism and the Interpretation of Culture*, edited by Cary Nelson and Lawrence Grossberg (Chicago: University of Illinois Press, 1988), pp. 271–316.

Summers, Lawrence H., 'Investing in All the People: Educating Women in Developing Countries', EDI Seminar Paper 45 [originally delivered at the 1992 Annual Meeting of The World Bank] (Washington DC: World Bank, 1994).

'Tears of the Sun: the Gold Rush at the Top of the World', The New Yorker, https://www.newyorker.com/magazine/2015/04/20/tears-of-the-sun (accessed 27 November 2023) April 13, 2015, pp. 54.

The Cunning of Gender Violence, edited by Lila Abu-Lughod , Rema Hammami, and Nadera Shalhoub-Kevorkian (Durham, NC: Duke University Press, 2023).

Wilson, Kalpana, *Race, Racism and Development: Interrogating History, Discourse, and Practice* (London: Zed Books, 2012).

10

Reimagining Home: Exile and Resilience in Chilean Film, 1970–90

Jennifer Alpert and Camila Gatica Mizala

There is a folk tale that explains how a Chilean community developed in Lausanne, Switzerland. When Chilean exiles arrived in the 1970s, the Swiss government placed them in different parts of the country, giving these new residents no input regarding *where* they would live. One day, a Chilean exile took a trip to Lausanne, which reminded him of the south of his country. He went back to his house, organized his fellow Chileans and they moved to the town that reminded them of home. This story captures an example of how Chilean exiles have historically resisted against lack of agency. Regardless of this tale's veracity, it illustrates that exile became another way of being Chilean beyond Chile, in places far away from what was once home. Home was a contentious space in Latin America in the second half of the twentieth century, since many civilians had to leave their countries when dictatorships sprung in the region and sowed violence and disruption.

The armed forces that took over various governments not only broke the social contract between democratically elected regimes and the people they represented, but also identified an enemy that was no longer outside the country—it had infiltrated its borders. In the Cold War context, this internal foe was the embodiment of all things politically left, which made the alleged enemy unpatriotic and foreign even though in most instances those persecuted were citizens. The illegitimate regimes used this line of thinking to justify the need to extirpate those deemed subversive to protect the nation. The eradication techniques that *de facto* governments employed included forced detentions, torture, assassination, disappearance, and exile, methods they applied systematically and built into governmental structures.

Within Latin America, Chileans were seemingly forced to abandon their country at a higher rate than others in the region. Patricio Orellana recounts that the Comisión Chilena de Derechos Humanos estimated that by 1982 approximately 200,000 people had left the country. However, military regime representative Carlos Varas claimed in 1988 that 200,000 was an unreasonable number and that this figure was only 352 exiles.[1] In contrast, Javier Campo notes that 'according to a report by the [...] Team for Denunciation, Investigation and Treatment of the Tortured and Their Families [...] published in 1989 [...] it was calculated that since [the coup in] 1973 1,600,000 Chileans had left the country for extended periods'.[2] These highly dissimilar figures evidence that no clear numbers regarding exiles exist due to legal, political, and economic issues, as well as a lack of counting accuracy of countries which welcomed displaced Chileans.[3] However, these tallies demonstrate the sheer magnitude of this displacement, one of the reasons why Chile has been the frequent focus of academic study in relation to exile. Scholarly works have discussed exile as a 'continuation rather than a cessation' of suffering, a bereavement, and 'a source of invisible pain'.[4]

1 Patricio Orellana, 'Exilio y desexilio', in *La represión en Chile 1973–1989* (Santiago: Senda, 2015), https://www.probidadenchile.cl/wp/la-represion-en-chile-7-cap-7-exilio-y-desexilio/ (accessed 30 June 2023). For general works on Chilean exile see Alan Angell, and Susan Carstairs, 'The Exile Question in Chilean Politics', *Third World Quarterly*, 9:1(1987), pp.148–67, doi:10.26409/2019MKbook01 (accessed 27 November 2023); Thomas C. Wright, and Rody Oñate, 'Chilean Political Exile', *Latin American Perspectives*, 34:4 (2007), pp. 31–49, doi:10.1177/0094582X07302902 (accessed 27 November 2023). Many of the people who left Chile immediately after 11 September 1973 were Brazilians, Argentines, Peruvians, and Bolivians who were themselves asylum seekers and had become key members in the development of intellectual centres such as Centro de Estudios de la Realidad Nacional (CEREN, PUC), Escuela de Artes y Comunicaciones (EAC, PUC), and the Centro de Estudios Socio-Económicos (CESO, Universidad de Chile). See Carla Rivera, 'Diálogos y reflexiones sobre las comunicaciones en la Unidad Popular. Chile, 1970–1973', *Historia y Comunicación Social*, 20:2 (2015), pp. 345–67, doi:10.5354/0719-1243.2022.67231 (accessed 27 November 2023).

2 Javier Campo, 'Documentary Film from the Southern Cone during Exile (1970–1980)', *Latin American Perspectives* 188, 40 (2013), p. 146.

3 Eugenia Palieraki, 'El año 1978 y el exilio chileno', in *Albornoz, Francisco, Gatica Mizala, Camila, and Rolle, Claudio* (1978) (manuscript).

4 Carlos J. Gonsalves, 'The Psychological Effects of Political Repression on Chilean Exiles in the US', *American Journal of Orthopsychiatry*, 60:1 (1990), 143–53, doi:10.1037/h0079176 (accessed 27 November 2023); Liliana Munoz, 'Exile as Bereavement: Socio-psychological Manifestations of Chilean Exiles in Great Britain', *British Journal of Medical Psychology*, 53:3 (1980),

These characterizations point towards an experience of endurance, which psychologists commonly refer to as resilience, a term that is prevalent in popular, governmental and academic discourses.[5]

Resilience as a concept has not always been germane to the humanities or the social sciences. The term, in its acceptation 'to rebound or recoil', was imported into the English language in the early seventeenth century from the Latin verb *resilire*.[6] English engineer Thomas Tredgold used the term in 1818 to explain why some types of wood (timber) could accommodate sudden and severe loads without breaking (McAslan, 'The Concept of Resilience'). From the natural sciences it has migrated to the humanities and the social sciences as a way to describe certain behaviours that enable people to quickly adapt to adverse situations. The American Psychological Association defines resilience as 'the process and outcome of successfully adapting to difficult or challenging life experiences, especially through mental, emotional, and behavioural flexibility and adjustment to external and internal demands'.[7] Resilience usually refers to the capacity to recover swiftly, to have a flexibility or elasticity that allows people (and originally objects) to bounce back.

It is not uncommon, then, to find many scholarly articles (particularly in the fields of psychology, political science, and education) that link resilience to refugees or experiences of loss. In their book *Resilient Life: The Art of Living Dangerously*, Brad Evans and Julian Reid identify the concept of resilience as a neoliberal ideal that aims to reduce the impacts of emotion

227–32, doi:10.1111/j.2044-8341.1980.tb02545 (accessed 27 November 2023); Jorge Barudy, 'A Programme of Mental Health for Political Refugees: Dealing with the Invisible Pain of Political Exile', *Social Science & Medicine*, 28:7 (1989), 715–27, https://doi.org/10.1016/0277-9536 (accessed 27 November 2023).

5 Some examples are as follows: 'Hacia un Chile resiliente frente a desastres: Una oportunidad', Center for Climate and Resilience Research, https://www.cr2.cl/informe-cnid-hacia-un-chile-resiliente-frente-a-desastres-una-oportunidad/ (accessed 29 June 2023); 'Chile Resiliente: Ciencia de Datos e Inteligencia Artificial para abordar los desafíos del cambio climático', Evento Chile Resiliente, https://eventochileresiliente.cl/ (accessed 2 June 2023); 'Chile, el país más resiliente de América Latina', Psicologos Online, https://www.psicologosonline.cl/articulos/chile-el-pais-mas-resiliente-de-america-latina (accessed 29 June 2023).

6 Alastair McAslan, 'The Concept of Resilience. Understanding its Origins, Meanings and Utility', *Torrens Resilience Institute*, 1(2010), https://www.flinders.edu.au/content/dam/documents/research/torrens-resilience-institute/resilience-origins-and-utility.pdf (accessed 29 June 2023)

7 'Resilience', American Psychological Association, https://dictionary.apa.org/?_ga=2.110647105.57727777.1685565970-1381700433.1685565963 (accessed 29 June 2023).

(specifically pain and mourning) in service of efficiency and productivity. This operation allows individuals to survive in a world where security is no longer the norm. Evans and Reid critique this model, since it reduces human subjects to the purpose of surviving rather than thriving and disempowers them, as they are meant to accept and exist within their conditions rather than change them.[8] Additionally, in the 2012 Intergovernmental Panel on Climate Change Report, resilience appears repeatedly, connected to ideas of precariousness and vulnerability in the context of managing risks of climate change.[9] The report defines resilience as 'the ability of a system and its component parts to anticipate, absorb, accommodate, or recover from the effects of a potentially hazardous event in a timely and efficient manner, including through ensuring the preservation, restoration, or improvement of its essential basic structures and functions' (C. B. Field et al., Managing, p. 34). Even as definitions of resilience change to respond to new perspectives and contexts, the concept reappears linked to the idea of returning to a previous state (status quo).

Chile often draws associations with resilience given a historic ability to recover from natural disasters (predominantly earthquakes), but the experience of exile during the dictatorship called for the act of resistance. While these two concepts are linked, they are distinct. If we take resilience as the capacity to bounce back, this action entails accepting structural conditions. On the other hand, resistance, the capacity to oppose or push back, is by definition a refusal.[10] Zuzana Pick argues that Latin America's 'collective consciousness is identified in the historical resistance to violence and oppression [...] Resistance is understood in terms of the struggle to construct and maintain a cultural specificity by appropriating elements that will characterise the diverse historical, social, cultural and political contexts'.[11] Resistance in the Latin American context is confrontational and the hallmark of an agentic fight to change the status quo. Cinema was part of that struggle.

8 Brad Evans and Julian Reid, *Resilient Life: The Art of Living Dangerously* (Cambridge: Polity, 2014), pp. 1–2. For another take on this point see Laura Quintana's chapter in this volume, where she characterises resilience with reference to a 'consensual' ideology.

9 C. B. Field et al., *Managing the Risks of Extreme Events and Disasters to Advance Climate Change Adaptation.* Special report of the Intergovernmental Panel on Climate Change (Cambridge: Cambridge University Press, 2012). https://www.ipcc.ch/site/assets/uploads/2018/03/SREX_Full_Report-1.pdf (accessed on 18 September, 2022).

10 On the distinction between resilience and resistance see also Nicolas Lema's contribution in this volume.

11 Zuzana Pick, 'Chilean Cinema in Exile, 1973–1986', in *New Latin American Cinema*, ed. Michael Martin (Detroit: Wayne State University Press, 1997), p. 45.

Exiled filmmakers were prolific and political in their cultural production. As Campo notes, 'Chileans have the most films from exile to their credit among Latin Americans and among the most in the world. In just the first 10 years of exile (1973–83), 178 films were made, including long and short films of fiction, animation, and documentaries' (Campo, 'Documentary Film', p. 148). Cinema instilled a form of resistance by constructing the possibility of a Chile that exists beyond the trauma of the coup, the dictatorship, and exile.

These films' national and political tenor has been contentious, partly because scholars have categorized them in a number of ways. Pick argues that 'only certain films produced in exile were classified as 'Chilean'. [...] The term 'Chilean cinema of the resistance' was used to 'categorize' mostly films produced in Spanish that were 'concerned with the Chilean situation' (Pick, 'Chilean Cinema in Exile', p. 41). As another way of classifying cultural production in exile, José Miguel Palacios makes a distinction between 'cinema of resistance' and 'exile cinema': 'cinema of resistance' insisted on the language and aesthetics of the past to organize and signify their present; 'exile cinema' confronted the historical and cultural conditions that defined their present.[12] Thus, for many Chilean filmmakers who left their countries, making films became a way to process and denounce the violence that displaced them. If resilience is tied to the tangible realm of a body that can bounce back to its original state, or a person that can eventually return to the once forbidden land, the intangibility of exile's affective journey and the irreversible change that this trauma generates became materialised through cinema, giving shape to a journey of no return for which resilience could not account. Thus, the old codes of the 'cinema of resistance' persist in exile, but also become reconfigured in 'exile cinema'. Both craft a resistance that looks to reconstruct not only the lost political project of the left, embodied in the Unidad Popular political coalition and its figurehead President Salvador Allende, but also a lost home.[13]

Films became a material reality (both in their quality as a physical object and the screen as a physical space) through which exiles could construct an idea of home. This home was at once tangible and imagined, tethering the

12 José Miguel Palacios, 'Resistances vs. Exile: The Political Rhetoric of Chilean exile Cinema in the 1970s', *Jump Cut*, 57 (2016), https://www.ejumpcut.org/archive/jc57.2016/-PalaciosChile/index.html (accessed 1 July 2023).

13 The Unidad Popular (UP) was a left political coalition. Its leader Salvador Allende became the elected president in 1970. As a project, it became internationally relevant because it was a left wing government whose aim was to instate socialism through democracy by introducing radical and structural social and economic changes. The UP government was cut short by a coup on 11 September 1973. The same day, President Allende committed suicide in Palacio La Moneda, the seat of the Chilean government as the military forces were closing in.

intangible affective journey of the traumatic experience of uprooting to a tangible location, whether a celluloid print, an analogue tape, or a theatre screen in which these images came to life. This home was created and projected, a literal space that allowed rootedness in something physical yet portable. These filmmakers' work combated this uprooting and reconfigured their position as exiles, creating versions of home that they could always conjure and access (and even carry with them) in observable, material ways, regardless of location. In these films, the idea of home becomes reimagined—in the dialectic between that which is physical and envisaged, itinerant yet fixed, Chilean filmmakers created a locus of resistance against violence and displacement as they reclaimed agency in their construction of spaces of belonging. Film then became a place in which to create new conceptions of home. Rather than being resilient and bouncing back in the midst of challenging circumstances, these exiles offered a way to challenge the status quo through filmic representational strategies.

I The meaning of exile, the creation of home

The dictatorship deeply fragmented the nation and attempted to strip agency from its people. In 1974, Augusto Pinochet's illegitimate regime codified exile as a practice into law-decree 604, which prohibited Chilean or foreign people who had 'dishonour[ed], defame[d] or vilely discredit[ed] the country, its Government and its people' to be in or allowed into Chile.[14] The junta saw the need to emphasize Chilean-ness as a key part of their duties. This characteristic translated into 'devotion to the Homeland, its sacred emblems and its historical traditions' (Decreto Ley 604), which predicated and constructed a particular way of being Chilean. The dictatorship considered everything that did not fit their prescribed idea of citizenship to be threatening, and something (or in this instance, someone) that needed to be cast out.

Exile represented a deeply unsettling experience that had the potential to rob agency from those displaced and redefine what being Chilean entailed. Whether it was forced or pragmatic, exile involved being barred from one's country (or city, if exiled internally), or having to leave for reasons related to survival.[15] In this context, exile also meant breaking, willingly or unwillingly,

14 'Prohibe el ingreso de personal al territorio nacional en los casos que indica', Decreto Ley 604, https://www.bcn.cl/leychile/navegar?idNorma=6225 (accessed 27 November 2023).

15 In this chapter, we focus on filmmakers who were in exile outside of Chile. Being displaced to another, often remote, region of the country (internal exile) was also a common practice.

ideas of identity linked to a territory (bound by territorial frontiers), which allowed for a questioning of the relationship between identity and place (Palieraki, 'El año 1978'). In this sense, being banished from one's country by a *de facto* regime turns the act of making a new home into mourning for an irreversible loss. Chilean exile implied a double loss, since staying in Pinochet's Chile would not have felt like home either. Chilean exiles also mourned the demise of the left's political project, as well as the possibility of a new Chile.

Territorial and political displacement generated a common experience. Zuzana Pick argues that 'the cultural filiation of Latin Americans, including its exiles, is not limited to a place but rather to the recognition of a subjective and collective relationship to a social, political, and historical formation—Latin America as a continental entity and its specific national components' (Pick, 'Chilean Cinema in Exile', p. 45). This filiation helped to bring Chilean exiles closer to other Latin Americans who were also far from their countries, reinforcing their identity and expanding and transforming an imagined community.[16]

Developing memories of the pain and violence the dictatorship inflicted on Chilean society was also crucial. Elizabeth Lira's work decodes the profound consequences that this brutality had on those who were directly affected and points out the importance of remembering and reparation as a way of healing.[17] Although she centres on how trauma developed in victims of physical violence (which some exiles also experienced), trauma can also

16 The term comes from Benedict Anderson, *Imagined Communities: Reflections on the Origin and Spread of Nationalism* (London and New York: Verso, 2006). Solidarity will play a key role in the expanding and transforming of the Chilean exile community. Mariana Perry has written several articles in which she explores Chilean exiles, as well as the solidarity networks that arose linked to the Chilean situation. See '"With a Little Help from My Friends": The Dutch Solidarity Movement and the Chilean Struggle for Democracy', *Revista Europea de Estudios Latinoamericanos y del Caribe*, 101 (2016), pp. 75–96; 'The Power of Solidarity with Chile. The British Left in Response to the Coup, 1973–1979', *Secuencia*, 108 (2021), doi:10.18234/SECUENCIA.V0I108.1823 (accessed 27 November 2023).

17 Elizabeth Lira and Brian Loveman, *Las ardientes cenizas del olvido: Vía chilena de reconciliación política 1932–1994* (Santiago: Lom, 2000); Elizabeth Lira, 'Trauma, duelo, reparación y memoria', *Revista de Estudios Sociales*, 36 (2010), pp. 14–28, doi:10.7440/res36.2010.02 (accessed 27 November 2023). On the topic of remembering and the Chilean dictatorship, see Steve Stern, *Remembering Pinochet's Chile: On the Eve of London 1998* (Durham, NC: Duke University Press, 2006); Stern (*Battling*); Steve Stern, *Reckoning with Pinochet: The Memory Question in Democratic Chile, 1989–2006* (Durham, NC: Duke University Press, 2010).

emerge from the distance with home and the loved ones who stayed. For Lira, remembering and exercising collective memory are key to unlocking those traumatic experiences, at home and abroad.

After being forced out, exiles (both legally expelled and self-imposed for the sake of preservation) attempted to make a home in another country. Steve Stern, a historian of Chile's dictatorship and the 1990s, has foregrounded 'the value of the work undertaken by many Chileans in exile—to mobilize international solidarity, to work professionally on themes of human rights, to build circuits of political dialogue [...] about the meaning of the Chilean experience'.[18] Chilean filmmakers in exile were stewards of these practices: their work materialised from a combination of memory, nostalgia, and imagination to construct an idea of home and with it, of Chile. They did so with agency: by mobilizing peers, contributing to social discourses, and readily condemning the dictatorship through fiction and documentaries alike.

In this sense, cinema can work as an important device to preserve memory, not only by capturing relevant images and showing a particular reality, but by playing an active role in the battle for *what* and *how* we remember. In a way, films can work as places/environments of memory akin to Pierre Nora's classification of *lieux de mémoire* and *lieux d'histoire*, as they allow a constant remembering through a 'reconstituted object beneath the gaze of critical history'.[19] Thus, filmmaking in exile served not only as a way to remember one's country but also to reconstruct it, turning the act of filming into a way to make a home away from home. Cinema offered a physical and symbolic space to place the idea of home, when for exiles it was now an emotional state. If home was a space of safety, a womblike embrace of belonging that exile had disrupted in exile, the dark theatres in which to view memories of one's country could offer an affective relationship through which to recognize that home was now mobile.

Moving from one country to another is often attached to the idea of 'starting from scratch' somewhere else, often with very few or no material possessions, making the process of installation critical in the formation of new identities as people begin a process of modelling new spaces of belonging.[20] Memory, in this context, becomes 'an important political tool,

18 Steve Stern, *Battling for Hearts and Minds: Memory Struggles in Pinochet's Chile, 1973–1988* (Durham, NC: Duke University Press, 2006).

19 Pierre Nora, 'Between Memory and History: Les Lieux de Mémoire', *Representacions*, 26 (1989), 12, access link:http://www.jstor.org/stable/2928520 (accessed 27 November).

20 Divya P. Tolia-Kelly, 'Locating Processes of Identification: Studying the Precipitates of Re-memory through Artefacts in the British Asian Home', *Transactions of the Institute of British Geographers*, 29:3 (2004), 314–29, doi:10.1111/j.0020-2754.2004.00303.x (accessed 27 November 2023).

grounding both individual memory and collective cultural heritage stories' (Tolia-Kelly, 'Locating Processes of Identification', p. 315). Adapting Divya Tolia-Kelly's concept of re-memory into the Latin American context, what emerges are new sites of identity-territory relations where memory-history gets activated in connection to the new place of settling, which signifies the notion of home as one that imbues the new space with memories and sentiment. Thus, home is not only a physical location, but a place that can be created when memories and sentiment are poured into it. Similarly, the bond between individuals and their homeland is not static, and it impacts how collective members remember their home country. In this context, the condition of exile greatly influences identities and narratives in the process of remembering, both in its meaning to create memory (remember) as well as reintegrating into a community (re-member).[21]

When it comes to home-making, material culture creates a safeguard that bridges the experience of feeling out-of-place in the new country and building a home. According to Macarena Bonhomme, home-making is the process in which individuals build and embody their own space, and transform it into a *home* through displaying their material possessions as well as performing their everyday practices.[22] In the context of displacement that being exiled entails, this transformation allows for individuals to have or feel their agency in an environment where they seem to have none.[23] Agency through home-making could also take place through cultural production, particularly filmmaking. Exiled Chilean directors made sense of a new territory and a new reality by displaying their memories onto films as a way of organizing personal and collective experiences of displacement.

II Cinema as a tangible expression of home

With the coup in 1973, Chile plunged into disarray, becoming a different place at the hands of a ruthless dictatorship that had little regard for freedom of expression. The new illegitimate government closed film schools, cinema clubs, Chile Films (a major public production and training centre),

21 Geert Franzenburg, 'Displaced Values: From Remembrance to Resilience', *Problems of Education in the 21st Century*, 56 (2013), pp. 59–65, doi:10.33225/pec/13.56.59 (accessed 27 November 2023).

22 Macarena Bonhomme, 'Exilio y retorno: dos procesos de integración desde el hogar', prepared for delivery at the 2014 Congress of the Latin American Studies Association (Chicago, May 21–24, 2014).

23 Anthony Giddens, *La constitución de la sociedad: Bases para la teoría de la estructuración* (Buenos Aires: Amorrortu, 2011).

and destroyed film material. The regime also detained and abducted filmmakers and people linked to the film industry, many of whom the dictatorship eventually disappeared (an emblematic case was Jorge Müller, who was the cameraman for *La Batalla de Chile* and films like *A la sombra del sol*). Renowned filmmakers that included Raúl Ruiz, Miguel Littín, Patricio Guzmán, Pedro Chaskel, Helvio Soto, and Sergio Castilla left Chile.[24] The filmmakers who stayed, such as Ignacio Agüero, began working in the very profitable advertising industry in combination with filmmaking in the 1980s.

The 178 films produced outside of Chile between 1973 and 1983 (most of which were documentaries) worked as a way to project an idea of Chile that helped exiled filmmakers cope with their uprooting.[25] It was in these films that they could project a narrative that allowed them to not only have agency as they reconstructed their home on screen, but also to deal with the trauma of displacement and the defunct dream of the left. The impulse to (re)construct a place of belonging in exile appeared through form and narrative, showing how filmmakers sought to reimagine their relationship with Chile, its land, and its history. These reconstructions and reimaginations took shape in three distinct ways, which appeared independently of or concurrently with each other in films made in exile: (a) making home tangible through community and belonging; (b) displacing space and time to replicate and reproduce a version of home; and (c) reimagining the past to create a material history of home.

a) Making home tangible through community and belonging

Building and exploring a community on screen became a critical way for exiled filmmakers to remake home. Palacios argues that filming was possible

24 In some cases, films also had an exile story, like *La batalla de Chile* (Patricio Guzmán 1975, 1976, 1979). Guzmán had actively filmed during the Unidad Popular years. He was detained in the National Stadium, but the film was hidden in the Swedish Embassy and sent by sea to Stockholm, and later to Cuba, where it was edited into what we see today. Behind this effort was filmmaker Chris Marker. See Mónica Villarroel and Isabel Mardones, *Señales contra el olvido: Cine chileno recobrado* (Santiago: Cuarto Propio, 2012).

25 As Campo notes, 'Chileans have the most films from exile to their credit among Latin Americans and among the most in the world. In just the first 10 years of exile (1973–1983), 178 films were made.' 'Filmografía en el exilio', Memoria Chilena, http://www.memoriachilena.gob.cl/602/w3-article-92833.html (accessed 20 June 2023).

precisely because of solidarity practices of peers and strangers.[26] The landmark film *Diálogos de exiliados* (Raúl Ruiz, 1974/5) thematises this solidarity in its foregrounding of community narratively and stylistically as it shows camaraderie as a form of belonging.[27] The film documents how a group of exiles kidnap a pro-Pinochet Chilean artist who visits Paris, and shows how efforts of coordination unite these activists towards a common goal. Stylistically, the film is composed almost exclusively of two-shots with additional group shots that construct and highlight communitarianism. The opening sequence begins with a shot of an empty space only populated with furniture and shortly after the camera slowly tracks toward two men, framed in a two-shot. In their conversation, one asks the other about his place of origin and insistently proposes different locations, to which the companion

26 For a more extensive account of the transnational solidarities of exiled Chilean filmmakers, see José Miguel Palacios, *Transnational Cinema Solidarity: Chilean Exile Film and Video after 1973* (Berkeley, University of California Press, 2025).

27 In the last fifteen years there has been an expansion of Ruiz studies: Verónica Cortínez and Manfred Engelbert, *La tristeza de los tigres y los misterios de Raúl Ruiz* (Santiago: Cuarto Propio, 2011); Valeria de los Ríos and Iván Pinto, *El cine de Raúl Ruiz: Fantasmas, simulacros y artificios* (Santiago: Uqbar, 2010); Valeria de los Ríos, *Metamorfosis: aproximaciones al cine y la poética de Raúl Ruiz* (Santiago: Ediciones Metales Pesados, 2019); Laura Jordán González and Nicolás Lema Habash, 'Raúl Ruiz's Now We're Gonna Call You Brother and the Problem of the People's Sonic Representation', in *Soundings: Documentary Film and the Listening Experience*, ed. Geoffrey Cox et al. (Huddersfield: University of Huddersfield, 2018), pp. 255–77; Miguel Marías, *Raúl Ruiz* (Madrid: Cátedra, 2012); Sergio Navarro Mayorga, *La naturaleza ama ocultarse: El cine chileno de Raúl Ruíz (1962–1975)* (Santiago: Ediciones Metales Pesados, 2019); Raúl Ruiz et al., *Conversaciones con Raúl Ruiz* (Santiago: Universidad Diego Portales, 2003); Raúl Ruiz and Bruno Cuneo, *Ruiz: Entrevistas escogidas, filmografía comentada* (Santiago: Eds. Universidad Diego Portales, 2013); Raúl Ruiz and Bruno Cuneo, *Diario: Notas, recuerdos y secuencias de cosas vistas* (Santiago: Ediciones Universidad Diego Portales, 2017); Cristián Sánchez, *Aventura del cuerpo: El pensamiento cinematográfico de Raúl Ruiz* (Santiago: OchoLibros, 2011); Adolfo Vásquez Rocca, 'Raúl Ruiz: Ontología de lo fantástico. Territorios, políticas estéticas y polisemia Visual' *Aisthesis,* 48 (2010), 31–47, doi: 10.4067/S0718-71812010000200003 (accessed 27 November 2023); Laura Jordán González and Nicolás Lema Habash, 'On the Cinematic Deconstruction of Logical Sounds: Raúl Ruiz's Quasi-Voice in *La maleta', Cultural Critique,* 121 (2023), 42–67; Ignacio Albornoz and Iván Pinto, Raúl Ruiz: Potencias de lo Múltiple (Santiago: Metales Pesados, 2023); Nicolas Lema Habash, 'De los usos políticos de la muerte en ;a expropiación de Raúl Ruiz', *Aisthesis,* 69 (2021), 103–30, doi:10.7764/69.5 (accessed 27 November 2023).

Figure 10.1 One of the many group shots in *Diálogos de Exiliados*.

repeatedly responds 'further than that' (he is Chilean). At one point, the man questioned requests to see his companion's papers, which reveal his Algerian nationality. Even though these two men are from different countries, the shot establishes their similarity by framing them together: from its initial scene, *Diálogos* suggests that even though they may be far from home, a shared identity as exiles links these characters in community. As the film progresses, audiences see additional permutations of community through different framings that include two or more characters. When characters appear alone, they do so briefly—either the camera moves slowly to include others in the frame, or off-screen characters swiftly move to enter the shot.[28] In this way, the shots' composition puts forth a sense of unity that builds a community of primarily Chilean exiles that approximates a sense of home.

However, *Diálogos* does not offer a one-dimensional, utopian portrayal of a community but rather provides a poignant example of the complex dynamics of exile. Ruiz depicts a plurality of experiences of displacement (and those displaced) and recreates Chile as well as its interpersonal and political relationships. In this sense, the film is less about the struggle and activism against the dictatorship, and more about demystifying the experience of exile and refusing to romanticize the efforts of the resistance.[29]

Diálogos shows the difficulties of political organization in exile, and offers an exegesis of how precarity can modify political practices. Ruiz provides a cynical counterpoint to romantic views of the resistance against the dictatorship by showing that individuals united towards a common goal still had personal material needs. A sequence in which money changes hands offers an example of the different relationships Chileans had with the resistance against the dictatorship.[30] A woman hands over an envelope with 10,000 USD that French comrades had donated for distribution to the comrades

28 Similarly, some of these singular shots also include an arm, or hair that signals a view from over the shoulder of an interlocutor.

29 For more on displacement see Nicolas Lema Habash, 'Against Purity: Spinoza and the Problem of Displacement in Raúl Ruiz's On Top of the Whale (1982)', in *Spinoza nella letteratura e nelle arti del Novecento*, ed. Daniela Bostrenghi et al. (Florence: Le Lettere, 2022), pp. 317–32.

30 Money is also an important element in the films of Valeria Sarmiento, who was crucial to the making of Ruiz's film (and his greater filmography).

from the Chilean far left revolutionary movement MIR, Movimiento de Izquierda Revolucionaria (Left Revolutionary Movement). The man who takes the envelope asks the woman if she thinks he could use part of the money to be reimbursed for expenses incurred taking care of newly arrived Chilean exiles. When the woman replies that she was handed the money to give to someone else, he replies that he cannot finance the resistance because his personal funds were scarce, and that he can offer her a signed receipt. The woman relays that it is his responsibility, and he retorts that it is the responsibility of the resistance. The man is the first of a sequence of exchanges during which different men remark on the need for reimbursement of expenses and offer to leave a signed receipt. Finally, the last man hands back the envelope to the woman waiting outside. She approaches the camera and addresses the audience directly, raising the envelope while saying 'here were US$10,000, at present there are US$9,800. Since I'm not the person responsible for making use of this money, I need to hand this to comrade Carlos. Because comrade Carlos is also not responsible for using this money, he will give it to comrade Lucho. Because comrade Lucho is also not responsible for making use of the money, he will hand it to comrade [...]'. The scene ends mid-sentence, suggesting that the long list of people who would receive and pass the envelope was never ending.[31] The implication is that there may be no money left at the conclusion of the envelope's journey. Regarding this scene, Ruiz has said 'the money for a cause can disappear without it being robbed... money that circulates by the mere fact of being used correctly can disappear' (Cuneo, *Ruiz: Entrevistas escogidas*, p. 292). Ruiz's words suggest that while the resistance was a collaborative endeavour, it did not supersede financial needs for some of the exiles depicted.

The envelope sequence reinforces the money's comings and goings and its lack of clear destination through an interplay of light and dark, as Ruiz portrays each exchange with the woman in a blue-tinged dark environment, and those between men in well-lit rooms. The woman shrouded in shadows is a newcomer whose financial situation may not yet be as dire as those who have been in exile for a longer period of time, thus the illuminated rooms signify a greater understanding of the material necessities of displacement.[32] In this way, the sequence critiques resistance movements that eschew pragmatism.

The dynamics that Ruiz shows offered a critical yet at times amusing representation of the complexities of everyday life for Chilean exiles like himself

31 'Diálogo de exiliados', La Cinémathèque française, https://www.cinematheque.fr/henri/film/60316-dialogue-d-exiles-raoul-ruiz-1974/ (accessed 28 June 2023).

32 The film also displays certain sexist attitudes and dialogue, though that is outside the scope of this chapter.

Figure 10.2a–d: The exchanges between the newly arrived woman and the man take place in the shadows, while the handoffs between more seasoned exiles happen in well-lit rooms, which signals a certain enlightenment.

and the people who took part in the film. On the one hand, Ruiz placed speech and behaviour (including slang and aspects of national identity) at the centre of his film, shedding light on how Chilean dynamics endured displacement and nurtured a sense of belonging among these exiles. Humorously, even the kidnapped pro-dictatorship musician says that 'he feels he is among friends' and even signs a letter supporting his expulsion from a leftist alumni group that censures his views. The performers, both 'French and Chilean, worked for free for solidarity reasons' as most were Ruiz's friends and exiled themselves.[33] On the other hand, Ruiz creates humorous situations as a result of characters that remain tethered to a pre-traumatic time and an old version of Chile that is no longer possible after the coup and Allende's demise.[34] This attitude is nowhere clearer than in a moment halfway

33 'Diálogos de exiliados', Memoria Chilena, http://www.memoriachilena.gob.cl/602/w3-article-97296.html (accessed 28 June 2023).

34 Ruiz stated that '[w]hat I wanted to show was the everyday life of exiles and their possible political perspectives. But politics in everyday life. Not political

through the film, when a voiceover simulates documentary form to narrate that 'in exile, the refugees continue behaving as if they were in Chile. In light of any small quotidian problem, they recur to the processes of participation and direct democracy, of assemblies that only made sense inside of the Chilean process'. In addition to a critique of the characters' attachment to a Chilean way of living that does not translate to exile, the film shows the material difficulties of life in another country. This manifests in the command of the French language, which some exiles barely speak, or in the way they live, sometimes many people to a room and finding space for others by springing them on unsuspecting visitors. The film does not shy away from revealing exiles' attempts to secure sources of lodging and sustenance.

Diálogos thus shows a contradiction between the shared sense of belonging among exiles on the heels of the coup (and subsequent dictatorship), nostalgia for the lost project of the left, and the precarity that forces the characters to act according to individual needs, which seems to undo a utopian commitment to the resistance. According to Michèle Arrué, Ruiz's incisive view did not provide a 'heroic and idealized vision of exiles, but rather [...] a disenchanted and mocking vision of what is supposedly the Chilean resistance of the militants of a Chilean left-wing party in France. In 1975, when the film opens, it is the target of many criticisms, causing a great scandal among Chileans. Some even want the director to destroy the film's negative'.[35] In response to this reaction, Ruiz said that he 'was convinced that it was an activist film, a call to unity, a sort of foresight of all the mistakes that could be made and that we should avoid'.[36] At the same time, Ruiz stated in different interviews that he did not 'understand very well political cinema's expression [...] The cinema I make is political cinema in another sense. For me, to film a movie is a political act [...]' (Cuneo, *Ruiz: entrevistas escogidas*, p. 29). For Ruiz, Chile had a 'culture of resistance', and the techniques of resistance had a non-verbal language of their own that could be translated ideologically through cinema. Ruiz used filming as a way to build contacts through this non-verbal language (Cuneo, *Ruiz: Entrevistas escogidas*, p. 29). Akin to the contradictions constitutive of exile, Ruiz's film depicts a sense of belonging that combines the building of

declarations, but what impression can be taken of people that live in a parodical situation, like they are still in Chile and still in power' (Ruiz y Cuneo, *Ruiz*, p. 292).

35 Michèle Arrué, 'Lejos de Chile, lejos de Francia: Los exiliados chilenos en Diálogos de exiliados de Raúl Ruiz', *Amérique Latine Histoire et Mémoire,* 37 (2019), paragraph 26, doi:10.4000/alhim.7813 (accessed 28 November 2023).

36 Jacqueline Mouesca, *Plano secuencia de la memoria de Chile: Veinticinco años de cine chileno (1960–1985)* (Madrid: Litoral 1988), p. 122.

a Chilean resistance movement abroad while taking into account the material realities of these exiles trying to make home in Paris.

Similarly, other filmmakers examined belonging outside of Chile in ways that differ from Ruiz's cynical standpoint. Among them is Marilú Mallet, who arrived in Canada as a political refugee after the coup in 1973. Most of her oeuvre, particularly work completed in the earlier part of her exile, examines uprooting and immigration. Mallet also takes on community, belonging, and the idea of home. In *Les Borges* (1978), she explores the lives of numerous Portuguese immigrants in Montreal, particularly the Borges family in Quebec. She 'exposes, with nuance and sensitivity, the problems that the condition of being an immigrant entails and shows how one learns to live in a country one wants to make one's own'.[37] Through the Borges' story, Mallet tells a version of her own while she expresses her desire to make home in exile. Continuing this thematic engagement, in *Unfinished Diary* (1982) she investigates the bonds exiles develop amid the profound isolation that this experience often generates. In this film, Mallet tells her own story directly alongside interviews with other exiles such as writer Isabel Allende (whose father was President Allende's first cousin). The genesis of these works can be found in *Il n'y a pas d'oubli* (*There is No Forgetting*, Rodrigo González, Marilú Mallet, and Jorge Fajardo, 1975), an episodic three-part film in which three directors spotlight the difficulties of survival in a new country as they offer vignettes of the lives of exiles in Quebec. Mallet directed the second segment titled 'Lentement' [Slowly], which represents a fitting prelude to her later work.

Il n'y a pas d'oubli frames and reframes the impulse to remake home and community. It does so in its very constitution: three Chilean exiled filmmakers join forces to create an episodic picture of life in Quebec. As Pick notes, 'Jorge Fajardo, Rodrigo González and Marilú Mallet each directed a short film to be brought together as a long feature. This film was made because of the intervention of the [National Film Board of Canada]'s unionized workers and the wider network of groups mobilized in solidarity with Chile' (Pick, 'Chilean Cinema in Exile', p. 39). Through each of the chapters in this triptych, directors González, Mallet, and Fajardo offer their own perspective and experience of the vicissitudes of exile in Canada, while constructing new communities and spaces of belonging that remake and reimagine the idea of home.

The film foregrounds the community as an antidote to the loneliness that so frequently accompanies displacement. In the opening sequence

37 'Les Borges', *Office national du film du Canada*, https://www.onf.ca/film/borges/ (accessed 29 June 2023). Authors' translation.

Figure 10.3 Comrades get together at a professor's house in the first segment of *Il n'y a pas d'oubli.*

of the film's first segment, titled 'J'explique certaines choses' [*I explain certain things*], González relies exclusively on group shots to create unity among the characters like Ruiz does in *Diálogos de exiliados.* The space becomes a rearticulation of home as the comrades toast to 'Chile's constitutional president, comrade Salvador Allende' under the tutelage of Ernesto 'Che' Guevara, whose poster seems to lend his blessing to the invocation of Allende's Unidad Popular. Even in Canada, the Chile before dictatorship becomes a unifying factor among these characters. A pre-traumatic Chile becomes transported to a professor's living room, suggesting that the country's project was mobile and longevous. The link between the words 'constitutional' and 'president' indicates a rebuke of Pinochet's authority, as does a surrogate Allende who remains alive in a poster in a different room, placed even higher on the wall than Guevara's.

Through a character that leaves after refusing to toast Allende (or rather, attempts to leave and after engaging in a brawl is asked to leave), González indicates that there is no room in this house for anybody who is not pro-Allende, which suggests that this new home establishes a continuity with a lost Chile. Thus, making home becomes both a material and ideological endeavour that aims to access what was lost. In this way, González remakes Chile in Quebec, proposing that unity under the banner of the left is a way to recover and reproduce a version of home that was no longer possible in Chilean soil under Pinochet's illegitimate rule.

'Lentement,' a story about adapting to exile, also showcases community-building. Like González's film, Mallet's segment makes use of group shots to show the everyday life of exiles, but also incorporates language as an element that brings two people together. The film showcases tender moments in which the protagonist teaches her companion how to pronounce Spanish words. This incorporation of Spanish, her native language, in a French-spoken film suggests another pathway towards building a home, bringing some of Chile with her to Quebec. The pace of her film, composed of slow, longer shots, shines a spotlight on human relationships and attempts at communication, rather than centring on action or conflict. Through these choices, the film reinforces that these bonds are the key to not only surviving but thriving, finding and building spaces of belonging that can help ameliorate the pain and isolation that exile often creates.

Jorge Fajardo's 'Jours de fer' ('Steel Blues') takes a different approach to the difficulties of exile, as it explores the strength that survival as a migrant or an emigrant entails as well as community through solidarity in the labour sphere. Pablo, an ex-professor, secures work at a steel mill despite a language barrier and no experience in that role as the hiring manager supplies work necessities (steel toed boots and a hard hat) that are not usually provided. Despite the isolation that both the cold lighting and arduous work of steel milling convey, his work takes place in a homosocial space, and the audiences access glimpses of community as the film shows labourers working collaboratively in pairs to stack steel bars and communing on breaks. Although Pablo cannot partake in the latter given the language barrier, halfway through the film we see his colleagues fetch him to take a break, get him a drink when he cannot work the vending machine, and pat him on the back as they return to work. Despite the isolation that the film shows, Pablo finds another glimmer of community with a Portuguese worker whose language is closest to his own. The latter mentions Allende and the Chilean workers after asking Pablo's country of origin and later addresses how he has not needed to learn much of either English or French despite being in Canada for twelve years, suggesting solidarity and understanding of the protagonist's newly arrived position.

While the film is not upbeat and does not shy away from showing the isolation of exile, it offers the possibility of reading its ending not only as a testament of the inescapability of the worker's struggle, but also as a liberatory instance of hope and agency. In this final scene, Pablo cuts a wire that holds steel bars together, and as he liberates them, they cascade down to be processed. This moment is particularly poignant as it follows a scene that takes place the night before, in which Pablo reads a letter from his wife Elena and looks through a magazine that has photos of protests, which trigger a flashback of him enduring the military's violence. The editing links the survival of the past to the arduous work of the present, which effectively translates the struggle of the Chilean left into the space of the Canadian factory, not only to create class solidarity but also to reaffirm the need to, as Pablo's comrade sings in the flashback, 'sink the bourgeois empire'.

Despite the cynical depictions and precarious conditions that both *Diálogos de exiliados* and *Il n'y a pas d'oubli* show, these films also evidence a way to find community in the act of adapting to a new culture. In doing so, exiled characters, as well as the filmmakers, construct spaces of belonging. Through stylistic means that convey community formation and different degrees of integration against the backdrop of isolation, filmmakers use images to remake an idea of home.

b) Displacing space and time to replicate and reproduce a version of home

Many filmmakers found ways to simulate the Chilean territory in other countries as a way to reclaim their home. A clear example is Valeria Sarmiento's *La dueña de casa*, a twenty-three-minute film about a housewife during the final days of the Unidad Popular.[38] In Paris, Sarmiento recreated an apartment in Providencia, one of the more affluent areas of Santiago, in an attempt to remember Chilean bourgeois women who protested by banging empty pans because of the lack of food products to buy.[39] Throughout the short, we only see parts of the apartment and views from the outside of the windows, which offer the audience clues to the kind of Chilean space Sarmiento recreates. In this same vein, the film also includes intertitles with quotes by Gustavo Leigh (Aviation General and its representative in the Junta), Teresa Donoso (journalist), and Lucía Hiriart (Pinochet's wife) about the bravery of these women who stood up to Allende throughout the Unidad Popular years. The film ends with a view of the opposite apartment, where a neighbour looks excitedly at the sky against the sonic backdrop of Hawker Hunters and bombing. Sarmiento's memory exercise of reconstructing an apartment in Providencia in this short allows her to avoid forgetting about the spaces that women who were against the Unidad Popular inhabited. By doing so, she commits to filming and reconstructing a way of living, thinking, and treating others (as the *dueña de casa* constantly class-shames her housekeeper)—in

38 Iván Pinto Veas, 'Valeria Sarmiento'. *La Fuga*, https://lafuga.cl/valeria-sarmiento/638 (accessed 27 June 2023). For a comprehensive look at Valeria Sarmiento's work see Bruno Cuneo and Fernando Pérez V, *Una mirada oblicua: El cine de Valeria Sarmiento* (Santiago: Universidad Alberto Hurtado, 2021). *La dueña de casa* was produced by Groupe de Recherche et Essais Cinématographiques, and Sarmiento has stated that this film was key in allowing her to realise that she was able to make films outside Chile (Jacqueline Mouesca, 'Una cineasta que no quiere ser transparente. Conversación con Valeria Sarmiento', *Araucaria de Chile*, 31 (1985), 115–16).

39 This historical event is called the *cacerolas* [saucepans] period. Regarding the actions and movement of right-wing women during the Unidad Popular see Margaret Power, *Right-Wing Women in Chile: Feminine Power and the Struggle against Allende 1964–1973* (University Park, PA: Pennsylvania State, 2002). Also see Teresa Donoro Loero, *La epopeya de las ollas vacías* (Santiago: Gabriela Mistral, 1974).

short, the everyday lives of many who were against Allende. The film then offers a version of Chile in which the soon-to-be overthrown political coalition is not all-encompassing but rather a large political actor in a landscape that entailed a number of sociopolitical forces.

Las tres coronas del marinero (Raúl Ruiz, 1983) provides another example of this transplanting operation, as Ruiz replicates the port of Valparaíso through images of Portugal.[40] The film's narrative, which tells the story of a young man who must escape his home after committing a crime, serves as an allegory of exile as it jumps from location to location to follow a physical journey that stands in for an emotional one.[41] According to Jacqueline Mouesca and Carlos Orellana, 'with each return, the city is recreated according to a different gaze, and as the distance increases, the optics begin to resemble those of a foreigner'.[42] By doing this, Ruiz offers commentary on the way distance has an effect on the perception of a place, how things change with each new gaze in the place that used to be home. In this sense, the film is not only about the experience of exile but also of 'its consecutive tearing' (Mouesca and Orellana, 'El caso Raúl Ruiz', p. 109). Exile is not only having to leave one's country, but also how it ripples beyond the act of leaving. In this instance, the separation from Chile lingers even years after, and becomes intertwined in how one makes sense of place and history.

Similarly, *Ardiente Paciencia* (Antonio Skármeta, 1983) constructs home abroad as it employs Portugal as a backdrop for Isla Negra, a small beach town in central Chile where the story takes place. The film begins in 1969, when Pablo Neruda moves to this town and mail circulation increases notably as a result. Mario, a young man who only recently became the town's postman, befriends the poet given his regular visits to deliver his mail and learns how to court his love interest through the writer's famous words. The film recreates Neruda's house, including recognizable elements like the ship figureheads he used as decor and the outdoor wooden structure with bells he rang to let his neighbours know when he was home. In brightly lit and colour saturated frames, the film constructs an idyllic setting that lends a hopeful atmosphere to a Chile on the brink of downfall. Through the narrative's central romance, Skármeta allegorizes a love letter to Chile and its political project with an exuberance that relives the halcyon days before

40 In the film, a character explicitly transplants Chile when he states that in Bilbao, there is a neighbourhood just like the one in which they are walking around in Valparaíso, with identical bars that have the same number of chairs but different names.

41 'It is a film full of quotes, but deep down it's a metaphor for exile [...]', in Cuneo and Ruiz, *Ruiz: Entrevistas escogidas*, p. 270.

42 Jacqueline Mouesca and Carlos Orellana, 'El caso Raul Ruiz', *Araucaria de Chile*. 12:23 (1983), 106–12 (p. 109).

Pinochet, and narrates the fateful events of 11 September 1973 (the day of the coup) in Isla Negra as well as the atmosphere in that small seaside town.

Las Actas de Marusia (Miguel Littín, 1976) also transplants space to recreate and investigate Chile while also condemning the dictatorship. Littín depicts the struggles of striking workers in a small nitrate town in the northern part of the country as he retells the story of the 1925 massacre, during which over 500 people (mostly workers and their families) died as a result of government repression.[43] Littín shot *Actas de Marusia* in Mexico, where he migrated after he escaped Chile. The Chihuahuan desert serves as an attempt to replicate the north of Chile, where the massacre transpired.[44]

It is not only space that cinema traverses to reconstruct Chile and with it, home. *Actas de Marusia* also travels in time to resignify a 1925 massacre as an allegory for the coup and subsequent dictatorship. The story's link to the junta's actions are not evident, but the themes of the film (mainly social justice) went hand in hand with elements such as worker's rights and social freedoms, which were pivotal during Allende's government. In the film, past and present meet through the brutal armed forces repression, which links 1925 and 1976, three years after Pinochet's dictatorship seizes power (although it is important to note that the magnitude of Pinochet's repression and systemic violence far surpassed the death toll of the Marusia massacre). Zuzana Pick remarks that the film inscribes 'actuality in history' as 'the workers' resistance to military intervention is told in images that recall the massacre at the Santa Maria de Iquique school in 1917. The violence of this episode and the brutal torture scenes that follow bring together the anecdotes of the film and the events of the 1973 coup' (Pick, 'Chilean Cinema in Exile', p. 50).

Films like Ruiz's, Skármeta's and, Littín's recreate an idea of Chile, and that recreation offers the possibility to construct a memory that allows filmmakers and audiences to cope with longing for their lost home. Out of necessity, Chile became a place that could be recreated and home became a space that needed to be simulated—cinema provided the means for both. Films offered a tangible way to build and access a home that had been lost, and could transport Chile to exile and exiles to Chile through the flicker of a projector.

43 *Las actas de Marusia* represented Mexico in the Oscar for Best Foreign Film since it was shot there. The film is an adaptation of Patricio Manns's book of the same title. Patricio Manns, *Actas de Marusia* (Santiago: P & P, 1993).

44 'Miguel Littín', Memoria Chilena, https://www.memoriachilena.gob.cl/602/w3-article-92834.html (accessed 20 June 2023).

c) Reimagining the past to create a material history of home

A number of films made in exile also reenact historical events only to recreate and reimagine them, which evidences the need to reproduce a version of home while also denouncing Pinochet's actions.[45] Whether it was through fiction or the many documentaries filmmakers produced during these years, there was an impulse to retake the narrative of the coup, of exile or even that of the Unidad Popular to make sense of the trauma of dictatorship. Their way to do so is to engage in a revisitation of the past. Exiled filmmakers presented a fictionalized version of the coup and the subsequent dictatorship. Examples abound, most notably Helvio Soto's *Llueve sobre Santiago* (1975), which reconstructs President Allende's last days and the military's uprising. Similarly, Sebastián Alarcón and Aleksandr Kosarev's *Noche sobre Chile* (1977) narrates how a politically unaffiliated man bears witness to the military's torture tactics when he is abducted and imprisoned at the Estadio Nacional (National Stadium). These recreations and reconstructions express the need to remember and generate a collective memory to begin healing.

Llueve sobre Santiago (1975) is an indicative example, as it suggests that the coup fundamentally changed Chile and the country could never be the same. As the film narrates the events of 11 September 1973, the day when the armed forces seized power, it implies that Chile is now different, foreign, unrecognizable. The film generates a sense of estrangement not only through its shooting location but also through its use of language. Director Helvio Soto transplants the fictional streets of Santiago to those in French and Bulgarian urban spaces, where he shot the film. Additionally, *Llueve sobre Santiago* combines character dialogue in French with visual signs and background chants in Spanish without acknowledging or calling attention to the language differences, instead treating them as a continuity. Beyond the logistical aspects of a film shot in, released, and circulated in Europe, *Llueve sobre Santiago* suggests that the Chile the filmmaker reconstructs can never be the one that he remembers.

Remembrances often take the form of nostalgia, itself a wistful desire to inhabit and reimagine the past, which became one of the most prevalent ideas in these productions. These films express and invoke nostalgia through a number of stylistic means, including music. Soto's *Llueve sobre Santiago*'s vivid soundtrack is the work of Astor Piazzolla, an Argentine composer and musician famous for his tangos. The film's tango music and its characteristic sounds of the bandoneón (an instrument akin to an

45 Nostalgia comes from the Greek compound of nostos (return home) and the word álgos or 'pain', 'ache'. See 'Nostalgia', *Oxford Learner's Dictionaries*, https://www.oxfordlearnersdictionaries.com/us/definition/english/nostalgia (accessed 20 June 2023).

accordion) activate the pathos of a bygone era. Or, as Florencia Garramuño puts it, tango 'delays itself in the nostalgia of a past and lost world'.[46] In this way, the soundtrack suggests a yearning for that which has been lost: the Chile of yesteryear and the home it used to be. Additionally, Piazzolla's musical style evokes the sense of something olden that has changed, as his ushering in of the *nuevo tango* musical style modernized traditional sounds through the incorporation of jazz and classical music. The soundtrack (as well as Piazzolla as a figure at the vanguard of tango music) reinforces the stylistic hybridity of the film, a fictionalized account of the 1973 coup which towards the end evokes documentary form through voiceover narration. Through these formal strategies, the film acknowledges a home that can no longer fulfil that function, while also transplanting Santiago to another location to indicate that home is not static.

Valeria Sarmiento's *La nostalgia* (1979) also explores memory and its title's emotion by narrating exiled children's lives in a Paris suburb and their attitude towards, as well as remembrances of, their country of origin. In an interview with Jacqueline Mouesca, Sarmiento recounts that although the apartments had all the amenities of modern life, the children missed their lives back in Chile, often stating that they 'wanted to go back to the same house they had' even though it was far more precarious (Mouesca, 'Una cineasta', p. 116). Prevalent in the interview is the idea that the subjects Sarmiento portrayed are '[p]eople from everywhere, people from nowhere'. This statement aptly describes the difficulties and challenges of acclimatizing to life away from Chile, even for children, who are often more adaptable than adults.[47] This documentary short was a commission for the United Nations, which evidences a consciousness of the dire situation of exile and uprooting in the international stage, and the need for home as a crucial developmental element in children. In the nostalgic attachment to the past, the films' subjects constantly make and remake a home that lives in their memory, and now in Sarmiento's film.

These reconstructions served to create a material history of home, now embodied in celluloid. Through these different reimaginings of the past, the films invited their directors, protagonists, and viewers to inhabit and

46 Florencia Garramuño, *Modernidades primitivas: Tango, samba y nación* (Buenos Aires: Fondo de Cultura Económica de Argentina, 2007), p. 15.

47 *La nostalgia* was not Sarmiento's first attempt to make a film about the exiled. Right after *La dueña de casa,* she filmed a documentary about exiles financed by the Centre Bruxellois de l'Audiovisuel which was never shown because of its avant-garde style. In it, Sarmiento never showed people's faces, only filming their bodies. She also kept dialogue to a minimum. The director's main aim was to show that 'all bodies suffer the same under the same conditions of life' (Mouesca, 'Una cineasta', p. 116).

yearn for a home that had invariably changed, but which could be accessed through a projector. In the remembrance and the reinvention of the subjects' and the characters' space and time, cinema allows access to a Chile that has been lost.

IV A home away from home

In 1985, an interviewer asked Sarmiento about coming back to Chile after being exiled for almost ten years. She answered that she did not recognize her country, especially when it came to everyday life during the dictatorship. In particular, she discussed Valparaíso (the city where she was born), and stated that it was unrecognizable except for Chileans' grace and slyness, highlighting this was the only human aspect she could identify. When asked if she would like to film in Valparaíso, she mentioned that it was too hard to film in Latin America due to censorship issues, but that she was going to include several aspects of that city in her new film (Mouesca, 'Una cineasta…', p. 122). In a way, the technique of transplanting places and home was one of the lasting characteristics of the Chilean style of filming in exile. When home was no longer there (geographically or because it was no longer the same), film could help bring it back, recreate, and project home. Cinema became a way to mediate the difficulties and the experience of exile and build a home away from home to make displacement more tolerable.

Exile created an irretrievable loss, as the dictatorship transformed a nation (physically and emotionally) to shape it according to Pinochet's illegitimate whims. It was a double loss: displacement accompanied the end of the dream of the Unidad Popular, and with it, the promise of a better Chile. As the dictatorship bore down on the country's people, there was an imperative to conform to a narrow, unilaterally-imposed vision of Chileanness.

Exiled filmmakers used their productions to regain control of the narrative of their recent history, and cinema was a medium to make those dreams and experiences tangible. In that action, they were able to adapt, but without bouncing back to a norm that would beckon them to uphold the status quo. Exile did not allow for a return to normal: it disrupted the norm, so there was no way for these filmmakers to go back home. They were not resilient, but rather mounted a process of resistance through the act of filming, which served as a collective memory on screen. As they searched for agency in the act of making a home away from home, exiled Chilean filmmakers effectively used images and sounds to shorten the physical and psychological gap between them and Chile.

Bibliography

Albornoz, Ignacio, and Iván Pinto, *Raúl Ruiz: Potencias de lo múltiple* (Santiago: Metales Pesados, 2023).

Anderson, Benedict, *Imagined Communities: Reflections on the Origin and Spread of Nationalism* (London and New York: Verso, 2006).

Angell, Allan, and Susan Carstairs, 'The Exile Question in Chilean Politics', *Third World Quarterly*, 9:1 (January 1987), pp. 148–67, doi:10.26409/2019MKbook01 (accessed 27 November 2023).

Arrué, Michèle, 'Lejos de Chile, lejos de Francia: Los exiliados chilenos en "Diálogos de exiliados de Raúl Ruiz"', *Amérique Latine Histoire et Mémoire*, 37 (2019), doi: https://doi.org/10.4000/alhim.7813 (accessed 28 November 2023)

Barudy, Jorge, 'A Programme of Mental Health for Political Refugees: Dealing with the Invisible Pain of Political Exile', *Social Science & Medicine*, 28:7 (1989), 715–27, https://doi.org/10.1016/0277-9536 (accessed 27 November 2023).

Bonhomme, Macarena, 'Exilio y retorno: Dos procesos de integración desde el hogar', Prepared for delivery at the 2014 Congress of the Latin American Studies Association (Chicago, May 21–4, 2014).

Campo, Javier, 'Documentary Film from the Southern Cone during Exile (1970–1980)', *Latin American Perspectives*, 188, 40 (2013), p. 146.

'Chile, el país más resiliente de América Latina', Psicologos Online, https://www.psicologosonline.cl/articulos/chile-el-pais-mas-resiliente-de-america-latina (accessed 29 June 2023).

'Chile resiliente: Ciencia de datos e inteligencia artificial para abordar los desafíos del cambio climático', Evento Chile Resiliente, https://eventochileresiliente.cl/ (accessed 2 June 2023)

Cortínez, Verónica, and Manfred Engelbert, *La tristeza de los tigres y los misterios de Raúl Ruiz* (Santiago: Cuarto Propio, 2011).

Cuneo, Bruno, and Fernando Pérez V, *Una mirada oblicua: l de Valeria Sarmiento* (Santiago: Universidad Alberto Hurtado, 2021).

'Diálogo de exiliados', La Cinémathèque française, https://www.cinematheque.fr/henri/film/60316-dialogue-d-exiles-raoul-ruiz-1974/ (accessed 28 June, 2023).

'Diálogos de exiliados', Memoria Chilena, http://www.memoriachilena.gob.cl/602/w3-article-97296.html (accessed 28 June, 2023).

Donoro Loero, Teresa, *La epopeya de las ollas vacías* (Santiago, Chile: Gabriela Mistral, 1974).

Evans, Brad, and Julian Reid, *Resilient Life: The Art of Living Dangerously* (Cambridge: Polity, 2014), pp. 1–2.

Field, C. B., V. Barros, T. F. Stocker, D. Qin, D. J. Dokken, K. L. Ebi, M. D. Mastrandrea, K. J. Mach, G.-K. Plattner, S. K. Allen, M. Tignor, and P. M. Midgley, eds, *Managing the Risks of Extreme Events and Disasters to Advance Climate Change Adaptation. Special Report of the Intergovernmental Panel on Climate Change* (Cambridge: Cambridge University Press, 2012).

'Filmografía en el exilio', Memoria Chilena, http://www.memoriachilena.gob.cl/602/w3-article-92833.html (accessed 20 June, 2023).

Franzenburg, Geert, 'Displaced Values: From Remembrance to Resilience', *Problems of Education in the 21st Century*, 56 (2013), pp. 59–65, doi:10.33225/pec/13.56.59 (accessed 27 November 2023).

Garramuño, Florencia, *Modernidades primitivas: Tango, samba y nación* (Buenos Aires: Fondo de Cultura Económica de Argentina, 2007).

Giddens, Anthony, *La constitución de la sociedad: Bases para la teoría de la estructuración* (Buenos Aires: Amorrortu, 2011).

Gonsalves, Carlos J., 'The Psychological Effects of Political Repression on Chilean Exiles in the US', *American Journal of Orthopsychiatry*, 60:1 (1990), 143–53, doi:10.1037/h0079176 (accessed 27 November 2023).

'Hacia un Chile resiliente frente a desastres: una oportunidad', Center for Climate and Resilience Research, https://www.cr2.cl/informe-cnid-hacia-un-chile-resiliente-frente-a-desastres-una-oportunidad/ (accessed 29 June 2023)

Jordán González, Laura, and Nicolas Lema Habash, 'Raúl Ruiz's Now We're Gonna Call You Brother and The Problem of the People's Sonic Representation', in *Soundings: Documentary Film and the Listening Experience*, edited by Geoffrey Cox and John Corner (Huddersfield: University of Huddersfield, 2018), pp. 255–77.

Jordán González, Laura, and Nicolas Lema Habash, 'On the Cinematic Deconstruction of Logical Sounds: Raúl Ruiz's Quasi-Voice in "La maleta"', *Cultural Critique*, 121 (2023), 42–67.

Lema Habash, Nicolas, 'De los usos políticos de la muerte en *La expropiación* de Raúl Ruiz', *Aisthesis*, 69 (2021), 103–30, doi:10.7764/69.5. (accessed 27 November 2023).

Lema Habash, Nicolas, 'Against Purity: Spinoza and the Problem of Displacement in Raúl Ruiz's *On Top of the Whale* (1982),' in *Spinoza nella letteratura e nelle arti del Novecento*, edited by Daniela Bostrenghi, Cristina Santinelli and Stefano Visentin (Florence: Le Lettere, 2022), pp. 317–32.

Lira, Elizabeth, 'Trauma, duelo, reparación y memoria', *Revista de Estudios Sociales*, 36 (2010), pp. 14–28, doi:0.7440/res36.2010.02 (accessed 27 November 2023).

Lira, Elizabeth, and Brian Loveman, *Las ardientes cenizas del olvido: Vía chilena de reconciliación política 1932–1994* (Santiago: Lom, 2000).

Marías, Miguel, *Raúl Ruiz* (Madrid: Cátedra, 2012).

McAslan, Alastair, 'The Concept of Resilience. Understanding its Origins, Meanings and Utility', *Torrens Resilience Institute*, 1(2010), https://www.flinders.edu.au/content/dam/documents/research/torrens-resilience-institute/resilience-origins-and-utility.pdf (accessed 29 June 2023).

'Miguel Littín', Memoria Chilena, https://www.memoriachilena.gob.cl/602/w3-article-92834.html (accessed 20 June, 2023).

Mouesca, Jacqueline, 'Una cineasta que no quiere ser transparente. Conversación con Valeria Sarmiento', *Araucaria de Chile*, 31 (1985), 115–16.

Mouesca, Jacqueline, *Plano secuencia de la memoria de Chile: Veinticinco años de cine chileno (1960–1985)* (Madrid: Eds. del Litoral, 1988).

Mouesca, Jacqueline, and Carlos Orellana, 'El caso Raul Ruiz', *Araucaria de Chile*, 12:23 (1983), 106–12.

Muñoz, Liliana, 'Exile as Bereavement: Socio-psychological Manifestations of Chilean Exiles in Great Britain', *British Journal of Medical Psychology*, 53:3 (1980), 227–32, https://doi.org/10.1111/j.2044-8341.1980.tb02545 (accessed 27 November 2023).

Navarro Mayorga, Sergio, *La naturaleza ama ocultarse: El cine chileno de Raúl Ruíz (1962–1975)* (Santiago: Ediciones Metales Pesados, 2019).

Nora, Pierre, 'Between Memory and History: Les Lieux de Mémoire', *Representacions*, 26 (1989), 12, http://www.jstor.org/stable/2928520 (accessed 27 November 2023).

Palieraki, Eugenia, 'El año 1978 y el exilio chileno', in *1978*, ed. Francisco Albornoz, Camila Gatica Mizala, and Claudio Rolle (1978) (manuscript).

Pick, Zuzana, 'Chilean Cinema in Exile, 1973–1986', *New Latin American Cinema*, edited by Michael Martin (Detroit: Wayne State University Press, 1997), p. 45.

'Prohibe el ingreso de personal al territorio nacional en los casos que indica', Decreto Ley 604, https://www.bcn.cl/leychile/navegar?idNorma=6225 (accessed 27 November 2023).

Orellana, Patricio, 'Exilio y desexilio', in *La Represión en Chile, 1973–1989* (Santiago: Senda, 2015), http://www.probidadenchile.cl/ver_articulo.php?art=144&cat=2 (accessed 30 June, 2023).

Palacios, José Miguel, 'Resistances vs. Exile: The Political Rhetoric of Chilean Exile Cinema in the 1970s', *Jump Cut*, 57 (2016), (https://www.ejumpcut.org/archive/jc57.2016/-PalaciosChile/index.html) (accessed 1 July 2023).

Palacios, José Miguel, *Transnational Cinema Solidarity: Chilean Exile Film and Video after 1973* (Berkeley, University of California Press, 2025).

Perry, Mariana, '"With a Little Help from My Friends": The Dutch Solidarity Movement and the Chilean Struggle for Democracy', *Revista Europea de Estudios Latinoamericanos y del Caribe*, 101 (2016), pp. 75–9.

'The Power of Solidarity with Chile. The British Left in Response to the Coup, 1973–1979', *Secuencia*, 108 (2021), doi:10.18234/SECUENCIA.V0I108.1823 (accessed 27 November 2023).

Pinto Veas, Iván, 'Valeria Sarmiento', *La Fuga*, https://lafuga.cl/valeria-sarmiento/638 (accessed 27 June, 2023).

Power, Margaret, *Right-Wing Women in Chile: Feminine Power and the Struggle against Allende 1964–1973* (University Park, PA: Pennsylvania State, 2002).

'Resilience', American Psychological Association, https://dictionary.apa.org/?_ga=2.110647105.57727777.1685565970-1381700433.1685565963 (accessed 29 June 2023).

Rivera, Carla, 'Diálogos y reflexiones sobre las comunicaciones en la Unidad Popular. Chile, 1970–1973', *Historia y Comunicación Social*, 20:2 (2015), pp. 345–67, doi:10.5354/0719-1243.2022.67231 (accessed 27 November 2023)

Ríos, Valeria de los, *Metamorfosis: Aproximaciones al cine y la poética de Raúl Ruiz* (Santiago: Ediciones Metales Pesados, 2019).

Ruiz, Raúl, and Bruno Cuneo, *Ruiz: Entrevistas escogidas, filmografía comentada* (Santiago: Universidad Diego Portales, 2013).

Ruiz, Raúl, and Bruno Cuneo, *Diario: Notas, recuerdos y secuencias de cosas vistas* (Santiago: Ediciones Universidad Diego Portales, 2017).

Ruiz, Raúl, Eduardo Sabrovsky, and Christine Buci-Glucksmann, *Conversaciones con Raúl Ruiz* (Santiago: Universidad Diego Portales, 2003).

Sánchez, Cristián, *Aventura del cuerpo: El pensamiento cinematográfico de Raúl Ruiz* (Santiago: OchoLibros, 2011).

Stern, Steve, *Battling for Hearts and Minds: Memory Struggles in Pinochet's Chile, 1973–1988* (Durham, NC: Duke University Press, 2006).

Stern, Steve, *Reckoning with Pinochet: The Memory Question in Democratic Chile, 1989–2006* (Durham, NC: Duke University Press, 2010).

Tolia-Kelly, Dyvia P., 'Locating Processes of Identification: Studying the Precipitates of Re-memory through Artefacts in the British Asian Home', *Transactions of the Institute of British Geographers*, 29:3 (2004), pp. 314–29, doi:10.1111/j.0020-2754.2004.00303.x (accessed 27 November 2023).

Vásquez Rocca, Adolfo, 'Raúl Ruiz: Ontología de lo fantástico. Territorios, políticas estéticas y polisemia visual', *Aisthesis*, 48 (2010), 31–47, doi:10.4067/S0718-71812010000200003 (accessed 27 November 2023).

Villarroel, Mónica, and Isabel Mardones, *Señales contra el olvido: Cine chileno recobrado* (Santiago: Cuarto Propio, 2012).

Wright, Thomas C., and Rody Oñate, 'Chilean Political Exile', *Latin American Perspectives*, 34:4 (2007), pp. 31–49, doi:10.1177/0094582X07302902 (accessed 27 November 2023).

11

'A Time that Has Not Yet Been'. Futurity and Survival in Marta Aponte's Caribbean Archive

Carlos Fonseca

Towards the end of Marta Aponte's 2018 book *PR 3 Aguirre* we read of her return to the old company town of Aguirre after the devastating impact of Hurricane María, which had struck the Puerto Rican archipelago one month earlier, 16 September 2017: 'Un año después, a pocas semanas de haber pasado el huracán, volví a Aguirre, donde los vientos dejaron el rastro de una destrucción caprichosa.'[1] The image of the narrator walking through the ruins of the ghostly town, anxiously inspecting what remained of the place whose history of exploitation she had wished to tell, closes a book that from its very get go plays out the relationship between catastrophe and its aftermath. The scene concretizes the post-catastrophic mood that prevails throughout the book, in which the long story of the company town of Aguirre, established in the late nineteenth century to develop a sugar cane manufacturing business, runs parallel to the history of another more enduring social and ecological catastrophe: that of colonialism and its enduring legacy. For a writer like Aponte, who has always inscribed her work within the broader Caribbean literary tradition, writing history means learning to live after the founding catastrophe of colonialism whose resonance still prevails today under different guises and names. What becomes visible in that final walk through Aguirre is precisely the political task of the Caribbean writer, the call to refigure the remnants that have been left behind by catastrophe and to shape with them post-colonial futures capable of redeeming the past: '[E]l fervor de recoger las señales que alguien dejó en los márgenes de un

1 Marta Aponte, *PR 3 Aguirre* (Cayey: Sopa de Letras, 2018), p. 232.

país destrozado y ver qué puede hacerse con ellas…' (Aponte, PR 3 Aguirre, p. 348). Faithful to Kamau Braithwaite's post-colonial dictum—'Art must come out of catastrophe'[2]—Marta Aponte asks us to carefully examine how the traces of history survive beyond catastrophe, sketching a poetics of survival that resounds powerfully within our present world, where the omnipresent eschatological figure of the end of the times sometimes seems to preclude the possibility of imagining new futures and new beginnings.

PR 3 Aguirre is then a book about legacies: a book about what it means to inherit a catastrophic past and the struggle to make sense of it. Divided into two parts, entitled 'Boston' and 'Las islas', it shuffles between telling the story of the four Bostonians who in 1901 acquired the business and transcribing the witness accounts of its present day inhabitants. At the heart of this long story of ownership and dispossession, of inheritance and disinheritance, Aponte significantly includes the story of a painting: J. W. M. Turner's 1840 *Slavers Throwing Overboard the Dead and Dying—Typhoon Coming On*, most commonly known as *Slave Ship*. The true story of the late eighteenth century British Ship *Zong*, whose captain had thrown overboard unhealthy slaves only in order to collect insurance, is woven here into a broader history of colonial exploitation that ties the history of the Caribbean to that of the world. Tracing the painting's routes as it changed proprietors across the Atlantic, Aponte sketches the cartography of ownership that led to it being in the possession of one of the founders of Aguirre, William Sturgis Lothrop. One can almost feel the resonance of the painting's title weaving together the social and ecological histories of exploitation Aponte wanted to tell, with the typhoon standing both for colonialism understood as social catastrophe as well as for the ecological catastrophe of the plantation system. By the time Aponte visited the ruins of Aguirre, Turner's prophesized typhoon must have resonated deeply with the hurricane which had recently struck the archipelago, unearthing in turn the colonial layers that the island had for long tried to cover. However, this uncovering of catastrophe was not to be understood as a melancholic song of defeat or as an elegy sung at the end of the world, but rather as opening the possibility for a new poetics of survival. As Marta Aponte would later tell critic Julio Ramos in an interview: 'Se dice que el huracán reveló las entrañas ocultas del dominio colonial. También demostró lo que un pueblo puede hacer para no dejarse morir…'[3] *PR 3 Aguirre*

2 'Poetics, Revelations, Catastrophes: An Interview with Kamau Braithwaite', Rain Taxi, https://www.raintaxi.com/poetics-revelations-and-catastrophes-an-interview-with-kamau-brathwaite/ (accessed 13 December 2023).

3 Julio Ramos, 'PR 3 Aguirre: Entrevista a Marta Aponte', *Caracol*, 18 (2019), p. 32, access link: https://www.revistas.usp.br/caracol/issue/download/11320/1684 (accessed 13 December 2023).

sketches, from both a social as well as an ecological perspective, what it means to write this struggle to endure and to outlive catastrophe.

In what follows I will explore Marta Aponte's poetics of survival as an art of traces that rewrites the post-colonial archive, highlighting those erasures that are inherent to the colonial historical regime, and positing against them the testimonial voices of those silenced by history. In dialogue with discourses of resilience, as well as with Jacques Derrida's insights into the connection between the trace, the archive and survival, *PR 3 Aguirre* shows what it would mean, nowadays, to escape the eschatological discourses regarding the end of the world, instead foreshadowing new beginnings after the so-called end of history. This post-catastrophic literary aesthetic, which remains faithful to Braithwaite's call, points to a revolutionary temporality of reading, one which points to the future by looking to the past:

> Este libro no quiere ser una elegía a la isla desparecida. Lo que se desconoce por tachado pertenece más bien a un tiempo que no ha sido todavía. No forma parte del tiempo perdido, sino de la potencialidad que el conocimiento de lo censurado desata. Sus lectoras, sus lectores será de un momento que aún no existe cuando escribo. (Aponte, *PR 3 Aguirre*, p. 15)

Aponte's poetics of survival then consists of her capacity to unravel, through writing, the censured potentiality that lies at the heart of this 'crossed out time', where past historical erasures serve as index of a redemptive time yet to come. *PR 3 Aguirre* is, in that sense, a clear example of both what an archival novel and a testimonial novel could mean nowadays, in our post-testimonio era, where the archive becomes a site for exhuming the testaments of those lives forgotten by history: a place for hearing what the phantoms of the dead have said in order for their claims to continue echoing beyond death.

I *La huella testamentaria*: Reading and Writing the Surviving Traces

> The disaster is related to forgetfulness... (Maurice Blanchot)[4]

If there is a figure that recurs not only throughout the pages of *PR 3 Aguirre*, but across Marta Aponte's oeuvre as a whole that is the figure of the trace as a site where both reading and writing are made possible. Attentive inheritor

4 Maurice Blanchot, *The Writing of the Disaster*. Translated by Ann Smock (New York: University of Nebraska Press, 1995), p. 3.

of the archival impulse present in W. G. Sebald's novels, Aponte remains faithful as well to the crucial intuition present in the works of the French writer Pierre Michon, whose *Vies minuscules* showed that no matter how small and insignificant a life might seem within the annals of world history, it nonetheless leaves a biographical trace that bears a buried potential. Born far away from Michon's French countryside, Aponte has instead decided to focus her attention on the biographical traces of those lives that have marked the complex global history of the Caribbean. If in *Sexto sueño* she had turned her attention to the biography of one of the infamous authors of the 'crime of the century', Nathan Leopold, and in *La muerte feliz de William Carlos Williams* she had restored to life the biography of Raquel Hélène Hoheb, Williams' mother, in *PR 3 Aguirre* this biographical impulse reaches its true potential, as Aponte rewrites the lives of those erased from history. Focusing on what she calls the 'huella testamentaria'—that is, the testamentary trace—she begins to 'read' the southern route PR 3 as a site of a fundamental erasure:

> [U]na zona semejante a un terrario que en lugar de especies naturales acumulara ausencias, rastros de voces, ruinas modernas, celajes de muertos exóticos. En esa zona hay huellas de la historia mundial de varios siglos, pero el mundo no lo sabe. (Aponte, *PR 3 Aguirre*, p. 9)

This landscape of 'modern ruins' becomes then the palimpsest where Aponte aims to read the erased biographical traces of those disinherited by history, as part of her wish to rewrite global history from the perspective of the Caribbean. This is a book that, as she states early on, is centred on '... las vidas que pasaron por un tramo de la carretera PR 3...', and not only on those lives, but rather on the historical traces they left behind (Aponte, *PR 3 Aguirre*, p. 12). Within Aponte's poetics of survival the biographical trace always outlives the biographical subject: the biographical trace is always a testamentary trace and it is the task of the writer turned historian to read and write that legacy. For a region like the Caribbean, whose history, as Michel-Rolph Trouillot has explored, is marked by silences and erasures, this act of unearthing the buried potential hidden behind a set of names forgotten by history coincides with a broader political call to reconfigure world history from the perspective of the Caribbean itself.[5] Like Édouard Glissant, who saw the Caribbean as a microcosm that stood for the totality of the world relation, as that which he called the *tout-monde*, Aponte finds in the Caribbean a space where the relations of the modern world emerged as a

5 Michel-Rolph Trouillot, *Silencing the Past* (20th Anniversary Edition) (Boston: Beacon Press, 2015), p. 15.

result of the paradoxically globalizing forces of colonialism.[6] As Julio Ramos has stated in his reading of the book, what is fascinating about Aponte's approach to the history of this coastal landscape is her capacity to see there a confluence of global and local forces that both founded modernity and turned it into a landscape of ruins:

> ...litoral caribeño —enclave abierto al tránsito y ocupación de varios imperios, fugas cimarronas y contrabandos de todo tipo— cobra un sentido particular en *PR 3 Aguirre*. Esa costa es una instancia localizada de fuerzas globales, comprimidas en esa mínima encrucijada planetaria donde se superponen y se entremezclan —como estratos geológicos del territorio— los tiempos múltiples de una modernidad colonial en ruinas. (Ramos, 'Entrevista a Marta Aponte', p. 24)

Building on Aponte's previous trope of the coastal landscape as a terrarium of absences, Ramos highlights the geological angle of the book, suggesting that the coast works as a stratified landscape where different temporalities lay superimposed upon one another. The trace becomes then the site where the 'multiple times of a colonial modernity in ruins' can be read in their clashes and struggles, unearthing in turn the potentiality of that 'crossed out time' which the author had mentioned. Framing the story being told against the history of colonialism and its spectres allows the book to interweave the social and ecological histories being told within a single narrative that reconfigures what is meant by historical document and by testamentary trace. In *PR 3 Aguirre* the ruinous traces found in the landscape echo the witness accounts, underlying the superimposition of the past and the present: 'William Sturgis Hooper Lothrop, Francis Dumaresq, John Dandridge Henley Luce, Henry DeFord. Nombres, sombras, sonidos, aunque la obsesión de permanencia haya dejado rastros'(Aponte, *PR 3 Aguirre*, p. 78). The names of the founders of Aguirre are presented here as evidence of the impulse of survival that drags the past into the present, forcing us to reconsider the documentary trace as the cornerstone at the heart of Aponte's poetics of survival: 'La huella documental misma, sus dimensiones, refleja el lugar reservado al desaparecido en la jerarquía ciudadana' (Aponte, *PR 3 Aguirre,* p. 78). The testamentary trace is the sign for a past that stubbornly refuses to be simply erased by the catastrophic passage of history, but rather insists on bearing witness to the violence inherent to that history. To write is then akin to sketching, for the writer's task is to uncover the half-erased past impressions, tracing the contours of a subaltern history whose echoes still prevail today.

6 Édouard Glissant, *Poetics of Relation.* Translated by Betsy Wing (Michigan: University of Michigan Press, 2021).

Building a poetics out of this dialectic between impression and erasure, Marta Aponte underlines that writing is never set either in the past, the present or the future exclusively, but rather in the overlapping temporality that the testamentary trace presupposes. Having explored the role of the spectre in some of her other novels, she is well aware that the writer turned historian works with the phantoms of history, with history as the remnants of what survives. As Michael Naas has remarked in an essay on Derrida: 'Every trace is a living death, a sur-vivance...'[7] Exploring Derrida's notion of survival (*survivre*), Naas highlights that survival lies at the heart of the trace. More important for Aponte's work and her act of rewriting Caribbean history is his remark that this temporal outliving of the trace is precisely what founds, according to Derrida, the possibility of the archive:

> This survivance is broached from the moment of the first trace that is supposed to engender the writing of a book. From the first breath, this archive as survivance is at work. But once again, this is the case not only for books, or for writing, or for the archive in the current sense, but for everything from which the tissue of living experience is woven, through and through. A weave of survival, like death in life or life in death, a weave that does not come along to clothe a more originary existence, a life or a body or a soul that would be supposed to exist naked under this clothing.[8]

Namely, the testamentary trace founds the archive as site of survival. *PR 3 Aguirre* could then be read as an archaeology that tries to explore the potentiality inherent to the Caribbean archive.

II The Surviving Archive: The Precarity of Caribbean History

> The unearthing of silences, and the historian's subsequent emphasis on the retrospective significance of hitherto neglected events, requires not only extra labour at the archives, but also a project linked to an interpretation. (Michel-Rolph Trouillot, *Silencing the Past*, p. 58)

Praising her capacity to weave history and fiction, Áurea María Sotomayor has referred to Marta Aponte as 'la archivista fantasiosa'.[9] This title seems

7 Michael Naas, *The End of the World and Other Teachable Moments: Jacques Derrida's Final Seminar* (New York: Fordham University Press, 2015), p. 132.

8 Jacques Derrida, *The Beast and The Sovereign*. Translated by Geoffrey Bennington (London: University of Chicago Press, 2011), p. 131.

9 'Áurea María Sotomayor Reseña 'PR3 Aguirre', '*El Roommate: Colectivo de lectores*, elroommate.com/2020/06/21/

to fit perfectly Aponte's proposal in *PR 3 Aguirre*, where the factual historical facts are intricately woven into fictional narratives that allow history to dream its way through its blindspots. As the author has stated in interviews, there is a reason for this. Namely, the precarity of Caribbean history, either erased by the catastrophe of colonial history or threatened by the self-hatred of the post-colonial subject: '[N]uestros pueblos sin archivos o con archivos precarios, sin identidades que no hayan sido destrozadas por el auto desprecio. Sin embargo, se obstinan en sobrevivir. Ni la aniquilación furiosa de la memoria ni la gozosa asimilación de los pueblos y culturas del mundo han sido posibles' (Ramos, 'Entrevista a Marta Aponte', p. 58). Against both this 'furious annihilation of memory' resulting from colonialism and the 'joyous assimilation of cultures' characteristic of globalization, the archive appears as the site where the survival of another history becomes possible.

In *PR 3 Aguirre* Aponte relinquishes the traditional position of the author as original creator in order to reposition herself as fanciful archivist. Temporally, she places herself not at the origin of history but rather in its catastrophic aftermath, gathering the remnant traces left behind by what Benjamin would call the storm of progress. In her case, the Angel of History's attempt to 'reawaken the dead' out of the 'pile of debris' left behind by the storm of progress gains a particular density when confronted with the writing of a book that found in the aftermath of Hurricane María its natural conclusion, but which had already been written, before the storm hit, from the perspective of such catastrophic aftermath.[10] Amid such remnants, inscribing herself into the narrative, the narrator walks gathering as many traces as possible, losing herself within a Caribbean archive that quickly expands far away from Aguirre, forcing her to follow the global routes determined by such an archive. As Jeffrey Lawrence has noted, she does not hide her role as archivist but rather stages it: 'En *PR3 Aguirre*, estas inquietudes llevan a una nueva estrategia narrativa en la cual la dramatización de la búsqueda de la documentación histórica por parte de la narradora—aquí otra vez identificada con la autora—resulta tan imperante como la lectura esa documentación.'[11] Whether we follow the narrator on her trips to Boston, in search of the biographical archives of the founding fathers of Aguirre, or whether we follow her in her research into the archives of Aguirre or in her search for the transatlantic routes traced by Turner's painting, in each case

aurea-maria-sotomayor-resena-pr3-aguirre-dossier-marta-aponte-alsina/ (accessed 13 December 2023).

10 Walter Benjamin, *Illuminations.* Translated by Harry Zorn (London: The Bodley Head, 2015), p. 55.

11 Jeffrey Lawrence, 'Los gringos de Marta Aponte Alsina', *El Roommate: Colectivo de Lectores*, elroommate.com/2020/06/14/jeffrey-lawrence-los-gringos-de-marta-aponte-alsina-dossier-marta-aponte-alsina/ (accessed 13 December 2023).

we witness how the writer finds in the archive a site of potentiality, namely, surviving remnants or traces that allow for a rewriting of official history, as Sotomayor suggests in her excellent reading of the book:

> La carretera de la modernidad serviría quizá para trazar su zigzagueo en el tiempo, pero también sus intentos de sobrecubrir a manera de palimpsesto el trayecto de lo que un camino traza: huellas, principalmente, que aquí asumen la forma de un archivo escrito, hablado, imaginado. (See 'Áurea María Sotomayor Reseña "PR3 Aguirre"')

Palimpsest of a modernity in ruins, in its archival search for traces, *PR3 Aguirre* ends up establishing an archive in itself. Aponte ends up gathering the found traces within a book that both holds the history of the Caribbean and opens it to the world. This paradoxical double nature of the archive, which as Gabriela Nouzeilles has pointed allows it both to gather and to disperse, to be both the site of an inscription and an itinerancy, permits Aponte to sketch the complex routes that ended up forming the Caribbean as a space where the global flows of modernity nonetheless intersected.[12] Attentive reader of Glissant, whose emphasis on routes rather than roots she has elsewhere praised, she has found in the Caribbean archive a site of entanglement, where identity is always staged at the crossroads of the Atlantic. A precarious archive, however, that is always at the verge of disappearing or being silenced.

Throughout the book there seems to be always a looming fear: that Aguirre might disappear before its story is exhumed and told. When the narrator returns to the old company town a month after the hurricane, it is with the fear that the town might have been erased by the winds and that the story she wished to tell had been once again silenced and erased. This frailty and precarity is characteristic, for Aponte, not only of Aguirre, but of the Caribbean archipelago itself where 'los archivos son frágiles y la memoria traumatizada se reprime' (Ramos, 'Entrevista a Marta Aponte', p. 32). Once and again, however, what she finds is the resilience of history, its capacity to endure in the aftermath of catastrophe: 'Pasear hoy por Aguirre es ver ruinas habitadas de las que salen voces humanas, donde conviven niños con nidos de palomas' (Aponte, *PR 3 Aguirre*, p. 298). As both ruinous archive and as an archive of ruins, Aguirre stages the possibility of witnessing after catastrophe, bridging the otherwise distant worlds of *testimonio* and of the archive.

12 Eduardo Cadava and Gabriela Nouzeilles, *The Itinerant Languages of Photography* (New York: Yale University Press, 2013), p. 45.

III *Las Voces Humanas*: On Testimony, Testaments and Futurity

The archive pre-occupies the future... (Jacques Derrida)[13]

Faithful to its testamentary nature, *PR3 Aguirre* remains singular in its attempt to bridge the world of the human voice and the world of the written archive. The passage from its first half, devoted to the written records tracing the lives of the founders of Aguirre, to its second half, dedicated to transcribing the interviews with the remaining residents of the old company town, stages the book's attempt to find a new literary modality of witnessing that is able to weave together two important literary traditions within Latin American literature: that of *testimonio* and that of the archival novel. Just like a will turns a person's final wishes regarding their estate into a legal document expressing how the estate will be distributed, *PR 3 Aguirre* plays with this passage between living word and written will, between life and what outlives life. If, as Áurea María Sotomayor has remarked, this is a book about property and about legacy, it could also be said that it is in turn about disinheritance and debt. A book about 'La rareza de las voces que protestan en el desierto de las cenizas' (Aponte, *PR 3 Aguirre*, p. 228). And so, if ashes are precisely what asks the question of survival at its limits, the question regarding the possibility of voicing a protest from within such a postcolonial desert is the question concerning the very possibility of witnessing. If, in the first part of the book, the author follows the archives containing the written accounts of the lives of the founders of Aguirre who, due their wealth and standing, left a visible mark within the annals of history, in the second part what is sketched are the voices that protest against oblivion and disinheritance: 'Lástima que nadie escribió la biografía de Marcelo J. Obén Sánchez. Queda la palabra testimonial' (Aponte, *PR 3 Aguirre*, p. 201). The testimonial word becomes the anchor that allows Aponte to reinscribe what the colonial archive has forgotten. It is against those archival silences that the novel gains the possibility of becoming a counter-archive: 'Esa desmemoria, esa tachadura, entristece, pero es inevitable, e incluso libera espacios que de otra manera languidecerían en el limbo de las conmemoraciones oficiales, que se cumplen sin saber qué significan, con hastío' (Aponte, *PR 3 Aguirre*, p. 222). Against official history understood as a 'desert of ashes', the testimonial word makes possible a new modality of survival: one that reinscribes

13 Jacques Derrida, 'Cinema and its Ghosts: An Interview with Jacques Derrida', in *Discourse*, transl. Peggy Kamuf (Detroit: Wayne State University Press, 2015), p. 22.

within the archive that which has been crossed out by both colonialism and by capitalism.

As Luis Othoniel Rosa has noted, the curious thing for a book about testimony and about the archive, is that *PR3 Aguirre* never surrenders to melancholy. Rather, as he goes on to argue: 'Aguirre, como todas las ruinas, también funciona como una alegoría en el libro. Una alegoría sobre algo que el lector deberá decidir por sí mismo, porque al visibilizar Aguirre, Marta Aponte parece querer decirnos algo sobre el futuro y no tanto sobre el pasado.'[14] The voices we find within this landscape of modern ruins are directed not only to the past but rather to the future. Their testimonial impulse seems to lead in the direction of an archive to come, reminding us of the poetic statement found early on in the book: 'Este libro no quiere ser una elegía a la isla desaparecida. Lo que se desconoce por tachado pertenece más bien a un tiempo que no ha sido todavía' (Aponte, *PR 3 Aguirre*, p. 15). This is a book about 'el futuro de Aguirre' precisely because the true history of Aguirre, a space disinherited by history like so many places in the Caribbean, is something that remains to be told. Aponte's book is merely the first attempt to rescue the surviving traces that will one day constitute its counter-archive:

> Son resquicios, voces turbadoras que descuadran los lugares comunes del sujeto colonial y de la historiografía del nacionalismo colonialista. Invitan a un desentumecimiento de la imaginación. Sin imaginación no son posibles las acciones políticas. (Ramos, 'Entrevista a Marta Aponte', p. 54)

Disturbing the colonial imagination and its historiographical commonplaces, the testimonial voices here summoned act, according to Aponte's interview remarks, as a catalyst for the post-colonial mind, energizing it into action. Against the apocalyptic imagery that often prevails in the Caribbean, where apocalyptic discourses often hide an end of history political apathy, here the counter-archive is instead seen as a stimulus for action. Beyond a mere melancholic revival of the past as it truly was, the testimonial word here enlivens the archive, pushing it towards the future, the possibility of redemption lies awaiting. Moreover, as Derrida has explained in *Archive Fever*, this archival impulse of survival is always staged against a horizon of catastrophe. Against either the death drive or oblivion, it opens the time for a future yet to come: '...the question of the archive is not, we repeat, a question of the past [...] It is a question of the future itself, the question of a response, of a promise

14 'Luis Othoniel Rosa Reseña 'Pr3 Aguirre', *El Roommate: Colectivo de lectores*, elroommate.com/2020/06/14/luis-othoniel-rosa-resena-pr3-aguirre-dossier-marta-aponte-alsina/ (accessed 13 December 2023).

and of a responsibility for tomorrow'.[15] It is there, in that 'tiempo que no ha sido todavía' that the testimonial counter-archive find its true temporality and its true home, part of a 'testamentary desire ... that something survive, be left, be transmitted—an inheritance'.[16]

PR3 Aguirre is then a book written *beyond* the figure of the end, heralding a new beginning. Not only a new beginning for the Latin American novel, with its bridging of *testimonio* and the archive, but also a new beginning for a community that for many years has felt disinherited by history. In this sense, the book's fragmentary structure mimics the attempt to make whole a history that has been torn apart by the violence of both colonialism and capitalism: '¿Cómo pensar las paradojas de la comunidad que se conjuga o se re-articula mediante una escritura fragmentaria?' (Ramos, 'Entrevista a Marta Aponte', p. 54). Marta Aponte has written a book that rearticulates Caribbean history, reminding us of Kamau Brathwaite's verses in his poem 'Caribbean Man in Space and Time': 'The unity is submarine/breathing air, our problem is how to study the fragments/whole.'[17] An archipelagic relationship between fragment and whole that reminds us of the mangroves and their capacity to withstand the violence of tropical storms.

IV Of Mangroves and Trees: A Conclusion

> ... to imagine new ways to live in the wake of slavery, in slavery's afterlives, to survive (and more) the afterlife of property. (Christina Sharpe, Aponte, *PR 3 Aguirre*, p. 300)

'Si Aguirre ha de sobrevivir...', we read in the concluding pages of the book, as we witness the narrator strolling through the post-hurricane ruins of the old company town.[18] We then realise that *PR3 Aguirre* was, from the very get go, a book about survival and about learning to live in the aftermath of that great catastrophe that was colonialism and its aftermath. It is not

15 Jacques Derrida, *Archive Fever: A Freudian Impression*. Transl. Eric Prenowitz (London: University of Chicago Press, 2005), p. 36.

16 Kas Saghafi, 'The Desire for Survival?', in *Desire in Ashes: Deconstruction, Psychoanalysis, Philosophy*, ed. Simon Morgan Wortham and Chiara Alfano (London: Bloomsbury, 2015), p. 141.

17 Edward Kamau Brathwaite, 'Caribbean Man in Space and Time', *Small Axe*, 25 (2021), p. 91, https://www.muse.jhu.edu/article/863462 (accessed 13 December 2023).

18 Christina Sharpe, *In the Wake: On Blackness and Being* (New York: Duke University Press, 2016), p. 18.

surprising that Marta Aponte had spent months tracing the transatlantic routes of Turner's 1840 painting *Slave Ship*, for in a way what the book traces is the long wake that follows that ship. Learning to live in such a wake, as Christina Sharpe has recently suggested, is one of the tasks that this book takes head on, conscious that the wake is here both an act of mourning the past as well as an act of awakening to a new post-catastrophic future. It is this double task that Aponte assigns to all of us readers, when she hands us '...un libro como este, de apuntes rasgados entre tumbas y sobrevivientes' (Aponte, *PR 3 Aguirre*, p. 245). Her poetics of survival lie in her capacity to see how the testimonial trace allows us to reconfigure the Caribbean archive, opening a space for a reading that speaks of a time yet to come.

In a book so deeply indebted to the works of Sebald, and so deeply entrenched in the question of the archive, it is not surprising to find a series of photographic images accompanying the text. As George Didi-Huberman has recently highlighted, the photographic image is, at the end of the day, staged against that spectral logic of survival which pervades *PR3 Aguirre.*[19] More surprising is the fact that many of these images are of trees, as if the tree—that figure which in the aftermath of María must have seemed painfully absent from the landscape—was a stand-in for memory. In a book about genealogies and about families, this is undoubtedly the case: the tree is an archive, reminding us that nature is also a giant archive. Walking throughout the post-hurricane ruins of Aguirre, with its barren landscape devoid of vegetation, Aponte must have felt that the site encapsulated a catastrophe that was as much social as it was ecological. In fact, as Julio Ramos has noted, this capacity to weave the ecology into the history of exploitation of Aguirre what makes the book unique:

> ... la crítica del tiempo acumulativo del progreso manifestada en términos afines a las discusiones actuales sobre el ecocidio y el antropoceno en las economías planetarias del monocultivo agroindustrial, donde las derivas ontológicas que produce el *laboratorio colonial* dificultan incluso cualquier distinción elemental entre naturaleza y cultura o artificio. (Ramos, 'Entrevista a Marta Aponte', p. 25)

Most of the images that appear throughout *PR3 Aguirre* are interestingly pictures of barren trees, as if the archive itself was in peril, as if a catastrophe had befallen the archive. As if the branches, like the archive, were in ruins: 'La noche de nuestro encuentro con Claudio Paco soñó con una ciudad en ruinas, de edificios abandonados [...] Yo desperté preguntándome cómo será pasar la noche en Aguirre. Tantas ruinas con sus árboles cubiertos de

19 Georges Didi-Huberman, *The Surviving Image: Phantoms of Time and Time of Phantoms* (London: Pennsylvania State University Press, 2017).

enredaderas parásitas, que arropan el aire sobre las casas, tamizando la luz' (Aponte, *PR 3 Aguirre,* p. 241). But these ruins seem to face, not so much the past, as the future. They are a sign not of a melancholic rehearsal of the past, but rather a sign of survival, symbols for a nation that refuses to surrender. For, as Aponte has stated in an interview: 'Somos una nación de sobrevivientes, de misterios íntimos de familias destrozadas cuyos sentidos reinterpretamos en soledad, de aquella memoria rota que describió Arcadio Díaz Quiñones' (Ramos, 'Entrevista a Marta Aponte', p. 546). The ruins of Aguirre bear witness, then, not so much to the catastrophic end of a history, but rather to its survival and to the dawn of a new beginning.

Among the many trees photographically depicted throughout the book there is one that always catches my attention. In it we see the mangroves that populate Pozuelo, the southern coastline Aponte's esteemed Luis Palés Matos admired in his memoir *Litoral.* Among all the trees present in the book, their branches suggesting the bifurcations of Aguirre and its history, it is perhaps here where the image of the precarious Caribbean archive and its survival is rendered most clearly. Protecting the middle of the island from the gusts of the storms that often assail it, the mangrove presents us with a final image of what Marta Aponte's poetics of survival is: an archive that proposes an archipelagic unity to history, beyond the classical progressive logic of modernity, beyond the logic of ends. The mangrove, resilient against the winds of progress, reminds us indeed of what Glissant once posited as the transversal logic of Caribbean history: 'Submarine roots: that is floating free, not fixed in one position in some primordial spot, but extending in all directions in our world through its network of branches'.[20] As an image of both entanglement and resilience, of roots becoming routes, the mangrove remains a figure for the possibility of survival beyond catastrophe.

Bibliography

Aponte, Marta, *PR 3 Aguirre* (Cayey: Sopa de Letras, 2018).

Áurea María Sotomayor Reseña 'PR3 Aguirre', *El Roommate: Colectivo de lectores,* elroommate.com/2020/06/21/aurea-maria-sotomayor-resena-pr3-aguirre-dossier-marta-aponte-alsina/ (accessed 13 December 2023).

Benjamin, Walter, *Illuminations.* Translated by Harry Zorn (London: The Bodley Head, 2015).

Blanchot, Maurice, *The Writing of the Disaster.* Translated by Ann Smock (Lincoln: University of Nebraska Press, 1995).

20 Édouard Glissant, *Caribbean Discourse: Selected Essays.* Transl. J. Michael Dash (New York: University Press of Virginia, 1989), p. 67.

Brathwaite, Edward Kamau, 'Caribbean Man in Space and Time', *Small Axe*, 25 (2021), pp. 90–104, https://www.muse.jhu.edu/article/863462 (accessed 13 December 2023).

Cadava, Eduardo, and Gabriela Nouzeilles, *The Itinerant Languages of Photography* (New Haven: Yale University Press, 2013).

Derrida, Jacques, 'Cinema and its Ghosts: An Interview with Jacques Derrida', in *Discourse*. Translated by Peggy Kamuf (Detroit, MI: Wayne State University Press, 2015), pp. 22–39.

Derrida, Jacques, *Archive Fever: A Freudian Impression*. Translated by Eric Prenowitz (London: University of Chicago Press, 2005).

Derrida, Jacques, *The Beast and The Sovereign*. Translated by Geoffrey Bennington (London: University of Chicago Press, 2011).

Didi-Huberman, Georges, *The Surviving Image: Phantoms of Time and Time of Phantoms* (London: Pennsylvania State University Press, 2017).

Glissant, Édouard, *Caribbean Discourse: Selected Essays*. Translated by J. Michael Dash (New York: University Press of Virginia, 1989).

Glissant, Édouard, *Poetics of Relation*. Translated by Betsy Wing (Ann Arbor: University of Michigan Press, 2021).

'Los gringos de Marta Aponte Alsina', *El roommate: Colectivo de lectores*, elroommate.com/2020/06/14/jeffrey-lawrence-los-gringos-de-marta-aponte-alsina-dossier-marta-aponte-alsina/ (accessed 13 December 2023).

'Luis Othoniel Rosa Reseña "Pr3 Aguirre"', *El roommate: Colectivo de lectores*, elroommate.com/2020/06/14/luis-othoniel-rosa-resena-pr3-aguirre-dossier-marta-aponte-alsina/ (accessed 13 December 2023).

Naas, Michael, *The End of the World and Other Teachable Moments: Jacques Derrida's Final Seminar* (New York: Fordham University Press, 2015).

'Poetics, Revelations, Catastrophes: An Interview with Kamau Braithwaite', Rain Taxi, https://www.raintaxi.com/poetics-revelations-and-catastrophes-an-interview-with-kamau-brathwaite/ (accessed 13 December 2023).

Ramos, Julio, 'PR 3 Aguirre: Entrevista a Marta Aponte', *Caracol*, 18 (2019), p. 32, access link: https://www.revistas.usp.br/caracol/issue/download/11320/1684 (accessed 13 December 2023).

Saghafi, Kas, 'The Desire for Survival?', in *Desire in Ashes: Deconstruction, Psychoanalysis, Philosophy*, edited by Simon Morgan Wortham and Chiara Alfano (London: Bloomsbury, 2015), pp. 139–60.

Sharpe, Christina, *In the Wake: On Blackness and Being* (Durham: Duke University Press, 2016), p. 18.

Trouillot, Michel-Rolph, *Silencing the Past (20th Anniversary Edition)* (Boston: Beacon Press, 2015).

12

Beyond Resilience: Débrouillardise in Civil War Novels

Hannah Grayson

Abstract

How do novels reflect and respond to political catastrophe? How do people 'get by' during conflict? How does a city wear the fractures of civil war? How might a poetics of movement illuminate the practice of negotiating ever-changing circumstances? In this chapter on two novels from Ivory Coast I focus on navigating the quotidian during civil war. My argument, sketched out in this chapter, is that the notion of *débrouillardise* is a useful lens for reading this kind of navigating. I define *débrouillardise* as a form of situated, creative expertise, and here set it against the more commonly circulated concept of resilience.

Quand on refuse on dit non (*When You Refuse You Say No*, Ahmadou Kourouma, 2005) and *Matins de couvre-feu* (*Curfew Mornings*, Tanella Boni, 2005) present a diverse picture of survival and negotiation in civil war. These Ivoirian French-language writers gesture towards a particular practice of coping and living that goes beyond the individualistic, strength-based limitations of resilience. This practice centres on networked, mobile acts which are generated within a collective commitment to renewal and shift. I situate my reading within a frame of Patrice Nganang's *romans de detritus*, AbdouMaliq Simone's reading of ensemble work in cities and Achille Mbembe's analysis of decolonisation on the African continent. The fiction of Ivory Coast and its tumultuous recent history draws our attention to new vocabularies that help interrogate the concept of resilience and its relationship to catastrophe.

Keywords: resilience; débrouillardise; civil war; mobility; Ivory Coast; literature

I Introduction

A reign of terror had taken hold of the city, with the infamous 'death squads' roaming the streets after curfew, army officials encouraging citizens to report 'suspicious activity' to telephone hotlines, and the destruction of poor neighbourhoods and slums. Northerners in popular neighbourhoods were subjected to regular roundups in which they were stripped to the waist, relieved of their documents, and carted off in trucks like cattle. It was not uncommon to drive by a naked corpse on the side of the road in the early morning, hands tied behind the back and a bullet in the back of the head.[1]

Describing Abidjan, Ruth Marshall-Fratani writes of the escalation of events she observed in horror as an eyewitness in 2002. A nine-year conflict saw the southern-led government of the Ivory Coast fight groups traditionally hailing from the north, such as the Malinke and Senoufo ethnic groups, that complained of marginalisation and exclusion. That year, the then president Laurent Gbagbo had launched the Opération Nationale d'Identification instructing all Ivorians to return to their 'village of origin' in order to be registered there as citizens. All persons who could not claim a village of origin within the country were to be considered as immigrants and would therefore lose their citizenship. This was but the latest step in years of conflict around the category of autochthony that split the nation in two. This term (being of the soil) has been used as a basis for ivoirité in Ivory Coast and, ideologically, makes citizenship status subject to being at home in the soil or national space. A colonial model reinvigorated by projects leaning into a vision of the postcolonial nation-state, autochthony undoes the principle of equality by dividing laws of belonging 'into "pure" citizenship (that of the native born) and borrowed citizenship (one that, less secure from the start, is now not safe from forfeiture)'.[2]

In *Manifeste d'une nouvelle littérature africaine*, Patrice Nganang (2007) sets out what he sees as the defining terms of contemporary African literature. His primary reference point for authentic experience of precarious life in the twenty-first century is *la rue*, or the street. To hold this focus on context alongside an examination of movement is to avoid the over abstraction present in some nomadic thought (e.g. Braidotti, Deleuze). Yet it also moves beyond the dangerous entanglement of soil and citizenship by seeing *la rue* not as a condition for belonging, but as a defining reference point that informs a way of being in the world. The apparent paradox that

1 Ruth Marshall-Fratani, 'The War of 'Who is Who?': Autochthony, Nationalism and Citizenship in the Ivorian Crisis', *African Studies Review*, 49:2 (2006), 9–43, doi:10.1353/arw.2006.0098 (accessed 19 November 2023).

2 Achille Mbembe, *Necropolitics* (Durham: Duke University Press, 2019), p. 3.

Nganang—much like AbdouMaliq Simone—seeks to untangle is that space being both the churning seat of detritus and 'an infinite space of possibilities birthed from disorder'.[3] Following Lydie Moudileno, who has argued for African literature as a unique locus for catching glimpses of 'the considerable complexity of the place',[4] this chapter takes two twenty-first-century Ivoirian novels as a way into looking beyond resilience in the space of civil war.

Ahmadou Kourouma's novel *Quand on refuse on dit non*,[5] written as a sequel to the more widely read *Allah n'est pas obligé* follows two characters fleeing the violence of civil war. Published in 2004, there is a marked intensity to the country's unravelling political situation and the disdain directed at it in the novel through parody. Published the following year, *Matins de couvre-feu* by exiled Tanella Boni plunges the reader into the heart of that violence in a similarly satirical way. The unnamed protagonist narrates from her home where she is under house arrest for having broken one of the myriad rules of the *Anges suprêmes* (Supreme Angels), the party who track the movements of all citizens of Zambaville, Boni's fictionalisation of Abidjan. Taken together, these two novels allow us a look at the specific navigation of space during civil war, a context described by Boni as 'a society which survives in corruption, *débrouillardise*, and is always on its toes, women and children are situated at risk on the front line'.[6]

This chapter addresses whether in such a context, the omnipresent terminology of resilience makes sense. That is to ask, whether resilience—as a widespread behavioural descriptor and societal target—is useful for framing life in and around (Ivoirian) crisis; life, for Boni's women and children, 'on the front line'. I align my views with those of International Relations scholars David Chandler, Julian Reid and Charles Amo-Agyemang here, in seeing resilience discourse as perpetuating core assumptions of Eurocentric or Western thinking, particularly around notions of individual autonomy and regularity in space and time. 'Western policies of resilience', Chandler writes, 'understood as automated adaptation to the world, close off and are

3 Patrice Nganang, 'Un espace infini de possibilités qui naissent du désordre', in *Manifeste d'une nouvelle littérature africaine: Pour une littérature préemptive* (Paris: Homnisphères, 2007), p. 265. My translation.

4 Lydie Moudileno, 'Penser l'Afrique à partir de sa littérature', in *Penser et écrire l'Afrique aujourd'hui*, ed. Alain Mabanckou (Paris: Éditions du Seuil, 2017), pp. 137–47 (p. 147): 'la considérable complexité du lieu'. My translation.

5 Ahmadou Kourouma, *Quand on refuse on dit non* (Paris: Éditions du Seuil, 2004).

6 Tanella Boni, *Que vivent les femmes d'Afrique?* (Paris: Éditions du Panama, 2008), p. 94: 'une société qui survit dans la corruption, la débrouillardise et toujours sur le qui-vive, les femmes et les enfants se trouvent exposés en première ligne' (my translation).

antithetical to' understandings of communities as relationally open (after Glissant) and communities as situated in and amongst a world of flux and flows.[7] The seemingly incessant recourse to resilience discourse currently plaguing us is incontestably Eurocentric in both of its disciplinary origins: on the one hand, applications of systemic resilience stem from ecology, and on the other, individual resilience is based on psychology.[8] The co-option of this analytical framework by small-scale institutions up to national governments has seen a pressurising of the individual subject or group to be unbreakable and efficient in the face of struggle. This neoliberal framing threatens to romanticise community strategies for coping at the edge of crisis, while promoting self-responsibility as self-determination and empowerment in a strength-based lexicon which overlooks ongoing systemic injustice and oppression and remains fixed in a teleological understanding of time.[9] The term's colonial heritage emerges in ongoing 'interventions' within the fields of development, economics and international policy around disaster response, but also entraps 'vulnerable' communities when they are characterised as especially adapted to coping with rapid change. Chandler's decolonising critique of resilience discourse gestures towards some of the creativity and mobility my work sketches with a view to building alternative vocabularies of resilience. In this chapter, I additionally draw on the work of AbdouMaliq Simone and Achille Mbembe who conceptualise some of the issues I explore in relation to understandings of *débrouillardise*.

II *Débrouillardise*

To address some of the limitations of the concept of resilience, I propose the alternative concept of *débrouillardise* (see Boni, *Que vivent*, p. 94). The term is used by citizens of Kinshasa, Democratic Republic of Congo to describe a spirit of survival characterising everyday life in the city. By using this term I mean more than a capacity for problem solving; rather, something like

7 David Chandler, 'Decolonising Resilience: Reading Glissant's *Poetics of Relation* in Central Eurasia', *Cambridge Review of International Affairs*, 35:2 (2021), 158–75, doi:10.1080/09557571.2021.1944984 (accessed 29 July 2023).

8 Susan Moser et al., 'The Turbulent World of Resilience: Interpretations and Themes for Transdisciplinary Dialogue', *Climatic Change*, 153:1–2 (2019), 21–40, doi:10.1007/s10584-018-2358-0 (accessed 19 November 2023).

9 Charles Amo-Agyemang, 'Decolonising the Discourse on Resilience', *International Journal of African Renaissance Studies—Multi-, Inter- and Transdisciplinarity*, 16:1 (2021), 4–30, doi:10.1080/18186874.2021.1962725 (accessed 28 July 2023).

situated, creative expertise informing a way of being in the world. Situated, because unlike nomadic ontologies critiqued for being overly abstracted or metaphorical, *débrouillardise* emerges from specific (most often precarious) contexts.[10] And creative, because it is more than an impulse of reactive repairing.[11] It includes strategic devices, gestures and rhythms and disavows the apolitical nihilism of a resilient subject in a permanent struggle to accommodate itself to the world (Evans and Reid, 'Dangerously Exposed'). AbdouMaliq Simone (whose work on urban life in the Global South seeks to move beyond their dominant presentation as failed cities) asks: 'How many actions are undertaken seemingly indifferent to the survival of the subject that undertakes them?'—in other words, crucially, the direction of life is not only set towards surviving, but, as Simone puts it, 'in their extension toward a liveliness of things in general [...] as techniques of prolonging'.[12] To return to Nganang's *rue*, the city is the key site fiction has provided for examining *débrouillardise*, something that goes beyond survival. Boni's text is set in 'a city where the fight for life is the rule to follow': 'for life', rather than a fight, merely, to live.[13] Simone describes the city as 'a conjunction of seemingly endless possibilities of remaking'[14] for variously located actors who manoeuvre

10 An Yountae, *The Decolonial Abyss: Mysticism and Cosmopolitics from the Ruins* (New York: University of Virginia Press, 2016).

11 By this I mean to contest the assumptions of 'crisis' and 'resilience' that signify (1) there has been an error and (2) there is a preferred baseline/target to which we must either return or move forward. See An Yountae, *The Decolonial*, who argues that the telos of progress, the process of learning from errors that marks the transcendental subject of European philosophy, does not hold the future open but is a 'totalitarian' closing of the imagination. The future in this case is built on history-as-teacher, a past regarded as a 'reservoir of multiplied experiences which the readers can learn and make their own'. Reinhart Koselleck, *Futures Past: On the Semantics of Historical Time* (New York: Columbia University Press, 2004), p. 27. See also Brad Evans and Julian Reid: 'Resistance here is transformed from being a political capacity aimed at the achievement of freedom from that which threatens and endangers to a purely reactionary impulse aimed at increasing the capacities of the subject to adapt to its dangers and simply reduce the degree to which it suffers.' 'Dangerously Exposed: The Life and Death of the Resilient Subject', *Resilience,* 1:2 (2013), 83–98, doi:https://doi.org/10.1080/21693293.2013.770703 (accessed 28 July 2023).

12 AbdouMaliq Simone, *Improvised Lives: Rhythms of Endurance in an Urban South* (Oxford: Polity Press, 2018), p. 19.

13 Tanella Boni, *Matins du couvre-feu* (Paris: Serpent à Plumes, 2005), p. 185, 'une ville où la lutte pour la vie est la règle à suivre' (my translation).

14 AbdouMaliq Simone, *For the City Yet to Come: Changing African Life in Four Cities* (Durham, NC: Duke University Press, 2004), p. 9.

and resituate themselves, though it must be noted he is explicit about not romanticising the chaos of the African city.

My description of such practice as a kind of expertise is elaborated in the examples below, where it is set against colonial systems of knowledge formation that are openly derided. In Michel de Certeau's gestures towards the artful nature of knowing (*connaître*) a city ('space is a practised place'), character-agents condition space through their ways of being.[15] What becomes clear with *débrouillardise* is that transformation from place to space is conditional on an expertise not accessible to everyone. This embodied knowledge, the shift away from strength and survival, the play and creativity, indicate some of the ways I am drawing distinctions between resilience and *débrouillardise*. As such, it moves us away from the assumption of a status quo which after any given catastrophe subsides is returned to, along with the stable, predictable future apparently subsumed within the assurances of resilience discourse. It also moves African subjects out of the reductive bounds of vulnerability and victimhood they have so often been tied into. It has relevance for levels of the individual, the collective and the city. As such, *débrouillardise* stands as a way to bring *la rue* into some kind of focus, as a way to render visible forms of action and life left opaque when during conflict, spaces of civil war may be seen only as battlegrounds or stalled and fractured infrastructure.

Drawing on the aforementioned novels, I will illustrate this kind of expertise as it emerges in two ways, first, in mobility, and second in networks.

III *Débrouillardise* as mobile expertise

Moving away from a concept of resilience as a return to status quo or stability requires us to acknowledge the intrinsic role of mobility. *Débrouillardise* relies on shift and flux, and helps us see that instability is not a temporary state (for a nation in upheaval or an individual) but is intrinsic to a way of being. This emerges at three levels in the novels: nation, city and individual. The historical implications of migration in Ivory Coast—its policies and practices—are evident in the violence described above. The eruptions of violence since 2002 stemmed from colonial and postcolonial policing of territory and belonging, particularly around the question of who is a 'foreigner'.[16] The Gbagbo regime set about turning back the clock of

15 Michel de Certeau, *L'invention du quotidien* (Paris: Gallimard, 1990), p. 173: 'L'espace est un lieu pratiqué' (my translation).

16 'Who is a 'foreigner' and who is an Ivoirian in the country today? This distinction is at the heart of the conflict, and this debate, perpetually postponed since independence, and exacerbated both by economic crisis and the process of

Ivoirian history, promoting nativist identity over the migration so favoured during Houphouët-Boigny's forty-year reign. Immigration has thus given rise to highly ambivalent discourses in Ivory Coast: on the one hand, valorized as the basis for the Ivoirian miracle, the country's economic and moral superiority (whose cornerstones were pan-Africanism, fraternity, generosity); and on the other, tirades against the supposed ungratefulness and greed of the strangers formerly beckoned in.[17] Then at the level of the cities themselves (in these novels Abidjan or 'Zambaville', Daloa and Bouaké) are continually weathering (in)security, precarious economies and the in- and out-bound flux of populations. Within these urban spaces, the protracted and substantial history of movement has opened up new circuits through which actors operate (Simone, *Impoverished Lives*, p. 118). Finally, we see individuals and communities who are using movement as a strategy, and moving all the time. This seemingly basic notion must be emphasised; else it is foreclosed—however subtly—by the assumptions of linearity and stability often inherent in resilience discourse. If instability is merely a temporary pause on an otherwise linear timeline of progress, we bypass the possibilities for alternative worlds opened up by breaks and disruptions. For Achille Mbembe,[18] mobility is what conditions the development of postcolonial Africa. It goes without saying that this movement must not be the subject of indiscriminatory acclamation. The lines Mbembe sketches are 'frenetic lines, in truth, which break endlessly, continually change direction, opening the way to whirlwind movement—accidents rather than vents, spasms, stretching out from below, movement on the spot, and in any event, complication and ambivalence' (Mbembe, *Sortir*, p. 203).[19]

These frenetic lines of interruption are evident throughout Kourouma's novel, an open-ended text published posthumously since the author died before it was finished. The story in *Quand on refuse on dit non* is a journey taken by Birahima and Fanta from Daloa in the south of the country towards

democratization, has become increasingly radicalized over the years of the conflict.' (Marshall-Fratani, 'The War of 'Who is Who?', p. 11).

17 For a helpful overview of this issue in the history of Ivory Coast, see John, Akokpari, '"You Don't Belong Here"—Citizenship, the State and Africa's Conflicts: Reflections of Ivory Coast', in *The Roots of African Conflicts: The Causes and Costs*, ed. Alfred Nhema et al. (Oxford: James Currey, 2008), pp. 85–105.

18 Achille Mbembe, *Sortir de la grande nuit: Essai sur l'Afrique décolonisée* (Paris: La Découverte, 2013).

19 'Lignes frénétiques, à la vérité, qui se brisent sans cesse, changent continuellement de direction, ouvrant la voie à un mouvement tourbillonnaire—l'accident plutôt que l'événement, les spasmes, l'étirement par le bas, le mouvement sur place et, dans tous les cas, la complication et l'équivocité' (my translation).

Bouaké to the northeast. Following a massacre in her town, one of multiple expulsions in the novel, Fanta seeks safety with relatives further north.[20] Birahima is a (former) child soldier (having fought in Liberia), a Muslim, who volunteers to travel as a guardian for Catholic Fanta, with whom he is besotted. As the pair stop off overnight and continue on their way, their repeated refrain (in Kourouma's Malinké-inflected French) reads 'nous avons pris pied la route' (took our feet on the way). The repetitious, pedestrian nature of the text illustrates the length of the journey, where threats of violence are so frequent they become commonplace. Yet in that phrase there is also a commitment to shift; to keep moving forwards. They are propelled to leave Daloa in the first place: 'la ville de criminels et de barbares' (the city of criminals and barbarians) which refugees flood out of 'comme s'il y avait la peste' (as if there was the plague) (Kourouma, *Quand on refuse*, p. 37). Leaving one city under stress, plagued by violence, they are nonetheless propelled towards another, in the promise of opportunities (or Simone's possibilities) that await there. The pull-push between cities demonstrates that the city remains the reference point Nganang identifies, even when not the explicit backdrop. For both protagonists, Daloa has been a training ground that proves more or less helpful on their journey.

In Kourouma's text, Birahima's *débrouillardise* is a streetwise modus operandi set in stark contrast to Fanta's stultifying discourse on the story of the nation. Fanta uses the journey to educate Birahima in her version of the history and politics of Ivory Coast. Where her valuing of a pacifist word has been set against Birahima's so-called barbaric weapons and violence, I would offer a less reductionist view of the so-called uneducated boy's value.[21] His experiences have seen him ready and able to navigate 240km of road and save Fanta's life on numerous occasions. His expertise is mobilised, whereas hers is deadening, and unlike resilience it does not rely on the kind of formulaic templates derided in the novel.

To take one example, when the pair are set on by sixteen young rebels armed with machetes, Birahima shoots his Kalashnikov to scare them off. The two laugh once the rebels flee and the very next sentence reads, 'Fanta continued teaching the history of the Ivory Coast' (Kourouma, *Quand on*

20 This is the territorial outworking of a conflict over *ivoirité* that has been both cultural and political. Former (internal and external) migrants to the south, broadly grouped together as Dioulas (Malinkés, Sénoufos, Mossis, Gourounsis) were attacked and mistreated by the Bétés in a bid to oust them from the land of 'true Ivoirians'.

21 Isabelle Constant, 'Quand on refuse on dit non: Roman du dire cruel, ou Comment écrire la guerre?', *Nouvelles Études Francophones*, 22:2 (2007), 34–43, doi:10.2307/25702066 (accessed 20 November 2023).

refuse, pp. 104–5).[22] Appearing indifferent to the danger to their lives, Fanta resumes her pages-long passages of history lessons in a parody of the oral epic. Her verbosity and objective, history-textbook, style is at the heart of Kourouma's irony as the woman in mortal danger is almost unresponsive such is her commitment to imparting official history.

The primacy of a (French) education and colonial forms of knowledge is parodied in such a way that allows alternative forms of expertise to emerge. Fanta's lessons are always followed by a coarse summary on the part of Birahima; his interpretation more often than not delivered in vulgar language and a derisive tone.

> In the same way, Fanta's lecturing narrative waters down the terror in an enumeration of facts, whereas Birahima condenses it and presents it in all its horror: 'Heads without necks over here, arms without bodies over there, and elsewhere men without heads or legs. It took four massive graves to bury all these horrors' (Constant, 'Quand on refuse on dit non' , p. 39).[23]

Moving along this double narrative the reader is removed rhythmically from the violence, and then thrown back close to it. As such, the history lesson is seen to be a distraction from the dangerous journey they are undertaking. The official discourse is parodied as it is imposed; the text highlights its irrelevance for survival even as it unveils the dire consequences of the colonial and postcolonial manipulations of Ivory Coast. Kourouma is highlighting the impact of political past whilst arguing the value of other forms of knowledge: more mobile, equipped and streetwise, for surviving the present.

Birahima chimes in self-deprecation and in a bid to impress Fanta, his bravado promises place all hope on his eventual 'brevet, bac et licence' (French national education qualifications). 'Me, little Birahima, I caught it all without understanding it all. Whatever I haven't understood for now will be well

22 'A la sortie d'un village, un jeune homme nous a barré la route. Il voulait nous fouiller pour savoir si nous n'emmenions pas chez nous au Nord l'argent du Sud de la Côte-d'Ivoire ... brusquement sont sortis de la foret une quinzaine de jeunes comme lui, tous armés de coupe-coupe. Ils nous encerclèrent en hurlant "Dioulas voleurs !" et en balançant leurs armes.'

Moi, petit Birahima, je n'ai rien dit. Je me suis courbé, j'ai tourné deux fois et, tout à coup, j'ai sorti la kalach et j'ai tiré en l'air. Les jeunes gens ont hurlé, beaucoup sont tombés dans les fossés avant de disparaitre dans la forêt. Nous avons éclaté de rire et nous avons continué notre pied la route. Fanta a continué à enseigner l'histoire de la Côte-d'Ivoire' (Kourouma, *Quand on refuse*, 104–5).

23 'De même, la narration professorale de Fanta dilue l'effroi sous l'énumération des faits, alors [que] Birahima la condense et la livre dans toute son horreur: "Des têtes sans cou par ci, des bras sans corps par-là, et ailleurs des hommes sans tête ni jambes. II a fallu quatre immenses charniers pour enterrer toutes ces horreurs"' (my translation).

understood with my dictionaries once I'm real good for the [high school certificates])' (Kourouma, *Quand on refuse*, p. 87).[24] He seems to attribute these objects of French education with a kind of magic, but repeated eleven times in the novel, his humble rhetoric is saturated with irony. Alongside his rhetorics of praise for 'le français français des vrais Français de France,' (the French French of real French people from France) (Kourouma, *Quand on refuse*, p. 19) he moderates and vulgarises the language continually.

Kourouma makes Birahima as primary narrator the guide through the text, another marker of his expertise. The boy's no-nonsense telling of the story and his ironic mediations indicate he is wiser than he makes out. Birahima declares repeatedly that he is ignorant, but his knowledge of the violent landscape and the realities of war and death, is what keeps them alive. He is the guide through the narrative and the physical journey, acting as guarantor of safety. Ultimately the value of his knowledge is shown in his ability to move fast and protect them (*se débrouiller*), allowing them to continue on their way, and for the more physically vulnerable Fanta to remain safe. The juxtaposition of two forms of knowledge, one derided and one enhanced by an experience of mobility, forms a pointed critique of colonial and postcolonial knowledge-power practices. Against the cerebral accumulation of facts, Birahima is best equipped for navigating these spaces; his awareness of the provisional is an embodied expertise, in 'a living body with a specific shape, flesh, and history' (Yountae, *The Decolonial*, p. 3).

The primary distinction between the two is a reliance on the known versus a preparedness for the unknown. Birahima is a wandering subject, who 'produces himself in the unknown, by means of a chain of effects that is at times calculated but that never materializes exactly in the ways foreseen. It is within the unexpected, and within radical instability, that he creates and invents himself'.[25] It is in an experience and ongoing practice of mobility that Birahima is débrouillard, ready to navigate what is unknown unlike Fanta, who blindly recites what is apparently known. The fact that the two do not reach their destination is the ultimate undercutting of reason and certainty. As Mbembe writes,

Destinations may be the predetermined stages of a journey, and yet paths do not always lead to the desired destinations. What is important is where one ends up, the road travelled to get there, the series of experiences in

24 'Moi, petit Birahima, j'ai tout retenu sans tout comprendre. Ce que je n'ai pas compris pour le moment sera bien compris avec mes dictionnaires quand je serai fortiche pour le brevet élémentaire et pour le bac' (my translation).

25 Achille Mbembe, *Critique of Black Reason* (Durham, NC: Duke University Press, 2017), p. 149.

which one is an actor and to which one is witness, and, above all, the role played by the unexpected and the unforeseen (Mbembe, *Critique*, p. 144).

The targets of critique here are the same as in the closing pages of *Matins de couvre-feu*, discussed below. Both novelists take aim at France's *mission civilisatrice* and the postcolonial reincarnation of similar agendas in CURDIPHE (Cellule Universitaire de Recherche et de Diffusion des Idées et Actions du Président Konan Bédié) which expounded a restrictive and ethnonationalist vision of citizenship. In contrast, what Birahima shows is that

> the effective actor is he who, unable to kill with the first blow, shows himself to be cleverer than the other. Having prepared the trap, he must draw the other in through intelligence and ruse. The goal each time is to immobilize the other by enticing his body into a snare. Central to the *work for life* is the body. (Mbembe, *Critique*, p. 143)

Birahimia is certainly violent, and Constant reads this as a purely reactive form of survival expressed in monstrous actions. Birahima seems unremorseful in killing, and indeed more generally numbed by exposure to violence, but his actions are undoubtedly more than reactionary.[26] To return to Simone, this is a way of being that is open to more than survival. In a *débrouillardise* founded on experience of movement, there is an assumption of provisionality that becomes embodied knowledge. The expert mover, Birahima, is able to adapt to a wide range of territories but neither in a nihilistic expectation of no escape, nor a return to a status quo, nor a glamorous escapism. Rather, in these openings there is a way of being in the world, a step towards possible futures as yet unknown.

Movement is a subtext that sits in friction with ideas of resilience that are based on an ideal of stability and knowability, but it also undermines the very notion of autochthony. These two novelistic evocations of insistent movement refute that adherence to formulaic templates. When Séri Wayoro, the director of identification within Gbagbo's Opération National d'Identification claims that originally, 'people [in Ivory Coast] were sedentary, they stayed on their homelands' (Marshall-Fratani, 'The War of "Who is Who?"', p. 27), it is clear to see how an active erasure of histories of migration is used to serve the purposes of a politics of ethno-nationalisation. But

26 Isabelle Constant contends that 'Birahima's life circumstances make him a purely reactive character, making his actions at once monstrous and essential in the context of his survival.' ('Les circonstances de vie de Birahima en font un personnage purement réactif, rendant ses actions à la fois monstrueuses et nécessaires dans le contexte de sa survie') ('Quand on refuse on dit non', p. 43). My translation.

Kourouma and Boni's texts inscribe such histories by foregrounding mobility, mixed ancestry and multilayered networks.

IV *Débrouillardise* as networked expertise

I turn now to discuss *débrouillardise* as a way of being which is reliant on connections with others that are actively and creatively renewed and drawn on. In other words, it is a networked expertise. This necessarily moves us away from concepts of survival as autonomous and resilience as a developed individualism which shores up a subject against any possible outside influence. Rather, I posit *débrouillardise* as an active, networked stance (not as a loyalty to normative categories of race, gender, religion or class, necessarily, but) towards who is with you where you are with what you have (Simone, *Improvised Lives*, p. 30). In the intensified uncertainties of urban settings, Simone elaborates on the informalisation of large portions of everyday life. Within this, he refers to people's disparate and temporary relations as 'ensemble work'. I am taking his framework to read the networks in Boni's novel as

> comings-together, where rhythm is produced [...] from the efforts of the connected and disconnected to create refrains, momentary stabilities that offer up a repertoire of vernaculars, gestures, and sensibilities that can then be taken up to twist and turn a place into some malleable yet steady arena for people to pay attention to each other, engage each other, or not. (Simone, *Improvised Lives*, p. 18)

On one hand *Matins de couvre-feu* is a novel about multiple imprisonments: psychological, familial, social and political. In this novel people's mobility is under threat. The ruling party use immobilising tactics as their most effective tool of control: people's vehicles are apprehended, those considered suspicious are imprisoned, the protagonist is under house arrest. Another character, Enée, is thrown in jail for supposedly disguising himself as a taxi driver. Despite being a male autochthon whose citizenship rights are theoretically unhindered by his gender or origin, Enée's civil rights are withdrawn by the State and as a consequence he loses his wife and sense of direction (Boni, *Matins*, 289). In the extensive way it is targeted and curbed, freedom of movement is shown to be threatening in its potential.

However, *Matins de couvre-feu* is also a novel of overlapping and multilayered networks. The novel contains multiple interwoven strands of a family's story, extending branches of that same family's tree, webs of lies and deceit, a double-layered network of surveillance, and polysemic economies of objects which circulate and form links to transfer information and power. The most notable of these objects are taxis and telephones, which are managed by Timothée, a lead member of the *Anges suprêmes* and master of surveillance. The protagonist discovers that Timothée owns 1,387 phone boxes across the city, and that he employs people at each one to record who calls whom, and beyond that to wiretap private phones, noting all information in a notebook that proves to be 'a database worthy of the greatest spy networks'. His fleet of taxis is used for a similar purpose: 'there too Timothée excelled at hunting every word, even the most trivial, that flew around the streets' (Boni, *Matins*, p. 182).[27] He manipulates these networks to gather evidence which he hoards, and the resultant threat of such power-knowledge is clear: 'Such that in Zamba we're all the potential disappeared' (p. 57).[28]

Timothée, whose bedroom wall is covered in the phone numbers he scrawls there daily, embodies an obsession with knowing. The ever-growing number of phone boxes and taxis in his fleet signify his thirst for information; the more he knows, the greater his sense of control. This is underscored in the text by a proliferation of terms such as 'strings', 'links', 'channels' and 'chains', which Timothée seeks to strengthen just as he follows trails of information to establish some kind of supreme knowledge.

Ultimately this assumption of reality as knowable is undermined by the text moving as it does in so many directions, following the protagonist's own journey of discovery as she pieces together fragments of her family history. In its peripatetic narrative, the novel's form foregrounds shifting grounds of knowledge and potential ensembles. As Simone writes, 'urban collaboration does not simply reflect and institutionalise clearly identifiable social processes and forms. There are gaps and openings, room for negotiation and provocation, and thus collaboration can take many forms' (*For the City*, p. 12). Indeed, against these networks of knowledge hording, used to coerce and control, there exists a parallel ensemble more open to the provisional and creative.

What emerges is a female network of *débrouillardes* that is connected by a more-than-survival ethic and circulation of stories (by word of mouth and by letters). The nameless (and thus somewhat unknowable) protagonist, a successful businesswoman, takes herself to a rough area of Zambaville in a bid to find a way out of her stifling situation. The *débrouillardise* she finds there stands in stark distinction to any abstracted, autonomous existence of uninfringeable resilience. Here the description of the Bas-fonds is a crystallisation of the precarity and crush of Abidjan.

27 'Une base d'informations dignes des plus grands réseaux d'espionnage [...] là aussi excellait Timothée dans la traque de toutes les paroles même anodines, qui s'envolaient dans les rues' (my translation).

28 'Comme quoi nous sommes tous des disparus potentiels à Zamba' (my translation).

> In this district, no road was tarmacked. There were cracks everywhere which turned into muddy pools in the rainy season. And the dyers were set up, close to one another, on this bit of cramped land between the houses and the lagoon which, to be honest, had no banks [...] And all year long it was there that malaria found fertile soil for its rampant spread. (Boni, *Matins*, pp. 186–7)[29]

The sense of precarity, danger, overcrowding and dirt is almost tangible. Yet it is also here ('Pourtant, c'est là aussi') that she finds 'women on their feet, conscious of their fate and of their interests'.[30] It is specifically within this city space that opportunities for developing *débrouillardise* lie: 'And yet it's in this incredibly overcrowded setting that' they work[31] (*Matins*, pp. 186–8). The repetition of 'pourtant' (and yet) is an insistence of these women's ethic: a commitment to lucrative, creative work. And Boni then describes the repeated, plural actions as a systematic process of waxing, dying, cleaning, drying, beating and folding, which is, in Simone's apt words, 'adding something different to the fabric of mere survival' (*Improvised Lives*, p. 16):

> women covered wax over the cloth, so as to draw numerous patterns, here that they plunged the white cloth into mixes of carefully measured pigments, that they ridded the cloth of all its impurities, that they dried in the sun. Once dried, they had to beat it with a piece of wood to render it more workable and to brighten the colours, they had to fold it as many times as necessary [...]
>
> And they were there, these women, ready to get down to work, from morning to nightfall, carrying out moves whose origins got lost in the twists of time. At times they used indigo, the ancient pigment with an intensely blue blue that enhanced the cloth's beauty. But this matchless blue would leave stains on hands and body parts that came into contact with the dye. These were multicoloured women, not sad at all. Humanity that was well and warm and resistant to every ordeal worked in this unexpected place. (Boni, *Matins*, p. 188)[32]

29 'Dans ce quartier, aucune rue n'était bitumée. Il y avait des crevasses partout qui, en saison des pluies, se transformaient en mares boueuses. Et les teinturières étaient installées, les unes près des autres, sur cette portion de terre exiguë entre les maisons et la lagune, qui, à vrai dire, n'avait pas de rive... Et la malaria trouvait là, à longueur d'année, un terrain propice à son expansion galopante' (my translation).

30 'Des femmes debout, conscientes de leur sort et de leurs intérêts' (my translation).

31 'Pourtant, c'est dans ce décor incroyablement surchargé que...' (my translation).

32 'Les femmes passaient la cire sur le tissu, en vue de dessiner des motifs variés, qu'elles trempaient le tissu blanc dans les mélanges de pigments délicatement

The marketplace persists despite polluted waters; fabric is coloured despite the overcrowding. Simone writes that in circumstances of intense volatility, residents cannot be viewed as simply adding to the repetition of an endless grind of drudgery and dissolution (*Improvised Lives*, p. 16). It is here that the creative act of waxing and dying is crucial; it is productive in the face of decay in a seemingly effortless deployment of collective knowledge. And this knowledge is an expertise formed in the unknown, rather than set against it. It is in the heart of this network of women's work that the protagonist finds her own allies. Her self-sufficiency, learnt young, shifts from autonomy into collaboration as she finds Aya, another entrepreneur whose exceptional management, memory and cuisine the text celebrates.[33] The two go on to run a successful restaurant together which becomes a favourite in the city. If for Mbembe autochthony is 'an otherless universe' ('*le rêve fou d'un monde sans autrui*'),[34] then *débrouillardise* is an other-oriented stance, open to ensemble work.

What is more, as Tanella Boni writes elsewhere, those who navigate the marketplace need to know its specific rules, how to pull the strings and work its reach (beyond the city, beyond the nation) (*Que vivent les femmes?* p. 31). Porosity and openness to the global is part of this network's strength. The cloths dyed by Boni's *teinturières* circulate within a whole system of signs and significances that must be learnt: navigated and bent *in situ* with gestures and turns. Unlike the taxis and telephones, the cloths are not merely circulated in an accumulation of power. Their patterns have known names and meanings, some classic, known far and wide (like 'jalousie' or 'Addis-Abeba')

---

dosés, qu'elles débarrassaient le tissu de toutes ses impuretés, qu'elles le séchaient au soleil. Une fois séché, il fallait battre le tissu, avec un morceau de bois afin de le rendre plus malléable et de raviver les couleurs, il fallait le plier autant de fois que nécessaire [...].

Et elles étaient là, les femmes, à pied d'œuvre, du matin jusqu'à la tombée du crépuscule, accomplissant des gestes dont l'origine se perdait dans les méandres du temps. Parfois, elles utilisaient l'indigo, le pigment ancestral dont le bleu intensément bleu rehaussait la beauté du tissu. Mais ce bleu incomparable laissait des traces sur les mains et sur les parties du corps entrant en contact avec la teinture. C'étaient des femmes multicolores et pas tristes du tout. L'humanité saine et chaleureuse et résistante à toute épreuve travaillait à cet endroit imprévu.'

33 'This way I learned to walk, setting my feet where they should go' ('Ainsi j'appris à marcher en mettant les pieds là où il faut.') (Boni, *Matins*, p. 164). Aya's food and memory set her power apart from male colleagues who write things down, within the network of men's obsession in the text with recording and surveillance (Boni, *Matins*, p. 195). It is also thanks to Fanta's (religious and paternal) networks in *Quand on refuse on dit non* that the travellers receive hospitality each night of their journey.

34 Mbembe 'À propos des écritures africaines de soi', p. 25, doi:10.3917/polaf.077.0016 (accessed 26 November 2023).

and others requiring more complex decoding.[35] This practice of decoding is another element of the ruse of *débrouillardise* which extends beyond reading the camouflage of pagnes; in this too, Boni's protagonist becomes expert:

> Well, you had to survive, in some way, in this African megalopolis that was neither a desert nor a mountainous landscape with horses but a real jungle with goodies and baddies on the hunt for dosh. The glitch is that all of them concealed their game. Everyone, even the worst criminals, moved about under the cover of innocence. How to know who is who? I'd also learnt for myself how to skirt around the law. Whose fault was that? (Boni, *Matins*, p. 174).[36]

Once again then, *débrouillardise* emerges as a form of adeptness: skills, knowledge, language, at once playful and expert, collectively informed.

A final element of this gendered *débrouillardise* is the circulation of stories between women. From her house arrest, the protagonist receives letters from her sister-in-law, which inform and expand her understanding of their wider family. The correspondence builds a bigger picture for the reader, but at the same time, the protagonist herself learns more detail of her history.[37] The epistolary relationship lends a deeply reflective, personal tone to those sections of the novel, so different from Fanta's rote-learnt narrative of history in *Quand on refuse on dit non*. In turn, the protagonist recounts the story of her own mother, from whom, beyond the grave, she draws inspiration for a débrouillarde life.[38] Crucially, this network of *correspondance* is active across the openings of absence and different generations: 'my bedroom walls were

35 For example, '"Guineafowl" (*ko'ndjé-ko'ndjé*, as we say in Ivory Coast) symbolises the independent woman, elusive, rebellious, like the well-known bird. Isn't wearing the "guineafowl" pagne a way of telling everyone who we are? The language of *pagnes* is to do with both play and defiance' ('"pintade" [*ko'ndjé-ko'ndjé*, comme on dit en Côte-d'Ivoire] symbolise la femme indépendante, insaisissable, insoumise, comme l'oiseau familier de ce nom. Porter un pagne "pintade" n'est-ce donc pas dire à tous qui l'on est? Le langage des pagnes semble relever à la fois du jeu et du défi.') (Boni, *Que vivent*, p. 3). My translation.

36 'Or, il fallait survivre, tant bien que mal, dans cette mégalopole africaine qui n'était pas un désert ou un paysage montagneux avec des chevaux mais une vraie jungle avec des bons et des méchants à la recherche de fric. Le hic, c'est que les uns et les autres camouflaient leur jeu. Tout le monde, même les pires criminels, avançait masqué sous la silhouette de l'innocence. Comment savoir qui est qui? J'avais appris, moi aussi, à contourner la loi. A qui la faute?' (my translation).

37 The influence of Mariama Bâ is to be noted in the exchange of letters building understanding of the female experience whilst one is trapped at home (though under very different circumstances). Cf. *Que vivent*, p. 151, where Bâ is quoted by Boni.

38 'They knew all the secrets of the forest and the tree-filled savannah and were capable of defending themselves' ('Elles connaissaient tous les secrets de la

permeable to visits from those who, according to non-believers, no longer inhabit our world' (Boni, *Matins*, p. 239).[39] An openness to a plurality of worlds is critical for expanding our understanding of the multiple ways in which the 'vulnerable' become 'resilient', and the ways in which that 'resilience' draws on and re-activates stories from the past. Timothée's narrow, obsessive focus on technological objects overlooks a plurality of epistemologies actually central to *débrouillardise* as more than survival. Boni critiques that blind embeddedness in global capitalist markets and the patterns of coercion that come with them.

Against the ruling party's coercive control, this female network burgeons—over boundaries of space and (precolonial) time (house arrest, letters, memories, words from the dead). As Moudileno writes: 'But it's also fiction which allows us to imagine resistance to dictatorships by making us hear voices which cannot be reduced to silence.'[40] There is an emphatic distinction between the système D of Timothée and his *Anges* who watch, record, imprison and seem bent on curbing energy and life, between that and this network of women dyeing, writing, building businesses (cf. Boni, *Matins* pp. 173, 179, 315). The contrast we saw in Kourouma's text, between two forms of knowledge, is echoed here; the one set on immobilising, on overpowering, on recording, the other, stemming from and oriented towards 'a whirling movement' ('*un mouvement tourbillonnaire*') (Mbembe, *Sortir*, p. 203). The former is epitomised at the novel's end in the creation of 'an Academy whose members all had to be expert surveyors in the art of calculating their own interests' (Boni, *Matins*, p. 315),[41] an unambiguous slight aimed at Bédié's infamous attempt to develop an academic base for *ivoirité* through the Cellule Universitaire de Recherche et de Diffusion des Idées et Actions du Président Henri Konan Bédié. In both authors, a critique of (post)colonial forms of knowledge and control is rendered through acute attention to the 'ensemble work' of mobile and networked *débrouillardise*.

forêt et de la savane arborée et étaient capables de se défendre') (Boni, *Matins*, p. 88). My translation.

39 'Les murs de ma chambre étaient perméables à la visite de ceux qui, aux yeux des profanes, n'habitent plus notre monde.' My translation.

40 Lydie Moudileno, 'Penser l'Afrique à partir de sa littérature', in *Penser et écrire l'Afrique aujourd'hui*, ed. Alain Mabanckou (Paris: Éditions du Seuil, 2017), pp. 137–47 (p. 142). 'Mais c'est aussi la fiction qui permet d'imaginer des résistances aux dictatures en faisant entendre des voix impossibles à réduire au silence' (my translation).

41 'Une Académie, dont les membres devaient être tous des géomètres experts dans l'art du calcul de leurs propres intérêts' (my translation).

V Conclusion

Birahima, the child soldier escorting Fanta to a seemingly safer city in *Quand on refuse on dit non*, and the imprisoned, entrepreneurial protagonist of *Matins de couvre-feu*, could be described as resilient. Against the odds, they survive in the violence of civil war. However, that descriptor forecloses some of what I have shown to be in evidence, that is to say, some of the possibilities and gestures which make up their way of being. Rather than merely surviving in a reach towards a stable future resembling a universal status quo, they are on the move responding to the intensified uncertainties of their urban lives. By recourse to the concept of *débrouillardise* we can bring the city into a kind of focus that reveals strategic and networked ways of navigating precarious life that operate at the margins of power (here embodied by a child soldier and women). I have argued that *débrouillardise* (and particularly its expression in mobility and ensembles) extends our thinking beyond the limitations of resilience in the way it foregrounds dynamic and fluid life and relations as opposed to mechanistic existence in an ontology of stability. In Ivory Coast specifically, revitalised modes of thinking through subjecthood and citizenship are urgently required, given the destructive history of autochthony and its divisive reliance on a dichotomy of 'pure' and 'borrowed' citizenship.

Bibliography

Akokpari, John, '"You Don't Belong Here"– Citizenship, the State and Africa's Conflicts: Reflections of Ivory Coast', in *The Roots of African Conflicts: The Causes and Costs*, edited by Alfred Nhema and Paul Tiyambe Zeleza (Oxford: James Currey, 2008), pp. 85–105.

Amo-Agyemang, Charles, 'Decolonising the Discourse on Resilience', *International Journal of African Renaissance Studies - Multi-, Inter- and Transdisciplinarity,* 16:1 (2021), 4–30, doi:10.1080/18186874.2021.1962725 (accessed 28 July 2023).

Boni, Tanella, *Matins du couvre-feu* (Paris: Serpent à Plumes, 2005).

Boni, Tanella, *Que vivent les femmes d'Afrique?* (Paris: Éditions du Panama, 2008).

Certeau, Michel de, L'Invention du quotidien (Paris: Gallimard, 1990).

Chandler, David, 'Decolonising Resilience: Reading Glissant's *Poetics of Relation* in Central Eurasia', *Cambridge Review of International Affairs,* 35:2 (2021), 158–75, doi: 10.1080/09557571.2021.1944984 (accessed 29 July 2023).

Constant, Isabelle, 'Quand on refuse on dit non: Roman du dire cruel, ou Comment écrire la guerre?', *Nouvelles Études Francophones,* 22:2 (2007), 34–43, doi:10.2307/25702066 (accessed 20 November 2023).

Evans, Brad, and Julian Reid, 'Dangerously Exposed: The Life and Death of the Resilient Subject', *Resilience,* 1:2 (2013), 83–98, doi:10.1080/21693293.2013.770703 (accessed 28 July 2023)

Kourouma, Ahmadou, *Quand on refuse on dit non* (Paris: Éditions du Seuil, 2004).

Koselleck, Reinhart, *Futures Past: On the Semantics of Historical Time* (New York: Columbia University Press, 2004).

Marshall-Fratani, Ruth, 'The War of "Who is Who?": Autochthony, Nationalism and Citizenship in the Ivorian Crisis', *African Studies Review,* 49:2 (2006), 9–43, doi:10.1353/arw.2006.0098 (accessed 19 November 2023).

Mbembe, Achille, 'À propos des écritures africaines de soi', *Politique Africaine,* 77 (2000), 16–43, doi:10.3917/polaf.077.0016 (accessed 26 November 2023).

Mbembe, Achille, *Sortir de la grande nuit: Essai sur l'Afrique décolonisée* (Paris: La Découverte, 2013).

Mbembe, Achille, *Critique of Black Reason* (Durham, NC: Duke University Press, 2017).

Mbembe, Achille, *Necropolitics* (Durham, NC: Duke University Press, 2019).

Moser, Susan et al., 'The Turbulent World of Resilience: Interpretations and Themes for Transdisciplinary Dialogue', *Climatic Change* 153:1–2 (2019), 21–40, doi:10.1007/s10584-018-2358-0 (accessed 19 November 2023).

Moudileno, Lydie, 'Penser l'Afrique à partir de sa littérature', in *Penser et écrire l'Afrique aujourd'hui,* edited by Alain Mabanckou (Paris: Éditions du Seuil, 2017), pp. 137–47.

Nganang, Patrice, 'Un Espace infini de possibilités qui naissent du désordre', in *Manifeste d'une nouvelle littérature africaine: Pour une littérature préemptive* (Paris: Homnisphères, 2007), p. 265

Simone, AbdouMaliq, *For the City Yet to Come: Changing African Life in Four Cities* (Durham, NC: Duke University Press, 2004).

Simone, AbdouMaliq, *Improvised Lives: Rhythms of Endurance in an Urban South* (Oxford: Polity Press, 2018).

Yountae, An, *The Decolonial Abyss: Mysticism and Cosmopolitics from the Ruins* (New York: University of Virginia Press, 2016).

13

Resilience in the Latin American Anthropocene Western

Leidy Paola Bolaños Florido and Wolfgang Fuhrmann

The rise of ecological awareness has gained major relevance since Paul Crutzen and Eugene Stoermer coined the term Anthropocene in 2000.[1] In contrast to Rachel Carson's influential book *Silent Spring* (1962), that drew attention to mankind's responsibility for nature, the term Anthropocene stands for a man-made geological epoch that challenges humanity's ability to survive and for resilience in an increasingly hostile environment, for example, due to climate change.

The debate around the Anthropocene and what it could mean takes on other nuances in Latin America. The Anthropocene discourse cannot be cut off from historical power relations and social inequalities in the region, nor of the struggles of its inhabitants to face their destructive effects.[2] Understanding the approaches towards the Anthropocene in Latin America should consider both the specific detrimental outcomes of this era and the practices attempting to confront them. As Maristella Svampa points out, when thinking about the link between nature and society in Latin America, feminist, Indigenous, and environmentalist narratives arise, which propose other ways of inhabiting the earth. Following Donna Haraway, Svampa notes: 'It is true that successive extinctions wiped out an important part of

1 Paul J. Crutzen and Eugene F. Stoermer, 'The "Anthropocene"', *Global Change Newsletter*, 41 (2000), 17–18.

2 Astrid Ulloa, 'Dinámicas ambientales y extractivas en el siglo XXI: ¿Es la época del Antropoceno o del Capitaloceno en Latinoamérica?', *Desacatos,* 54 (2017), 58–73 (p. 60) (accessed 23 January 2024).

species due to exogenous factors (climate change and/or major catastrophes), but life on earth has always shown a great capacity for resilience.'[3] In this sense, when thinking about the Anthropocene in the region, the concept of resilience allows us to explore the way of exercising the common by using intangible goods such as peace, local justice, traditional knowledge, or those material goods that are not subordinated to exclusively economic and destructive interests and serve as a basis to sustain and develop life. Due to historical conditions in Latin America, resilience can be applied to the lives of many people who have developed their own strategies in order to be resilient to fragile constitutional legality caused by dictatorships, organised crime, and state corruption.

According to French psychiatrist and ethologist Boris Cyrulnik, resilience is 'the ability of human beings subjected to the effects of adversity to overcome it and even to emerge stronger from the situation'.[4] Novelist Gilmer Mesa relates this capacity to Baruch Spinoza's notion of 'conatus', which refers to the 'power to persevere in one's being', a kind of 'appetite' or 'will' to preserve one's life despite difficulties (Mesa, '¿Quién y qué no es infierno?', p. 31). This power serves as a trigger for resilience and unfolds in people's actions and in the collective reconstruction of what is broken or altered. In this sense, we understand resilience as the capacity of people to overcome tragedies and traumatic experiences.

To explore the idea of resilience, this chapter puts three Latin American feature films in dialogue with the Anthropocene, resilience, and the Western genre: *Bacurau* (Juliano Dornelles and Kleber Mendonça Filho, BR/FR, 2019), *El Ardor* (*The Ardor*, Pablo Fendrik, USA/AR/MX/BR/FR, 2014), and *La terra degli uomini rossi* (*Birdwatchers*, Marco Bechis, IT/BR, 2008). These feature films from Latin American cinema are a few of a larger number of productions in which environmental topics, suffering, endurance, and resilience make an active part of the stories. Here, we propose that, in their aesthetics, these films refer to a specific film genre not immediately associated with Latin American cinema—the Western.

In the context of the Western genre, in which the protagonists are forced to defend themselves against an existential threat, defeat it, and start anew, we also suggest including the notion of resilience given by Colombian historian Ortiz Cassiani. Following the etymology of the word, Ortiz Cassiani

3 Maristella Svampa, 'Reflexiones finales. Dimensiones de la crisis sistémica', in *Las fronteras del neoextractivismo en América Latina: Conflictos socioambientales, giro ecoterritorial y nuevas dependencias* (Bielefeld: Bielefeld University Press, 2019), pp. 104–23 (p. 107).

4 Quoted in Gilmer Mesa, '¿Quién y qué no es infierno?', in *Resiliencia*, ed. Comisión de la Verdad (Bogotá: Comisión de la Verdad/Rey Naranjo Editores, 2020), pp. 26–38 (p. 26).

describes resilience as 'to overcome adverse situations—contexts of violence of all kinds, abuse, and extreme poverty—to rise above them, to cope with the situation, to use them as *a springboard*' (our emphasis). The metaphor of a springboard, not to return to the previous condition but to 'build enriching experiences, and come out stronger and in better conditions than the initial ones',[5] corresponds to the films' narrative trajectories in which successfully defeating the enemy at the end of the film means to start from a new social constellation, hoping that from now on things will get better.

The analysis of the films is based on the intersection of two proposals. First, as mentioned before, the discourse of the Anthropocene in Latin America differs from that of the Western world—the United States and Western Europe—and follows a different timeline. The Anthropocene, or anthropogenic outcomes, affects the life of many people in Latin America due to practices such as the devastating effects of land robbery, the deforestation of the Amazon rainforest, extractivism or mining—legal and illegal—inequality in the distribution of vital resources such as water, or the exploitative employment of cheap labour. The destruction of the living conditions of peasant and indigenous communities is inextricably linked to violence, forced displacement, and/or racism, and it has led to severe, even lethal, consequences for local populations that very often are unrepresented in political participation.

Second, in the Latin American context, the Western is a film genre that comes closest to showing the relationship between human activity and nature and the effects of the Anthropocene and highlights the resilience of the protagonists to the environmental effects and conditions that threaten their lives. Although the Western genre is usually associated with US history and is a staple of Classic Hollywood, it has many national varieties in Europe, Asia, and Latin America. From this perspective, a film genre is not a fixed but a dynamic category. Genres are flexible and subject to change. *Bacurau*, *The Ardor*, and *Birdwatchers* share characteristics of the Western genre, such as horses, knives or handguns, clothing, and violence as the ultima ratio to settle a social problem. Their stories are Western stories—the fight of an individual or a community in some remote region against a mighty landowner or a corrupt politician.

The three film examples, *Bacurau*, *The Ardor*, and *Birdwatchers*, follow popular genre patterns and not only deal with ecological issues such as water scarcity, the destructive power of global players, extractivism, or deterritorialisation, but also show, in the confines of the Western genre, how people's

5 Javier Ortiz Cassiani, 'Son de negros', in *Resiliencia*, ed. Comisión de la Verdad (Bogotá: Comisión de la Verdad/Rey Naranjo Editores, 2020), pp. 9–23 (p. 15).

resilience is changing history.[6] In other words, these films allow us to see the resilient practices of peasant and indigenous communities or vulnerable social groups and their capacities and abilities to face the effects of anthropogenic processes and reconstruct themselves to create conditions that allow sustaining the basis of their existence.

The Anthropocene and Latin America

The Anthropocene characterises a new epoch in which human intervention in the transformations of the biophysical world has become a new geological force. Its approach is linked to the anthropocentric view that defends that people are subjects of value, and plants, animals, and, in general, the non-human world that forms the ecosystem are an object and a commodity for the human species.

According to Svampa, 'we are witnessing imminent major anthropogenic and sociogenic changes on a planetary scale that have the potential to endanger life on the planet (Anthropocene)'.[7] For Paul Crutzen, the climate crisis caused by human activity began with the Industrial Revolution: the invention of the steam engine and the beginning of the exploitation of fossil fuels such as coal and oil. This first phase was followed by a second one called 'the great acceleration', which began after 1945 and is illustrated by many indicators of human activity that resulted, among others, in the atmospheric concentration of carbon and methane and a drastic loss of biodiversity.[8]

Since the 1980–90s, environmental legal frameworks have appeared in Latin America. They attempt to distance themselves from the postulates of classical anthropocentrism that separate nature and culture and claim the protection and conservation of nature.[9] Likewise, in the twenty-first century, the biocentric position is gaining strength—far from being the dominant

6 Pablo Fendrik's *The Ardor* is probably the most vivid example: the film is set in the present, but its setting makes viewers believe that the story takes place in the late nineteenth century.

7 Maristella Svampa, *Neo-extractivism in Latin America. Socio-environmental Conflicts, the Territorial Turn, and New Political Narratives* (Cambridge: Cambridge University Press, 2019), p. 12, https://www.memoria.fahce.unlp.edu.ar/libros/pm.5180/pm.5180.pdf (accessed 3 March 2024).

8 Crutzen quoted in Maristella Svampa, *Antropoceno: Lecturas globales desde el Sur* (Córdoba: Universidad Nacional de Córdoba, 2019), p. 11, https://www.memoria.fahce.unlp.edu.ar/libros/pm.5176/pm.5176.pdf (accessed 3 March 2024). Unless stated otherwise, all translations are by the authors.

9 Eduardo Gudynas, *Derechos de la naturaleza: Ética biocéntrica y políticas ambientales* (Lima: Programa Democracia y Transformación Global, 2014), p. 62.

one—which goes beyond the 'conservationist' legacy by declaring the right of people to a healthy environment, considering that nature has rights, and recognising that 'life on Earth has values in itself (synonyms: intrinsic value, inherent value)', and that these values are 'independent of the usefulness of the non-human world for human purposes'.[10]

Without ignoring that the effects of climate change are global, there are social, spatial, and environmental inequalities in terms of their impacts and the actions to face them. The debate on the Anthropocene in Latin America must take into account environmental injustice produced by processes of extraction of natural goods and services and their 'inequitable distribution … in a globalized world in which the different nations, peoples and communities world inhabit the planet under unequal ecological, economic and political conditions and among societies with differentiated values and senses of life'.[11] Thus, the Anthropocene appears more complex from a Latin American than a Eurocentric perspective.

The Anthropocene and Resilience in Film History

The critical examination of anthropocentric positions, ecological crises, the intervention and influence of human action on nature, and the relationship between the human and the non-human has recently been addressed by film and media studies.[12] However, the relationship between cinema and nature is as old as cinema itself.

The first film of the Lumière brothers, *Repas de bébé* (*A Baby's Meal*, FR, 1895), shows the feeding of a baby. Nevertheless, it did not fascinate the viewers due to the feeding but rather because of the leaves of a tree in the background. While natural catastrophes such as floods, deluges, or volcanic eruptions turned into cinematographic spectacles, avant-garde films such as *Rain* by Joris Ivens (NL, 1929) or *Arabesque* (FR, 1929) by female filmmaker Germaine Dulac depicted meteorological phenomena. In 1936, Pare

10 These positions were already held by Indigenous peoples who considered that territories are living beings and that they fulfil a function independent from human utilities (Naess and Sessions 1985, quoted in Gudynas, *Derechos de la naturaleza*, p. 53). Translations are our own.

11 Enrique Left, 'Racionalidad y justicia ambiental: La elusiva injusticia de la vida', *Historia Ambiental Latinoamericana y Caribeña (HALAC)*, 11 (2021), 19–38 (p. 23), https://doi.org/10.32991/2237-2717.2021v11i3.p19-38 (accessed 3 March 2024).

12 Jennifer Peterson and Graig Uhlin, 'In Focus: Film and Media Studies in the Anthropocene', *JCMS: Journal of Cinema and Media Studies*, 58–2 (2019), 142–6, doi:10.1353/cj.2019.0006 (accessed 8 January 2024).

Lorentz launched the famous informative film on the 'New Deal', *The Plow that Broke the Plains*, in which the environmental disaster known as the 'Dust Bowl' was heroically reversed by government planners. Film studies from cinema reformers such as Hermann Häfker's *Kino und Erdkunde* (*Cinema and Geography*) (1914) and Béla Balázs' *Der Film: Werden und Wesen einer neuen Kunst* (*The Film: The Emergence and Essence of a New Art*) (1949/1972) to Siegfried Kracauer's *Theory of Cinema* (1960/1989), all repeatedly placed the observation of nature at the centre of their considerations.

From a growing interest in ecocinema at the beginning of the new millennium, seminars on the Anthropocene in film and television studies have become commonplace.[13] Recently, Jennifer Fay pointed out the peculiar relation between the Anthropocene and feature films: 'Filmmaking occasions the creation of artificial worlds, unnatural and inclement weather, and deadly environments produced as much for the sake of entertainment as for scientific study and military strategy'.[14] She emphasises that films cannot give a 'totalizing explanation of climate change', but 'cinema helps us to see and experience the Anthropocene as an aesthetic practice' (Fay, *Inhospitable World*, p. 4).

In contrast to expensive settings on a studio's backdrop or digitally created landscapes that produce apocalyptic visions of climate change, such as *The Day After Tomorrow* (Roland Emmerich, USA, 2004), filmmaking in Latin America is different due to historical conditions in terms of production, distribution, and exhibition. It was only with the rise of a New Latin American cinema in the 1960s that documentaries such as *La hora de los hornos* (*The Hours of the Furnaces*, Fernando Solanas and Octavio Getino, ARG 1968),

13 A first wave of publications was published at the turn of the millennial. See Jhan Hochman, *Green Cultural Studies: Nature in Film, Novel and Theory* (Moscow: University of Idaho Press, 1998); David Ingram, *Green Screen: Environmentalism and Hollywood Cinema* (Exeter: University of Exeter Press, 2000). More recent publications are Paula Willoquet-Maricondi, ed., *Framing the World: Explorations in Ecocriticism and Film* (Charlottesville: University of Virginia Press, 2010); Nadia Bozak, *The Cinematic Footprint: Lights, Camera, Natural Resources* (New Brunswick: Rutgers University Press, 2011); Pietari Kääpä and Tommy Gustafsson, *Transnational Ecocinema: Film Culture in an Era of Ecological Transformation* (Chicago: Intellect, 2013); Stephen Rust, Salma Monani, and Sean Cubitt, eds., *Ecocinema Theory and Practice* (New York: Routledge, 2013); Ilka Kressner, Ana María Mutis, and Elizabeth Pettinaroli, eds., *Ecofictions, Ecorealities, and Slow Violence in Latin America and the Latinx World* (New York: Routledge, 2020); Carolyn Fornoff and Gisela Heffes, eds., *Pushing Past the Human in Latin American Cinema* (New York: State University of New York Press, 2021).

14 Jennifer Fay, *Inhospitable World: Cinema in the Time of the Anthropocene* (New York: Oxford University Press, 2018), p. 4.

Vidas secas (*Barren Lives*, Nelson Pereira dos Santos, BR, 1963), or *Chircales* (*The Brickmakers*, Marta Rodríguez, COL, 1966/1971) started to analyse the growing social-political conflicts on the continent, whereas filmic-political manifestos called for an independent self-conscious Latin American cinema that is not dominated by and dependent on hegemonic film industries.[15]

Marta Rodríguez' *Chircales* is an anthropological case study that shows the dehumanising life and working conditions of a brickmaking family—a couple and their eleven children—in Bogotá, Colombia. The film comments on the state of people's resilience in Latin America at that time, making it quite clear that, besides other aspects, labour exploitation creates a social inequality in the country that can easily translate into today's activities of global enterprises and extractivism. In contrast to a substantial amount of literature on the Anthropocene in film, a quick survey on the term resilience in them shows that the term is rarely used when referring to nature's resilience in the Anthropocene.[16]

However, the representation of the Anthropocene's effects and consequences for the people in Latin America is not absent and has been dealt with in various documentaries and experimental films. For example, *La sangre de Bolivia: De los Andes a la Amazonía* (*Be Water—From Andes to Amazonia*, Julia Blagny, BOL/FR, 2021) and *La hija de la laguna* (*Daughter of the Lake*, Ernestro Cabell Damián, PER, 2015) follow an activist agenda in which numbers, graphics, and testimonies of indigenous and non-indigenous communities address the drastic consequences of contamination, water dispossession, mining, and extractivism. *Daughter of the Lake* follows the fight of the Peruvian activist Nélida Ayay Chilón and her community against a global mining company to document how people organise their lives, given the continuous threat through the company and the police. These films can be considered Anthropocene cinema as they deal with the challenges of living under unexpected environmental conditions.

The apparent dominance of documentaries and experimental films raises the question of whether people's resilience in the Anthropocene era plays any role at all in Latin American feature filmmaking. Following David Ingram, one can ask 'whether one film style, genre or taste culture is more effective

15 See Glauber Rocha, 'Eztetyka da Fome 1965', *Hambre*, 15 September 2013, https://hambrecine.com/wp-content/uploads/2013/09/eztetyka-da-fome.pdf (accessed 8 January 2024); Fernando Solanas and Octavio Getino, 'Hacia un tercer cine. Apuntes y experiencias para el desarrollo de un cine de liberación en el Tercer Mundo', *Cine Club*, 1 (1970), 27–40.

16 Far from having made an in-depth analysis of the existing literature, the following publications were consulted: Stephen Rust et al., *Ecocinema Theory and Practice*; Daniel White, *Film in the Anthropocene*; Jennifer Fay et al., *Pushing Past the Human in Latin American Cinema*.

than another in promoting ecological understanding'.[17] Ingram argues that the relation between film and ecological awareness is not simply given. There is no empirical proof that, for example, art cinema offers the audience a better understanding of ecological problems than popular cinema. Audiences not trained to watch art cinema will not appreciate its characteristic aesthetics. Ingram criticises ecocinema for being too prescriptive and excluding aesthetics not approved by its advocates.

The directors of the films—Kleber Mendonça Filho and Juliano Dornelles from Brazil (*Bacurau*), Pablo Fendrik from Argentina (*The Ardor*), and Chilean-Italian director Marco Bechis (*Birdwatchers*)—are best known for their international festival successes in the art-house segment. However, all three films follow popular patterns from the Western genre that combine art and popular cinema with ecological topics, featuring issues such as water scarcity, the destructive power of global players, extractivism, or deterritorialisation. In the specific context of the Latin American Western, these films allow us to see the resilient practices of indigenous or peasant communities and their capacities to resist the effects of anthropogenic processes.

Genre and Western

The Western is one of the oldest genres in the history of cinema and has almost become extinct at various points in its history. Genre is one of the most problematic areas of film theory, which only seems conclusive at first glance. As Rick Altman notes, 'not all genre films relate to their genre in the same way or to the same extent'.[18] Traditionally, the Western is considered a genuinely US genre, and questions about its origin, evolution, and adaptation to other national cinematographies are underresearched. A closer look shows that it is by no means a clear-cut Hollywood genre, as traditional approaches suggest, but much more heterogeneous.

Regarding its existence in other cinematographies, Edward Buscombe concludes that 'the European Western, and by extension the Latin American and other geographically displaced Westerns, are capable of meanings which are not confined by American history, and in particular by its frontier

17 David Ingram, 'The Aesthetics and Ethics of Eco-film riticism', in *Ecocinema Theory and Practices*, ed. Stephen Rust et al. (New York and London: Routledge, 2013), pp. 43–61 (p. 43).

18 Rick Altman, 'A Semantic/Syntactic Approach to Film Genre', *Cinema Journal* 23 (1984), 6–18 (p. 12), doi:10.2307/1225093 (accessed 8 January 2024).

myth'.[19] In this vein, Dagmar Brunow argues that the Western has always been a global phenomenon that is possibly more 'hybrid, queer and transnational' than previously assumed and points out the influence of the Mexican vaquero on the iconography of the cowboy.[20] The anthology *Crossing Frontiers: Intercultural Perspectives on the Western* demonstrates that the Western is used in very different nationally specific contexts.[21] It shows that this genre is not about the history of the United States; instead, it has to be understood as a key to different national mythologies. Consequently, the Western migrated to other national cinematographies, including those of Latin America, even though this issue has received little attention to date.[22] As it will be argued, *Bacurau*, *The Ardor*, or *Birdwatchers* refer to the Western genre but also base their stories on national tales or mythologies, such as the cordel literature of Northeast Brazil, the genocide of indigenous groups, and local rituals.

In his seminal article 'A Semantic/Syntactic Approach to Film Genre', Rick Altman presents an approach seeking to understand the complexity and heterogeneity of film genres. His approach unites traditional genre analysis by combining semantic and syntactic genre analyses. While semantic analyses in genre theory concentrate on elements such as characters (cowboy, sheriff), clothing (hat, boots, waistcoat), objects (weapons, carriage), or situations (shootout, attacks on trains and stagecoaches by Indians), syntactic analyses focus on the frontier myth or binary oppositions, such as wilderness versus civilisation, law and order against outlaws, or good versus evil. In contrast to a semantic approach that is applicable to a range of films but has a weak explanatory potential, a syntactic analysis approach 'has a strong explanatory potential ..., but has a field of application that is often fairly limited in its coverage'.[23] Altman, therefore, argues in favour of thinking semantics and

19 Edward Buscombe, 'Is the Western about American History?', in *Crossing Frontiers: Intercultural Perspectives on the Western*, ed. Thomas Klein, Ivo Ritzer, and Peter W. Schulze (Marburg: Schüren, 2012), pp. 13–24 (p. 23).

20 Dagmar Brunow, 'Western', in *Filmwissenschaftliche Genreanalyse: Eine Einführung*, ed. Markus Kuhn et al. (Berlin/Boston: De Gruyter, 2013), pp. 39–61 (p. 39).

21 Thomas Klein et al., eds., *Crossing Frontiers: Intercultural Perspectives on the Western* (Marburg: Schüren, 2012).

22 Peter W. Schulze, 'Beyond Cowboys and Cangaceiros. Transculturations of the Western in Brazilian Cinema', in *Crossing Frontiers. Intercultural Perspectives on the Western*, ed. Thomas Klein et al. (Marburg: Schüren, 2012), pp. 163–93; see also Laura Lattanzi, 'El western en el cine argentino contemporáneo y los relatos fundacionales. Sobre el desierto negro y aballay el hombre sin miedo', *En la otra isla. Revista de Audiovisual Latinoamericano*, 3 (2020), 21–32.

23 Raphaëlle Moine, *Cinema Genre* (Malden, MA: Blackwell, 2008), p. 56.

syntax together, where 'semantic givens are the content of the film, and the syntactic situation the narrative structure in which the content inserts itself' (Moine, *Cinema Genre*, p. 56). A relevant aspect for the further analysis of Westerns, including Latin American Western, is that films can relate very differently to a given genre, as 'some actively contribute to the development of a syntax for the genre, others pick up in a less systematic way the traditional elements associated with a genre' (Moine, *Cinema Genre*, p. 57).

These 'different levels of genericity' (Moine, *Cinema Genre*, p. 57) allow us to expand Western film narratives and include, for example, issues of resilience and the Anthropocene into the genre. The films' stories are based on people's experience and endurance in difficult environmental living conditions: the struggle of a small community against a corrupt politician in *Bacurau*, a farmer against foreign mercenaries and an unknown global enterprise in *The Ardor*, and an indigenous group against a wealthy landowner and the state in *Birdwatchers*. They have learnt to be resilient, and the films' narratives start at a moment when these living conditions are threatened from the outside and require a reaction from the protagonists.

The conflict between the communities and the enemy marks a turning point in the narratives and is closely related to the experience and use of violence. Violence is an important structuring characteristic of the Western genre as it establishes or re-establishes the social order. In these films, the protagonists are confronted with violence and use violence to defend themselves. Violence becomes the protagonists' stories' springboards from which they start their new lives. Violence is used in *Bacurau* to recover the local water supply or to reclaim private or ancestral property, as in *The Ardor* and *Birdwatchers*. By using semantic elements of the Western, the films expand the syntactic range of the genre. *Bacurau*, *The Ardor*, and *Birdwatchers* are Latin American Westerns, given that they can be identified as Western films. These Western elements are placed differently concerning time, location, and narrative, as shown below.

Resilience in the Anthropocene Western: *Bacurau*, *The Ardor*, and *Birdwatchers*

Bacurau is Kleber Mendonça Filho's third feature film, which he codirected with his long-time collaborator Juliano Dornelles. In contrast to Mendonça Filho's previous films *O Som ao Redor* (*Neighbouring Sounds*) (2012) and *Aquarius* (2016), both of which deal with issues of social inequality/land robbery and real estate speculation, *Bacurau* is more specific but also more polemic in its aim to criticise the consequences of corruption in the country.

Bacurau makes references to Brazilian film history and folklore as well as to popular Hollywood cinema. The film was shot in the Sertão do Seridó, on the border between Rio Grande do Norte and Paraíba, in the region of Pernambuco. The *sertão*, which comprises an area within the Northeast Region of Brazil, is, together with urban favelas, the scenario that par excellence represents poverty and the unequal territorial distribution of resources.

The film tells the story of the people of Bacurau, who face water shortage due to a dam construction promoted by a corrupt mayor who plans his re-election. As if that was not enough, the major, who knows that the community neither believes nor respects him, hires unscrupulous foreigners to massacre the Bacurau community. Simultaneously, its inhabitants discover that the village has vanished from the map and been cut off from electronic communication so that its inhabitants cannot communicate with the outside world and warn about the threat. With the help of local bandit Lunga, who is wanted by the authorities for the murder of dam guards responsible for limiting the water supply, the community can defend itself and kill the mercenaries.

This representation of precariousness was portrayed by the Cinema Novo movement, which emerged in the 1960s, inspired by Italian post-war realism. Its iconic figure and spokesman, Glauber Rocha, described it as a movement operating with 'a camera in the hand and an idea in the head' that stood up against the parameters of Hollywood escapism. During the military dictatorship (1964–85), Cinema Novo sought to express the social problems of the peasants of the Brazilian northeast and the whole of America. In the words of Bruno Guaraná:

> [T]he sertão condemns its characters to live always on the verge of a crisis brought about by seasonal droughts. Survival becomes part of the everyday struggle, and death, a slow, inescapable process. In other words, the sertão has mostly appeared as an infertile, stifling land, with an aesthetic tuned to the struggles of characters in search of survival and escape.[24]

Although *Bacurau* has been compared to a science fiction film because its story takes place in the future and uses futuristic elements, it corresponds in many ways to a Western. On the semantic level, *Bacurau* concentrates on elements and situations such as cowboys, hats, desolate and dusty locations, weapons, shootouts, and armed attacks against a local community. On the syntactic level, the film evolves towards the struggle between the community and powerful and unscrupulous individuals who limit water consumption as a vital commodity. It is filmed in a dusty and hostile town, featuring mountains in the background. This village seems to be located 'nowhere'. It is an exotic

24 Bruno Guaraná, '"A Few Years from Now" in Western Pernambuco: *Bacurau*'s Vision of the Future', *Film Quarterly* 74 (2020), pp. 77–80 (p. 77), doi:https://doi.org/10.1525/fq.2020.74.2.77 (accessed 4 March 2024).

landscape, enveloped by a reality that is more present-day than dystopian, in which the inhabitants—the *sertanejos*—guard the last dispensations of water.

Facing above circumstances, this town, which seems to have been intentionally wiped off the map, defends itself. The inhabitants of Bacurau show their resilience through their awareness of their collective power and the reconstruction of the social fabric that was disrupted first by the theft of water and then by the presence of mercenaries. Thus, during a visit by the mayor to the village, all the inhabitants agree to vacate the streets to make the mayor's words fall on deaf ears. By ignoring the mayor's presence, they symbolically complain to him about the non-fulfilment of his electoral promises, which had to do with the fair distribution of essential resources such as water. The people not only mistrust the mayor; they go beyond that by organising community practices of self-management and care for water resources.

Such is the need to unite to face difficult situations that the inhabitants of Bacurau who break away from the community, as in other Western films, 'meet a violent and sudden end'.[25] Thus, different characters are killed when they break away from their group and try to flee or when they want to separate themselves from the community to which they belong. As Marcelo Ikeda points out, '*Bacurau* concerns several characters who complement each other and contribute different skills in their efforts towards a common goal: the very idea of community, and its salvation'.[26] This strength to resist surprises their assailants who have the racist vision that the inhabitants of the northeast are backward, defenceless, and ignorant, which correlates geography with social and racial prejudices.

As an element that accompanies resilience, the film shows the violent resistance of the protagonists to situations that threaten their lives. To defend themselves, the inhabitants of these arid and marginalised areas of Brazil—young and old, men and women—resort to war planning and the use of weapons. In the film, one can see how violent actions committed by one of the village leaders are broadcast on a screen hung on the back of a vehicle and applauded as heroic actions, even in the eyes of younger villagers.

Westerns deal with violence and expose the conditions in which it can become legitimate. In *Bacurau*, the showing of violence and its use (for example, when the *sertanejos* display in the museum antiquated firearms with which their ancestors defended themselves) take place in a territory where the protagonists use machetes and old arms, weapons that help people

25 Alejandro Núñez-Alberca, 'El territorio como forma de vida: la representación del sertão en la película Bacurau (2019) de Kleber Mendonça Filho y Juliano Dornelles', paper presented at V Congreso Internacional de Narrativas Audiovisuales, Trujillo, Peru, June 2023.

26 Marcelo Ikeda, 'The Ambiguities of *Bacurau*', *Film Quarterly* 74 (2020), 81–3, p. 82, doi:10.1525/fq.2020.74.2.81 (accessed 8 March 2024).

protect themselves from foreigners and corrupt politicians who arrive to extract resources from the region.

Different from *Bacurau*, which makes reference to Brazilian folklore with the representation of Lunga as a modern *Cangaceiro*, *The Ardor* and *Birdwatchers* base their stories on a local myth and an indigenous tradition. *The Ardor* and *Birdwatchers* deal with expulsion, dispossession, and deterritorialisation in Argentina.

The story of the Argentinian-Brazilian coproduction *The Ardor* takes place at the banks of the Paraná River, the second largest river in Latin America after the Amazon and one that passes through Brazil, Paraguay, and Argentina. The film does not clarify exactly where the story happens; however, the mixture of Spanish and some Brazilian-Portuguese words in dialogues suggests that the region and its people are less characterised by nationality than by a shared cultural heritage.

The film presents the story of shaman Kaí (Gael García Bernal), who comes to help and protect tobacco farmer João, his daughter Vania (Alice Braga), and his assistant Jara, who are all threatened by a group of mercenaries. João tells Kaí that every night another part of the jungle is set on fire, and neighbouring farmers are forced to leave their land and be killed. While the film does not specify under whose order the mercenaries stand, João indicates that their land is needed for a monoculture of pine and soya and the construction of a processing plant. After João gets killed and Vania kidnapped by the mercenaries, Kaí follows them, liberates Vania, and in a Western-like showdown, he kills the invaders so that Vania and Jara can continue their life and work on the farm.

In this film, Pablo Fendrik uses a range of characteristic elements of the Western genre to tell the film's story: rifles and handguns, knives, Western-like clothing and housing, and a typical soundscape of whistling wind during the shootout at the end of the film. On the syntactic level, the film evolves into a struggle between good and evil, the protection of nature versus its destruction. Fendrik's film takes a stand for the farmers who make a living from the modest farming of their land.

The opening sequence of *The Ardor* indicates that living in the region requires resilience. It starts with an intertitle that explains that the people living by the Paraná River have for centuries practised a ritual invoking Beings (*Seres*) for help in case of an invasion of their lands: 'Until today, people resort to this ritual when a threat is near.' What follows is an aerial shot over the Paraná River and the sheer limitless green of the Paraná tropical forest. It illustrates the isolation of the people living in the area and the region's botanical and potential economic and commercial value.

It is resilience that characterises João and his small family's daily life, who have survived against all odds over the years. João arrived with his father in the 1970s and purchased land after ten years of hard work. In the film, conversations are limited to the bare essentials, and they emphasise that labour outdoes social communication. Since we learn nothing about João's wife, Vania's mother, one can assume that João had to fulfil a double social role in the past: farming the land and raising his daughter.

The intertitle at the beginning of the film, in addition to the setting of João's house, emphasises even more the aspect of people's resilience in the region. *The Ardor* is set in the present, but its setting reminds us of the late nineteenth century and shows that people have adapted to difficult living conditions to live and work on their own property. João, his daughter, and Jara live in a timber house that does not appear to be very solid. Kitchenware and clothing do not correspond to modern standards. The daily food is yucca and bread, symbolising their modest way of living. It is just some of the mercenaries' clothes, a coloured football shirt and a baseball cap, that reminds viewers in the first few minutes of the film that the story is taking place in the present and that it deals with the current problem of land robbery for extractivist purposes in South America.

The term resilience is not only appropriate to characterise João and his small family; it can also be applied to his and Jara's decision to send for Kaí: they need Kaí's support to remain resilient and continue with the farm. Kaí is characterised as a tight-lipped Paraná *Pale Rider* who lives on his own in the jungle. As a victim of land robbery, all the members of his family were killed, and he has learnt to be resilient on his own. He knows how to survive in the jungle and use the jungle's resources, flora, and fauna.

In his fight against the mercenaries, Kaí is supported by a jaguar, 'tigre' in the people's word. The jaguar has been a characteristic animal of the Paraná River but today is threatened with extinction. The third party in the group to defend the land is João's assistant, Jara. He was a former mercenary who had to spy on João. He fell in love with Vania, quit his job, and turned against his employer to save João's farm and the region from destruction.

Kaí, the jaguar, and Jara represent different sides of the same environmental interest but also exemplify resilience that is at stake. Kaí stands for the protection and continuity of the peasants' life in the region, while the jaguar symbolises the extinction of flora and fauna at stake. Finally, Jara can be compared to a converted environmental activist who has understood that the destruction of the Paraná jungle does not bring any good and must, therefore, be preserved and protected. All three have learnt to adapt to their living conditions. They are resilient, but their resilience can also come to an end if they do not react in time and defend themselves.

In contrast to *The Ardor*, which thematises a peasant's fight against the destruction of his basis of existence, Marco Bechis' *Birdwatchers* deals with those who have lived for centuries in a country that is no longer theirs. The film was shot six years before *The Ardor*, but, in a way, it tells what happens when mercenary groups are successful in their work, and the original population of a territory is expelled.

Birdwatchers is based on real events and focuses on the decades of suffering of this indigenous population and how they have been discriminated against and maltreated by Brazilian society.[27] Like *The Ardor*, *Birdwatchers* starts with an aerial shot that, together with the following images, reminds the viewers that Brazil was populated before its conquest. The film shows an encounter between a group of tourists in a canoe, *Birdwatchers*, and a group of Guaraní-Kaiowá people at the riverbank. When the indigenous group attacks the boat with their bows and arrows, the tourist group escapes safely. The exposition plays with the viewer's expectation of an authentic encounter with a Latin American indigenous tribe. However, it is a fake 'authentic' encounter that rather demonstrates the discrimination against and omnipresent degradation of indigenous groups, which have become simple ethnic spectacles for a paying audience. After the attack, the camera stays with the Guaraní-Kaiowá, who return to a pick-up car where they change clothes and receive a fee for their tourist show.

Back in the reservation, the indigenous community decides to leave this place and settle next to a private territory where their ancestors once inhabited. However, the territory is no longer the same. What once was a dense forest has turned into eroded land for slash-and-burn agriculture, cattle breeding, and sugar beet owned by another settler, white wealthy landowner Moreira. For him, indigenous culture is merely décor, shown by his swimming pool, which is tiled with indigenous motifs.

In an interview, Marco Bechis explained that he chose a camera aesthetic close to the Western genre.[28] Besides static shots, the film also contains a range of Western elements: Indigenous people armed with bows and arrows, guards on horses with guns, and a conflict between a community and a wealthy landowner. However, Bechis reverses the syntax of a classic settler story. Moreira—himself a settler—considers the Guaraní-Kaiowá to be invaders and presents himself as the legitimate owner of the country: 'He represents the general notion that the settler culture is the normative and naturalised localised culture

27 Five years after its release, the film again received international attention when Ambrósio Vilhalva (Nádio), a Guaraní activist in real life, was stabbed to death in 2013. Vilhava's death was just one among many others; the Guaraní people suffer from one of the highest murder rates worldwide. 'Guarani-Mordrate: eine der höchsten weltweit', *Survival International*, 22 November 2023, https://www.survivalinternational.de/nachrichten/9757 (accessed 23 January 2024).

28 Cristina Nord, 'Edle Wilde gibt es nur für Touristen', *taz*, 15 July 2009, https://taz.de/Film-mit-brasilianischen-Indianern/!5159853/ (accessed 23 January 2024).

and the indigenous culture is the displaced and denaturalized culture in territories deemed useful land, here for agricultural purposes.'[29]

With this reversion, the film approaches the question of resilience from the perspective of the Guaraní-Kaiowá indigenous people, exemplified by the life of two youngsters, Ireneu and Osvaldo. The film's narrative starts at a moment when the community's resilience is put to the test. The reservation no longer provides a real home for the Guaraní. Frustration is drowned in alcohol, while, aside from performing the 'savage indigenous' act for tourists, the community does not have a regular income. They can resist the first time they receive the offer of working on a farm to gain some money; however, when they are asked the second time, they give in. The exploitation of cheap indigenous labour is also illustrated by the Moreira family's Guaraní housemaid, who must do absurd and humiliating work such as simply flipping the cushions of Moreira's wife's sun lounger in front of her. The most shocking, humiliating, and racist moment in the film relates in a drastic way to the dehumanisation of the Guaraní-Kaiowá. Moreira applies to them the same measures he applies to vermin to keep them off his land: he sprays the camp with poisonous pesticides.

The film is as much about the resilience of the Guaraní-Kaiowá as it is about their limits and the price for being resilient in a society of human and environmental injustice. When Ireneu and Osvaldo go hunting at the beginning of the film, they discover two girls who have hanged themselves in the forest. The girls' suicide refers to the high suicide rate among young Guaraní, which, according to the NGO Survival International, is nineteen times higher than the Brazilian average. Many young Guaraní do not see any sense in continuing a life that is full of deprivation and suffering.[30] For Ireneu and Osvaldo, suicide is not an alternative for the time being, but they are torn between living according to their tradition and breaking out of it. Ireneu tries to find a girlfriend in his community but gets rejected by the girl. When he buys new tennis shoes with the money he earned from a job at a farm, Ireneu is scolded by his father Nádio, the community's leader, because he does not contribute the money to the community. Full of frustration, Ireneu commits suicide and hangs himself.

29 Kerstin Knopf, 'Land Through the Camera: Post/Colonial Space and Indigenous Struggles in *Birdwatchers* (Terra Vermelha)', in *Biopolitics, Geopolitics, Life: Settler States and Indigenous Presence*, ed. René Dietrich and Kerstin Knopf (Durham, NC and London: Duke University Press, 2023), pp. 246–71 (p. 262).

30 'Der Selbstmord der Guarani—Wie die Trennung zwischen Mensch und Natur die Psyche beeinflussen kann', *Survival International*, https://www.survivalinternational.de/artikel/3586-guarani-selbstmorde (accessed 23 January 2024).

Not frustration but anger characterises Osvaldo's development in the film. He is trained to become the group's next shaman, a role that does not allow him to have contact with women. He practises his shaman exercises at a nearby river, where he meets Maria, Moreira's daughter. Both are attracted to each other, and they have sex one day. The relationship comes to an end when Moreira orders the killing of Nádio, and Osvaldo turns into a warrior and threatens Maria and her family. In desperation, Osvaldo decides to kill himself, but in the very last moment, he overcomes the evil spirit Anguè, who drives young Guaraní-Kaiowá to commit suicide.

Finally, the film's ending shows the community's reaction to the continuous humiliation that has caused suicides in their community. Ireneu's suicide motivates the community to take action. They become warriors and set up their camp on the territory that once belonged to their ancestors. This *retomada* (reclaim) is equivalent to restoring a new social order. The price the community pays for the liberating act is high: Nádio is murdered by contracted killers, and the victory is short lived. Moreira's support from a federal prosecutor, who wants the judiciary to be respected, makes it clear that the real decision of who owns the land will be made in court in Brasília. Unlike in the two previous films, the enemy is not fully defeated here. The community's future depends on the state's guarantees of non-repetition of violence against the Guaraní people and access to resources that previously belonged to them. In this sense, it is a bittersweet ending. The community's resilience has entered a new phase, but it can reach its limits at any moment.

Conclusion

Bacurau, *The Ardor*, and *Birdwatchers* are Latin American films that follow the patterns of the Western genre. Although their stories are based on different national contexts, they share a common social concern for people affected by anthropogenic crises. The starting point in all three films is people's resilience to anthropogenic processes such as water scarcity, land robbery, and deterritorialisation. In these films, their resilience is tested, and in the confines of the Western genre, their reaction is resistance and the use of violence.

Genre films are fictional products that tell fictional stories. It would be short-sighted to understand that the films favour using violence as a solution to real social problems and environmental injustices. Genre films, as Judith Hess Wright notes, 'resolve conflicts in a simplistic and reactionary way'.[31]

31 Judith Hess Wright, 'Genre Films and the Status Quo', in *Film Genre Reader II*, ed. Barry Keith Grant (Austin: University of Texas Press, 1995), pp. 42–50 (p. 42).

In contrast to Hess Wright's observation that one of the characteristics of genre films that make the films' resolutions plausible is that they never deal with current political issues (Hess Wright, 'Genre Films', p. 43), *Bacurau*, *The Ardor*, and *Birdwatchers* show that this characteristic does not necessarily apply to Latin American Westerns and that genre films have since evolved from a traditional understanding.

Resilience and the Anthropocene may be dry subjects for some film enthusiasts, who are unfamiliar with academic debates, and the topics are not particularly those that one would expect from popular cinema. It is worth thinking about the use of feature films in communicating the Anthropocene to a wider public. In addition to documentary or experimental filmmaking and their activist and artistic agenda, the three films show that genre films can also engage crucially, but in their own ways, with current debates that increasingly start to affect people in Latin America.

Bibliography

Altman, Rick, 'A Semantic/Syntactic Approach to Film Genre', *Cinema Journal*, 23–3 (1984), 6–18, doi:10.2307/1225093 (accessed 8 January 2024).

Bozak, Nadia, *The Cinematic Footprint: Lights, Camera, Natural Resources* (New Brunswick: Rutgers University Press, 2011).

Brunow, Dagmar, 'Western', in *Filmwissenschaftliche Genreanalyse: Eine Einführung*, edited by Markus Kuhn, Irina Scheidgen, and Nicola Valeska Weber (Boston: De Gruyter, 2013), pp. 39–61.

Buscombe, Edward, 'Is the Western about American History?', in *Crossing Frontiers: Intercultural Perspectives on the Western*, edited by Thomas Klein, Ivo Ritzer, and Peter W. Schulze (Marburg: Schüren, 2012), pp. 13–24.

Carson, Rachel, *Silent Spring* (Boston: Houghton Mifflin, 1962)

Crutzen, Paul J., and Eugene F. Stoerner, 'The "Anthropocene"', *Global Change Newsletter*, 41 (2000), 17–18.

'Der Selbstmord der Guarani—Wie die Trennung zwischen Mensch und Natur die Psyche beeinflussen kann', *Survival International*, https://survivalinternational.de/artikel/3586-guarani-selbstmorde (accessed 23 January 2024).

Fay, Jennifer, *Inhospitable World: Cinema in the Time of the Anthropocene* (New York: Oxford University Press, 2018).

Fornoff, Carolyn, and Gisela Heffs, eds., *Pushing Past the Human in Latin American Cinema* (New York: State University of New York Press, 2021).

Guaraná, Bruno, '"A Few Years from Now" in Western Pernambuco: *Bacurau*'s Vision of the Future', *Film Quarterly* 74 (2020), pp. 77–80, https://doi.org/10.1525/fq.2020.74.2.77 (accessed 4 March 2024).

'Guarani-Mordrate: eine der höchsten weltweit', *Survival International*, 22 November 2023, https://www.survivalinternational.de/nachrichten/9757 (accessed 23 January 2024).

Gudynas, Eduardo, *Derechos de la naturaleza: Ética biocéntrica y políticas ambientales* (Lima: Programa Democracia y Transformación Global, 2014).

Hess Wright, Judith, 'Genre Films and the Status Quo', in *Film Genre Reader II*, edited by Barry Keith Grant (Austin: University of Texas Press, 1995), pp. 42–50.

Hochman, Jhan, *Green Cultural Studies: Nature in Film, Novel and Theory* (Moscow: University of Idaho Press, 1998).

Ikeda Marcelo, 'The Ambiguities of *Bacurau*', *Film Quarterly*, 74 (2020), 81–3, doi:10.1525/fq.2020.74.2.81 (accessed 8 March 2024).

Ingram, David, *Green Screen: Environmentalism and Hollywood Cinema* (Exeter: University of Exeter Press, 2000).

Ingram, David, 'The Aesthetics and Ethics of Eco-film Criticism', in *Ecocinema: Theory and Practices*, edited by Stephen Rust, Salma Monani, and Sean Cubitt (New York and London: Routledge, 2013), pp. 43–61.

Kääpä, Pietari, and Tommy Gustafsson, *Transnational Ecocinema: Film Culture in an Era of Ecological Transformation* (Chicago: Intellect, 2013).

Klein, Thomas, Ivo Ritzer, and Peter W. Schulze, eds., *Crossing Frontiers: Intercultural Perspectives on the Western* (Marburg: Schüren, 2012).

Knopf, Kerstin, 'Land through the Camera: Post/Colonial Space and Indigenous Struggles in Birdwatchers (Terra Vermelha),' in *Biopolitics, Geopolitics, Life: Settler States and Indigenous Presences*, edited by René Dietrich and Kerstin Knopf (Durham, NC and London: Duke University Press, 2023), pp. 246–71.

Lattanzi, Laura, 'El western en el cine argentino contemporaneo y los relatos fundacionales', *En la otra isla. Revista de Audiovisual Latinoamericano*, 3 (2020), pp. 21–32.

Left, Enrique, 'Racionalidad y justicia ambiental: La elusiva injusticia de la vida', Historia Ambiental Latinoamericana y Caribeña (HALAC), 11 (2021), 19–38, doi:10.32991/2237-2717.2021v11i3, pp. 19–38 (accessed 3 March 2024).

Mesa, Gilmer, '¿Quién y qué no es infierno?', in *Resiliencia*, edited by La Comisión de la Verdad (Bogotá: Comisión de la Verdad/Rey Naranjo Editores, 2020), pp. 26–38.

Moine, Raphaëlle, *Cinema Genre*, translated by Alistair Fox and Hilary Radner (Malden: Blackwell 2008).

Nord, Cristina, 'Edle Wilde gibt es nur für Touristen', *taz*, 15 July 2009, http://www.taz.de/ !5159853 https://taz.de/Film-mit-brasilianischen-Indianern/!5159853/ (accessed 23 January 2024).

Núñez-Alberca, Alejandro, 'El territorio como forma de vida: La representación del sertão en la película *Bacurau* (2019) de Kleber Mendonça Filho y Juliano Dornelles', paper presented at V Congreso Internacional de Narrativas Audiovisuales, Trujillo, Peru, June 2023.

Ortiz Cassiani, Javier. 'Son de negros', in *Resiliencia*, edited by La Comisión de la Verdad (Bogotá: Comisión de la Verdad/Rey Naranjo Editores, 2020), pp. 9–23.

Peterson, Jennifer, and Graig Uhlin, 'In Focus: Film and Media Studies in the Anthropocene', *JCMS: Journal of Cinema and Media Studies*, 58–2 (2019), 142–6, doi:10.1353/cj.2019.0006 (accessed 8 January 2024).

Rocha, Glauber, 'Eztetyka da Fome 1965', *Hambre*, 15 September 2013, https://hambrecine.com/wp-content/uploads/2013/09/eztetyka-da-fome.pdf (accessed 8 January 2024).

Rust, Stephen, Salma Monani, and Sean Cubitt, eds., *Ecocinema: Theory and Practice* (New York: Routledge, 2013).

Schulze, Peter W., 'Beyond Cowboys and Cangaceiros. Transculturations of the Western in Brazilian Cinema', in *Crossing Frontiers. Intercultural Perspectives on the Western*, edited by Thomas Klein, Ivo Ritzer, and Peter W. Schulze (Marburg: Schüren, 2012), pp. 163–93.

Solanas, Fernando, and Octavio Getino, 'Hacia un tercer cine. Apuntes y experiencias para el desarrollo de un cine de liberación en el Tercer Mundo', *Cine Club*, 1 (1970), 27–40.

Svampa. Maristella, *Antropoceno: Lecturas globales desde el Sur* (Córdoba: Universidad Nacional de Córdoba, 2019), https://www.memoria.fahce.unlp.edu.ar/libros/pm.5176/pm.5176.pdf (accessed 3 March 2024).

Svampa, Maristella, *Neo-extractivism in Latin America. Socio-environmental Conflicts, the Territorial Turn, and New Political Narratives* (Cambridge: Cambridge University Press, 2019), https://www.memoria.fahce.unlp.edu.ar/libros/pm.5180/pm.5180.pdf (accessed 3 March 2024).

Svampa, Maristella, 'Reflexiones finales. Dimensiones de la crisis sistémica', in *Las fronteras del neoextractivismo en América Latina: Conflictos socioambientales, giro ecoterritorial y nuevas dependencias* (Bielefeld: Bielefeld University Press, 2019), pp. 104–23.

Ulloa, Astrid, 'Dinámicas ambientales y extractivas en el siglo XXI: ¿Es la época del Antropoceno o del Capitaloceno en Latinoamérica?', *Desacatos*, 54 (2017), 58–73, doi:10.29340/54.1740 (accessed 23 January 2024).

White, Daniel R. *Film in the Anthropocene: Philosophy, Ecology, and Cybernetics* (Cham, Switzerland: Palgrave Macmillan, 2018).

Willoquet-Maricondi, Paula, ed., *Framing the World: Explorations in Ecocriticism and Film* (Charlottesville: University of Virginia Press, 2010).

14

'Now Where Am I?': Endurance in Peter Loizos's *Sophia and Her People* (1985)

Ignacio Albornoz and Katerina Hatzikidi

In the current context of land occupations and openly territorial wars, such as those that the Russian invasion of Ukraine and the most recent chapter of the decades-long confrontation between Israel and Palestine have brought into the public eye once again, we turn our attention to an older, and perhaps largely forgotten, conflict that recently reached its fiftieth anniversary: the 1974 Turkish invasion of Cyprus. Taking place in Europe's Southeast Mediterranean margins, the division and occupation of Cyprus remain to this day an unresolved conflict, as the informal state established in the North by Turkish authorities after their military intervention continues to be contested by all major international instances.

In the present chapter, by delving into a short ethnographic film, we would like to approach a few aspects of this apparently frozen conflict, namely the ways it has been experienced over time by some refugees. Although there exists a major feature on the matter (Michael Cacoyannis's *Attila 74: The Rape of Cyprus*), we have preferred to concentrate here on a much lesser known production: *Sophia and Her People—Eventful Lives*, made by British anthropologist Peter Loizos in 1983 and released two years later, as one of the results of his long-term research carried out among Greek Cypriot communities, both before and after the Turkish occupation. Shot on 16 mm film, *Sophia and Her People* is an ethnographic featurette focusing on the life of the 1974 war refugee Sophia Paphitena, an 'internally displaced person' who was among the 180,000 Greek Cypriots, nearly two out of five, forced to leave their homes in August 1974.

Needless to say, our aim here is not to provide an all-encompassing, broad understanding of so complex a conflict such as this (one that inscribes itself on the one hand in the *longue durée* of history by its striking reminiscences of the 1922–23 population exchange between Greece and Turkey and has been, on the other hand, widely discussed in the specialised literature, from a whole range of disciplines). Rather, our modest objective is to illuminate the ways in which a particular cinematic object can, by the means inherent to its medium, help to reflect on certain specific questions linked to the more general theme of displacement and dispossession. We will do so by stressing mainly the temporal aspects at stake, which we will approach through the broad concept of *endurance*, a less pathos-charged, more future-oriented alternative to the tension between resilience and resistance. With its focus on both duration and strength, the concept of endurance seems like an adequate companion to Loizos's own anthropological work on Cyprus, a work developed over the course of several decades and in which the refugee experience is described less in terms of an everlasting, irreversible trauma than in terms of grievance and transcendence. Furthermore, endurance connects to experiences which are specifically cinematic, such as the passing of time and the oscillation between continuity and discontinuity.

The chapter begins with a short reflection on the dilemma posed by the tension between resistance/resilience, and its possible overcoming through the concept of endurance. Then we will move to a brief characterisation of Sophia Paphitena, the main protagonist of Loizos's film, by drawing upon some of his written work, both before and after the shooting of the film. We will proceed afterwards to a more detailed analysis of *Sophia and Her People*, focusing on rather specific sequences, shots or scenes, which will help us demonstrate how the film deals concretely with different temporalities and manages to bridge creatively between them.

I Resistance or resilience? Considering endurance

Resistance became an important analytical concept in social anthropology in the 1970s and 1980s, greatly influenced by Foucault, and perhaps most emblematically seen in the innovative work of James Scott in Southeast Asia.[1] Ethnographic studies attentive to resistance—vocal and organised, as

1 See James Scott, *The Moral Economy of the Peasant: Rebellion and Subsistence in Southeast Asia* (New Haven and London: Yale University Press, 1976); *Weapons of the Weak. Everyday Forms of Peasant Resistance* (New Haven and London: Yale University Press, 1985) and *Domination and the Arts of Resistance: Hidden Transcripts* (New Haven and London: Yale University Press, 1990).

well as that quietly found in small everyday acts—formed part of a broader turn in the discipline preoccupied with power in its different forms and manifestations. Following a boom in studies of resistance, however, the concept gradually came under increasing scrutiny. Anthropologists began calling for 'resisting resistance',[2] as they considered that excessive focus on resistance had not only side-lined other equally important aspects of the lives of the people they studied, romanticised or fetishised the term, and even essentialised people and their circumstances, but it also extended the term to include a wide diversity of situations and power dynamics that it risked explaining everything and nothing at all.[3] Sherry Ortner importantly highlights, however, that the term's conceptual plasticity may only provide part of the reason anthropologists at large moved away from it in their studies. As life in the 1990s became increasingly shaped by neoliberalism's harsh realities, resistance, writes Ortner, 'may have begun to seem a less realistic, even absurd, perspective, while "governmentality", the myriad ways in which people and populations are moulded and regulated, may have seemed increasingly relevant to the real-world conditions of life'.[4]

A new dominant interest in social anthropology now revolved around 'the harsh and brutal dimensions of human experience, and the structural and historical conditions that produce them'. Ortner calls the body of anthropological work produced around this preoccupation as 'dark anthropology' (Ortner, 'Dark Anthropology', p. 49). Joel Robbins, in another seminal essay, described it as an emphasis on the 'suffering subject'. Robbins, like others before him,[5] argued that the for-a-long-time central focus of the discipline on the 'exotic' or 'savage other' was replaced, in the last forty years or so, 'by the figure of humanity united in its shared vulnerability to suffering'.[6] To the extent that radical alterity was losing its ability to answer important

2 Michael Brown, 'On Resisting Resistance', *American Anthropologist*, 98–4 (1996), 729–35.

3 Lila Abu-Lughod, 'The Romance of Resistance: Tracing Transformations of Power through Bedouin Women', *American Ethnologist*, 17(1990), 41–55; Marshall Sahlins, 'Two or Three Things I Know about Culture', *Journal of the Royal Anthropological Institute*, 5–3 (1999), 399–421; Dan Rabinowitz, 'Resistance and the City', *History and Anthropology*, 25–4 (2014), 472–87; Susan Seymour, 'Resistance', *Anthropological Theory*, 6–3 (2006), 303–21.

4 Sherry Ortner, 'Dark Anthropology and its Others', *HAU: Journal of Ethnographic Theory*, 6–1 (2016), 47–73 (p. 61).

5 See Didier Fassin and Richard Rechtman, *The Empire of Trauma: An Inquiry into the Condition of Victimhood*, transl. Rachel Gomme (Princeton: Princeton University Press, 2009).

6 Joel Robbins, 'Beyond the Suffering Subject: Toward an Anthropology of the Good', *Journal of the Royal Anthropological Institute*, 19 (2013), 447–62 (p. 450).

questions about the anthropological (Western) self, Robbins suggests, the notion of 'trauma', with its 'universalistic quality', was gaining growing currency as 'it came to define a humanity without borders', allowing anthropology to move decisively away from its savage other past (Robbins, 'Beyond the Suffering Subject', p. 454). Acknowledging the contributions such works have made to the discipline, he nonetheless called for an 'anthropology of the good', which by focusing on such diverse issues as morality, affect, hope, well-being, care, among other things, would be able to offer insights into how people, individually and collectively, work towards improving their lives and their social worlds. Such insights would then help inform our own, learning, once again, from difference.

Sophia and Her People, as an ethnographic film produced in 1983, together with the bulk of Loizos's work on the people of Argaki can at first sight easily be placed among those studies primarily considering human suffering. After all, displacement and dispossession are key themes in his writing and filmmaking and Sophia, the protagonist, appears to be painfully longing for her return to her home and her orange groves. Yet Loizos, anticipating in a way anthropology's posterior move away from the suffering subject and towards ways of engaging with the good, takes distance from the notion of trauma as a possible analytical lens for what happened to his Argaki interlocutors. 'It is tempting to reach for the word trauma', he concedes, '[b]ut this hardly helps'.[7] Instead, he suggests that '[w]hile in the short-term the Argaki refugees were exposed to events which were massively disruptive', most of them were able to go about their lives in a meaningful, future-oriented way: '[t]heir world was not shattered, in spite of their unexpected and initially devastating losses of homes, land and a richly communal social life' (*Iron in the Soul*, p. 184).

Having accompanied many of these people over several decades, Loizos makes a compelling argument about their endurance in the face of disruption, and even about eventually transcending the initially devastating experience (Loizos, *Iron in the Soul*, p. 3). Using social capital theory as a framework for understanding the ways Greek Cypriot, and other war-affected populations, coped with displacement and loss, his analysis sometimes resorts to the term 'resilience' to describe how 'people have become skilled at avoiding the pain, shutting themselves off from it' (Loizos, *Iron in the Soul*, p. 186). Yet the term does not become a central one in his writings. A key question that has guided Loizos's work on forced migration is the extent to which people's lives continue to be marked by the experience of displacement with the passing of time. To that he acknowledges distinct

7 Peter Loizos, *Iron in the Soul. Displacement, Livelihood and Health in Cyprus* (New York, Oxford: Berghahn, 2008), p. 184.

intensities and non-linear trajectories, as well as that different factors can influence the ways a person who has experienced such pain and distress may find a way to overcome their condition of suffering. An indispensable element towards endurance and healing, however, is to maintain and create new 'bonds of affinity, moral communities, social entanglements of a solidary and cumulative character'.[8]

Paradoxically, loss of hope in the eventual return to the homes from which they were evicted, did not increase despair among Greek Cypriot refugees but was instead a factor of mitigating displacement. It forced them to engage in nurturing social relations in exile, and 'rebuild their lives and livelihoods as best they could'.[9] The radical break that came about in the summer of 1974, drawing a frontier that violently separated home from exile, became less sharp as life away from the village was invested with affect and acts of proximity with others in their resettlement. This is not to say that displacement, loss, and grievance were no longer relevant to these refugees' lives but that at some point their dispossession was no longer their primary meaning-making modality. Towards this change of consciousness, 'the labouring body, the senses, the need for food and drink, for rest and sleep, for sexual and emotional intimacy, for social contacts' (Loizos, *Iron in the Soul*, p. 186), were all necessary and important aspects of daily life that eventually, and through their very routineness, helped dissipate a permanent feeling of loss.

The argument Loizos makes that by investing in building strong affective communities in exile, internally displaced Greek Cypriots were able to move away from suffering without breaking; that their memories of the past did not 'incapacitate' them (Loizos, 'Ottoman Half-lives', p. 238) because they relied on and got support from the kinds of social relations they cultivated and the everyday acts they engaged in, is not a description of resilience. It seems to us that it is substantially more than a simple act of adaptation. Owning to the fact that the anthropologist and filmmaker himself avoids the term to describe Greek Cypriot attitudes and realities after 1974, and agreeing with a view that sees the notion of resilience as deeply entangled with 'the adaptive imperative',[10] we propose the notion of endurance as a lens that allows us to closely approach and analyse *Sophia and Her People*, without imposing

8 Peter Loizos, 'Ottoman Half-lives: Long-term Perspectives on Particular Forced Migrations', *Journal of Refugee Studies*, 12–3 (1999), 237–63 (p. 256). See also: Renée Hirschon, *Heirs of the Greek Catastrophe: The Social Life of Asia Minor Refugees in Piraeus* (New York and Oxford: Berghahn, 2023 [1989]).

9 Peter Loizos, 'The Loss of Home. From Passion to Pragmatism in Cyprus', in *Struggles for Home: Violence, Hope, and the Movement of People*, ed. Stef Jansen and Staffan Löfvig (New York and Oxford: Berghahn, 2009), pp. 65–84 (p. 67).

10 This is the position defended by Nicolas Lema Habash in his chapter included in this volume.

any normative assumptions or moral evaluations with regards to the process of building a home away from home. In doing so, we are considering time as an important nodal point in the multiple constructions of standing up and enduring, as well as in the setbacks and shortfalls along the way.

As an alternative to both the notions of resilience and resistance, which this volume mostly grapples with, in this chapter we propose the less controversial concept of 'endurance', which is to be understood in its etymological origin in Middle French, as a way of being *in-the-duration*. The word *duration*, as we know, emanates from the Latin *durare*, via the French verb *durer* (to last). By using this term we seek to emphasise firstly the capacity for a person or idea to be or to exist continuously in time. However, we also take into consideration the fact that the Latin verb *durare* was itself subjected to some ambiguity of meaning from early on, due to its homophony and similarity with the radical of the noun *durus* (hard, solid). When we speak of 'endurance', thus, we will be actually thinking of two possible meanings: on the one hand, the capacity of something or someone to extend itself, to continue in time, and, on the other, its ability to indurate, that is to say to harden, to grow harder or to establish firmly. It is our contention here that both aspects of the word are emphasised in Loizos's work, whether in writing or in film.

II *Sophia and Her People*: From word to film

Much of Peter Loizos's ethnographic work—mostly in writing but also in film—has been centred around the people of Argaki, a village in the northern part of the island where his own father hailed from.[11] The anthropologist has followed the lives of many of Argaki's people from the time when they still lived in the village until many years after their displacement. In that, he paralleled Elizabeth Colson's pioneering work, who followed the Gwembe Tonga people for many years on end, offering ground-breaking insights into the complexities of forced migration.

Sophia Paphitena, the protagonist of *Sophia and Her People*, is an Argaki villager to whom Loizos frequently returned and a key figure in his ethnographic work on Cyprus. She has been depicted primarily in his 2008 book *Iron in the Soul: Displacement, Livelihood and Health in Cyprus*, but she also makes a short appearance, in a two-page vignette, in his 1981 monograph *The Heart Grown Bitter: A Chronicle of Cypriot War Refugees (Loizos)*.

11 Peter Loizos, *The Heart Grown Bitter. A Chronicle of Cypriot War Refugees* (Cambridge: Cambridge University Press, 1981), p. 10.

Born in 1924 in the village of Argaki, in what is today Northern Cyprus, Sophia is at the time of shooting the film a visibly elderly woman, even though she is barely approaching the age of 60. At that point, almost ten years after displacement, she has already found herself a rather comfortable position as a baker in a family business which runs smoothly and provides the whole family with jobs and a good, steady income. After the initial shock of displacement and the overwhelming anxiety of the early months spent as a refugee, Sophia seems now more or less at peace with her new life situation.

In his 2008 book, Loizos describes Sophia's life trajectory as follows:

> Sophia Paphitena [...] came from a poor, hard-working family and had learned bread-making from her mother. [...]. In Argaki she had run a small bread-making business from her home, to supplement her husband's unpredictable earnings as a freelance lorry driver. They needed a steady income: they had six children, two boys and four girls. [...]. Sophia was selling a hundred loaves of bread a day to her fellow villagers in the early 1970s, and looked back on this as a time when she had 'a pocket full of money'. [...] In August 1974 she and her family left the village in confusion like everyone else. The children were mostly still of school age. Sophia had two brothers already resident in Nicosia and they agreed to take two children each, so they could get on with their schooling or start working. One daughter was already studying in Athens. Sophia and her youngest, a son, fetched up in Deftera village, some miles outside Nicosia, in an empty dilapidated village house, while her husband was off in Paphos with his lorry seeking work in the grape harvest. (Loizos, *Iron in the Soul*, pp. 119–20)

The stay at the Deftera village, in 1975, is Sophia's *nadir*, her lowest point of distress and sorrow. This seems only natural, as the shock of dislocation was still fresh and the conditions under which she suddenly found herself outside her village were adverse to say the least. Her only consolation, then, was to speak profusely about her days in Argaki and to try to fill the gap of absence by means of remembrance. 'She felt very sorry for herself', writes Loizos, 'and [...] wanted to talk at length about the good days in the village, the shock of losing it all, the pain of separation from her children. When she talked about Argaki life, which she recalled [...] in detail, her new situation felt bleak and futile. She wept frequently' (Loizos, *Iron in the Soul*, p. 120).

But other than that immediate emotional reaction to abrupt dislocation, what was exactly the reason behind Sophia's deep feeling of distress during her Deftera sojourn? From where did that relentless sadness steam concretely? In his writings, Loizos puts the blame mainly on day-to-day loneliness and isolation, which in spite of a rather moderate geographic displacement (Deftera is only 30 kms away from Argaki, and around 7 to 8 hours by foot), made the contrast between her old and her new life very hard to swallow:

> To go from living in a village of 1,500 people where she had known everyone by name, and was related to many people, being known to all by virtue of her bread, to being an unknown person, a nobody in a village of strangers, was very hard to bear. Her son was very young, her older daughters were not under her roof, and she had no telephone; she undoubtedly felt she had no intimate companion on a day-to-day basis with whom to share her deepest feelings. Back in the village, her older daughters, and her women neighbours would have supplied this companionship. (Loizos, *Iron in the Soul*, pp. 120–1)

Together with this feeling of isolation and strangeness came stagnation and a feeling of abandonment. Loizos perceptively notes that 'by her normal standards, [Sophia was] inactive and unproductive' (Loizos, *Iron in the Soul*, p. 133) during her Deftera period. A few projects were envisioned and put into practice at the time to keep her busy, both by her husband and by other relatives, but to no avail. Luckily, a sense of self-discipline eventually prevailed and once Sophia started to bake again, with the support of her family, things started to get back on track little by little, as '[she] found people bought her rolls and that she could make more money than working for wages' (Loizos, *Iron in the Soul*, p. 133). In this period of slow economic and emotional recovery, the film provides an eloquent testimony, backed up by Sophia's own recollections. Towards the first half of the film, she recalls her experience at large, from a state of lethargy to a new life gained at and from her work:

> My husband brought me some goats to mind, but I didn't like that. [...] I went to find work, and got a job in a kiosk, selling soft drinks but I didn't like that either, so I went to my sister, who had a refugee house with an oven that held 15 loaves. I made a basket of rolls which I took to my kiosk to sell. I was earning £10 a week at the kiosk but that wasn't enough for our needs. [] After a few days' baking at my sister's I decided to build an oven here in the (refugee) house they had given me. We started building the oven, and a man came from Town Planning to knock it down for me "It's not allowed", he said. "Knock it down. Knock it down". I got upset and said: "I won't knock it down". "It's the only living for me and mine! I must do this work".

Loizos's film offers, as we can see, a snapshot of Sophia and her family's everyday life. In so doing, images and memories of the radical break of displacement are interwoven with the ethnographic present. Those filmed are often seen (and frequently encouraged to) reflect on what, materially and affectively, they lost by being forced to leave behind: their village, Argaki,

Sophia's sun-washed balcony where she planned to be spending her afternoons in the company of her daughters, the orange groves, their neighbours, their old home and bakery. Yet the film is undoubtedly situated in the present, with Sophia and her family projecting onto the future: talking about their work and daily routine, seeing their children and grandchildren grow, hoping business will prosper, enjoying a summer afternoon before the next shift.

III Stressing continuities

There is little to no information available on the films Loizos made in Cyprus, nor on his previous activity as a documentary filmmaker for the BBC. Other than his own scarce notes and accounts in interviews, such as the one he gave to Paul Thompson,[12] the testimonies are indeed pretty rare. About *Sophia and Her People*, in particular, only a short review by Peter S. Allen, written for the *American Anthropologist* journal in 1988 appears to have circulated. Loizos's film is qualified there as both a 'modest videotape' and an 'outstanding production', whose main merit is to convey 'the emotional toll of warfare on noncombatants through an examination of one family's circumstance'.[13] Anthropologist Michael Herzfeld, for his part, has qualified *Sophia and Her People*, together with Loizos's previous film, *Life Chances*, as 'ethnographic classics',[14] but does not provide any argument in support of his affirmation.

What we know from Loizos's own testimony is that *Sophia and Her People* represents a willing departure from *Life Chances*, both 'technically and conceptually' (Thompson, 'Interview'). While the first film he shot in Cyprus was done with a silent 16 mm camera and a pervasive voice over recorded *après-coup* which oriented the whole flow of the narrative, the second was set to adopt a more 'observational' approach, with synchronous sound, no voice-over narration and a series of short intertitles. *Life Chances*, in that sense, is a monological film, in which, says Loizos, 'my voice is the only voice you really hear' (Thompson, 'Interview with Peter Loizos'). *Sophia and Her People*, on the other hand, strikes the viewer as a more dialogical

12 Paul Thompson, 'Interview with Peter Loizos', in *Pioneers of Social Research*, pp. 1–377, doi:10.5255/UKDA-SN-6226-6 (accessed 16 February 2024).

13 Peter S. Allen, 'Sophia's People—Eventful Lives', *American Anthropologist. New Series*, 90–3 (1988), p. 782.

14 Michael Herzfeld, 'Social Anthropology: Openings and Expansions in the Age of Exclusion', *Byzantine and Modern Greek Studies*, 40–1 (2016), 99–113 (p. 104), doi:10.1017/byz.2015.11 (accessed 5 March 2024).

or polyphonic enterprise, as it collects the direct testimonies of an array of people, in different time periods.

Although certainly a modest one by its means and length, Loizos's 1985 film is far from being a straightforward or simplistic account of refugee life in post-occupation Cyprus, partly thanks to its dialogical nature. Despite an apparent effortlessness, the film manages to interweave various aspects and dimensions of what was at stake at the time for refugees. Besides the polyphony of voices, the most patent of those aspects is perhaps temporality.

The chronology of the film fluctuates indeed with some liberty, as Loizos puts together footage actually corresponding to three different time periods. There is in the first place the footage from what we may call the 'ethnographic present', set in April 1983 and shot in full colour, mostly against the background provided by the suburban area of Nicosia and the accommodation built there in order to rehouse the refugees coming from the North. A second set of images, this time presented in something like black and white, shows Sophia around 1972 or 1973, in her hometown Argaki, where she ran a much smaller bakery, also with the help of her relatives. These images display a blueish colour-scheme with little to no nuances and a rather high contrast, which betrays a different source of recording than that of the rest of the film. There is finally a third time period, broadly corresponding to 1975, that is after the occupation, with the members of the family dispersed and a severely demoralised Sophia, living by herself in a dilapidated house somewhere in the Deftera village. This latter period is depicted mostly through still monochromatic images, which are accompanied by a sound recording in which we can hear the main character's grievances, half obscured by her sobbing.

This tripartite division is however far from being clear cut in terms of the temporalities involved. Further analysis reveals in fact that each one of the three time periods schematically described above actually has its own complexities and internal divisions, which intermingle sometimes in quite paradoxical ways. For instance, what we have depicted in the previous paragraph as the third time segment of the film, with the still images of a disheartened Sophia inside her Deftera house, is indeed a composite sequence, made out of sparse material, stemming from different moments in time. Loizos himself recalls this particular sequence in his own book on ethnographic film, when speaking of the paradoxes and ethical implications of wanting to revive painful memories through the re-enacted return to the actual places where they occurred. From his own testimony we learn that the photographic images of the Deftera house were actually the result of a sort of *mise en scène*, a re-enactment in which the protagonist was explicitly asked to go back to her transitory dwelling in order to trigger the memory of past experiences. Loizos writes:

> I asked [Sophia] to re-visit a house she had lived in shortly after becoming a refugee, so that some still photographs could be taken to suggest the depression she had felt at the time. When she got to the house, she was immediately filled with painful memories, and the photographs taken then show this very clearly. […] [F]rom the period of her depressed sojourn, I had a sound tape in which she had frequently wept, but had no appropriate images.[15]

While Loizos acknowledges the problematic aspects of stimulating traumatic memories for the sake of re-enactment, he dismisses them as a minor compromise in the specific case of Sophia. Her suffering, although vocally expressed in the tape recordings, remains a relatively mild one for Loizos, as it is less extreme than other forms of suffering which involve for instance violent deaths, physical torture or repeated harassment. Loizos's aim here, in any case, is merely to 'suggest' Sophia's depression, and not to mislead the spectator into believing that the photographs correspond in reality to the time period which the sound recording is evoking. Perhaps involuntarily, however, what this sequence ends up suggesting is the inevitable layering of temporalities and the constant blurring of its frontiers in the experience of refugees.

This is a rather interesting way to put forward exclusively by cinematic means the continuity of it all, as well as the impossibility of conceiving of the refugee experience as one determined only by irreparable ruptures and perfectly circumscribed events. Rather, what comes to the surface here is an acute contrast between the tape recording—dated in September 1975—and Sophia's body, visibly the same as that in the 'ethnographic present' of 1983.

Let us now turn to the 'ethnographic present' of the film. This section displays its own internal divisions as well, at least in terms of the strategies of *mise en scène* imagined by Loizos: to a quite discrete set of talking-head and mostly frontal interviews (around six in total, with Andreas, Sophia's brother; with Nikos, Sophia's elder son; and with Sophia herself) follow here and there some exterior scenes—although only a few of them—where the members of the family run different errands around town. In those, we can see for instance Sophia's daughters, inside a car, strolling around the streets of Nicosia, or one of her grandchildren, being cared for by his paternal grandmother.

Then there are scenes of everyday life inside the bakery. During these scenes, the focus is placed on the chores and the manual work of the staff. Here, the camera patiently films the gestures of some of the workers: getting the bread in and out of the oven, scoring it, selecting it and finally preparing it for transportation. These gestures are emphasised by a clever montage of the 1973 footage, which establishes some very transparent equivalences with

15 Peter Loizos, *Innovation in Ethnographic Film. From Innocence to Self-consciousness 1955–1985* (Chicago: University of Chicago Press, 1993), pp. 62–3.

the chores of the past, as if the current bakery was in a way nothing more than a continuation, or even an exact replica of the one the family ran in Argaki. This seems to be Theodoros Rakopoulos's interpretation, when he writes that Loizos's film describes precisely 'the desire to assert family sovereignty among displaced [Greek Cypriots], embedded in the construction of a village furnace identical to the one left behind in their North Cyprus village'.[16]

One very telling moment of patent visual equivalence between the past and the present is when Loizos edits in succession the ritual burning of blessed olive leaves against misfortune and envy, through the gestures and movements of one of Sophia's daughters. First we see her in the ethnographic present, sideways, burning the leaves and passing them through the room in a small bowl, which she then takes outside to smoke the bakery's van. A simple cut gives way after a while to a frontal shot, now in black and white, in which we see Sophia's daughter in 1973, in Argaki, participating in the same ritual burning, but filmed now with a much tighter framing, which perhaps responds to the narrowness of the place and the small number of people involved.

Image-wise, it is worth noticing that Loizos chooses to present the setting of the 'ethnographic present' section of the film with a panoramic high angle shot of the suburban accommodations built for the refugees. In a way, this choice relates to a viewing strategy he himself had developed during his first sojourn in Argaki, which had taken place towards the mid-1960s (as he describes it in Loizos, *The Heart Grown Bitter*, 1981). In fact, Loizos recalls his initial impressions of Argaki as that of a rather dull-looking place, neither pretty nor picturesque by any conventional standard. To get a better, more poignant view of the small village Loizos comes up with an ingenious trick. The village, he argues, must be looked at from a very particular angle to be properly appreciated: that of a rooftop, the only place from where the gaze of the observer can arbitrarily focus on the intricate set of motifs punctuating the landscape and discover complexity. His description of Argaki may well correspond to the establishing shot of Nicosia.

> Unless you looked at it *in a rather special way*, [Argaki] looked drab and flat, hot and dusty, with neither the striking terraced settings of the mountain villages, [...] nor the whitewashed nestling compactness of some villages in the Kyrenia foothills [...]. The way to *see the village at its best* was to get high up on someone's roof, and then look at small areas of houses, concentrating on arbitrary sections, where several different planes criss-crossed each other, with a courtyard wall running at an oblique angle to the

16 Theodoros Rakopoulos, 'Property as Sovereignty in Micro: The State/ Property Nexus and the Cyprus Problem', *Journal of the Royal Anthropological Institute*, 28–3 (2022), 769–87 (p. 774).

> roof of another house. *The eye had to concentrate* and pile up the dwellings one upon another, as a telephoto lens would do, in order to *discover* the complex textures. (Loizos, *The Heart Grown Bitter*, p. 12)

It is very telling indeed that Loizos's first cinematic glance at the new refugee neighbourhood in which Sophia and Her People now dwell goes back to this early recollection of the landscape and viewpoints of Argaki. Here again, we find that it is endurance as continuity in time which explains and irrigates the image of the ethnographic present, as if the only way to gain a better understanding of it was to set it against the backdrop of the past, in continuity with it.

The centrality of time, in more general terms, is expressed throughout the film in the conversations themselves, which revolve quite often around explicit day-to-day time schedules and the specific length of chores and shifts established for each activity. During a car ride through Nicosia, Eleni rapidly goes through the programme of the day: 'By the time we get home, it will be mid-day. I'll pick up my kid, give him a bath and we'll eat at about 1:00 PM. Then it will be time for a bit of rest. Maybe if there's time later, we could go shopping. [...] we could have a stroll, until the evening. If there's enough time ...'. Just before that, we could see Loizos inside the bakery asking Sophia at what time she came to work («Τι ώρα ήρθες δουλειά σήμερα;») and at what time will she end her shift («Ιντα ώρα θα σχολάσεις;»). The same questions are addressed then to Eleni, who is supposed to start her shift again at midnight, after taking care of her little son. Between work and family life, time appears in each testimony as a flying, scarce commodity which demands organisation, the agendas being by default extremely tight. This is what Nikos's testimony, towards the end of the film, makes explicit when he recalls for Loizos his brief 'personal strike', during which he withdrew from the bakery: 'the reason I left the job [...] was the working hours. I thought the shifts should be rotated, so that if I had been working from 2:00 P.M. till 11:00 P.M., next week I should work from 2 A.M. till 11 A.M., so I could sleep, then have my afternoon free to go out, to move freely, and not be bound to the bakery's time'.

IV Sophia's laments: A creative output for hurtful memories

There is yet a third kind of scene, which is also a form of re-enactment. On those, Sophia is shown alone, often in a room where the only movement is that of her arms working with dough in striking contradistinction to the bakery scenes bustling with people and movement. Sophia sings what Loizos calls 'poems of lament' (Loizos, *Iron in the Soul*, 172), often improvised in rhyme, about her former life in Argaki. She does so while kneading the dough with her body half bent over a wooden bucket. These scenes punctuate the film from the beginning to the end and are naturally of the utmost interest.

The image of Sophia punching down the dough while calling to mind her old life is in the first place highly allegorical, for it materialises the hardships of life in displacement through the resistance of the dough, as well as Sophia's will to accommodate matter to her own will, to 'bend', mould, or to malaxate it, by means of her own strength, cunning and *savoir-faire*. These scenes reflect once more Sophia's endurance (as continuity) in the sense that they pose a direct link to her previous life in Argaki, both by the content of the laments and the gesture of kneading. At the same time, though, they encapsulate quite eloquently her 'induration', the ability she has shown through her refugee experience to grow harder and to firmly establish herself once again, to lay new roots.

Although the poems sung by Sophia seem to be mostly improvised, their performance is far from being completely spontaneous, as one of the last chant sequences clearly shows. At some point, just before the sequence where Nikos relates his time away from the bakery, Loizos asks Sophia to sing a lament in relation to that incident. 'Give us the song about Nikos', he requests abruptly while off camera. The idea seems to disturb the women, who are all busy making the filling for the stuffed bread and therefore not directly engaging with the camera. 'A song?' asks then Sophia with the spurt of an embarrassed giggle, as the camera pans from her bustling hands to her face, visibly self-conscious. Sophia fears that the song is not appropriate for the moment and expresses her reluctance to indulge the filmmaker. Loizos then intervenes to reassure her by saying that the song would indeed be very suitable, an affirmation with which one of the daughters finally agrees, in good spirit: 'OK, so let him hear it then!' Despite Xenia's clearance, Sophia still hesitates, but finally caves in. She proceeds then to sing the song somehow begrudgingly, after having signified with a brief gesture of her head her discomfort.

This short performative moment of the film resonates in various ways. Its most obvious implication is that the film ceases to appear from then on as a pure observational documentary, the performance of Sophia's laments being ultimately the result of some form of negotiation that Loizos is not afraid in the least to show on the screen. But most importantly, the fact that this fleeting moment of conflict arises precisely and only when invoking Nikos's strike, demonstrates that the weight of the initial dislocation has given way now to other more poignant or painful memories, which are felt more vividly. By not editing out this moment of discomfort, then, Loizos makes it clear that in the current situation of the 'ethnographic present' the hierarchy of events past has somehow been modified. So that while Sophia gladly agrees to sing her laments on her Argaki life, which punctuate most of the film, the much more recent strike and distancing of her son Nikos emerges as an unlikely unsettling topic.

More broadly, this sequence reveals that Loizos's commitment to his field site and interlocutors, however, was in no way a straightforward affair. In his writings, he repeatedly muses on the delicate and often fragile nature of relationships with Argaki villagers. On the one hand, being a 'partial insider'[17] offered him the advantage of being warmly received and mostly trusted, as well as the authority to speak of local matters, as anyone with blood-linkage to the place would equally do. On the other, he was also a researcher, an Englishman, and someone who often openly disagreed with many of the political benchmarks his interlocutors, and Greek Cypriots more broadly, shared, a situation of mutual discomfort about which he wrote in some detail, and in a confessional tone, in a reflexive text on research ethics.[18]

V Conclusions

In this chapter we have reflected on Peter Loizos's 1985 film *Sophia and Her People—Eventful Lives*. By stressing mostly the way in which Loizos works in merging different temporalities, both by tools of editing and *mise en scène*, we have discussed how the film manages to show that grieving and longing can actually coexist with some form of transcendence and overcoming, and that the two do not necessarily exclude one another. Sophia's trajectory is a perfect example of that, as it is not a monolithic one of pure incapacitating suffering, nor one of evident, mere prosperity: the dreamed success story of a former refugee. In fact, it moves constantly along the two, back and forth, at different degrees. This is not far from what Edward Said considers to be the *contrapuntal* nature of exile, which constitutes one of exile's paradoxical 'pleasures', one of its possible positive outcomes:

> For an exile, habits of life, expression, or activity in the new environment inevitably occur against the memory of these things in another environment. Thus both the new and the old environments are vivid, actual, occurring together contrapuntally. [...]. There is also a particular sense of achievement in acting as if one were at home wherever one happens to be. [...] Perhaps this is another way of saying that a life of exile moves according to a different

17 Peter Loizos, 'User-Friendly Ethnography?', in *Europe Observed*, ed. João de Pina-Cabral and John Campbell (London: The Macmillan Press, 1992), pp. 167–87 (p. 171).

18 Peter Loizos, 'Confessions of a Vampire Anthropologist', *Anthropological Journal on European Cultures*, 3–2 (1994), 39–53.

> calendar, and is less seasonal and settled than life at home. Exile is life led outside habitual order. It is nomadic, decentered, contrapuntal.[19]

If exile and dislocation can in fact, as Said argues, give birth to 'an awareness of simultaneous dimensions', where everything that happens in the now of the present is happening as well against the memory of events past, they can also be the source for an 'originality of vision', which fosters acts of creativity. According to Loizos, Sophia's laments correspond to such acts, as he considers that 'her painful feelings about the loss of the village came out creatively and movingly in a series of laments [...]' (Loizos, *Iron in the Soul*, p. 123).

Ultimately, the possibility of overcoming a traumatic experience such as forced displacement may have more to do with what Loizos has called 'experiential time', which in our perspective could be viewed as a form of endurance, both as continuation-in-time and as rooting. 'Experiential time' designates the complex system of balances under which the experiences lived in one particular time and place can be 'compensated' or 'surpassed' by new, more recent and vivid ones, which tend to gain in quantity and importance as time goes by. The result of these complex negotiations, both at the social and at the personal level, is what Loizos refers to when he speaks of the 'half-lives' of displaced people, understanding by that 'a power that goes on being active for many years but slowly loses its force' (Loizos, 'Ottoman Half-lives', p. 238). In a way, *Sophia and Her People* reflects on experiential time and the half-lives of refugees in a very concrete manner when distributing and limiting its own durations, giving more exposure to the ethnographic present than to previous time periods, whether it is the 1975 isolation in Deftera or the 1974 silent snippets of life in Argaki.

Of course, a lived experience as complex and multifaceted as that of forced displacement cannot be simply transcended or overcome. It is therefore important to reiterate the necessity of nuances, of degrees and situatedness, in approaching and understanding a refugee past, present and future, and the extent to which endurance may be a key concept that can help us unpack such experiences. For the case at hand, as our discussion has shown, it appears to be a useful concept indeed. Sophia and Her People are struggling and thriving, each in their own way, in their everyday life structured around their work at the bakery, as portrayed in Loizos's short film. They appear to be enjoying, worrying, and deeply caring for everything they have built after 1974. They appear proud to have been able to reconstruct their lives, to maintain continuities, and to forge new affective relationships after the radical break the invasion produced. And they always remember Argaki.

19 Said, Edward, 'Reflections on Exile', in *Reflections on Exile and Other Essays* (Cambridge, MA: Harvard University Press, 2003), pp. 173–86 (p. 186).

It is worth noting in passing that for a film that looks at the lives of refugees nine years after displacement, any mention of politics is conspicuously absent. Was that too delicate a topic to be addressed? Were Loizos and his interlocutors more concerned by other questions? Or was perhaps discussion of politics already implicit in the composed and dispassionate description of the everyday? As mentioned in the introduction, the 'Cyprus Problem' is largely considered an insoluble one, especially after the 2004 referendum, which saw the vast majority of Greek Cypriots rejecting the UN unification plan. While a 'frozen' conflict carries with it the impossibility of a desired and awaited resolution, it also, not uncontroversially, bears a liberating permission to dispense with the necessity to engage with a thorny problem, a permission for a lull in the fighting. This lull, tentative and uncertain as it may be, offers the potential for throwing oneself in the here and now, and in a future outside of displacement and dispossession; the potential of enduring without dwelling in suffering.

Our reading of *Sophia and Her People*, reflected in the notion of endurance, conveys precisely the idea of an embodied memory, carried forward and passed on to the next generations, that informs but does not cripple a life of an individual or that of a community. In the film, Sophia's son, Nikos, speaks about 'feeling' Argaki, the village he left in his teens: 'it lives in my soul, there is no way I can forget about it'.[20] At the same time, deeply personal and spontaneous and shared and predetermined, Nikos's testimony verbalises and visualises Loizos's own perspective on displacement: a condition of varying intensity that depends on a multiplicity of factors, a life of endurance that does not, in the long term, necessarily find in the identity of refugee its primary meaning-making modality.

This perspective is best encapsulated by the very first sentence in Loizos's *Iron in the Soul*, through a formulation that did not shy away from ambiguity: 'Forced Migration hurts. But how badly it hurts, what heals those hurts, or what keeps them septic, depend on many things' (p. 1). In *Sophia and Her People*, Loizos certainly points in that same direction, and that is maybe one of the film's main assets: to pinpoint, through the different cinematic strategies that we have analysed here, some of the complexities and contradictions that underlie the unsettling experience of forced displacement.

20 Our translation.

Bibliography

Abu-Lughod, Lila, 'The Romance of Resistance: Tracing Transformations of Power through Bedouin Women', *American Ethnologist,* 17 (1990), 41–55.

Allen, Peter S., 'Sophia's People–Eventful Lives', *American Anthropologist. New Series*, 90–3 (1988), 782.

Brown, Michael, 'On Resisting Resistance', *American Anthropologist*, 98–4 (1996), 729–35.

Fassin, Didier, and Richard Rechtman, *The Empire of Trauma: An Inquiry into the Condition of Victimhood*, translated by Rachel Gomme (Princeton: Princeton University Press, 2009).

Herzfeld, Michael, 'Social Anthropology: Openings and Expansions in the Age of Exclusion', *Byzantine and Modern Greek Studies*, 40–1 (2016), 99–113, doi:10.1017/byz.2015.11 (accessed 5 March 2024)

Hirschon, Renée, *Heirs of the Greek Catastrophe: The Social Life of Asia Minor Refugees in Piraeus* (New York and Oxford: Berghahn, 2023[1989]).

Loizos, Peter, *The Heart Grown Bitter. A Chronicle of Cypriot War Refugees* (Cambridge: Cambridge University Press, 1981).

Loizos, Peter, 'User-Friendly Ethnography?', in *Europe Observed*, edited by João de Pina-Cabral and John Campbell (London: Macmillan Press, 1992), pp. 167–87.

Loizos, Peter, *Innovation in Ethnographic Film. From Innocence to Self-consciousness 1955–1985* (Chicago: The University of Chicago Press, 1993).

Loizos, Peter, 'Confessions of a Vampire Anthropologist', *Anthropological Journal on European Cultures*, 3–2 (1994), 39–53.

Loizos, Peter, 'Ottoman Half-lives: Long-term Perspectives on Particular Forced Migrations', *Journal of Refugee Studies*, 12–3 (1999), 237–63.

Loizos, Peter, 'Are Refugees Social Capitalists?', in *Social Capital: Critical Perspectives*, edited by Stephen Baron, John Field, and Tom Schuller (Oxford and New York: Oxford University Press, 2000).

Loizos, Peter, 'Misconceiving Refugees?', in *Therapeutic Care for Refugees: No Place Like Home*, edited by Renos K. Papadopoulos (London and New York: Routledge, 2002), pp. 41–56.

Loizos, Peter, *Iron in the Soul. Displacement, Livelihood and Health in Cyprus* (New York, Oxford: Berghahn, 2008).

Loizos, Peter, 'The Loss of Home. From Passion to Pragmatism in Cyprus', in *Struggles for Home: Violence, Hope, and the Movement of People*, edited by Stef Jansen and Staffan Löfvig (New York and Oxford: Berghahn, 2009), pp. 65–84.

Ortner, Sherry, 'Dark Anthropology and its Others', *HAU: Journal of Ethnographic Theory*, 6–1 (2016), 47–73.

Rabinowitz, Dan, 'Resistance and the City', *History and Anthropology*, 25–4 (2014), 472–87, doi:10.1080/02757206.2014.930457 (accessed 16 February 2024).

Rakopoulos, Theodoros, 'Property as Sovereignty in Micro: The State/Property Nexus and the Cyprus Problem', *Journal of the Royal Anthropological Institute*, 28–3 (2022), 769–87.

Robbins, Joel, 'Beyond the Suffering Subject: Toward an Anthropology of the Good', *Journal of the Royal Anthropological Institute*, 19 (2013), 447–62.

Sahlins, Marshall, 'Two or Three Things I Know about Culture', *Journal of the Royal Anthropological Institute*, 5–3(1999), 399–421.

Said, Edward, Reflections on Exile', in *Reflections on Exile and Other Essays* (Cambridge, MA: Harvard University Press, 2003).

Scott, James, C., *The Moral Economy of the Peasant: Rebellion and Subsistence in Southeast Asia* (New Haven and London: Yale University Press, 1976).

Scott, James, C., *Weapons of the Weak. Everyday Forms of Peasant Resistance* (New Haven and London: Yale University Press, 1985).

Scott, James, C., *Domination and the Arts of Resistance: Hidden Transcripts* (New Haven and London: Yale University Press, 1990).

Seymour, Susan, 'Resistance', *Anthropological Theory*, 6–3(2006), 303–21, https://doi.org/10.1177/1463499606066890 (accessed 16 February 2024).

Thompson, Paul, 'Interview with Peter Loizos' in *Pioneers of Social Research* (London: University of Essex, 1996–2018), 1996–2018, pp. 1–377, doi:10.5255/UKDA-SN-6226-6 (accessed 16 February 2024).

15

When I'm Down I Just Get up—or Do I? Contentiousness of Resilience in the Face of Natural Disasters in Jamaica

Victoria Carpenter and Lakhbir Singh

If Gilles Deleuze had come across the field of resilience studies he would undoubtedly rephrase himself and state, 'There is no resilience and never has been'—and this sentiment would be echoed by many in support and by more in opposition. From the abundance of definitions, interpretations, stances and views on resilience, one can only conclude that either resilience is an amazing morphing quality that becomes anything and everything to each stage of recovery or it is an artificial construct that conflates different qualities thus obscuring or ignoring some of their aspects. In short, are we trying to define the undefinable? Is the term resilience wishful thinking or can it be reimagined from a novel theoretical perspective that will give it a new lease on life within the uncertainty and fluidity of present-day social orders?

We argue that 'resilience' is an empty signifier that obscures the complexity of a rather strained relationship between the social actors involved in recovery after natural disasters—government agencies responsible for recovery process and local communities affected by disasters. Rather than attempting to build 'resilient communities' able to handle the aftermath of regular disasters (hurricanes, earthquakes, tsunamis, and so forth), we need to analyse the discourses produced by the state, media and public in response to hurricanes, and propose a framework that allows the key social actors to collaborate successfully during recovery—something that is currently not the case.

I Pinning a Definition on Resilience

Resilience is a rather hard term to pin down—like with many terms that encompass a significant variety of behaviours, cultural norms, and political stances, there are as many definitions of resilience as there are studies attempting to define it. Originally referring to material's ability to restore its original form after being affected by an external force, resilience migrated from physics and engineering to psychology, and branched out across social sciences, humanities, area studies, and creative arts,[1] often combining disciplines to create an illusion of cross-disciplinary applicability.[2] We will not join this bandwagon; instead, we will consider the key stumbling blocks posed by resilience studies.

In very general terms, resilience to disasters means that affected communities recover quickly and improve their living conditions,[3] with the proviso that 'a community participates fully in the recovery process and … has the capacity, skills and knowledge to make its participation meaningful'.[4] But whose understanding of the capacity, skills and knowledge are we talking about? Who determines the meaningfulness of participation? The issue

1 C. S. Holling, 'Resilience and Stability of Ecological Systems', *Annual Review of Ecology and Systematics*, 4 (1973), 1–23, http://www.jstor.org/stable/2096802 (accessed 12 December 2023); Peter Timmerman, *Vulnerability, Resilience and the Collapse of Society* (Toronto: Institute of Environmental Studies, 1981); Markus Keck and Patrick Sakdapolrak, 'What is Social Resilience? Lesson Learned and Ways Forward', *Erdkunde*, 67 (2013), 5–19, doi:10.3112/erdkunde.2013.01.02 (accessed 12 December 2023).

2 See, for example, Steven Southwick et al., 'Resilience: Definition, Theory and Challenges', *European Journal of Psychotraumatology*, 5 (2014), 1–14, doi:10.3402/ejpt.v5.25338 (accessed 12 December 2023).

3 Graham Tobin, 'Sustainability and Community Resilience: the Holy Grail of Hazards Planning?', *Global Environment Change Part B: Environmental Hazards*, 1 (1999), 13–25, doi:10.3763/ehaz.1999.0103 (accessed 12 December 2023). Anita Chandra et al.,'Building Community Resilience to Disasters: A Way Forward to Enhance National Health Security', *Rand Health Quarterly*, 1 (2011), https://www.ncbi.nlm.nih.gov/pmc/articles/PMC4945213/ (accessed 25 January 2023); Dennis Parker, 'Disaster Resilience—a Challenged Science', *Environmental Hazards,* 19 (2019), 1–9, doi: 10.1080/17477891.2019.1694857 (accessed 12 December 2023)

4 Eve Coles and Philip Buckle, 'Developing Community Resilience as a Foundation for Effective Disaster Recovery', *Australian Journal of Emergency Management*, 19 (2004), 6–15 (p. 6), doi:10.3316/ielapa.375435145094637 (accessed 12 December 2023); see also Paul Ward, 'Participatory Development in Jamaica: Does It Work in Practice?', *Social and Economic Studies*, 59 (2010), 167–96, doi:10.2307/41803732 (accessed 12 December 2023).

of knowledge sharing and acceptance of knowledge by the social actors involved in recovery, and the difficulties associated with this process is widely recognised although there is no consensus on how to mitigate this or avoid it altogether—or whether it is even possible.[5]

Jones et al. see resilience and recovery going hand in hand but rather than bouncing back (which could mean returning to a position of vulnerability): 'resilience has been modified to consider a "bounce forward" ability, moving, therefore from a disaster to a more stable, less vulnerable state'.[6] And this would mean that all members of the communities affected by a disaster need to be involved in the process of 'building back better'—which is an excellent plan but then in actual practice, this process falls back onto structured approaches even when community involvement is professed to be at the heart of the process.[7] While seeing 'a more inclusive and structured recovery process' (Jones et al, 'Building Back Better', p. S155) as a more viable alternative to the status quo, this study ends up promoting structured planning led by the government and once again communities are left to buy into these plans for some reason that remains unknown to them.

A slowly growing number of studies question the completely structured approach to recovery, arguing that the communities affected by natural disasters should have a say in what recovery projects they need and, more importantly, who will be bearing the costs of running and maintaining them.[8] Pelling and Uitto's study of the resilience of small-island nations led to an

5 Kirstie Méheux and El Parker, 'Tourist Sector Perceptions of Natural Hazards in Vanuatu and the Implications for a Small Island Developing State', *Tourism Management*, 27 (2006), 69–85, doi:10.1016/j.tourman.2004.07.009 (accessed 12 December 2023); Barbara Carby, *Jamaica's Experience with Hurricane Ivan: The Case for Mitigation and Preparedness Programmes* (Kingston: Caribbean Disaster Emergency Response Agency, 2005).

6 Eleanor Jones et al., '"Building Back Better" in the Context of Multi-hazards in the Caribbean', *Disasters*, 46 (2022), pp. 151–65. See also Jeanne Leroy et al., 'Vulnerability and Social Resilience: Comparison of Two Neighborhoods in New Orleans after Hurricane Katrina', E3S Web of Conferences, 7 (2016), article 08002; Adolfo Lucero Álvarez et al., 'Recognition of Factors that Promote Resilience to Hurricanes', *Regions and Cohesion*, 11:2 (2021), 26–56, doi:10.3167/reco.2021.110203 (accessed 12 December 2023).

7 Loretta Pyles, 'Community Organizing for Post-disaster Social Development: Locating Social Work', *International Social Work*, 50 (2007), 321–33, doi:10.1177/0020872807076044 (accessed 12 December 2023).

8 Alpaslan Özerdem, 'Disaster as Manifestation of Unresolved Development Challenges: The Marmara Earthquake, Turkey', in *Natural Disasters and Development in a Globalizing World*, ed. Mark Pelling (London: Routledge, 2003), pp. 199–213; Evelyn B. Harrell and Michael J. Zakour, 'Including Informal Organizations in Disaster Planning: Development of a Range-of-Type

inescapable conclusion that these vulnerable states need all the help they can get to build up resilience, since they tend to rely on tourism for growth and suffer from years of economic and social instability. They conclude that this process is very much policy-based and plagued with internal problems faced by these states,[9] so it would be logical to suggest that the onus of the process of increasing their resilience would lie on their governments.

Thierry Ribault's article 'Resilience in Fukushima' (2019) and his more recent (and much more compelling) book *Contre la résilience* (2021) argues passionately against saddling the communities with the responsibility to become resilient on their own dime (directly and metaphorically speaking), especially when these communities are among the most underserved and historically overlooked in wider recovery efforts (mostly because they do not contribute to the country's tourist industry). Ribault sees resilience as a firmly hegemonic construct built around structured power hierarchy ensuring consent to participation, which 'establishes through comanagement of the aftermath [of a disaster] the deresponsibilization of those responsible'.[10] Unpicking the narrative of the Fukushima disaster and its aftermath, Ribault warns against glorifying resilience as an end all and be all of recovery, especially if the toughness and resistance to damages caused by a disaster mean that 'only she or he who knows how to suffer has the ability and the right to survive' (Ribault, 'Resilience', p. 97). While rejecting a fully structured approach to resilience building, Ribault is equally unsympathetic to full decentralisation of the process, considering it as a source of 'illusion of participation', leading to further hegemonic subordination of the already subordinate populations. Osei offers an equally critical view of a decentralised approach to recovery in the CARICOM nations. When Hurricane Ivan made landfall in Jamaica in 2004, the decentralisation of recovery was not managed accordingly, which meant local organisations were not empowered

---

Measure', *Tulane Studies in Social Welfare*, 21:2 (2000), 61–83; Méheux and Parker, 'Tourist Sector Perceptions', pp. 80–3.

9 Mark Pelling and Juha Uitto, 'Small Island Developing States: Natural Disaster Vulnerability and Global Change', *Environmental Hazards*, 3 (2002), 49–61, doi:10.1016/S1464-2867(01)00018-3 (accessed 12 December 2023). See also Boyeong Hong et al., 'Measuring Inequality in Community Resilience to Natural Disasters Using Large Scale Mobility Data', *Nature Communications*, 12 (2021), article 1870, doi:10.1038/s41467-021-22160-w (accessed 12 December 2023); Denise Thompson, 'Compounding Challenges for Disaster Resilience in Small Island Developing States', *Disaster Prevention and Resilience*, 1 (2022),doi:10.20517/dpr.2021.04 (accessed 17 July 2023).

10 Thierry Ribault, 'Resilience in Fukushima', *Alternatives: Global, Local, Political*, 44 (2019), 94–118, doi:10.1177/0304375419853350 (accessed 12 December 2023).

to do anything meaningful and did not have the resources or the knowledge to do so anyway.[11]

However, a number of studies do not have such a grim view of resilience, recognising that there needs to be equitable contribution from both the government agencies and local communities. Collodi et al. emphasise the importance of involving those affected by disasters in the planning process: 'This is necessary for democratic—respecting local agency and ensuring the legitimacy of recovery—and pragmatic—recognising the value of experiential knowledge to learning and building back better—reasons.'[12] While this is a laudable proposition, the practicalities of carrying it out remain a mystery, as many studies turn yet again to the structured top-down approach and put the onus of investment into Emergency Operations Sectors (EOCs), education programmes, emergency operation plans, and recovery efforts back onto the communities' shoulders.[13]

Like Ribault, Manyena et al. note that 'the emergence of the resilience concept has shifted the focus to self-reliance as a counter to vulnerability, particularly for the poor and the marginalised'.[14] This study follows Jones et al.'s view that the bounce back should be not to pre-disaster conditions but to '"bounce forward" and adapt in order to survive by changing its non-essential attributes and rebuilding itself'(Manyena et al., 'Disaster Resilience',

11 Philip Osei, 'Policy Responses, Institutional Networks Management and post-Hurricane Ivan Reconstruction in Jamaica', *Disaster Prevention and Management: An International Journal*, 16 (2007), 217–34.

12 Jason Collodi et al. 'How Do You Build Back Better So No One Is Left Behind? Lessons from Sint Maarten, Dutch Caribbean, following Hurricane Irma', *Disasters*, 45 (2021), 202–23 (p. 204), doi:10.1111/disa.12423 (accessed 12 December 2023). See also Raven Marie Cretney, 'Towards a Critical Geography of Disaster Recovery Politics: Perspectives on Crisis and Hope', *Geography Compass*, 11 (2017), article E12302, and Colin H. Davidson et al., 'Truths and Myths about Community Participation in Post-disaster Housing Projects', *Habitat International*, 31 (2007), 100–15, doi:10.1016/j.habitatint.2006.08.003 (accessed 12 December 2023).

13 See, for example, Christine Beve, 'Introduction to Conceptual Insights and Applications of Resilience', in *Disaster Resiliency: Interdisciplinary Perspectives*, ed. Naim Kapucu et al. (New York: Routledge, 2013), pp. 15–20, doi:10.4324/9780203102459 (accessed 12 December 2023); Frances Edwards, 'All Hazards, Whole Community: Creating Resiliency', in *Disaster Resiliency: Interdisciplinary Perspectives*, edited by Naim Kapucu, Christopher Hawkins, and Fernando Rivera (New York: Routledge, 2013), pp. 21–47, doi:10.4324/9780203102459 (accessed 12 December 2023).

14 Siambabala Bernard Manyena et al., 'Disaster Resilience: A Bounce Back or Bounce Forward Ability?', *Local Environment*, 16 (2011), 417–24 (p. 418), doi:10.1080/13549839.2011.583049 (accessed 12 December 2023).

p. 419). While in principle this is an attractive proposition, who would determine which attributes are 'non-essential'? And would rebuilding itself mean that the community is the one helping itself? Would that then mean that any funding from outside is withdrawn if the community is deemed to be disaster resilient? In some cases, that would be right; in others, the community may only have limited resources rationed among its members—would they be able to bounce forward as successfully as their richer counterparts?

Unfortunately, neither Ribault nor others sharing (or refuting) his view offer solution to what is surely a highly problematic situation that, if left unresolved, can result—and so far, has done so repeatedly—in a long-term social conflict, damaging most significantly those affected the most by disasters. As a result, the concept of resilience emerges from heated academic debates not as a cogent framework ready to provide meaningful support for recovery studies and practice, but as a contentious space of power struggle between the government and the public. In the face of concrete damage by a hurricane, the notion of resilience becomes too ephemeral to be useful. What is resilient for one is a matter of course for another. And what use is an abstract idea of resilience to someone who is bailing water out of their house, hoping they can protect their most valued possessions? We will therefore engage in a theoretical discussion to explore this struggle further and propose an alternative to this stalemate. From Ernesto Laclau's notion of empty signifiers underpinning hegemonic order we will move to the posthegemonic shared emotional spheres and position recovery vis-à-vis these seemingly mutually exclusive power structures in the space where they come together collaboratively rather than confrontationally.

II Resilience as an Empty Signifier?

In *Emancipation(s)*, Laclau argues that a hegemonic relationship is determined and characterised by the process when 'a particular content becomes the signifier of the absent communitarian fullness'[15]—or the signifier that does not have a corresponding signified because it (the signified) does not exist as such. The mechanism of articulation—adapting parts of the discourse to the needs of each subject—becomes the principal characteristic of a class or a party or a political stance (see Ribault, 'Resilience', p. 98). Part of that articulation is the production of empty signifiers: 'The logic of the "empty signifier" [is] the tendential emptying and transcendence of one element within a given signifying chain'[16]—but no signifier can be completely empty, just like

15 Ernesto Laclau, *Emancipation(s)* (London: Verso, 2007), p. 43.

16 Jon Beasley-Murray, *Posthegemony: Political Theory and Latin America* (Minneapolis: University of Minnesota Press, 2010), p. 48.

there is no absolute hegemony. As a signifier is emptied of its meaning, it is filled by another meaning—if it is not it becomes too 'precarious', unable to sustain itself as an articulation space completely void of articulating properties—and when this happens the empty signifier gets hijacked by another power node. And another, and another. And in the end, there is a signifier with multiple fillings, suited to the interests of specific power nodes—much like resilience, the definition of which is a conglomerate of fillings from different power nodes, dominated by structured power on the one hand and by diffused power on the other. This precarious balancing act has no resolution and therefore no usefulness beyond the power node that created it.

Laclau posits that 'the hegemonic operation would be the presentation of the particularity of a group as the incarnation of that empty signifier which refers to the communitarian order as an absence, an unfulfilled reality'(Laclau, *Emancipation(s)*, p. 44). Because of this, hegemony is an unstable construct, 'penetrated by a constitutive ambiguity' (Laclau, *Emancipation(s)*, p. 44). So, resilience in this sense is a hegemonic articulation, 'contingent, precarious and pragmatic' (Laclau, *Emancipation(s)*, p. 90), in that it is never fully realised but designed from the get-go as an achievably useful characteristic of a 'fully constituted structure' of hegemonic order (see Ribault, 'Resilience', p. 97). And by the virtue of being hegemonic, it excludes posthegemonic features of the social condition when knowledge distribution-based power structures are not sustainable because of a significant effect on the social routine. Its rupture and subsequent release of emotions unite the affected social groups into shared emotional spheres with no discernible power locus other than the degree of the emotion they house that replace (at least, for a period of time) the existing knowledge distribution-based structured power of hegemony.[17] As a result, resilience cannot be achieved when posthegemonic order is in full swing—it cannot even be achieved after the initial effect subsides because 'something always escapes' (Beasley-Murray, *Posthegemony*, p. 293). In the case of recovery after a natural disaster, that 'something' is the discourse of the community that needs to reconcile restoring its livelihood with the emotional fallout from the disaster, which, if left unaddressed will continue to be a barrier to the realisation of structured recovery plans when hegemonic order is, at least partially, restored.

But are emotions a barrier? Do shared emotional spheres prevent hegemony from regaining its power? Should they? The answer is probably yes to all three questions but that's because hegemony alone does not support the process of recovery. It is not flexible enough, nor does it account for

17 See Beasley-Murray, *Posthegemony*, pp. 133–37; Victoria Carpenter, *The Tlatelolco Massacre, Mexico 1968, and the Emotional Triangle of Anger, Grief and Shame: Discourses of Truth(s)* (Cardiff: University of Wales Press, 2018), pp. 149–51.

the variety of factors imbuing this period. But—and this is more important than hegemony's inherent inflexibility—there should not be a single order dominating society at this point because there is no hierarchy left. It is either washed away in the storm surge as everyone in the area is being exposed to the same rainfall, wind or storm surge, or it splits into multiple power loci, each carrying with it what is deemed important by those populating it. A local strongman may hold the knowledge necessary to help a community recover but he is not going to share it with the government agencies because he does not trust them as an authority—he is the authority locally and he will not concede it to an outsider. Alternatively, a government agency comes to a community with recovery plans designed without the community's involvement and expects to be received as an authority solely on the strength of them being a government body.

While the state sees resilience as 'an unfulfilled reality' (Laclau, Emancipation(s), p. 44), something to strive for in the face of (and, as Ribault would see it, with the help of) repeated disasters, from the community's perspective resilience is not an external add-on—it is something that is already in the public's character regardless of circumstances, something not related to what the state does. And so it rejects the state's resilience—it has its own and this resilience has nothing to do with the government's agenda. In short, resilience as part of the articulation process of recovery guided by the needs of a structure power node does not work for both social actors because its emptying and refilling excludes the social actors for whom it is apparently devised. These social actors fill it with their own meaning without the input of the structured power node—and so two resiliences end up fighting it out in the articulation field of hegemonic order in an attempt to regain control after the affective clash of social bodies. What can be done to stop or, at least, diminish this conflict? We cannot abandon one meaning to privilege the other, otherwise we will face the problem of unmet demands leading to 'an internal antagonistic frontier separating the "people" from power',[18] which leads to the creation of the enemy construct and whatever rift emerging between the 'people' and structured power deepens to the point of a long-term social conflict. And this is what we are trying to avoid—or, at least, avoid adding to the existing social conflicts by mishandling the complex and perilous period of recovery.

Thus, we propose that a different power sphere governs the recovery process—the one where neither hegemonic nor posthegemonic power structure is in full control. We call it a transhegemonic sphere: it combines the complexity of hegemonic and posthegemonic orders with the instability of transcultural space. Transhegemony arises during the period in between

18 Ernesto Laclau, *On Populist Reason* (London: Verso, 2005), p. 74.

the turmoil of posthegemonic affective clash and the stability of hegemonic knowledge distribution—the period when neither order can sustain control over the uncertainty of the relationship between the two social actors navigating this space. This is a period of precarious balance between the two orders, fraught with potential conflicts but also offering the promise of collaboration: '[t]ranshegemony extends this period of balance to allow both sides to shed their preconceived roles of domination/subordination and for the collaborative stability to allow the period of recovery to run its course quickly and efficiently'.[19] It is populated by knowledge exchange and shared emotions in equal measure; it is also characterised by a balance between turmoil and stability.[20] The turmoil aspect of transhegemony is in the language of the shared emotions of frustration, unity, defiance, pride, self-investment, determination, and planning, of which defiance and pride are at the centre of the transhegemonic space (see Carpenter, 'Dancing in a Hurricane'). The stability of transhegemony is in the combination of the language of balance, empathy, and 'you'; these factors temper the turmoil of emotions so that they do not spill into a conflict. There is a gradual shift from the dominance of shared emotions with little knowledge exchange from frustration and unity (the strongest posthegemonic factors) to determination and planning (the strongest hegemonic factors).

III State Discourse of Recovery: Jamaica = Resilience

The theme of resilience appears in a number of texts from the state discourse of recovery after hurricanes in Jamaica, starting with Gilbert (1988), the worst hurricane in twentieth-century Jamaica and the second worst in the country's history (following the Great Storm of 1780). This Category 5 storm made landfall in Jamaica on 12 September 1988 and zigzagged across the island before progressing to the Yucatán peninsula in Mexico. It killed forty-nine people, destroyed three quarters of Jamaica's housing stock, and devastated the country's agriculture and tourism industry.[21] The next hurricane of similar proportions was Ivan (2004), skirting the island on 9–12 September without making landfall. However, rain and high winds (with

19 Victoria Carpenter, 'Dancing in a Hurricane: State and Public Responses to Hurricane Gilbert in Jamaica', *Caribbean Quarterly*, 68 (2022), 44–66 (p. 61).

20 See Gareth Williams, *The Other Side of the Popular: Neoliberalism and Subalternity in Latin America* (Durham, NC: Duke University Press, 2002), p. 26.

21 See Klaus Meyer-Arendt, 'Hurricane Gilbert: The Storm of the Century', *GeoJournal*, 23 (1991), 323–35, doi:10.1007/BF00193605 (accessed 12 December 2023).

gusts up to 340 km/h) caused widespread floods, killing fifteen people and wreaking havoc across the island to the cost of eight per cent of Jamaican GDP, or J$38 billion.[22] Ivan was followed by Dean, the ninth worst hurricane in the history of Atlantic storms. Dean made landfall in Jamaica on 19 August 2007, destroying crops, flooding the low-lying areas of St Thomas and St Catherine parishes, and damaging sixty per cent of the country's housing stock.[23]

In the state discourse of recovery, resilience is a common term used to denote a desirable quality of a community fighting back after being devastated by the forces beyond its control. In the wake of Hurricane Gilbert (1988), Prime Minister Michael Manley released the following statement:

> [Gilbert] tested the courage, fortitude and resilience of Jamaicans. It was a test, while difficult, our nation passed with flying colours. This is not to say that all the damage done by the hurricane has been repaired. ... However, in the main, the Jamaican people were able to pick themselves up and start anew with vigour and determination. ... As I write today, six months after the hurricane, Jamaican people are rapidly putting the finishing touches to plans that will not just restore economic activity to pre-Gilbert levels but surpass them. Again it is a testimony to the nation's resilience.[24]

Resilience is associated with 'vigour and determination', being able to 'rapidly' work on plans to restore the economy and to 'surpass [pre-Gilbert levels of economic activity]'. This is seen as 'the nation's resilience'—while not defined, it is definitely something to be proud of ('passed with flying colours', 'testimony to the nation's resilience'). It is also a trait that unifies the country ('our nation'). 'Pick themselves up' indicates the ability to react with positive action to the destruction caused by Gilbert. 'Start anew' suggests that the destruction was significant—but people are working to build back

22 'Hurricane Ivan: Vulnerability of Women and Children', University of the West Indies, https://www.uwi.edu/ekacdm/node/277 (accessed 17 July 2023). See also Anthony McKenzie, 'Beach Responses to Hurricane Impacts: A Case Study of Long Bay Beach, Negril, Jamaica', *Caribbean Journal of Earth Science*, 43 (2012), 51–8; Belkis Enidian Romero Pino, 'Impacto económico a largo plazo de los huracanes Iván y Dean en Jamaica', *Revista de Economía del Caribe*, 29 (2022), 50–75, doi:10.14482/ecoca.29.041.423 (accessed 12 December 2023).

23 Donovan Campbell and Clinton Beckford, 'Negotiating Uncertainty: Jamaican Small Farmers' Adaptation and Coping Strategies, Before and After Hurricanes—A Case Study of Hurricane Dean', *Sustainability*, 1 (2009), 1366–87, doi:10.3390/su1041366 (accessed 12 December 2023).

24 Bob Hill, Bob Ogley, and Joan Hooley, *Hurricane Gilbert* (Westerham: Froglets Publications, 1989), p. 95.

better, to use a rather hackneyed phrase. To sum up, resilience for Manley is a combination of bounce back and speed of action, both very desirable on the one hand (because they speed up recovery), and potentially psychologically damaging, as Ribault argues, because they necessitate 'the people to look only to the future—a key feature of the resilience paradigm—and to keep all their experiences silent' (Ribault, 'Resilience', p. 100). However, as we will see, this is not necessarily the case for Jamaica. My previous analysis of the state, media and public discourses of recovery after Gilbert indicated that these components are steeped in the original experience of the storm and its aftermath, so it is logical to conclude that all three discourses rely to varying degrees on the emotional components of recovery when negotiating this contentious space (Carpenter, 'Dancing in a Hurricane').

In an analysis of response strategies after natural disasters in the Caribbean, Jeremy Collymore (coordinator of the Caribbean Disaster Emergency Response Agency (CDERA)), focuses on how best to create a recovery plan fit for purpose across the small-island nation territory. This report, written in 2008, compiles data on major floods, storms and hurricanes affecting Jamaica between 1979 and 2005. During this period, the two most destructive hurricanes were Gilbert (1988) and Ivan (2004); of these, Gilbert was by far the worst of the two, costing Jamaica sixty-five per cent of its GDP.[25]

When discussing successful ways of addressing recovery after natural disasters, Collymore sees the need for 'a set of core values and principles that inform the phenomenology, which underpins the development process. Hence, the issue of governance becomes central, as we seek to address the issues of organisational and distributional equity that will naturally surface in this realignment of the development agenda' (Collymore, 'Beyond Humanitarianism', p. 250). The use of 'we' suggests unity of action not just by relevant agencies but by all involved in the process of recovery. However, whose values is he referring to? And how will equity surface 'naturally'? Is there a belief that the values and principles will be the same on both sides, formulated the same way and meaning the same thing? Since Collymore's focus is on the government structure and national infrastructure rather than communities, there is no evidence that his proposal goes beyond national governance and economic development. One could argue that with a robust infrastructure and support communities will flourish and recover quicker

25 Jeremy Collymore, 'Beyond Humanitarianism: Building Resilient Communities, Revisiting the Development Dialogue', in *Enduring Geohazards in the Caribbean: Moving from the Reactive to the Proactive*, ed. Serwan M. J. Baban (Kingston: University of the West Indies Press, 2008), pp. 244–54 (p. 246), doi: 10.3763/ehaz.2011.0002 (accessed 12 December 2022), citing CDERA, 'Caribbean Community Regional Programme Network 2005–2015', Second World Conference on Disaster Reduction (Kobe, 2005).

after hurricanes. But that is not a given, especially since there is plenty of evidence that these plans have never been translated fully into actions—and where they have they did not benefit all strata of society.[26]

Following the aforementioned focus on risk management and disaster effect reduction, Collymore sees resilience as 'tak[ing] away the emphasis from disaster losses and focus[ing] it in a search for patterns of human organization and relationships that may reduce the cost of disaster' (Collymore, 'Beyond Humanitarianism', p. 251). This suggests both a top-down and bottom-up approach—top-down in that there is an indication of assessment of cost (best done in a planned and informed way), and a reference to human relationships, which would point to community collaboration (people getting together to help each other out). But the top-down structured approach prevails in the sense of planning ('patterns' and 'organisations'), so bottom-up collaboration is secondary to it.

Another quote suggests a combination of top-down and bottom-up approaches but then leans almost immediately to the former: 'Two critical steps are necessary to pursue a development dialogue anchored in the principles of resilience: Formulation of a national disaster management policy. … Development of a national economy preparedness programme and plan. This will outline the steps in implementing the national disaster management policy' (Collymore, 'Beyond Humanitarianism', p. 251). The dialogue, it would seem, is going to be between various government entities rather than between government entities and local population. Emphasis on 'a development philosophy and approach centred on the generation of resilience, in all aspects of the society and economy, [acting] as a bridge for structuring a pragmatic agenda for reshaping the loss profile of our national economies' (Collymore, 'Beyond Humanitarianism', pp. 253–4) supports this interpretation—resilience is about economy plans rather than communities. And this is fine, as long as this process is equitably beneficial for all social strata without becoming an abstract notion of improving 'the loss profile of our national economies'.

The combination of top-down and bottom-up approaches to community improvement is at the core of the Jamaican Social Investment Fund's (JSIF) mission. Established in 1996, JSIF is an agency managing a national partnership between central government, parish councils, private and international funders, and local communities to deliver community improvement projects.[27] While not involved directly with recovery projects, JSIF works to

26 Pelling and Uitto, 'Small Island Developing States'; Cretney, 'Disaster Recovery Politics'; Thompson, 'Compounding Challenges'.

27 See Philip Osei, 'The Community Leadership Model and Country Ownership of Local Development in Jamaica', *Social and Economic Studies,* 59 (2010),

improve community infrastructure so that it can withstand regular impacts of natural disasters and last longer under constant use. In an interview with two project managers (hereafter JS1 and JS2) in 2019, it was noted that recovery is more important than response because it provides long-term stability and may rectify other problems, like poverty: 'focus right on improving adaptation', 'improve the resilience of the community'; vulnerability of low-income female-headed households is rooted in long-term poverty and unemployment (JS1). JSIF also ensures that the community owns the project from the onset:

> There are other projects that are open, where we get the funding to fund specific types of activity, to improve roads, water, agriculture, and then the community will determine what their NEEDS are and then they apply to us instead of what we need, this is what the community needs and we go and do the assessment to ensure that whatever they are saying is legitimate and we have discussions and we fund the project if it meets the requirements. So, it comes sometimes from top down, other times from bottom up. (JS1).

> I think a big part of all these projects is that even if the persons who are trained they leave or pass on, it's really building their capacity so it's hoped as best as possible that they transfer the knowledge and skills to other persons in the community. Of course, that might be the area where we can trace so many people and do more, literally. But we definitely try to have that as part of every single project because it is really for them to be resilient and to have an interest in what is presented to them and this is why the approach that we take is taken, literally because we don't want to just give them something and say here you look after it. You want to be involved from the start, you want to be involved from even picking it or deciding what is exactly the scope, so when it's left it's not like someone just came and invaded—you are part of it, it's for you, it's yours. (JS2)

In JS2's quote, 'their capacity' is closely related to self-reliance; then buy-in is added ('have an interest in what is presented to them'), so resilience combines owning the project and continuing to implement it because it is now 'their' project. Ownership is part of self-reliance: if a community owns a project and its outcomes they make it part of their space and rely on it later to help them get through the recovery period. Whatever is adopted becomes 'yours'—but is it for sure that what is adopted is what is given in the first place? Do the givers know what to give so that the takers can adopt it and make it theirs and use it later? In the case of JSIF's work, this is indeed the case and their success in building relationships with local communities attests

97–126 (p. 111), access link: https://www.jstor.org/stable/41803729 (accessed 12 December 2023).

to it and indicates self-investment on behalf of the communities. However, if we consider a wider practice and the current state of play in the recovery and resilience literature, the answer is, unfortunately, no.

When JSIF managers were asked what resilience meant, their responses were very similar: it is 'about your capacity or ability to get back to where you were or to move past the situation that you got yourself into ...; [it] is the ability to bounce back' (JS2); 'it's to be able to sustain regardless of whatever, being able to overcome whatever adversity you go through, whether it is from climate change, a natural disaster, you're able to recover and be better than you were even before ... Being able to survive whatever the issue is' (JS1). There is a strong sense of determination in JS1's response: the use of 'whatever' in 'whatever adversity you go through' and 'whatever the issue is' indicates strength of character and defiance in the face of any challenge. This combination of bounce back and determination reflects Michael Manley's view of Jamaican resilience.

In summary, the state discourse of recovery after hurricanes presents the emotional spectrum associated with resilience as unity, pride, self-investment, determination and planning. Pride dominates this spectrum and resilience is seen as a desirable trait to develop and foster in the underserved communities.

IV Media Discourse of Recovery: Making Do with What Little Is Left

Another significant contribution to the discourse of resilience comes from the media coverage of Jamaican hurricanes. Situated between the state and public discourses, the media holds a two-pronged position. A previous analysis of the state, media and public reaction to Hurricane Gilbert hitting Jamaica in 1988, concludes that while leaning heavily towards the state view of the disaster and its aftermath, 'newspapers' own narrative ... could be construed ... as representing either the state or the public sentiment' (Carpenter, 'Dancing in a Hurricane', p. 51).[28] We shall follow the same path of enquiry, indicating where the newspaper coverage of recovery after hurricanes represents the views of Jamaican government or local communities. To this end, we will consider the coverage of Hurricane Gilbert in the *Daily Gleaner* (renamed *The Gleaner* in 1992). Founded in 1834, it is Jamaica's main newspaper and key source of information across the island and in expat communities. Outside Jamaica, *The Weekly Gleaner* and *The*

28 See also Brittany Forsythe, 'Tensions between Media Censorship and Regulation in Jamaica', *Media Development*, 66:3 (2020), 44–7, for a wider discussion of media regulation and freedom of expression in Jamaica.

Weekly Gleaner with North America Extra publish the main news of interest to the West Indian communities in the UK and USA respectively.[29]

The media presents self-reliance as a synonym for resilience; Carl Stone's article 'A Story of Resilience', published in *The Gleaner* on 29 November 1988, just over two months after Gilbert, is a telling example of this approach. Self-reliance surfaces because government aid is slow in reaching the affected communities, so 'for the time being people are surviving on the basis of self-reliance'. It is a necessary evil rather than a desirable characteristic—one has to do what is necessary to recover because help is not forthcoming. And for some, it will not be forthcoming for a long time: 'in December 1988 it was reported that an estimated 1,000 households were still living in various shelters throughout the island. The number dwindled slowly but in March there were 180 Gilbert victims under the concrete shelter of the national stadium in Kingston and the minister responsible made it clear that every effort was being made to relocate them' (Hill et al., *Gilbert*, p. 93). It is unclear how many people the 1,000 households entailed but it is clear that, while 'hotels re-opened and the tourist industry prepared for a successful year' (Hill et al., *Gilbert*, p. 7), the immediate problem of making sure everyone still in shelters could go back home to decent accommodation was not solved. One cannot help wondering whether the financial benefits of letting tourists come back to the island outweighed the government's responsibility to serve all of its citizens, as pledged by Sir Florizel Glasspole, Jamaica's governor general, when he took office in 1962.[30]

Stone sees this self-reliance as the trait specific to the poor population: 'a quiet, unrecorded effort by people in poor communities to help themselves in the absence of the tangible help from government'. Those who have the least have to improvise the most, be the most self-reliant (read: resilient), so that they minimise the suffering of their families, friends, and so forth, while the government is bickering about whose face should appear on the aid packages in the run-up to the 1988 elections. Stone's reaction to this is rather bitter: 'The hardships being experienced are reinforcing that understanding, that after the politicians have got their votes and won elections, the poor for the most part have to fend for themselves.' This is why shifting the onus of developing resilience onto the most underserved is a cop-out: the government stepped up its efforts when it needed to and then the poor can fend for themselves because they are no longer important to the

29 See Linda Cameron, ed., *The Story of the Gleaner: Memoirs and Reminiscences* (Kingston: Gleaner Co., 2000) for more information on the history of *The Gleaner* and its impact in Jamaica.

30 See David Clement, *An Analysis of Disaster: Hurricane Gilbert* (Kingston: Institute of Social and Economic Studies, University of West Indies, 1990), p. vii.

government's agenda. There is a strong sense of frustration with the lack of action on behalf of the government, who chooses to 'bicker' instead of helping those directly affected by Gilbert.

Out of the necessity to survive, people in underserved communities come together and help each other with what little they have (however it was purloined)—but this is not a sustainable way to recover after a disaster. It is to be commended with pride—'the quiet initiatives towards self-reliance, in which poor people have relied on their own effort to put their lives back into some ordered pattern … is the untold positive story about "Gilbert" that more than balances all the negatives that have been covered in the media'—but it cannot be the only way forward. Perhaps '[the country's poor people's] resilience and survival instincts rather than the state handouts … is the basis of the rapid strides towards normality', but when communities are left with no choice but to help themselves by whatever means necessary we should turn to the government agencies for answers rather than just applaud the people's efforts. A similar sentiment is expressed in the story of an initiative in the Portland parish on the eastern coast of Jamaica—a rural area some way away from the capital, where 'the "woeful" lack of preparedness' led to the local population feeling abandoned by the centre 'and the parish quickly established its own hurricane relief association in an attempt to improve supplies to those in dire need' (Hill et al, *Gilbert*, p. 92). The quote presents frustration ('the "woeful" lack of preparedness'), pride ('quickly'), self-investment ('its own'), and planning ('in an attempt to improve supplies'). While it is laudable that a relatively poor parish could put its resources together to help those worst affected, the lack of centralised effort to help everyone regardless of how close they are to Kingston contributes to the misery of the communities trying hard to keep going after losing their dwellings and livelihood.

There is plenty of pride of the communities not sitting and waiting for handouts. This pride is not calling attention to itself when Stone notes that 'quiet initiatives' become 'the basis of the rapid strides towards normality'. It is also mixed in with defiance: the communities do this because they need to and they do not expect anyone to applaud their efforts. Defiance is also seen in how government aid is described: 'state handouts', 'while the politicians gear up for massive aid programmes'—it is either seen as demeaning ('handouts') or too much of an effort on the government's part to be of practical use. And in the end it is accepted (grudgingly perhaps) but is seen as an add-on. However, if we compare this view to JSIF's perspective discussed above, the same notion of owning recovery efforts can be seen as both a cross to bear because of the lack of help from the state and a desired outcome of a jointly created and run community improvement project. Regardless of the reasons for self-reliance, it is a reason to feel proud of oneself and one's community.

Resilience is also alluded to in the final paragraph of 'The reconstruction of the economy' by Peter Phillips (*The Gleaner*, 25 October 1988). He connects self-reliance as an 'attitude of mind' to the need to 'determin[e] our own priorities for action'—which indicates planning based on critical evaluation of what is in place and what is needed. There is also defiance in 'our OWN priorities'—the communities are the ones determining them, not waiting for someone to come along and do it, thus making the community comply with something they do not own. This stance is echoed in JSIF managers' responses, which emphasise the need for the community to buy into the project from the onset and own its outcomes. Pride and self-investment are evidence in 'our own'—we create these, we know what we are doing and we are proud of this, along with the fact that our 'attitude of mind' makes it possible. Pride is also implied in the derision towards 'handouts from abroad' ('determining our own priorities for action, rather than waiting on handouts from abroad')—a perspective similar to Stone's mention of 'handouts' from the government.

Stone's article 'The Challenge of Rebuilding' (*The Gleaner*, 4 October 1988) adds another dimension to pride by pairing it with the feeling of derision:

> Wringing our hands and wallowing in self-pity about being hit by the most powerful storm in this hemisphere since this century are hardly going to help us to recover by discovering the inner resources and determination needed to bounce back. Aid and outside assistance will help a great deal but if the whole exercise becomes another chapter in the book of total dependence on external solutions and the ever-present hat in hand to receive aid, we will not recover.

The images of 'wringing hands', 'wallowing in self-pity', and 'the ever-present hat in hand' reveal deep disdain for inaction, whereas 'inner resources and determination' speak to the unified image of Jamaica as a nation willing and able to look after itself. However, both sets of images refer to the same country: 'we' are both guilty of wringing our hands and expecting handouts, and proud of being capable to deal with our problems ourselves. This self-contradictory image of Jamaica is absent from both the state and public discourses: they present Jamaica's self-reliance as its key trait to be proud of. However, the press sees self-reliance as a result of the population being trapped in the conditions of abject poverty and disillusionment with the government that does not serve all its citizens equitably. It also considers self-pity and helplessness just as intrinsic to the country's nature as self-reliance and determination, offering a much more complex view of Jamaica's national character than that painted in the state discourse.

The emotional spectrum of the media discourse of recovery is frustration, unity, defiance, pride (accompanied by derision), self-investment and planning. The pride/derision combination drives this spectrum, adding a significant degree of self-criticism, largely absent from the state and public discourse. Self-reliance is used as a full synonym of resilience at the expense of all other factors, and presented as a survival tool used out of sheer desperation in the face of the government's inaction.

V Public Discourse of Recovery: Where Has Resilience Gone?

In the public discourse, the term resilience is all but non-existent. In 2019 and 2022 we collected six group and individual interviews with residents in Portmore and Old Harbour Bay (St Catherine parish), Yallahs (St Thomas parish), Rocky Point (Clarendon parish), and Trench Town (St Andrew parish), totalling twenty-eight participants. Of these, there is only one transcript where a respondent uses the word 'resilience'; other texts contain the components of resilience without directly referring to it. It is possible that the term is not used widely in spoken language; it is also possible that the term is so strongly associated with the state discourse as to be all but meaningless outside of it.

We will start by considering the only text containing the word 'resilience'. A group interview was conducted with ten representatives of Rocky Point (hereafter RP1—RP10), a small fishing community of around 3,000 in Clarendon Parish, Jamaica. Located in the low-lying area on the southern shore of Clarendon, this village is in the path of hurricanes and tropical storms; with no mountains to protect it, it suffers frequent wind damage when a storm passes. Many residents have had their houses damaged or destroyed by high winds during various hurricanes; the most common damage caused by a hurricane or tropical storm is to the roof. If the roof is torn off the house the rest of the structure either collapses or is rendered uninhabitable unless a new roof is installed. And this takes time and money, which means that interim measures have to be taken to ensure that at least some possessions are kept safe and people have somewhere to sleep. In some cases, a makeshift roof of tarpaulin and plywood would be erected and remain in place for years. While for some residents this was a cause of constant frustration, others saw this ability to make do with what they had a positive trait uniting the community:

> Well, if I may say, Rocky Point people are very resilient. They do not really wait that much for help to come. They try to help themselves. And so when help come it's just additional. As soon as the storm was over people were out there, trying to get back their lives together whatever they could find, they were trying to put something back together to start the ball rolling,

> trying to see what they could save and as soon as it was possible to go back to venture out they were out. Very resilient, very resilient. (RP5)

Here, collective effort in the form of self-investment and determination is about giving one's time and resources to help others and doing so together as a community; this attitude is similar to that expressed in Carl Stone's article 'A Story of Resilience'. The feeling of pride and defiance is very strong: the community fends for itself because nobody will help it so it defies others' expectations that the residents will sit and wait for help. Instead, the community helps itself with what limited resources it has after a destructive storm ('whatever they could find'). But to do so means planning and sharing knowledge with those involved in the process: 'start the ball rolling' implies that there is a starting point and therefore a general plan as to what happens next.

This stance is similar to that of a respondent from Portmore, a large residential community (over 160,000) on the outskirts of Kingston. It consists of two parts: a less populated hilly zone and a denser populated shoreline area in the low-lying reclaimed land; this zone is prone to flooding and standing water after storms. When asked about his experience with recovery after hurricanes, he began with 'we in the community—well, that's the important one—we in the community we like to help ourself'. He expresses defiance in the face of the government's actions not accepted by the community ('what's wrong now, the government said it wants to take us out of the community and want to put us in um … you'd call it place of safety'). The reference to being taken 'out of the community' suggests forceful displacement rather than protection, so the community does not consent even if it is the best option. The community rallies together: 'nobody would sleep, everybody would like cook and give one another and if your clothes wet, you know, here's the neighbour clothes and such delight'. Sharing and working together is a positive action ('such delight'), even though there is a tinge of irony here because the circumstances are not the most positive ones: you might not want to wear your neighbour's clothes but you do not have many other options if all your clothes are wet. And government help is not forthcoming, not even well after the hurricane: 'they didn't send anybody to fix up anybody's house, we have to do it yourself'; this echoes Stone's depiction of poor communities rallying together when help was not coming quickly enough. Local politicians are not particularly involved in supporting Portmore beyond getting votes during election time ('when voting time you see them come around and them want to know all these things and tell you, remember to vote for me'). But when it comes to action, the community does it: 'when [local government] are supposed to chuff up the place nothing like that happen. They're supposed to clean the gulley—we, individuals who live in the community, we shuffle and clean the gulley'. 'Shuffle' suggests a degree of frustration with having to do someone else's job but it gets done by the community anyway because the community needs it. While this is similar to JSIF's focus on the community's interest in the projects, the problem is that there is no governmental input in Portmore. Here, the locals are supposed to be 'resilient' by the virtue of not only owning community projects but also initiating them and investing into them. While it may be fine to invest one's time, what about the equipment and materials needed to deliver? It would appear that the community is expected to provide this from what little they may have.

In a letter to the editor of *The Gleaner* on 18 October 1988, a month after Hurricane Gilbert, Tanya Green adds to the discussion of the community supporting each other: 'hurricane Gilbert has helped Jamaicans to unite and come together as one to build back one big, beautiful Jamaica'; people have been able to 'organise humbly and communicate together in time of trouble.' This echoes what Respondent 5 from Rocky Point and the representative from Portmore were saying about working together. Also, Green's admiration for 'so many people visiting each other's homes, finding out what is needed and if they are able to help' is similar to the account from Portmore about people cooking together and sharing dry clothes and furniture with those less fortunate.

Overall, the language of resilience in the public discourse is dominated by self-reliance and unity of action in the face of the government's inaction (either real or perceived). This is somewhat similar to the media's view; however, the public discourse associates resilience with the sense of both frustration and pride, combining the state and media perspectives. This suggests that all three discourses agree to a certain degree on the nature of resilience and emotions associated with it.

VI Conclusion: From Self-reliance to Collaboration

Comparing the language used by the state and the public to describe resilience, we note that both social actors present resilience as self-reliance allowing those affected by hurricanes to return to a relatively normal life that is expected to be an improvement on the communities' previous socio-economic conditions. Both the state and public texts concede that the recovery period requires structured organisation and emotional commitment in equal measure—the structured aspect will establish the order of actions needed to restore the living conditions and make them more sustainable than before the hurricane, and the emotional aspect will make sure this order is taken up by its beneficiaries and accepted fully, like the JSIF projects established by JSIF and maintained by the community. In fact, JSIF's work is a good example of transhegemonic coordination with both sides making equal contribution in terms of effort and commitment, and the government providing most of materials and finances to support the projects.

Self-reliance in all three discourses is characterised by the full range of emotions associated with the transhegemonic space. The areas where the state, media and public discourses converge fully are unity, pride, self-investment and planning. Our analysis has also shown that the language used to express these emotions is similar across the three discourses; this offers a possibility of establishing shared emotional spheres populated by the four emotions through the use of combined language. In practice, this can be accomplished by compiling a language pack of the shared emotions and using it to develop a mediation training programme designed to present the participants of negotiations during recovery periods with the vocabulary encompassing language of the emotional spectrum from both social actors. By using this language, those participating in the negotiation will generate a shared emotional sphere in which both social actors' language of specific emotions will be accommodated, thus making them feel and express the same emotions in the same way. This should lead to the formation of stable transhegemonic space where the two social actors experience the same emotions, voice them with the same language, and collaborate rather than fall into confrontation.

Bibliography

Beasley-Murray, Jon, *Posthegemony: Political Theory and Latin America* (Minneapolis: University of Minnesota Press, 2010).

Beve, Christine, 'Introduction to Conceptual Insights and Applications of Resilience', in *Disaster Resiliency: Interdisciplinary Perspectives*, edited by Naim Kapucu, Christopher Hawkins, and Fernando Rivera (New York: Routledge, 2013), pp. 15–20, doi:10.4324/9780203102459 (accessed 12 December 2023).

Cameron, Linda, ed. *The Story of the Gleaner: Memoirs and Reminiscences* (Kingston: Gleaner Co., 2000).

Campbell, Donovan, and Clinton Beckford, 'Negotiating Uncertainty: Jamaican Small Farmers' Adaptation and Coping Strategies, Before and After Hurricanes—A Case Study of Hurricane Dean', *Sustainability*, 1 (2009), 1366–87, doi:10.3390/su1041366 (accessed 12 December 2023).

Carby, Barbara, *Jamaica's Experience with Hurricane Ivan: The Case for Mitigation and Preparedness Programmes* (Kingston: Caribbean Disaster Emergency Response Agency, 2005).

Carpenter, Victoria , *The Tlatelolco Massacre, Mexico 1968, and the Emotional Triangle of Anger, Grief and Shame: Discourses of Truth(s)* (Cardiff: University of Wales Press, 2018).

Carpenter, Victoria, 'Dancing in a Hurricane: State and Public Responses to Hurricane Gilbert in Jamaica', *Caribbean Quarterly*, 68 (2022), 44–66.

CDERA, 'Caribbean Community Regional Programme Network 2005–2015', Second World Conference on Disaster Reduction (Kobe, 2005), https://www.preventionweb.net/files/27593_caribbeancommunityregionalprogramme.pdf (accessed 27 March 2024).

Chandra, Anita, Joie Acosta, Stefanie Howard, Lori Uscher-Pines, Malcolm Williams, Douglas Yeung, Jeffrey Garnett, and Lisa S. Meredith, 'Building Community Resilience to Disasters: A Way Forward to Enhance National Health Security', *Rand Health Quarterly*, 1 (2011), https://www.ncbi.nlm.nih.gov/pmc/articles/PMC4945213/ (accessed 25 January 2023).

Clement, David, *An Analysis of Disaster: Hurricane Gilbert* (Kingston: Institute of Social and Economic Studies, University of West Indies, 1990).

Coles, Eve, and Philip Buckle, 'Developing Community Resilience as a Foundation for Effective Disaster Recovery', *Australian Journal of Emergency Management*, 19 (2004), 6–15. doi:10.3316/ielapa.375435145094637 (accessed 12 December 2023).

Collodi, Jason, Mark Pelling, Arabella Fraser, Maud Borie, and Simone Di Vicenz, 'How Do You Build Back Better So No One Is Left Behind? Lessons from Sint Maarten, Dutch Caribbean, following Hurricane Irma', *Disasters*, 45 (2021), 202–23, doi:10.1111/disa.12423 (accessed 12 December 2023).

Collymore, Jeremy, 'Beyond Humanitarianism: Building Resilient Communities, Revisiting the Development Dialogue', in *Enduring Geohazards in the Caribbean: Moving from the Reactive to the Proactive*, edited by Serwan M. J. Baban (Kingston: University of the West Indies Press, 2008), pp. 244–54, doi:10.3763/ehaz.2011.0002 (accessed 12 December 2022).

Cretney, Raven Marie, 'Towards a Critical Geography of Disaster Recovery Politics: Perspectives on Crisis and Hope', *Geography Compass*, 11 (2017), https://doi.org/10.1111/gec3.12302 (accessed 17 June 2024)

Davidson, Colin, Cassidy Johnson, Gonzalo Lizarralde, Nese Dikmen, and Alicia Sliwinski, 'Truths and Myths about Community Participation in Post-disaster Housing Projects', *Habitat International*, 31 (2007), 100–15, doi:10.1016/j.habitatint.2006.08.003 (accessed 12 December 2023).

Edwards, Frances, 'All Hazards, Whole Community: Creating Resiliency', in *Disaster Resiliency: Interdisciplinary Perspectives*, edited by Naim Kapucu, Christopher Hawkins, and Fernando Rivera (New York: Routledge, 2013), pp. 21–47.

Forsythe, Brittany, 'Tensions between Media Censorship and Regulation in Jamaica', *Media Development*, 66:3 (2020), 44–7.

Harrell, Evelyn B., and Michael J. Zakour, 'Including Informal Organizations in Disaster Planning: Development of a Range-of-Type Measure', *Tulane Studies in Social Welfare*, 21:2 (2000), 61–83.

Hill, Bob, Bob Ogley, and Joan Hooley, *Hurricane Gilbert* (Westerham: Froglets Publications, 1989).

Holling, C. S., 'Resilience and Stability of Ecological Systems', *Annual Review of Ecology and Systematics*, 4 (1973), 1–23, http://www.jstor.org/stable/2096802.(accessed 12 December 2023).

Hong, Boyeong, Bartosz Bonczak, Arpit Gupta, and Constantine Kontokosta, 'Measuring Inequality in Community Resilience to Natural Disasters Using Large Scale Mobility Data', *Nature Communications*, 12 (2021), article 1870, doi:10.1038/s41467-021-22160-w (accessed 12 December 2023).

'Hurricane Ivan: Vulnerability of Women and Children', The University of the West Indies, https://www.uwi.edu/ekacdm/node/277 (accessed 17 July 2023).

Jones, Eleanor, Kristina Doughorty, and Pietra Brown, '"Building Back Better" in the Context of Multi-hazards in the Caribbean', *Disasters*, 46 (2022), 151–65.

Keck, Markus, and Patrick Sakdapolrak, 'What is Social Resilience? Lesson Learned and Ways Forward', *Erdkunde*, 67 (2013), 5–19, doi:10.3112/erdkunde.2013.01.02 (accessed 12 December 2023).

Laclau, Ernesto , *On Populist Reason* (London: Verso, 2005).

Laclau, Ernesto, *Emancipation(s)* (London: Verso, 2007).

Leroy, Jeanne, Jim Amdal, Marc Vuillet, Jean-Marie Cariolet, Youssef Diab, and Vincent Becue, 'Vulnerability and Social Resilience: Comparison of Two Neighborhoods in New Orleans after Hurricane Katrina', E3S Web of Conferences, 7 (2016), article 08002.

Lucero Álvarez, Adolfo, Columba Rodríguez Allison, Oscar Fausto Martínez, José Luis Aparicio López, Alejandro Díaz Garry, and Maximino Reyes Umaña, 'Recognition of Factors that Promote Resilience to Hurricanes', *Regions and Cohesion*, 11:2 (2021), 26–56, doi:10.3167/reco.2021.110203 (accessed 12 December 2023).

Manyena, Siambabala Bernard, Geoff O'Brien, Phil O'Keefe, and Joanne Rose, 'Disaster Resilience: A Bounce Back or Bounce Forward Ability?', *Local Environment,* 16 (2011), 417–24, doi:10.1080/13549839.2011.583049 (accessed 12 December 2023).

McKenzie, Anthony, 'Beach Responses to Hurricane Impacts: A Case Study of Long Bay Beach, Negril, Jamaica', *Caribbean Journal of Earth Science*, 43 (2012), 51–8.

Méheux, Kirstie, and El Parker, 'Tourist Sector Perceptions of Natural Hazards in Vanuatu and the Implications for a Small Island Developing State', *Tourism Management*, 27 (2006), 69–85, doi:10.1016/j.tourman.2004.07.009 (accessed 12 December 2023).

Meyer-Arendt, Klaus, 'Hurricane Gilbert: The Storm of the Century', *GeoJournal*, 23 (1991), 323–35, doi:10.1007/BF00193605 (accessed 12 December 2023).

Osei, Philip, 'Policy Responses, Institutional Networks Management and post-Hurricane Ivan Reconstruction in Jamaica', *Disaster Prevention and Management: An International Journal*, 16 (2007), 217–34.

Osei, Philip, 'The Community Leadership Model and Country Ownership of Local Development in Jamaica', *Social and Economic Studies*, 59 (2010), 97–126, https://www.jstor.org/stable/41803729 (accessed 12 December 2023).

Özerdem, Alpaslan, 'Disaster as Manifestation of Unresolved Development Challenges: The Marmara Earthquake, Turkey', in *Natural Disasters and Development in a Globalizing World*, edited by Mark Pelling (London: Routledge, 2003), pp. 199–213.

Parker, Dennis, 'Disaster Resilience—a Challenged Science', *Environmental Hazards*, 19 (2019), 1–9, doi:10.1080/17477891.2019.1694857 (accessed 12 December 2023).

Pelling, Mark, and Juha Uitto, 'Small Island Developing States: Natural Disaster Vulnerability and Global Change', *Environmental Hazards*, 3 (2002), 49–61, doi:10.1016/S1464-2867(01)00018-3 (accessed 12 December 2023).

Pyles, Loretta, 'Community Organizing for Post-disaster Social Development: Locating Social Work', *International Social Work*, 50 (2007), 321–33, doi:10.1177/0020872807076044 (accessed 12 December 2023).

Ribault, Thierry , *Contre la résilience. À Fukushima et ailleurs* (Paris, L'Échappée, 2021).

Ribault, Thierry, 'Resilience in Fukushima', *Alternatives: Global, Local, Political*, 44 (2019), 94–118, doi:10.1177/0304375419853350 (accessed 12 December 2023).

Romero Pino, and Belkis Enidian, 'Impacto económico a largo plazo de los huracanes Iván y Dean en Jamaica', *Revista de Economía del Caribe*, 29 (2022), 50–75, doi:10.14482/ecoca.29.041.423 (accessed 12 December 2023).

Southwick, Steven, Ann Masten, George Bonanno, Catherine Panter-Brick, and Rachel Yehuda, 'Resilience: Definition, Theory and Challenges', *European Journal of Psychotraumatology*, 5 (2014), 1–14, doi:10.3402/ejpt.v5.25338 (accessed 12 December 2023).

Thompson, Denise, 'Compounding Challenges for Disaster Resilience in Small Island Developing States', *Disaster Prevention and Resilience*, 1 (2022), doi:10.20517/dpr.2021.04 (accessed 17 July 2023).

Timmerman, Peter, *Vulnerability, Resilience and the Collapse of Society* (Toronto: Institute of Environmental Studies, 1981).

Tobin, Graham, 'Sustainability and Community Resilience: The Holy Grail of Hazards Planning?' *Global Environment Change Part B: Environmental Hazards*, 1 (1999), 13–25, doi:10.3763/ehaz.1999.0103 (accessed 12 December 2023).

Ward, Paul, 'Participatory Development in Jamaica: Does It Work in Practice?', *Social and Economic Studies*, 59 (2010), 167–96, doi:10.2307/41803732 (accessed 12 December 2023).

Williams, Gareth, *The Other Side of the Popular: Neoliberalism and Subalternity in Latin America* (Durham, NC: Duke University Press, 2002).

Contributors

Albornoz, Ignacio is a postdoctoral researcher at the College of Fellows, University of Tübingen. He holds a PhD in film studies from Université Paris VIII (France). His research explores, among other things, the documentary culture of the 1970s in Chile and beyond, as well as archival practices in Latin America and the aesthetic role of objects in the first-person documentaries of the post-memory generation. Ignacio has edited two collective volumes on the work of French-Chilean filmmaker Raúl Ruiz: *Potencias de lo multiple* (Metales Pesados, 2023), co-directed with Iván Pinto, which brought together more than 40 essays on the lesser-known films of the director, and Ruiz de lejos, *27 artefactos críticos* (Bastante, 2024), devoted to the critical reception of Ruiz's 1980s films in the French- and English-speaking worlds, which was the result of extensive archival work. Ignacio also works as a translator specializing in film history and theory.

Alpert, Jennifer is Assistant Professor of Film Studies at Oregon State University and serves as managing editor for the *Journal of Cinema and Media Studies Teaching Media Dossier*. Her research centres on how popular cinema and media address and represent marginalized groups, with a focus on human rights in Latin America and its diaspora. She is currently completing a book on film genre in post-dictatorship Argentina titled *Collective Reconstructions: Genre and Historical Trauma in Argentinean Cinema*. She received her PhD in film and media from the University of California, Berkeley, and was a Provostial Research Fellow at Stanford University (2023–2026).

Baard, Patrik has a PhD in philosophy from the Royal Institute of Technology, Stockholm, Sweden. He has conducted research in analytical philosophy at Malmö University, the Swedish University of Agricultural Sciences, and the University of Oslo. His primary focus has been on topics related to environmental ethics and climate change, from the perspectives of ethics, political philosophy, and epistemology. He has published nearly 40 peer reviewed papers in journals such as the *Journal of Applied Philosophy*, *Ethical Theory & Moral Practice*, and *Ethics, Politics & Environment*. He has also published a monograph called *Ethics in Biodiversity Conservation* (Routledge, 2022).

Bolaños Florido, Leidy Paola has a doctorate in history and a master's degree in cultural studies and in history. She is an editor at the Faculty of Social Sciences, Universidad de los Andes (Colombia) and a recipient of a Ministry of Culture (Colombia) grant for research publication and editorial work on Colombian cinema and audiovisual media, awarded for the book *Cine silente: Una historia de Hollywood en Colombia (1910–1930)*. Her research focuses on cultural history, history of cinema, media studies, and the intersections between media, politics, and society in Latin America. Recent publications include: with Gisela Cramer: 'Más allá de la punta del iceberg: las intervenciones de la oficina Rockefeller en la prensa colombiana y latinoamericana (1940–1946)'. *Historia* (Santiago) 2023, 56, 2, http://dx.doi.org/10.4067/s0717-71942023000200209; *Lo cultural y lo popular en la Radio Nacional de Colombia, 1940–1985.* Historelo.rev.hist.reg.local. 2021 13, 27, 146–181, https://doi.org/10.15446/historelo.v13n27.89101; 'La censura de Garras de oro y la propagación de la antiamericanización en los años veinte: un asunto internacional'. *Secuencia* (106), 2020, https://doi.org/10.18234/secuencia.v0i106.1695.

Carpenter, Victoria, PhD (Hull, 2000) is Head of Research Development at the University of Bedfordshire and specializes in the relationship between emotions and factual accuracy in the narratives of violent and catastrophic events, and power distribution in first-person narratives of 1960s Mexican literature. Recent publications include *The Tlatelolco Massacre, Mexico 1968, and the Emotional Triangle of Anger, Grief and Shame: Discourses of Truth(s)* (Cardiff: University of Wales Press, 2018); collected volumes on the representation of historical and violent events in Latin American literature; and articles on modern Mexican and Argentinean literature. She is the founder of the Latin American Literary Studies Association (LALSA).

Cussen, Celia is a professor at the Universidad de Chile. She received her degrees from Stanford University and the University of Pennsylvania. Her publications include *Black Saint of the Americas: The Life and Afterlife of Martin of Porres* (Cambridge University Press), as well as numerous articles on the social and economic aspects of slavery in Chile and Peru, and the evangelization and religiosity of African descendants in the region. She is currently working on a global history of the twentieth-century devotion to Martin of Porres. Cussen has held fellowships at the John Carter Brown Library, the Center for Latin American Studies at Stanford University, the Hutchens Center for African and African American Studies and the David Rockefeller Center for Latin America at Harvard University. In 2025–2026 she held the Randall Distinguished Professorship in Christian Culture at Providence College, Rhode Island.

Fonseca, Carlos is a writer and academic. He is Assistant Professor of Postcolonial Latin American Literature and Culture in the Spanish and Portuguese Section at the University of Cambridge and a Fellow of Trinity College. He is the author of the academic monograph *The Literature of Catastrophe* (Bloomsbury), as well as several works of fiction, including *Coronel Lágrimas*, *Museo animal*, and *Austral*, which have been translated into multiple languages. His writing has received international recognition, including the Anna Seghers Prize. His research focuses on literature and art in the aftermath of catastrophe, archival practices, and Caribbean and Latin American cultural theory.

Fuhrmann, Wolfgang holds a PhD in film studies and is an independent researcher based in Medellín, Colombia. His research interests include transnational film history, Latin American cinema, and German colonial and postcolonial cinema. He is the author of *Imperial Projections: Screening the German Colonies* (New York and Oxford: Berghahn Books, 2015). He has held teaching positions in Germany, Switzerland, and the Americas.

Gatica Mizala, Camila is an assistant professor at the Universidad de Chile's Departamento de Ciencias Históricas. She has a PhD in History from University College London. Her first monograph *Modernity at the Movies: Cinema-going in Buenos Aires and Santiago, 1915–1945* was published with University of Pittsburgh Press in 2023. She is one of the editors of the volume *Soft Power beyond the Nation* (Georgetown University Press, 2024). She has published articles on the Americanization of Chilean society, cultural diplomacy in Argentina and Chile, and film reception in Latin America. Her current research project focuses on the Office of the Coordinator of Inter-American Affairs and its policies towards Argentina and Chile.

Geidel, Molly is an associate professor of women's, gender, and sexuality studies at Dartmouth College. She has a PhD in American Studies from Boston University. She is the author of *Peace Corps Fantasies: How Development Shaped the Global Sixties* (University of Minnesota Press, 2015); *The Development Film in The Americas* (University of California Press, 2025); and *Theory of the Counterinsurgent Girl* (Cambridge University Press, 2026).

Grayson, Hannah is senior lecturer in French and Francophone studies at the University of Stirling. Her work on African fiction in French explores living in the wake of crisis. More broadly she seeks to explore the politically loaded language of vulnerability and resilience. She has published *Beyond Resilience in the Arts, Humanities and Social Sciences: Research on Critical Terms* (Routledge, 2026), and a forthcoming monograph on the poetics of movement in the writing of Tierno Monénembo.

Hart, Stephen M. (PhD, Cantab), is a professor of Latin American Film, Literature and Culture at University College London. Recent publications include '"World" Literature vs. "National" Literature', in *Reimagining the Humanities: Chinese and Western Perspectives*, edited by Suk-Ying Wong, Hua Yang, Weiwen He, Lúcia Nagib, and Matthew Reynolds (Beijing: The Commercial Press, 2024), Vol. II, pp. 89–115; 'The Magical-real Videogame', *Journal of Foreign Language and Culture*, 8.2 (2024), 91–102; 'The Historical Evolution of Saint Rosa de Lima's Nine Miracles (1586–1617)', in *The Dominicans in the Americas and the Philippines (c. 1500–c. 1820): Devotional Life, Catholic Literary Culture, and Models of Holiness*, edited by David T. Orique, Rady Roldán-Figueroa, and Cynthia Folquer (London: Routledge, 2025), pp. 27–41; 'César Vallejo: la dialéctica trotskista de una muerte política', in *César Vallejo: poesía reunida: Edición conmemorativa* (Madrid: Real Academia Española, 2025), pp. 269–289; *The 'Hidden' Story of Latin America and China* (Newcastle-upon-Tyne: Cambridge Scholars, 2025), 269 pp.; and *The Life of St Rose of Lima* (Tamesis, forthcoming, 2026).

Hatzikidi, Katerina (DPhil, Oxon) is a social anthropologist at the University of Tübingen. Her work explores political and social transformations with a special focus on Brazil. In 2023, she was Visiting Professor at the Federal University of Rio de Janeiro (IFCS/UFRJ). Among other publications, Katerina has co-edited the volumes *The Faces of Authoritarianism and Strategies of Dissent in Contemporary Brazil* (UCL Press, 2025), *Populism and Conspiracy Theory. Case Studies and Theoretical Perspectives* (Routledge, 2024), and *A Horizon of (Im)possibilities: A Chronicle of Brazil's Conservative Turn* (London University Press, 2021). Her monograph *Conservatism and Conspiracism in Brazil. A Time of Awakening* is forthcoming with Routledge.

Legeay, Vincent is Maître de conférences at the University of Paris Est-Créteil Créteil and a specialist in the history of modern philosophy, focusing on Hobbes, Descartes, and Spinoza. His research explores the long history of socio-scholastic judgment categories (such as aptitudes and competencies), their contemporary uses, and offers a Spinozist critique of these practices by tracing their pragmatic socio-biological implications. He is the author of *L'Éducation intégrale contre l'éducation nationale. Si l'école est gratuite, c'est vous qui êtes le produit* (Le Bord de l'Eau, forthcoming April 2026) and *'Être apte' chez Spinoza. Histoire, significations, usage biologique contemporain* (Classiques Garnier, 2020). He has also edited *La Philosophie efficace. Du concept de finalité organique comme héritage conceptuel et instrument de travail scientifique* (Éditions Matériologiques, 2023) and *Spinoza et l'essence plastique* (Publications de la Sorbonne, 2018).

Lehner, Andrea is an associate professor in the Department of Philosophy at Universidad de los Andes in Bogotá, Colombia. She has a PhD in philosophy from Nanterre University in Paris. Her research focuses on environmental philosophy, political ecology, and the intersections between philosophy of nature and ecological thought.

Lema Habash, Nicolas is an associate professor in the Department of Philosophy at the Universidad de los Andes, Bogotá, and an associate member of the Centre d'histoire des philosophies modernes de la Sorbonne. He holds a doctorate in philosophy from the University of Paris 1 Panthéon-Sorbonne and a master's in ancient philosophy from the University of Oxford. Previously, he studied philosophy, history, and aesthetics. His research focuses on modern and contemporary philosophy, critical theory, aesthetics, and Latin American thought and film. He is the author of *Duratio vitalis. Figures et variations de la vie dans la philosophie de Spinoza* (Paris, 2022).

Quintana, Laura is a professor in the Department of Philosophy at Universidad de los Andes (Colombia). Her books include *The Politics of Bodies* (Herder, 2020; Rowman & Littlefield, 2020), *Rabia* (Herder, 2021), *Esos afectos voraces* (Tusquets, 2022), *Espacios afectivos* (Herder, 2023), and *El tiempo que queda* (Ariel, 2025). For more information and other publications, see: https://uniandes.academia.edu/LauraQuintana

Singh, Lakhbir is a Senior Lecturer in Marketing at the University of the West of Scotland. Dr Singh completed his PhD at the University of Derby in 2017. His research looked at the issue of trust before, during and after the financial crisis incorporating Cultural Theory and Marketing theory. Dr Singh's research interests include the concept of trust, financial crisis and cultural theory. Prior to pursuing a career in academia, Dr Singh worked in industry working on various projects relating to public and private sectors.

Wienhues, Anna is an assistant professor in Environmental Philosophy at RIPPLE (Research in Political Philosophy and Ethics Leuven); part of the Institute of Philosophy at KU Leuven. She is also the editor-in-chief of environmental values. Her research focuses on environmental philosophy specializing in moral and political philosophy, and she is the author of *Ecological Justice and the Extinction Crisis: Giving Living Beings their Due* (Bristol University Press: 2020). She holds a PhD in political theory from the University of Manchester, as well as an MSc from University College London, and a BA from the University of Essex.

Index

Accommodation 74, 77, 78 79, 80, 81, 82, 84, 85, 86, 299, 301, 323
Adaptation 1, 6, 8, 30, 31, 32, 33, 34, 35, 36, 37, 43, 47, 49, 50, 51, 52, 58, 61, 62, 80, 81, 124, 137, 143, 145, 147, 149, 164, 212, 229, 253, 277, 294, 318, 321
Adaptive Management 134, 135
African descended peoples 162, 164, 335
Agency 28, 57, 59, 143, 144, 146, 174, 176, 181, 193, 194, 197, 210, 214, 216, 217, 218, 226, 232, 311, 313, 316, 319, 320, 246
  Cultural agency 176
Anthropocene 2, 12, 13, 61, 97, 140, 270, 271, 272, 273, 274, 275, 276, 279, 287
Aponte, Marta 11, 237, 238, 239, 240, 241, 242, 243, 244, 245, 246, 247, 248, 249
Aptitude 9, 82, 85, 86
ability 4, 5, 6, 10, 29, 38, 49, 50, 51, 63, 70, 79, 85, 86, 90, 95, 119, 121
archival novel 236, 237, 238, 239, 240
Autochthony 252, 261, 262, 265, 268, 269

Bachelard, Gaston 71, 72, 86, 87
Bacurau 271, 272, 273, 278, 279, 280, 281, 282, 286, 287, 289
Banana plantation 10, 11, 50, 177, 178, 181, 182
Barnet, Miguel 177, 187
Barrios de Chungara, Domitila 196, 200, 201, 202, 205
Bechis, Marco 18, 271, 273, 277, 284, 288
Behavioural psychology 175
Biografía de un cimarrón 177, 187
biology 72, 73, 76, 78, 79, 87, 132, 143
biopolitics 28, 33, 34, 35, 36, 148, 288
Birdwatchers 18, 271, 272, 277, 278, 279, 282, 283, 284, 285, 286, 287, 288
Bolivia 196, 197, 201, 202, 203, 207, 210, 276
Boni, Tanella 18, 56, 251, 253, 254, 255, 257, 261, 262, 263, 264, 265, 266, 267, 268
bounce back / bouncing 4, 6, 8, 11, 14, 15, 24, 25, 26, 27, 28, 32, 38, 39, 44, 49, 52, 70, 72, 73, 74, 76, 77, 78, 80, 84, 146, 147, 155, 156, 174, 175, 187, 188, 193, 211, 212, 213, 214, 232, 311, 313, 318, 322, 325, 331
Buendía, Aureliano 185
Byers, Andrew 164, 171

Cabral, Amílcar 8, 24, 39, 40, 41, 42, 44
Callicott, J. Baird 115, 128
Canary Islands 177
Capabilities approach 98, 99, 102, 109, 110, 146
capitalism 19, 28, 29, 30, 31, 34, 37, 44, 48, 58, 67, 68, 97, 131, 147, 149, 154, 155, 157, 186, 199, 201, 245, 247, 249

Caribbean 8, 11, 12, 44, 45, 177, 186, 237, 238, 240, 243, 244, 247, 249, 309, 311, 312, 319
Caribbean Archive 11, 237, 239, 242, 243, 244, 245, 246, 248, 249
Carr, David 164, 172
catastrophe 12, 13, 23, 24, 31, 34, 35, 36, 38, 41, 42, 43, 56, 130, 131, 150, 237, 238, 239, 243, 244, 246, 247, 248, 249, 251, 256
Catholic Church 162, 163
Ciénaga, Colombia 10, 177, 185, 186, 187
Clarendon parish 326
Closure of the future 30, 58
Colombia 10, 11, 16, 58, 59, 60, 62, 63, 66, 174, 175, 176, 177, 178, 179, 180, 181, 183, 184, 186, 187, 189, 271, 276
colonialism 12, 39, 40, 41, 60, 237, 238, 240, 241, 243, 246, 247, 274
Coloniality of power 58
Communist party 186
complex adaptive systems 149
consensual logic 30, 45, 48, 49, 51
Construction/construct 4, 5, 13, 18, 40, 41, 42, 59, 280, 282, 301, 312
constructivism 114, 128
Cortés Vargas, General Carlos 178, 179, 185, 186, 188
critical political ecology 143
Critique 1, 3, 4, 7, 10, 15, 17, 23, 29, 30, 37, 38, 44, 48, 78, 79, 82, 86, 88, 90, 92, 96, 97, 105, 108, 109, 142, 194, 202, 223, 248, 261, 267, 269
Cuba 177, 199, 218
Cyprus, and occupation of, and Greek Cypriots 290, 291, 292, 293, 294, 295, 296, 297, 298, 299, 300, 301, 302, 303, 304, 305, 306, 307, 308
débrouillardise 8, 12, 15, 251, 253, 254, 255, 256, 258, 261, 262, 263, 264, 265, 266, 267, 268
depoliticization of disasters 57, 141
Derrida, Jacques 239, 242, 245, 246, 247, 250
Descartes, René 73, 84
Destruction/destruct 14, 18, 23, 24, 26, 31, 32, 40, 41, 42, 43, 46, 47, 51, 54, 55, 58, 64, 65, 82, 131, 135, 136, 252, 272, 282, 283, 318
Development Film 190, 195
disappeared 180, 186, 218, 263
Disaster 4, 5, 13, 14, 18, 23, 42, 49, 55, 56, 57, 58, 65, 96, 97, 98, 130, 131, 138, 139, 140, 141, 142, 144, 147, 149, 150, 164, 173, 174, 192, 193, 212, 239, 254, 275, 309, 310, 311, 312, 313, 314, 315, 316, 319, 320, 322
Disciplinary power 34, 35
displace / displacement 11, 13, 51, 164, 210, 213, 214, 215, 217, 218, 220, 221, 222, 232, 272, 291, 293, 294, 295, 296, 297, 303, 305, 306, 327
Dispossession 13, 54, 58, 63, 238, 276, 282, 291, 293, 294, 306
Documentary/documentaries 11, 15, 190, 191, 194, 195, 196, 197, 202, 206, 210, 213, 218, 219, 230, 231, 235, 241, 275, 276, 287, 298, 303
Dornelles, Juliano 271, 277, 279, 281
Dragon's tail 183

Ecological limits (Earth's carrying capacity, planetary boundaries) 46, 55, 94, 101, 109
Ecological-biophysical research 175
Economics 91, 92, 110, 150, 175, 254
ecosystems 5, 6, 9, 47, 50, 51, 61, 93, 95, 98, 99, 101, 102, 103, 112, 113,

114, 115, 117, 118, 120, 122, 123, 126, 127, 132, 134, 135, 138, 144, 150, 153
El Espectador 179, 187
Elasticity 5, 71, 72, 86, 174, 211
Empire building 175
Empty signifier 13, 16, 309, 314, 315
Endurance 13, 15, 162, 200, 203, 211, 255, 269, 271, 279, 290, 291, 292, 293, 294, 295, 302, 303, 305, 306
Ensemble 86, 251, 262, 263, 265, 267, 268
environmental effects 272
environmental ethics 9, 112, 113, 114, 115, 117, 118, 120, 121, 127
ethnographic film 13, 290, 293, 299
Etymology 174, 271
Exile 11, 15, 209, 210, 211, 212, 213, 214, 215, 216, 217, 218, 219, 220, 221, 222, 223, 224, 225, 226, 227, 228, 229, 230, 231, 232, 233, 234, 235, 253, 294, 304, 305
expertise 12, 251, 255, 256, 258, 259, 260, 262, 265

Fajardo, Jorge 224, 225, 226
Femininity 193
Feminist documentary 196, 197
Fendrik, Pablo 271, 273, 277, 282
Food sovereignty
Foucault, Michel 3, 8, 17, 33, 34, 35, 36, 37, 44, 56, 67, 139, 148, 155, 291
Function 72, 79, 88, 100, 101, 118, 124, 133, 135, 143, 274

Gaitán, Jorge Eliécer 186
García Márquez, Gabriel 10, 11, 15, 173, 174, 176, 177, 178, 179, 180, 181, 182, 183, 184, 185, 186, 187, 188, 189
Georges, Norbert, OP 167, 168, 171
Ghost 177, 178, 181, 183, 184, 186, 187, 188, 245
Girl Rising 190, 191, 192, 193, 194, 204, 205, 206, 207
Glasspole, Sir Florizel – Governor General of Jamaica 323
Glissant, Édouard 240, 241, 244, 249, 250, 254, 268
Global Links: Women in the Third World 194
Global South 8, 11, 46, 54, 55, 56, 58, 67, 146, 190, 193, 194, 195, 202, 203, 255
Global North 11, 46, 54, 55, 56, 146, 192, 193, 201
González, Rodrigo 224, 225
Governance of uncertainty 10, 57, 134, 135, 137, 139, 140, 141, 144, 145, 147, 153, 154, 317
Green capitalism 47

Hickel, Jason 46, 47, 54, 55, 67
Holism 4, 19, 112, 114, 117, 118, 119, 120, 127, 134
Holling, C.S. 5, 6, 9, 18, 50, 51, 68, 95, 109, 131, 132, 133, 134, 135, 137, 138, 152, 153, 155, 156, 310, 331
Home 11, 52, 192, 198, 199, 209, 213, 214, 215, 216, 217, 218, 220, 224, 225, 227, 228, 229, 230, 231, 232, 236, 247, 252, 266, 285, 294, 295, 296, 302, 304, 305, 307, 323, 328
Hope 226, 259, 294
Hughes, Edward, OP 168, 169
Human Development Index 98, 105, 111
Hurricane Katrina 23, 193, 311
Hurricane Dean 318, 335
Hurricane Gilbert 317, 318, 322, 323, 328, 330, 331, 332

Hurricane Ivan 311, 312, 313, 318, 329, 331, 332
Hurricane María 237, 243

Ideal theory 103
non-ideal theory 103, 106
Imperialism 54, 67, 186
Imperialist Feminism 194, 202
Invisibility 176
Ivory Coast 12, 251, 252, 256, 257, 258, 259, 261, 266, 268

Jamaica 9, 13, 14, 309, 310, 311, 312, 313, 317, 318, 319, 320, 322, 323, 325, 326, 328, 330, 331, 332, 334
Jamaican Social Investment Fund 320
Kearns, John Chryostom, OP 169, 171
Justice 2, 13, 88, 89, 90, 91, 94, 97, 98, 99, 100, 101, 102, 103, 104, 106, 107, 144, 149, 154, 162, 169, 187, 271, 274, 286
distributive justice 91, 101, 102, 103
intra-human justice 89, 90, 98, 102, 103
interspecies justice 89, 98, 99, 102, 103
intergenerational justice 89, 90, 102, 103

Kingston 311, 319, 323, 324, 327, 329, 330
Kourouma, Ahmadou 12, 251, 253, 257, 258, 259, 260, 262, 267, 269

Laclau, Ernesto 314, 315, 316, 331
Latin American cinema 212, 235, 271, 275, 276, 287, 336
Latin American Western 13, 277, 279, 287
Leaf Storm 184
Littin, Miguel 218, 229, 235
Loizos, Peter 13, 290, 291, 293, 294, 295, 296, 297, 298, 299, 300, 301, 302, 303, 304, 305, 306, 307

Macondo 182
Magical realism 176, 184, 188
Mallet, Marilú 224, 225
Mangrove 247, 249
Manley, Michael – Prime Minister of Jamaica 318, 319, 322
Mbembe, Achille 12, 251, 252, 254, 257, 260, 261, 265, 267, 269
McKeon, Richard M., SJ 170, 171
Medina, Bernardo de, OP 165, 166, 167, 171
Memory 63, 175, 180, 188, 189, 215, 216, 217, 227, 229, 230, 231, 232, 235, 236, 243, 248, 265, 299, 304, 305, 306
Mendonça Filho, Kleber 271, 277, 279, 281, 289
Metaphor 96, 108, 124, 163, 175, 181, 183, 205, 216, 228, 255, 272, 312
Migration 256, 257, 261, 293, 294, 295, 306, 307
Miracle 165, 175, 188, 189, 257
Montejo, Esteban 177
movement 8, 12, 13, 33, 39, 40, 60, 61, 64, 65, 73, 76, 77, 84, 99, 110, 176, 186, 196, 197, 215, 221, 224, 227, 235, 251, 252, 253, 257, 261, 262, 267, 280, 294, 301, 302, 307

Naturalization of uncertainty 142
Neoliberalism 3, 6, 8, 11, 24, 31, 32, 33, 34, 35, 36, 37, 48, 61, 96, 138, 148, 156, 192, 193, 206, 292, 317, 333

Obama, Barack 26, 27, 37, 38, 39
Observer effect 71
Observer-dependence 113, 114, 115, 117, 118, 122, 127

Observer-independence 113
Official story 179
One Hundred Years of Solitude 173, 176, 177, 178, 179, 181, 182, 183, 184, 185, 186, 187, 188, 189
Onion cutter 183
Ontological relationality 176
Overcoming 65, 66, 82, 86, 163, 170, 171, 193, 202, 291, 304, 305

Pathetic fallacy 186
Physical sciences 174
Physics 5, 70, 71, 84, 310
places/environments of memory 216
Political philosophy 88, 89, 90, 91, 97, 100, 109
Political thought 9, 88, 89, 90, 91, 95, 97, 100, 101, 102, 103, 107
Popular cinema 277, 287
Popular culture 176
Porres, Martin of 10, 15, 161, 162, 163, 164, 165, 166, 167, 168, 169, 170, 171, 172
Portland parish 324
Posthegemony 314, 315, 329
PR 3 Aguirre 11, 12, 237, 238, 239, 240, 241, 242, 243, 244, 245, 246, 247, 248, 249, 250
Pueblo 11, 174, 181, 184, 186, 238, 243
Puerto Rico 11

Rancière, Jacques 8, 49, 68
Re-existence 8, 45, 58, 59, 60, 62, 64, 65
Refugees 13, 211, 223, 233, 258, 290, 293, 294, 295, 299, 300, 301, 305, 306, 307
Resilience
- climate resilience 175
- social-ecological resilience 96, 98, 104, 107, 109, 120
- ecological resilience 2, 50, 95, 96, 98, 101, 132, 133, 138
- resilience transition 104, 107
- resilience as a governance strategy 141
- resilience of socio-ecological systems 136, 144
- Latin American resilience 10, 173

Resistance 7, 8, 10, 11, 12, 13, 23, 24, 30, 37, 38, 39, 40, 41, 42, 43, 45, 48, 50, 59, 63, 139, 155, 163, 201, 212, 213, 214, 221, 223, 224, 229, 232, 235, 255, 267, 281, 286, 291, 292, 295, 303, 307, 308, 312
Ribault, Thierry 14, 312, 313, 314, 315, 316, 319, 332
Robbins, Richard 190, 191, 207
Rolston, Holmes 113, 115, 129
Ruiz, Raúl 63, 68, 218, 219, 220, 221, 222, 223, 224, 225, 228, 229, 233, 234, 235, 236

Saldaña, Antonio 178, 188
Saldaña, José
Santa Sofía de la Piedad 185, 186
Sarmiento, Valeria 220, 227, 231, 232, 233, 235, 236
Security logic 35, 36, 37, 52, 56
Segundo, Aureliano 185, 186
Segundo, José Arcadio 177, 182, 183, 184, 185, 186, 187
Simone, AbdouMaliq 12, 251, 254, 255, 257, 258, 261, 262, 263, 264, 265
Skármeta, Antonio 228, 229
Solberg, Helena 194, 196, 197, 198, 199, 200, 201, 205, 206, 207
Soto, Helvio 218, 230
Spinoza, Benedictus de 8, 29, 44, 72, 73, 74, 76, 77, 78, 79, 80, 81, 82, 84, 86, 87, 220, 271
St Catherine parish 318, 326
State legitimacy 88, 91, 101, 105, 107

Stiegler, Barbara 8, 61
Survival 11, 26, 29, 30, 164, 200, 204, 205, 214, 224, 226, 237, 238, 239, 240, 241, 242, 243, 245, 246, 247, 248, 249, 250, 251, 254, 255, 256, 259, 261, 262, 263, 264, 267, 280, 284, 285, 287, 288, 324, 326
Sustainability
weak and strong sustainability 9, 89, 91, 101, 130
waste-and supply-side sustainability 93, 94, 102, 103
sustainable development 45, 46, 47, 52, 88, 89, 90, 91, 92, 93, 94, 97, 104, 105, 107, 108, 110, 131
sustainability transition 103, 104, 106, 107

Test/testing 1, 7, 10, 12, 14, 146, 285, 286, 318
testimonio 161, 162, 166, 196, 197, 199, 200, 201, 202, 205, 207, 239, 244, 245, 246, 247, 276, 297, 298, 299, 302, 306, 318
The Double Day 194, 195, 196, 197, 198, 199, 200, 201, 202, 203, 204, 205, 206, 207
The Gleaner – also, The Daily Gleaner 322, 323, 323, 328, 329
The Ardor 271, 272, 273, 277, 278, 279, 282, 283, 284, 286, 287
Thorén, Henrik 95, 110, 113, 118, 119, 120, 124, 125, 126, 129
Time 4, 5, 8, 11, 13, 15, 16, 20, 23, 30, 38, 39, 45, 71, 77, 78, 83, 122, 126, 127, 132, 133, 151, 162, 166, 169, 174, 182, 184, 194, 205, 222, 229, 237, 239, 246, 247, 255, 261, 287, 290, 291, 295, 296, 299, 300, 302, 305, 323, 326, 327, 328
Trace 12, 194, 239, 240, 241, 242, 248, 321
Tragedy 10, 11, 52, 137, 173, 174, 180
Trauma 5, 6, 8, 11, 14, 17, 24, 25, 27, 28, 38, 42, 43, 48, 52, 57, 66, 68, 164, 184, 194, 200, 203, 213, 214, 215, 216, 218, 222, 225, 230, 234, 244, 271, 291, 292, 293, 300, 305, 307
Trouillot, Michel-Rolph 240, 242, 250

Unidad Popular 210, 213, 218, 225, 227, 230, 232, 236
United Fruit Company 178

Valdez, José Manuel 166, 167, 171
Vargas Ugarte, Rubén, SJ 167, 171
Vulnerability 6, 7, 17, 18, 46, 47, 52, 53, 55, 57, 95, 137, 143, 144, 146, 149, 174, 188, 212, 256, 292, 310, 311, 312, 313, 318, 321, 331, 332, 333

War 5, 12, 56, 63, 131, 140, 195, 207, 209, 251, 252, 256, 257, 260, 261, 269, 280, 281, 290, 295, 307
Western genre 271, 272, 277, 278, 279, 282, 284, 286
Western stories 272
Women in Development 194, 195, 196, 197, 199, 201

www.ingramcontent.com/pod-product-compliance
Lightning Source LLC
LaVergne TN
LVHW011351260826
846528LV00027B/258
* 9 7 8 1 6 4 8 2 5 1 8 5 6 *